THE POLITICAL WRITINGS
OF
Harold D. Lasswell

☆

Psychopathology and Politics

☆ ☆

POLITICS: Who Gets What, When, How

☆ ☆ ☆

Democratic Character

1951 · THE FREE PRESS · GLENCOE · ILLINOIS

PUBLISHER'S FOREWORD

In modern political science two volumes have made a special impact because of their originality of content and brevity of expression. One is Professor Lasswell's *Psychopathology and Politics* (1930) and the other is his *Politics: Who Gets What, When How* (1936). These books are made conveniently accessible in the present publication, together with a third book, a wholly new treatment of *Democratic Character*.

Political science is one of the social sciences that has been revolutionized by the epochal advances that have been made in recent years in the study of human personality. Medical psychology has been the greatest source of deeper knowledge of the mind of man, especially since the discovery of psychoanalysis by Sigmund Freud. Lasswell's *Psychopathology and Politics* was the earliest full-scale application of the principles of psychopathology to politics. It was much more than a simple re-statement and formal application of psychopathology to a special topic. With the cooperation of eminent physicians in this country and abroad the intimate life histories of active politicians were collected and analyzed in the light of the insights provided by modern psychiatry. One of the leading sponsors of the research, for example, was the late Dr. William Alanson White who was the superintendent of St. Elizabeth's Hospital, Washington, D. C., the chief government hospital for the care and study of the insane.

In the *Psychopathology* a sharp distinction is drawn between individuals active in politics, and "political personalities." The latter are driven by inner motivations to prefer politics above all other careers. Professor Lasswell develops some fundamental hypotheses about the "political man" as a social type, and about some of the sub-types, such as the "agitator," "theorist" and "administrator." The intensive study of political leaders disclosed the working of "non-rational" influences in politics, and indicated that special precautions were necessary if political judgments are to be made on a relatively rational basis. The *Psycho-pathology* emphasizes the "politics of prevention" as a means of liberating the constructive potentialities of man.

It has often been pointed out that the examination of politics from the standpoint of modern psychology has revitalized the scientific study of political behavior by freeing political science from excessive "legalism." It was the purpose of *Politics: Who Gets What, When, How* to clarify the nature of politics "in a new key." Instead of defining political science as the "science of the state," Lasswell conceived of politics as the shaping and sharing of values. Among these values were named such "representative" ones as "safety, income and deference." In a limited sense, of course, political scientists might concentrate on "power," defined as the making of important decisions. The essential point in any case is to view political behavior as part of the entire stream of behavior of man in society.

Professor Lasswell once characterized *Politics: Who Gets What, When, How* as an expansion of the first paragraph of the systematic volume originally published in 1935 and called *World Politics and Personal Insecurity* (republished in 1950 in *A Study of Power*, together with related studies by Professors Charles E. Merriam and T. V. Smith). The aim of the expansion was to provide concrete examples of how to conceive of the political process.

PUBLISHER'S FOREWORD

When we contemplate the ebb and flow of public life, it is possible to make sense of it as marking the rise or fall of social "classes," or "skill" groups, or "attitude" groups, or "personality" types. If we think of politics from a "manipulative" standpoint, it is appropriate to consider the strategy and tactics of handling "violence," "goods," "symbols," and "practices." The succinct and abundant examples used in the *Politics* made it comprehensible to students and laymen alike.

For the present volume Professor Lasswell has dealt at some length with the special problem of *Democratic Character*. The author begins by showing that Plato and Aristotle were keenly aware of the importance of "character" and "constitution," even asserting that "constitutions" could be shaped by "character." However the classical tradition has been denied by the subsequent thinkers who oppose "material" to "ideological" factors, and see nothing in the mind but what has been left by past contact with "material" elements. Lasswell suggests that such sharply conflicting interpretations may arise in part from the ambiguous way in which the relation between "psychological" and other factors is often stated. He goes on to say that nothing can be gained by opposing the "inner" to the "outer," since the important elements of politics and society are combinations of both. Human behavior is composed of patterns which are often in conflict; and the conflict is between one "inner-outer" pattern and another of the same kind. It is safe to say that the discussion of *Democratic Character* will be of interest far beyond the circle of professional students and teachers of government in this country and abroad.

The new political science is a synthesis of modern empirical inquiry with the tradition which began, so far as the Western world is concerned, in classical Greece. The connection is more closely worked out in Professor Lass-well's *Democratic Character* than in his other books and articles where it has been "taken for granted." Hence there is some special interest attached to this new discussion, which we are glad to make available to a larger audience at the same time that the older works are presented in more accessible form.

Contents

Psychopathology
and Politics

BY HAROLD D. LASSWELL

☆

THE FREE PRESS · GLENCOE · ILLINOIS

PREFACE

An understanding of political life can be sought by examining collective processes distributively or intensively. In my *Propaganda Technique in the World War* (New York and London, 1927), I undertook to analyze the factors which modified collective attitudes by examining the symbols to which many millions of people had been exposed, without paying heed to the order in which these symbols entered into the experience of any particular person. In this preliminary treatise on *Psychopathology and Politics*, I am likewise concerned with the factors which impinge upon collective attitudes, but the method of procedure is radically different. It is no longer a question of inspecting the symbols to which innumerable individuals have been exposed; the present starting-point is the lengthy scrutiny of the histories of specific individuals. The procedures and findings of psychopathology are relied upon for the purpose in hand, since they are the most elaborate and stimulating contributions to the study of the person which have yet been made.

Candor enjoins me once more to express my indebtedness to my former teacher and present chief, Charles E. Merriam, of the University of Chicago, who some time ago sensed the importance of psychopathology for political science, and who has been willing to encourage my own forays in the field, without, of course, feeling bound to indorse my results either in principle or in detail. Through him it became possible to have facilities for special work with Professor Mayo, of Harvard University, whose perception of the bearing of psychopathology upon the un-

PREFACE

derstanding of social life is bearing fruit in novel and important experiments in business. The tenure of a Social Science Research Council Fellowship (1928–29) made it possible to continue my studies abroad.

Circumstances have thus been such as to bring me in contact, sometimes fleeting and sometimes prolonged, with men who represent divers standpoints in psychopathology. Many of these have kindly placed their minds and their facilities at my disposal, and I hereby return thanks for the generosity and patience with which they treated an inquiring, if somewhat innocent, investigator. No one who knows the lay of the land in modern psychology, deeply pitted by the trenches and shell-holes of battling schools, will imagine that all the men whom I am to name see eye to eye with one another, or that they will look with equanimity upon the results of my explorations. To name them is, I hope, not unduly to incriminate them.

Among those from whom assistance has been received are to be included: Dr. William Healy, Judge Baker Foundation, Boston; Dr. William A. White, superintendent of St. Elizabeth's Hospital, Washington, D.C.; Dr. Ross Chapman, superintendent of Sheppard and Enoch Pratt Hospital, Towson, Maryland; Dr. Earl D. Bond, superintendent of the Pennsylvania State Hospital, Philadelphia; Dr. Mortimer Raynor, superintendent of Bloomingdale Hospital, White Plains, New York; Dr. C. MacFie Campbell, superintendent of the Boston Psychopathic Hospital, Boston; Dr. Harry Stack Sullivan, formerly of Sheppard and Enoch Pratt Hospital; Dr. N. D. C. Lewis, St. Elizabeth's Hospital; Dr. Samuel W. Hamilton, Bloomingdale Hospital; Dr. Gregory Zilboorg, Bloomingdale Hospital; Dr. F. L. Wells, Boston Psychopathic Hospital; Dr. Edouard Hitschmann, Vienna; Dr. Paul Federn, Vienna;

PREFACE

Dr. Alfred Adler, Vienna; Dr. Wilhelm Stekel, Vienna; Dr. S. Ferenczi, Budapest; Dr. Theodor Reik, Berlin; Dr. Franz Alexander, Berlin (now of the University of Chicago). My colleagues, Dr. Stewart B. Sniffen and Professor Leonard D. White, made valuable suggestions during the process of editing the manuscript, several of which I adopted.

Permission to quote freely from my previous publications was received from the editors of the *American Political Science Review, American Journal of Psychiatry, Journal of Abnormal and Social Psychology, International Journal of Ethics*, and from the University of Chicago Press and the Chicago Association for Child Study and Parent Education.

I wish especially to express my gratitude to those who cannot be singled out by name, but whose co-operation in submitting themselves to prolonged scrutiny was of the greatest possible help.

It ought to be pointed out that the cases actually cited are only a fraction of those which I have examined, or which I have in my possession. Only enough cases have been abstracted to serve the purposes of exposition, to supply a background for the theoretical material. The obscurities which result from an unlimited multiplication of "little Willie stories" have been sought to be avoided by curtailing their number and their extent.

The first part of the book proceeds in rather dogmatic fashion, and this no doubt tends to obscure the highly unsatisfactory nature of the materials and methods of contemporary psychopathology. The later chapters are given over to the critical and constructive discussion of these matters, and should fully indicate the highly provisional, though potentially significant, character of the whole.

H. D. L.

CONTENTS

CHAPTER I

LIFE-HISTORIES AND POLITICAL SCIENCE

Political biography as a field of political science has long been relied upon to furnish a vivid corrective to the overemphasis laid upon the study of institutional "mechanisms," "structures," and "systems." The legal and customary position of the House of Commons, the House of Lords, the monarch and the electorate, as expounded in the commentaries of Gneist and Dicey, suddenly take on new meaning when viewed through the lens of Morley's Gladstone, Strachey's Victoria, or Lee's Edward VII. The German imperial system of Laband is more fleshly and less transcendental when one has studied the lives of Bismarck or William II. An institutional account of the constitutional development of the United States without a life of Marshall and a life of Lincoln would be but the dregs of a rich and ebullient history. Political science without biography is a form of taxidermy.

When the tumultuous life of society is flayed into precedents and tanned into principles, the resulting abstractions suffer a strange fate. They are grouped and regrouped until the resulting mosaic may constitute a logical and aesthetic whole which has long ceased to bear any valid relation to the original reality. Concepts are constantly in danger of losing their reference to definite events. Notions like liberty and authority require a new birth of meaning after they have followed the tempting path of abstraction but a little way. If conceptions are to serve and not to

1

master the mind, their terms of reference must intermittently undergo the most rigorous scrutiny.

The use of "institutional" categories in describing political life is indispensable, but the publicists who employ them have little to say about the "personal" influences which modify the expected behavior of "legislatures," "executives," and "judiciaries." It is no news that "leadership" is an important variable in predicting the course of events, but the standard treatises on politics have next to nothing to offer about the traits of various kinds of agitators and organizers, and nothing to say about the kinds of experiences out of which these differences arise.

This limitation holds for the books about the theory of the state and of politics which are written by Englishmen like Sidgwick and Laski, Americans like Garner and W. W. Willoughby, and Europeans like Jellinek, Schmidt, Kjellén, and Kelsen. No doubt these men possess or have possessed a living sense of political realities. Of Sidgwick it is related that he was wonderfully adept in entertaining his circle for hours with incisive comments and amusing anecdotes about public men. But of this "humanity" of politics there is little to be found in what he wrote. Political biography has been relied upon chiefly to convey a sense of the unpredictable in human affairs, and to adorn an after-dinner tale. At its best, political biography has contributed to an understanding of the factors which differentiate one human personality from another. But it is no secret that the literary biography or autobiography omits or distorts much of the intimate history of the individual, and that many of the facts which modern investigators have found to be important are numbered among the missing.

Where is it possible to secure a supply of life-histories in which the usual conventionalities are ignored, and which are taken by specialists in the sociological, psychological, and somatic influences which play upon the individual? There exist in modern society sizeable collections of such material which have hitherto been accorded slight attention by students of social science. I refer to the case histories of those individuals who have been ill, and especially those who have been cared for in hospitals and sanitariums.[1]

The richest body of psychological and sociological facts is found in the files of the institutions for the care of the mentally disordered, although the material available in general hospitals is of value. The case history of a patient in a good mental hospital is a document to which many have contributed. There is a report of the physical condition of the patient as it is revealed in the routine examination on his admission to the institution. This may be supplemented by transcripts of previous and subsequent examinations. There is also to be found the rating attained by the subject on several general-intelligence and special-aptitude tests. There is a report of the preliminary interview and the diagnosis by the psychiatrist. This is amplified by a summary of the proceedings at staff conferences to which the patient is presented, and which is attended by the whole body of physicians and psychiatric social workers attached to the hospital. The usual routine is for the physician and social worker in charge to present a summary of the case, to introduce the patient for observation, and to engage in general colloquy upon the diagnosis and therapy after the patient has been escorted out of the room. The patient may be brought before several staff

[1] See Harold D. Lasswell, "The Study of the Ill as a Method of Research on Political Personalities," *American Political Science Review*, November, 1929.

conferences for the purpose of discussing whether he is in a condition permitting of release, parole, or transfer. During his stay in the institution the nurses, as well as the physicians who make rounds, add their descriptive comments upon his behavior. The social service department gets in touch with relatives and acquaintances and prepares a biography of the subject. Occasionally the patient will volunteer an autobiography, which is filed with the general record. Correspondence with individuals who have interested themselves in the case will often disclose valuable details. The exhibits frequently include letters written by the patient before, during, and after his illness, together with published works, drawings, paintings, and plastic productions. In some instances the record of a single patient who has been admitted, released, or transferred becomes very voluminous.

It is due to the growing emphasis upon the importance of understanding the personality as a functioning whole that modern medical men are willing and anxious to assemble data about the behavior of the individual in his family, business, and recreational relations. Such facts are often useful to the physician in making his diagnosis and in deciding how to handle the patient. The modern emphasis upon the rôle of reverie in developing one's traits and interests has led to the inclusion of data about night dreams, daydreams, ambitions, grievances, enthusiasms, and loyalties of the subject. Not infrequently the productions of the patient are recorded in his own words by a stenographer who is present during certain interviews with physicians. All these psychological and sociological data increase the significance of the case record for the individual who studies it for the purpose of understanding the total developmental history of the person.

Sometimes the case histories concern people who are without mental disorder, but who have, for one reason or another, been committed for observation. The German government was not the only one in the late war which sometimes resorted to the expedient of avoiding the appearance of internal dissension by referring pacifists to a mental hospital. The records of the kind obtained under these circumstances are often of men and women without pathology, and serve to control the conclusions which rest on the study of pathological cases.

Quite often the specifically pathological features in the record of a sick person are very meager. Thus, one prominent politician, the mayor of a large city, was brought to a mental hospital suffering from an alcoholic psychosis,[2] delirium tremens. He was only "insane" (to use a non-scientific term) when he was passing through this acute alcoholic episode, and was soon released. But the record of what he said and did during the delirium casts a brighter light on the deeper motivations of his political career than many pages of conventional biography. The hallucinations and delusions which he experienced were not entirely stereotyped for the disease. Since he was no longer able to maintain his repressions, his inner fantasy life came out in the clear, and his personality structure stood revealed. Another politician showed nothing abnormal except a propensity for collecting women's shoe heels, which he found sexually stimulating. He came to the medical psychologist to be freed from his fetishist perversion, and in so doing he made possible the preparation of a document which intimately revealed the origin of certain political interests. From the point of view of the political

[2] "Psychosis" means the more serious mental disturbances; "neurosis" means the less serious ones.

scientist the most valuable parts of his history happened to be quite far removed from the narrowly circumscribed pathological symptoms.

The value of some records is enhanced by the fact that, besides the pathological productions of the patient, they contain much information which is volunteered by the person when he is himself again. Some forms of mental disorder show recurrent intervals of disturbance and normality, and during the "clear" interludes the patient is quite competent to furnish autobiographical data. Often the "remissions" in the individual's condition extend over several years, although they may be momentary. Another form of mental disease is characterized by the fact that the sufferer's difficulties center about a single system of ideas which, if left untouched by the interviewer, permits him to be dealt with as an ordinary individual. It should be evident from the foregoing that, contrary to popular impression, the histories to be found in institutions for the care of the sick are by no means exclusively confined to pathological subjects or to the merely pathological aspects of the person.

Some of the life-histories which are summarized in this monograph come from mental hospitals. Others have been collected from volunteers who were outside mental institutions and who were aware of no serious mental pathology. They have been undertaken on the understanding that our knowledge of human nature in politics would be advanced if "normal" individuals were studied with the same care which is often bestowed on the abnormal.

So the book includes persons who are "sick" and persons who are "well." In the main the material is printed for the first time. There are no retrospective interpretations of historical personages. The chief unity of the study lies in the fact that it is restricted to politically interesting people who have been studied while alive by specialists under conditions of unusual intimacy.

The purpose of this venture is not to prove that politicians are "insane." Indeed, the specifically pathological is of secondary importance to the central problem of exhibiting the developmental profile of different types of public characters. Our job is not to catalogue the symptoms at the expense of the main patterns of the personality. We have not finished when we know that a modern Rousseau suffered from paranoia; that a modern Napoleon has partly atrophied genitalia; that modern Alexanders, Caesars, and Blüchers are alcoholic; that a modern Calvin is plagued by eczema, migraine, and kidney stones; that a modern Bismarck is hysterical; that a modern Lincoln shows depressive pathology; that a modern Robespierre displays a eunuchoid habitus; or that a modern Marat suffers from arthritis, diabetes, and eczema. "Psychopathography" is legitimate and useful, but pathography is not our aim.[3]

Nor is it the purpose of this book to make a hit-and-miss collection of isolated anecdotes about the relation between early experiences and specific political traits and interests. Not that this sort of thing is not a liberalizing experience. Our conventional schemes of "political motivation" seem curiously aloof from the manifold reality of human life when we discover the private basis of public acts. John B, to choose a random instance, is a busy, aggressive, and successful salesman who spends a great deal of time and money on the care of the blind. He takes time away from

[3] The best summary of this literature is Wilhelm Lange-Eichbaum, *Genie-Irrsinn und Ruhm*. See also the works of Ireland, Lombroso, Möbius, and Gould.

his business to serve on the board of governors of institutions for the blind, and he handles many financial campaigns on their behalf. Measures looking toward the improvement of public or private care for these unfortunates are certain of his support before legislative committees, on the platform, and in personal conference. The study of his early memories finally revealed the incident in which his ardent interest in the blind was rooted. When he was between three and four years of age, his little sister pulled an eye out of his favorite cat, and he was terribly distressed. His concern for the safety of his pets was the original drive toward protective work for the blind which matured into his adult activity. It would be possible to fill many pages with reports of "critical experiences" of this kind, and their importance is far greater than is usually supposed.

If diagnostic labels and isolated anecdotes do not satisfy us, what do we want? The answer can be succinctly stated thus: We want to discover what developmental experiences are significant for the political traits and interests of the mature. This means that we want to see what lies behind agitators, administrators, theorists, and other types who play on the public stage. Can we conceive the development of the human personality as a functioning whole, and discern the turning-points in the growth of various patterns of political life? Can we uncover the typical subjective histories of typical public characters? Can we place this subjective history in relation to the physical and cultural factors which were developmentally significant?

Even this ambitious project does not exhaust the scope of this study. We want to see whether the intensive investigation of life-histories will in any way deepen our understanding of the whole social and political order. The life-story of a Hottentot or an American reveals the concrete reality of images and moods as they are experienced seriatim by those whose life is caught up in the web of violently contrasting cultures. The trained student of society discerns a wealth of culture patterns whose full meaning in human experience can only be revealed by securing the subjective history of those who are exposed to them. In some cultures the child is slapped, switched, and beaten; in some cultures the child is rarely the target of corporal punishment. Does this mean that the children in the first culture will harbor revenge and welcome violence in social life? In some cultures, parental control is negligible from the fourth to the fourteenth year, and in other cultures supervision is strict and continuous. What difference does this make in the developing view of the world in successive generations? Those who are within the same culture are exposed to many minor variations in social practice, and we may hope to ascertain the consequences of these differences for the minds of those who undergo them.

This book is in harmony with a trend which has been growing in strength in the social sciences. Social science has been moving toward the intensive study of the individual's account of himself. This is a movement which is poorly conveyed by the phrase, "an interest in human biography," because the term "biography" is full of irrelevant literary and historical connotations. The person's own story is not a chronology of everything he thought and did, nor is it an impressionistic interpretation of what he experienced. The life-history is a natural history, and a natural history is concerned with facts which are *developmentally* significant. The natural history of the earth is not a rehearsal of every event included within the series, but a selective account of major changes within the series. Dated events matter, but they matter not because they have dates but because they mark phases. When biography is treated as natural history, the purpose is to pick and choose the principal epochs of development and to identify their distinctive patterns.

The study of life-histories as natural histories is a very recent phenomenon. The social sciences have barely begun to exploit this approach. It is of very great significance that Comte, after spending a lifetime in the preparation of his great system, finally saw that the capstone was missing, and at the time of his death was frantically trying to improvise it. His projected treatise was to deal with personality development and differentiation (*La morale*). It was never finished. There is something symbolic of the history of the social sciences in this story of Comte's long preoccupation with institutions, his belated recognition of the possibilities of personality study, his hurried effort to make good the omission, and the fragmentary nature of the results achieved. Social science is in the belated-hurried-fragmentary phase of growth.[4]

Comte's fragment was never expanded by French sociologists. The comparative morphology of culture became all-absorbing, and this was concerned with the pantomime of what men did, and sporadically with what men thought. Comte executed his earlier volumes only too well. When the mental processes of primitives came to be studied by Durkheim and the Durkheimians, these "primitive mentalities" were examined for the sake of revealing highly

[4] See De Grange's excellent treatment of this matter in his paper on the methodology of Comte, Analysis 1, *Methods in Social Science: A Case Book.*

abstract "forms" of thought, and not to reveal the individual sequence of human experience under different social
conditions. The efforts which have been made to fill the
gap have rested upon no massing of empirical data and
have been fortified by no critical reflection on the methodological problem of improving the reliability of the
data. The most promising sign of the times in France is
the synthetic approach to social psychology which is spon-
sored by Blondel at Strassbourg.

In Germany the social scientists were so occupied with
the *Streit um Marx* and the triumphs of the comparative
historical school that a comparative morphology of subjective histories, if one may indulge the phrase, did not
arise. The prodigious influence of Kant in the direction
of multiplying epistemological subtleties stereotyped a
penchant for high abstraction in the consideration of psychological phenomena. The great successes of the physical
sciences seemed to rest upon the ruthless division and re-
division of phenomena until they became amenable to
manipulation and control. The combination of Kantian
acuteness with scientific atomism was capable of producing the extremes of physiological psychology and the ob-
scurantist revulsion against submitting the sacred mystery
of personality to the coarse indignity of exact investigation.
Curiously enough, the modern era of personality study
was introduced as a protest against the laboratory emphasis, and meant a capitulation to the spirit of scientific
irreverance. Personalities could be compared and typolo-
gized. The pioneer was Dilthey, the philosophic historian;
but neither he nor those who followed him collected and
published actual accounts of intimate subjective experiences. Sociological overemphasis on the group was only
partially compensated in Simmel's theoretical exposition

of individuality, but there was no happy synthesis of category and fact in his work. The field ethnologists neglected to assemble autobiographical accounts, and only the fine sensibilities of Vierkandt made possible the utilization of fragments for the sake of comparing the inner life of primitive man with that of modern man, a task which was performed with rather more subtlety than by the French. The early social psychological impetus of Lazarus and Steindhal produced vast collections of folk-lore materials, but the task of threading folk lore and folk ways onto the developmental history of representative persons remained undone.

The great innovator in the subjective field was Freud. His book on dreams is one of the most unique autobiographies in history, and his publications set the pace for those who wanted to record the actual outpourings of the unrestrained human mind. Here at last was a truly scientific spirit who recorded everything of which the human mind was capable, and looked at it critically in the hope of finding the laws of mental life. He broke through the irrelevant barriers of conventionality and brought dark continents of data into the light of inquiry. He proposed theories which were supposed to be tested by the data, and devised a special procedure for securing data.

The scientific habilitation of the anonymous, intimate life-history document as a source for the study of culture was especially the work of William I. Thomas. He and Florian Znaniecki undertook and completed their remarkable study of *The Polish Peasant in Europe and America*. One volume was devoted to a long autobiography which included the most intimate facts in the life of a Polish immigrant to the United States. The work of Thomas left an abiding stamp on American sociology through the department at the University of Chicago. Franz Boas, dean of American ethnologists, has been keenly interested in the primitive's story of himself, and has collected and urged the collection of many such documents. Paul Radin published the life-story of a Winnebago chief in 1916. The importance of "the boy's own story" was early recognized by William Healy in his study of delinquents, and has been extended in every direction.

So, in stressing the value of the study of the concrete sequence of individual experience for political science, we are expressing a trend of interest which is already well founded in social science. Our quest for full and intimate histories has led to the exploitation of a relatively new source of material, the case-history records of hospitals. It has led to the application of psychopathological methods to the study of normal volunteers as a control on the inferences drawn from the institutional cases. It has led to a detailed study of the prolonged interview technique as a method of personality study (especially psychoanalysis), and to the formulation of improved methods of investigation. It has led to the statement of a functional theory of the state, a theory which springs directly from the intensive scrutiny of actual life-histories, and the realization of what political forms can mean when seen against the rich background of personal experience.

These studies are admittedly incomplete. The documents relied upon suffer from various shortcomings which have been specified in detail at an appropriate place. The number of documents on hand is limited. Caution would counsel deferred publication of even these materials. But the many objections to publication have been outweighed by certain positive advantages. The publication of such a collection of materials will serve to familiarize the professional students of government with the kinds of fact and interpretation which are now current among the specialists in important fields of study. Familiarization is especially necessary in dealing with personality histories because some of the material is unconventional and invariably produces initial emotional difficulties among unsophisticated readers. But science cannot be science and limit itself to the conventional. Some of the facts are not pretty, and they are not the topics of polite conversation. But the medical scientists who dabble with the excretions of the human body for the sake of diagnosing disease and understanding health are not bound by the limitations of banality and gentility in their work. And if political science is to become more of a reality and less of a pseudonym, there must be discipline in dealing objectively with every kind of fact which is conceivably important for the understanding of human traits and interests.

Familiarization, then, is one function of this set of studies. Another purpose is to set up tentative hypotheses about personality growth on the basis of available materials. The mere statement of these hypotheses about the growth of agitators and administrators will sharpen investigation. Perhaps those who have direct access to better histories will be impelled to use them in checking and revising the working conceptions herein set out.

The general scheme of presentation begins with some chapters which sketch the psychopathological standpoint in its historical setting and which review the current criteria of political types. Then comes selected life-history material. The concluding chapters discuss the bearing of personality studies on general political theory and criticize existing methods of study.

CHAPTER II

THE PSYCHOPATHOLOGICAL APPROACH

One of the standing obstacles in the path of personality research is the difficulty of describing the personality as a whole at any given cross-section of its development. In despair at the myriad difficulties of the task, academic psychology has long evaded the issue and concentrated its attention upon the minute exploration of detached aspects of the individual. The manuals of physiological psychology are full of painstaking accounts of how atomized aspects of the individual's environment (the "stimuli") modify the reactions of selected parts of the individual. What these manuals characteristically omit is a workable set of conceptions for the classification of the phenomena which are the objects of investigation in personality research. It is impossible to found a science of geology without inventing terms to distinguish plateaus, plains, mountains, and continental blocs, even though all these phenomena possess the common attributes of "matter." What matters for the geologist is how the differences and not the likenesses come to pass. Much of the academic psychology, in its quest for precision and prestige, has quit studying the problem with which it is ostensibly engaged, and has substituted a minor field of physiology therefor. In so doing, it has lost any criterion for testing the relevance of the results of particular researches for the understanding of personality because it has no master concepts of personality.

The psychopathologist has never been able to evade the

necessity of summing up the personality as a whole because he has been compelled to make important decisions about the future of the personality as a whole. The psychiatrist must continually decide whether John B and Mary C will, if released from careful supervision, commit suicide or murder, or whether they will be dependable members of the community. Thus the clinician has found it imperative to search for signs which have high predictive value in relation to the major social adjustments of the individual.

The psychopathologist has had the great advantage of seeing many trends of the personality which are normally subordinated to other trends when they have escaped from control and achieved Gargantuan proportions. The clinical caricature throws into imposing relief the constituent tendencies which make up the functioning person, and draws attention to their presence and their processes. "Normality" involves a complicated integration of many tendencies, a flexible capacity to snap from one mood, preoccupation, and overt activity to another as the changing demands of reality require. The pathological mind, if one may indulge in a lame analogy, is like an automobile with its control lever stuck in one gear: the normal mind can shift. One has a queer feeling as one passes around the wards of a hospital for the custody of the more seriously disordered patients that if one could assemble the scattered parts of the mind that one could create at least a single supermind. There in one corner is a melancholic who is stuck in the mood of despondency; in another corner is a manic who is expansive and elated; elsewhere is a man whose self-esteem has achieved cosmic dimensions; in the back wards is a deteriorated mind in perpetual repose. Every conceivable nuance of preoccupation and mood with which we are normally familiar seems to be dissatisfied with its minor rôle in a healthy integration, and intent upon autocratic mastery of the mind. The clinical caricature draws attention as sharply as possible to the components of the healthy mind. So every theory of pathological manifestations must presently become expanded or assimilated into a comprehensive account of human psychology.

The gross clinical material reveals the intimate interrelationships between soma and psyche. The patient who suffers from obsessive ideas may find relief from obsession by showing hysterical symptoms; and hysterical symptoms may clear up, only to make way for obsessive symptoms. "Pure pictures" are almost pure theories. The patient who is suffering from a definite organic lesion may complicate his troubles by "worry," and "worry" may be one of the factors in bringing about a physical disease picture. There is evidence that psychological factors are among those significantly operating in such diseases as common colds, asthma, catarrh, hay fever, hyperthyroidism, gall-bladder trouble, gastro-intestinal ulcers, irregular menstruation, and sexual impotence.

Fresh vitality has come into modern psychology from the clinic. The psychopathological approach has gradually vindicated itself as more and more of its conceptions find a permanent place in the vocabulary of psychology and social science. Modern psychopathology is itself a recent development, and undoubtedly the most revolutionary figure is Sigmund Freud.

The spectacular and influential nature of Freud's work is sufficient justification for devoting some space to a brief account of his standpoint and his innovation in method. As we shall have occasion to illustrate, his method is of more general application to practical problems of political research and political practice than is usually understood.

When Freud was a student in the University of Vienna, the triumphal progress of microscopic methods of studying cellular structure was sweeping all before it. Congeries of mental symptoms in the living were frequently found to be correlated with the discovery of certain definite cerebrospinal lesions on autopsy. The future seemed to rest wholly in the hands of those who used the dissecting knife and the lens. Before Freud graduated from the University, he became demonstrator to Brücke, the eminent physiologist; and he labored in the laboratory of Meynart, the distinguished psychiatrist of his day. Freud's first publication was a result of laborious laboratory work.

While materialism reigned, psychological phenomena were degraded to the status of trivial epiphenomena. But at this very time a revival of psychogeneticism arose in French psychiatry under the impetus of Charcot. Charcot had achieved eminence in pathological anatomy before he turned in middle life to the study of mental maladies. By 1883 he had demonstrated the possibility of producing hysterical symptoms by means of ideas (verbal stimuli). Time and again he hypnotized individuals and produced muscular contractures, hypersensitivity, and hyposensitivity, together with allied symptoms of hysteria.

Breaking away from the laboratories of Vienna, Freud journeyed to the Salpêtrière Hospital in Paris to work with Charcot, where he stayed from the autumn of 1886 to the spring of 1887. Here he was thrown in touch with the current of ideas which was giving concrete content to the notion of the "out of conscious" and its dynamic consequences for human behavior. Pierre Janet was busily accumulating the observations which were published to the world in 1889 under the title, *L'automatisme psychologique*. Early chapters appeared in the *Revue philosophique* as early as 1886. His work was submitted to the Sorbonne for the degree of Doctor of Philosophy. In view of subsequent controversies, it is worth observing that the scope of this research was confined to repetitive and dissociated phenomena. Words and movements of persons who were in somnambulistic, cataleptic, and similar states were described, together with studies of post-hypnotic suggestion, and of total and partial recall. Emphasis was laid upon the "restriction of the field of consciousness" and the "enfeeblement of consciousness."

In Paris Freud acquired a point of view which was bound to bring him into conflict with the materialistic pundits of Vienna. Hypnotism was itself looked upon as an artifice of charlatans. Wagner-Jauregg reflected the ruling tradition when, only a few years ago, he said, "The trouble with hypnotism is that you never know who is pulling the other fellow's leg." Freud was met by derisive laughter when he announced at the Medical Society of Vienna that male hysterics were to be found in Paris. For hysteria, as one of the pedants reminded him, was philologically derived from "hysteron," meaning uterus, and therefore couldn't possibly occur in males. This was an echo of the days when hysteria was supposed to be due to a migratory uterus and women were turned upside down to bring it back in place.

In 1881 and 1882 Breuer had treated a girl suffering from hysteria, and his interest was renewed in the case in conversation with Freud. Breuer remembered that when he treated the patient under hypnosis, she recalled the first episode in which a symptom had appeared, related it with every evidence of excitement, and discovered on waking that the symptom had disappeared. Breuer and Freud began to study hysteria from this point of view and published their results. Charcot had demonstrated that ideas could cause hysteria; Breuer had found that the discovery of pathogenic ideas could cure hysteria.

In 1889 Freud returned to France, this time to the other center of hypnotic research, Nancy, where Liébeault and Bernheim were doing remarkable things. Freud here saw something the full significance of which did not at once dawn upon him.

A subject was hypnotized and given a "post-hypnotic suggestion" to raise an umbrella at a certain signal after coming out of hypnosis. The subject was then awakened from hypnosis, and presently, when the stipulated signal was given, obediently raised the umbrella, although still inside the room. When asked why he raised the umbrella, *he said that he wanted to see whether it was his or not.* Thus did he rationalize (a concept later developed) the gratification of an impulse *which he did not himself at first recognize.* When challenged to explain himself, he merely produced a plausible interpretation of his own conduct.

The immense significance of this train of events is great enough. It at once raises the searching question: To what extent are we in ignorance of our own motives and accustomed to improvise merely plausible explanations of and to ourselves? But an even more notable phenomenon occurred. *If the subject was asked again and again to try to remember why he raised the umbrella, he sooner or later recalled (to his own surprise) that he had been commanded to do it.*

The full import of this observation did not instantly

dawn on Freud. But he continued to have difficulties with the patients whom he sought to hypnotize. They sometimes held out against his suggestions, even though they had accepted them many times before, and seriously impeded the progress of the search for the traumatic episode. He gradually abandoned hypnosis, leaving the patient in a waking state in a relaxed position with instructions to report every incident connected with the early appearance of the symptom under investigation. Vestiges of the hypnotic technique remained as late as 1895, when he would still lay his hand on the patient's forehead as a stimulus to recollection.

This method also encountered crippling difficulties. A patient would sometimes lie for hours without saying a word, totally unable to recover a relevant reminiscence. To meet this obstacle, Freud presently hit upon the simple expedient upon which he thenceforth relied. He instructed the patient to say anything and everything that popped in his head, regardless of its propriety, logic, or triviality.

Freud found that all ramblings of his patient could furnish him with clues to the underlying and unavowed impulses of the sufferer. He became able to guess the nature of the buried episode in which the impulse had received its present type of manifestation. Thus the patient might begin by saying that she had seen a red-headed man in the street and that she always despised red-headed men—except of course her dear brother. Day after day apparently random allusions would build out the picture of her great interest in anything reminiscent of her brother's looks and acts, all of which would be bitterly condemned. But if she were asked directly, she would maintain that her brother was a fine, upstanding man, and a credit to the family.

The analyst, after listening to the eddies of talk, and noting the patterns along which they seemed to whirl, would presently locate a hidden rock beneath the innocent surface of the stream—in this case, an unacknowledged load of hatred against her brother. Bit by bit, stories of real or fancied childhood tyranny would come floating along the stream. Then suddenly, amid tears and violent gestures, might come the story of a long-forgotten incident which involved an intimate aggression on the part of the brother. The patient, manifestly relieved, might speedily recover from her hysterical disabilities and return to the active responsibilities of life.

Freud's theory of what he saw began modestly enough, leaned heavily upon Charcot, Bernheim, and Breuer, and was mostly founded upon observations made upon patients who were handled by hypnosis and not by the new procedure which later was called psychoanalysis. He published a contribution to the theory of the psychoneuroses in which he laid down the proposition that a distinction could be drawn between one group, the anxiety neuroses, which depended on mental conflict, and the actual neuroses, which were not due to mental conflict but to masturbation and coitus interruptus. In the first case, mental energy was converted into bodily symptoms, and in the latter case bodily energy was supposed to be converted into bodily symptoms. In Freud's early articles there is little to forecast the course which he was to follow as his brilliant imagination viewed the behavior of the individual from the new vantage ground which he had discovered.[1]

Whether his particular theories survive or fall, the standpoint which he achieved by ruthlessly applying his

[1] What has been said above is current in the biography of Freud by Fritz Wittals, and in Freud's autobiographical sketches.

method is of the greatest value. His method, which grew from the necessities of an exasperated physician, led him *systematically to treat every manifestation of the individual as part of a related whole.* Freud's mental set had been furnished by the data of hypnosis, which seemed to show that patients suffer from reminiscences. When he dropped hypnosis and tried to force recollections, his mental set had not altered, for he was still in search of the original, the traumatic episode. When he asked his patients to say anything that came into their heads, he was still hunting the elusive memory of a definite early experience. But quite without realizing it, his original mental set had widened, and with momentous consequences for his own subsequent development. If one were given to exaggerations, one could say that the world of psychological investigation had suddenly begun to turn on a new axis.

What was the nature of this new mental set? Intently watching his patients, not for word for word accounts of what had happened, and looking upon everything else as "irrelevant," Freud learned to look for meanings and not for reports. Every dream, every phrase, every hesitation, every gesture, every intonation, every outburst began to take on significance as possible allusions to the "traumatic" episode. Allusions to hated objects, reminiscent of a brother, failure to mention a hated sister until days had passed, although other members of the family had been passed in review—every deviation from comprehensiveness—was eagerly scrutinized for the clue it might afford.

The technique of therapy consisted in using clues to facilitate the patient's search for relief. The problem was to discover the nature of the patient's conflict and to volunteer interpretations for the sake of helping the patient to dare to bring into full consciousness the unavowed impulse which had once frightened his socially adjusted self into frantic repression. This involved the interpretation of the symptom as a compromise product of the patient's ideal of conduct; and the out-of-conscious impulse, which, though denied access to the full consciousness of the sufferer, possessed enough strength to procure partial gratification. The symptom was thus a symptom of conflict between the socially adapted portion of the self and the unadapted impulses of the personality, and the symptom was a compromise between partial gratification of the illicit and partial punishment by the conscience. The particular form of the "conflict" depended upon the traumatic experience and the antecedent history of the individual.

Far more important than these therapeutic elaborations is the shift in standpoint which made them possible. Since Freud was on the search for the literal by way of the symbolic, he raised hitherto neglected manifestations of human behavior to the dignity of significant symbols, wrote them out, and introduced them into the literature of human behavior. There could be no sharper illustration of the prepotency of "mental set" for the seeing of "facts" than the difference between the clinical reports of Freud and Janet. Freud, convinced that the eluctable energies of the organism could betray themselves in every image and in every gesture, painstakingly recorded the dreams and day-fantasies of his patients. Janet, who continued to assume that dreams were nonsensical confusions attributable to the diminished tension of the sleeping organism, seldom made any allusion to dreams. His pellucid description of grimaces, gestures, sentiments, and theories of his patients led back to relatively recent moments when the patient failed of adjustment. This failure of the patient to mobilize his energies in smooth adaptation to the exigencies of social reality was then imputed to a defective biopsychical mechanism, to a lowered "psychological tension," due to a miscellany of possible causes, among which was mentioned "the exhaustive effects of emotional excitement." Therapy consisted in restoring the capacity of the individual to mobilize and deploy his energies at the highest "levels" of adjustment. This was to be achieved by a variety of means—by hypnotic suggestion, rest in a simplified environment, and the usual repertory of the psychotherapist.

But the golden flash of psychological insight eluded Janet. At bottom he had little respect for the concrete reality of the mental life of his patients. Although he talked the language of psychogeneticism, it had a poor and not a rich connotation in his mind. I think this is due to his too exclusive reliance upon hypnotism, for the mental set of the hypnotist is derogatory to most of the concrete productions of the patient. The patient, one feels with a shrug, will presently come to the important experience; why take the superimposed material too seriously? Then, too, the patient may be put in order by direct command. Janet relates with some pride how people in the waiting-room of his office would marvel when a woman, bent nearly double, would be admitted into his sanctum, presently to emerge, erect and cured—until the effect wore off.

Freud learned a new respect for the concrete reality of mental life in his concentrated effort to divine the hidden conflict without resorting to hypnosis. His weakness as a hypnotist was in a sense the beginning of wisdom. A patient who is deeply hypnotized is but infrahuman. Barring commands which do violence to the moral code of the individual, the subject will passively execute the commands of the hypnotist. The patient descends from a complicated "nearly normal" person to a waxy caricature of a human being. The unhypnotized patient of Freud is in relatively full possession of all the resources of the ordinary waking self, and must be dealt with as a complex human being.

The widest gateway to psychoanalytic development became the study of dreams. And here again we are dealing with something which came, not from laborious reflection upon underlying concepts, but from the urgencies of the clinical situation. Just as we found that Freud had taken up a new post of observation in practice before he discovered its implications in theory, we find that in such a detail as the investigation of dreams, his theoretical preoccupations contributed less than his everyday necessities. Freud's patients continually thrust their dreams upon him; and he, now in pursuit of clues to what lay behind, presently took them seriously, and found in them many helpful indications of unspoken things. He would assist the free-fantasies of the patient by asking what came into his mind about any detail of the dream, and he attentively followed the long chains of superficially meaningless associations.

It began to appear that Freud had stumbled upon, and then brilliantly elaborated the possibilities inherent in, a new way of using the mind. He trained his patients in a technique of free-fantasy which they could subsequently use for themselves as a supplement to the logical technique which society ostensibly tries to foster. It at once appeared that he had discovered a method of thinking which was applicable far beyond the confines of the clinic and which could be added to the repertory of the mind.

The interpretation of dreams was the bridge which brought Freud from the confines of the clinic to the analysis of the whole psychology of individual development.

The dreams of patients and the dreams of non-pathological persons showed such homogeneity of symbolism that the gap between the "normal" and the "sick" seemed to close. Popular lore already furnished a clue to dreams as wish-fulfilments, whether found in the "well" or "ill," but popular lore also treated them as reminiscences, prophecies, and omens, or as confusions, depending on the transitory context of the moment. Freud had a double orientation in dealing with the individual. He regarded him as motivated in the present by impulses which eluded his own consciousness. He regarded these motivations as having achieved their present form in concrete historical events in the life of the individual. The nature of the present could be made clear to the conscious mind if the organizing episode could be recalled. This recall could be greatly facilitated by paying special attention to the "irrational" or non-adjustive aspects of the person's present conduct. The "irrational" would seem rational enough if the unacknowledged motives were made manifest, and if the historical as well as the contemporary allusions were sought after. Sooner or later the unrecognized motives would disclose themselves in consciousness, if the individual waited attentively; but the process could be greatly helped by using a different style of thinking than the logical.

No one has more dramatically and repeatedly shown the limitations (as well as the advantages) of logical procedures of thought than Freud. No one has made a more important contribution to the technique of supplementing logical thought by other methods of thought than Freud. This is the aspect of Freud's work which has immediate and constant relevance to political as to every other sort of thinking, and to which it is important to devote more extended consideration.

CHAPTER III

A NEW TECHNIQUE OF THINKING[1]

The prevailing theory is that men who make important decisions in politics can be trained to use their minds wisely by disciplinary training in the practices of logical thought. Legal training is supposed to mold the mind to ways of dealing with the world which subordinate whim to principle. Formal instruction in the social sciences is intended to equip the mind for the detached consideration of social consequences, and everyone agrees that this implies a large measure of self-awareness for the sake of reducing the play of prejudice.

The nature of logical thought has been carefully examined by an array of able writers. Their conclusions may be provisionally reported by saying that logic is a guided form of mental operation. It is not something marked off from impulse, but a progressive elaboration and differentiation of impulse. It proceeds by the affirmation of a starting-point, which is in fact a vague indication of the goal to be reached, and develops by the criticism of the material which appears in consciousness according to its relevance to the end in view. If the judge begins by wanting to settle a controversy consistently with precedents, he has indicated in advance the shadowy outline of the desired termination of his efforts. If an administrator wants to reduce complaints against his handling of the postal service, he starts with a different mental set from the judge, but, like the mental set of the latter, his first

[1] Modified from "Self-Analysis and Judicial Thinking," *International Journal of Ethics*, April, 1930.

28

act is to bring into view the state of affairs which he hopes to find when he quits thinking. He is accustomed to guide the operations of his mind by this preliminary character- ization of the terminus sought. No thinker can haul into the center of attention the material which indicates how the terminal situation is to be attained. The thinker must wait attentively for whatever appears. If he wants to deal with such a simple practical matter as getting to the railway station, and his mind continues to fill with images of the one he left behind him, his accustomed means of asserting control is to reiterate the practical end and to hope that he can "keep his mind on" taxicabs or auto- busses. Alternating with periods of reiteration and ex- pectancy and illumination are episodes of "No" and "Yes," which evidence the existence of guided thought.

It would be misleading to stop with this formal de- scription of the characteristics of logical thinking. Logi- cal thinking is not a hocus-pocus to be applied here and there and everywhere. The previewing of events presup- poses familiarity with the sorts of events to which the previewing relates. It usually involves analysis of the con- tingent future in the light of analogies with the past, which is simply a means of refining general familiarity through systematic methods of inspecting reality. General knowl- edge of lending and borrowing must be supplemented, for many purposes, by detailed examination of the quantita- tive dimensions of various routines. The precise nature of the relationship between changes in the rediscount rate and the price of call money requires analysis far beyond impressionistic familiarity.

There need be no illusion that the specification of the terminal situation provides an immovable constant for thought. We can imply, as we have implied, that logical thinking begins by sketching a figure on the canvass and leaves the details to be filled in during the course of the thinking. But the starting-point is often subject to many shifts, and the initial sketch is more or less subject to re-making. The judge who starts in pursuit of consistency-with-precedent characteristically must add conformity-to-principles-of-policy. A plurality of ends is always involved, and usually appears.

Everybody knows that the pluralism of ends goes far beyond "official" ends. A sophisticated and discerning judge may discover an embarrassing conflict in the controlling precedents, and cast about for other social purposes than conformity-to-precedent to guide him. He may scrutinize the principal economic, cultural, and political changes in the society in which he operates, and discern the appearance of a new set of rising dominant values, and decide to diminish the cost of social change by seeking to facilitate their introduction. If this hypothetical judge believes that he should not consciously enact his private prejudices into law, and if the social values are so confused that uncertainty rules, the judge is well advised to flip a coin (in chambers) and govern his decision accordingly. If the judge finds himself favorably disposed toward any alternative to begin with, he will take himself as an object of investigation to determine the extent and origin of his prejudice. His logic thus involves the use of self-scrutiny for the exposure of private values which load the dice for or against a particular point of view. Besides the values which are "public," there are complicating values which are the residue of one's "private" history.

All these points are stressed in greater or less degree in the current writing on the use of the mind. The avowed purpose of our professional schools is to increase the amount of logical reflection in the world, and the set complaint is that people somehow or another manage to think very clumsily. In spite of our best efforts to disseminate logicality, people are always "letting their prejudices run away with them," even when they have a baggage of good intentions.

The stock alibi for the failure of the schools to improve the character of thinking among those who hold positions of power is that the human mind offers a perverse opacity to the rays of reason. Somehow or other our training doesn't take; but this is attributed not to the deficiencies of logic but to the resistances to it. All this is reminiscent of the reply of the Christian to the taunt that Christianity has failed. He says that Christianity isn't to blame, but the lack of it. The logicians say that the cure of bad logic is more and better logic. If the human mind refuses to be educated, that's just too bad.

Our thesis is that our faith in logic is misplaced. Exclusive emphasis upon logic (even where logic is adroitly used) incapacitates rather than fits the mind to function as a fit instrument of reality adjustment.

The supposition that emotional aberrations are to be conquered by heroic doses of logical thinking is a mistake. The absence of effective logic is a symptom of a disease which logic cannot itself cure. We have been misled by supposing that the mind can rely upon a single technique of operation when this isolated technique has serious limitations.

A totally different technique of thinking is needed to get on with the task of ridding the mind of the distorting results of unseen compulsions. Since our schools have found no place for the cultivation of this additional technique of thinking, our judges and administrators and policy-makers are turned loose on the world armed with faith in logic and incapable of making their minds safe for logic. Logical thinking is but one of the special methods of using the mind, and cannot itself achieve an adequate inspection of reality because it is unable to achieve self-knowledge without the aid of other forms of thinking.

The technique of free-fantasy offers many points of contrast with logical thinking. It is unguided rather than guided association. From a given starting-point, no effort is bent toward the exclusion of the trivial, the trite, the embarrassing, the filthy, the nonsensical. The mind is permitted to run hither and yon. It is hospitable to everything which germinates in the mind, and is subject only to the effort to steer clear of the molds of logical thinking. There is no specific definition of an objective, and no intermittent intervention in the flow of material to register its pertinence or impertinence to this rather specific objective.

Free-fantasy is not to be confused with free word associations which begin with simple stimulus words and end when the first few words which pop into the mind are put down. Free-fantasy is not a momentary relaxation of selective criticism, but prolonged emancipation from logical fetters.

Free-fantasy differs from the ordinary daydream, the night dream, and the visions which arise in sleeping or waking by the circumstance that it is embarked upon with the vague, generalized purpose of rendering available new subject matter for logical thought. The frequent interventions which characterize logical procedures are suspended, the better to serve the ultimate purposes of reality adjustment. Daydreaming which is not used for this general purpose does not represent a technique for using the mind.

The ultimate paradox of logical thinking is that it is

self-destroying when it is too sedulously cultivated. It asserts its own prerogatives by clamping down certain restrictive frames of reference upon the activity of the mind, and presently ends in impoverishing the activity which it purports to guide into creative channels. It becomes intolerant of the immediate, unanalyzed, primitive abundance of the mind, and by so doing destroys its own source.

More seriously, too, for the mind which is engaged with social life, logical procedures exclude from the mind the most important data about the self. Directed thinking, whether about the self or something else as an object, is impatient of the seemingly trivial, and this impatience with the seemingly trivial is the rationally acceptable guise in which the impulse to avoid rigorous self-scrutiny gets itself accepted. The mind which is freely fantasying produces distasteful evidence of the facts about the self which the socialized self wants to avoid. This is why free-fantasy is not learned by rote, but achieved through trying experiences, usually under prolonged supervision.

There are wide individual differences in acquiring the technique of free-fantasy. Logical controls are often so gradually released that progress is almost imperceptible for several weeks of daily contact with a psychoanalytic interviewer. Frequently, of course, the logical controls fall away quite rapidly, and the exposure of the underlying preoccupations proceeds apace. Freud developed the technique, and drills his subjects, largely in relation to their dreams, but this is in no sense its exclusive application. The purpose of the psychoanalytic interview is not served if the patient is merely relieved of a few annoying symptoms; its purpose is to equip him with a means of handling his mind which will enable him to go it alone. In developing the free-fantasy procedure, Freud added a powerful tool to the repertory of those who would use their mind with some hope of disentangling themselves from the compulsive domination of many vestigial remains of their "private" histories.

It is quite possible to train people to use the free-fantasy method with considerable success and to outfit them with a device which they can use in the ordinary problems of professional and private life.[2] The instances which I shall presently adduce are from the fantasies which were produced by a judge in the course of a series of interviews which he undertook after his curiosity about the method had been aroused by the therapeutic treatment of a member of his family. Any specific allusions are disguised.

One day the judge commented at the beginning of the interview that a certain attorney irritated him in some unexplained way. He found himself acutely conscious of his own prejudice against the man, and in trying to deal fairly with him often leaned over backward and showed him an embarrassing favoritism in sustaining his objections. There was always a struggle to hold the balance even. This seemed to indicate the conspicuous operation of some unrecognized set of motives in relation to this particular individual. The judge, who was already partly skilled in the use of free-fantasy, began to report whatever came into his mind at the mention of the attorney, without regard to logic or scruple. "Cigar smoke . . . . black cigar . . . . vile and pungent and stuffy . . . . corridor . . . . courtroom . . . . ," and so on and on. The word "corridor" reappeared several times in the course of his associations, and the interviewer initiated a new chain by using the word as a stimulus. After some time, there came up a

[2] The training should, of course, be conducted by a specialist alert to his responsibilities.

vivid memory of an incident in the corridor of the law school where the judge had studied. A fellow-student, who was a man with a great reputation as a promising mind, dropped cigar ashes by accident on the judge's overcoat. The judge remembered his angry impulse to "sock" the offender, an impulse which he instantly subdued, and that he accepted the apology, which seemed to end the incident. Associations were continued to find why the brilliant rival had so incensed the judge, and the trail led back to certain incidents and reveries in early adolescence, but this material is not relevant here. The connection of his hostility toward his former rival with the attorney before him was due to one of the attorney's mannerisms, which recalled the way the student had flecked ashes off the end of his cigar. When this tie was exposed, the compulsive animosity and the overcompensatory reactions disappeared from the attitude of the judge in relation to the attorney.

Another illustrative detail may be taken almost at random from the record. On one occasion the judge began to enumerate the three principal alternatives which lay before him in deciding a pending case. He remembered two of them but hesitated several seconds before the third came into his mind. This led him to remember that he had often casually noticed that this third possibility seemed to elude him, although on reflection he felt that it deserved as much attention as the other two. He began spontaneously to relax and report everything that crossed his mind, and produced a long string of catch phrases from law and politics like "freedom of contract," "life, liberty, and pursuit of happiness," "freedom of speech and assembly." He presently noted that a picture was forming of one of his old law-school classrooms. He felt that someone was just about to speak to him, and had to resist the temptation to turn around. Then there came across his mind a long series of incidents in which one of his law professors was the principal figure. This teacher was reputed to possess a mastermind and a caustic tongue; and the judge, though he had always wanted to make a great impression on him, had met with no particular success. The professor had a habit of using his most ironic tone of voice when he spoke of "this freedom of contract." Now it happened that the attorney who was arguing for alternative No. 3 before the court pronounced the word "freedom" with unction. This aroused in the judge's mind the ironic tone of the old professor's voice, and this in turn brought back the rather humiliating failure he had been in his efforts to impress the professor. He now exhibited a tendency to repress everything connected with the episode, including the attorney's argument.

The world about us is much richer in meanings than we consciously see. These meanings are continually cutting across our ostensible criteria of judgment, and compulsively distorting the operations of the mind whose quest for an objective view of reality is consciously quite sincere. Good intentions are not enough to widen the sphere of self-mastery. There must be a special technique for the sake of exposing the hidden meanings which operate to bind and cripple the processes of logical thought. With practice one may wield the tool of free-fantasy with such ruthless honesty that relevant material comes very quickly to the focus of attention which we call "waking consciousness."

It would be possible to fill many volumes with illustrations of the hitherto unseen meanings which have been discovered by men and women who have learned to use the free-fantasy technique. They have often been able to find how and why their emotions tended to be aroused favorably or unfavorably toward individuals of their own or the opposite sex who exhibited certain traits, and to understand why they tended to choose certain secretaries, to sponsor certain protégés, and to be impressed by certain witnesses and attorneys. They have been able to inspect the phraseology of law, politics, and culture, and to extricate themselves from many of the logically irrelevant private meanings which they read into it.

Freud developed the technique of free-fantasy well over a quarter of a century ago, but it is still beyond the pale of the schools. Our professional and graduate schools make no effort to readjust their methods to fit the minds of future men of authority for self-knowledge. The sententious admonitions to "know thyself" are no adequate substitute for special discipline in the ways of self-understanding.

We have tried to cure the failures of logical training by homeopathic doses of sermonizing, rather than by the discipline of supplementary techniques of using the mind. The mind is a fit instrument of reality testing when both blades are sharpened—those of logic and free-fantasy. Until this fundamental proposition is adequately comprehended, the professional training of our judges, administrators, and theorists will continue to furnish discipline in self-deception rather than self-analysis.

CHAPTER IV

THE CRITERIA OF POLITICAL TYPES

The free-fantasy method of exploring the mind is of very general application to the problems of life. In particular we are interested in examining the results of its use for the purpose of laying bare the natural history of personality growth and differentiation. All sorts of politicians are met with in society, and our special task is to relate the selection of these adult rôles to certain critical experiences in individual development. But before we can proceed farther, we need to examine the nature of the criteria which are currently used in identifying various political types.

The popular speech of every state and neighborhood swarms with names for varieties of political behavior and types of politicians. The study of political differences may very well begin by sifting the common vocabulary. Some of the popular images are derived from experience with government officials. Within the last hundred years the policeman has appeared over Western Europe, and a history of the popular conception of his rôle could be written around terms like "bobby," "cop," and *"Schupo."* Whatever differences in dress, manner, social position, and common humanity are supposed to exist between a "civil servant," a *"Beamter,"* and a *"fonctionnaire,"* there are common lineaments in the composite stereotype. A thick chapter in human experience could be entitled "The Bureaucrat," wherein would be recorded the innuendo of popular comment on a necessary evil. The "legislator" is identifiable through all the detailed contrasts between the "congressman," the "M.P.," and the "M.d.R."

The popular tongue is rich in expressions which fill out the official cast of characters in the political drama by peopling the public stage with figures whose traits are essentially irrelevant to their office. There are men of ideas —"anarchist," "socialist," "liberal," "communist,". "conservative." There are men of ideas and of action—"reformer," "revolutionary," "martyr." The history of American, British, French, German, medieval, Graeco-Roman, and every civilization could be written for the sake of showing how the carriers of public power figured in the eyes of the various groups within and without the culture.

This profusion of types in the popular firmament of politics is supplemented by the types which have been isolated by serious students of culture, who have sought to impose order upon the life of the past. Among the political forms which have been described by the historians, the "benevolent despot" of the eighteenth century, the "demagogue" of Athenian democracy, the "prince" of the Italian Renaissance, and the "despot" of the oriental empires spring at once to mind. The masterly sketch of the evolution of the public official with which Max Weber[1] has enriched social science is, it is to be hoped, the forerunner of many elaborate studies. The traits and arts of political leaders have been most systematically handled by Aristotle, Machiavelli, Robert Michels, Christensen, and Charles E. Merriam.[2]

These typologies, whether popular or scientific, possess

[1] "Politik als Beruf," in *Gesammelte Schriften*.

[2] I summarized some of this literature in "Types of Political Personalities," *Proceedings of the American Sociological Society, 1927*. Reprinted in *Personality and the Group* (edited by Burgess).

several features in common. They may converge to what is practically the same picture. When W. B. Munro described the "reformer," he filled out the popular image which arose in the American mind at a certain phase of American political evolution.[3] Practically every scientific conception is a refinement and generalization of some term in general circulation, though with local connotations.

The scientific and the popular typologies may include the same kinds of fact as their starting-points. The fact of supposed political conviction gave rise to the "liberal," but it is a far cry from the rather shadowy lines of the popular image to the finely wrought lineaments of Ruggiero.[4] The means employed in encompassing political objectives christen the "lobbyist," "propagandist," and "agitator." The idea that private motives are not merged in public motives is carried in "renegade," "sorehead," and "tyrant." The idea that private motives have been firmly fused into public purposes is one connotation of the "martyr." The fact of informal ascendancy is celebrated in the "boss." In the "bureaucrat" it is implied that the office has molded the man, and that the office tends to attract those especially likely to develop such qualities. The Western European idea of a judge almost necessarily refers to a functionary who carries certain paraphernalia and proceeds with ceremony. The leanness of the "fanatical agitator" figured in the popular mind long before Kretschmer gave it his scientific blessing.[5]

Both popular and scientific conceptions range from the particular to the general. The British "election agent" is closely bound to a recent, special social setting. The "lead-

[3] *Personality in Politics.*

[4] *The History of European Liberalism.*

[5] *Physique and Character*, chap. xiii.

er" keeps a stable nucleus of meaning for the description of a social rôle among widely separated peoples in widely separated periods.

Popular and scientific conceptions are at one in that they may present developmental and not merely descriptive implications. The notion of a lean and bitter agitator is not entirely a static, cross-sectional description of a fortuitous juxtaposition of traits, but a hypothesis that bodily irritations operate dynamically to foster the selection of forms of activity which enable the individual to give rather free vent to his animosities.

Both popular and scientific types may be taken as objects of study to determine the factors in their formation. The popular idea of a "reformer" in America bears a certain photographic resemblance to actual personalities who figured as public advocates of restrictive laws. It is possible to study the process by which the stereotype of the lean and spinsterly kill-joy arose, and to see why it persisted. Every body politic has its gallery of political mummers, and political history needs to be rewritten to explain the unique and the typical qualities of these popularly conceived rôles. Stuart A. Rice has developed a technique for the identification of contemporary stereotypes of this kind.[6] Rice took photographs of a senator, a bolshevik, and a bootlegger, and after obliterating the names asked various test groups to tell what designation best fitted each picture. By examining the erroneous identifications, it became possible to detect the mental pattern popularly associated with the class name.

An interesting contribution to social science would be the detailed examination of the factors affecting the rise and fall of those political typologies which have been seriously

[6] *Quantitative Methods in Politics*, chap. v.

proposed by scholars. The exaggerated picture of the omnipotent leader drawn by Carlyle no doubt had something to do with Carlyle's sexual impotence and his compensatory idealization of the potent; but the popularity which this exaggeration enjoyed among certain classes of English society was due to the dislocation of older economic institutions and the rise of threatening collective ideologies. The new business enterpriser felt the intoxicating vanity of the self-made man, and the decayed landlords felt the necessity of individualistic protests against the age of cities and machines.

Suppose we examine in more detail the intellectual structure of scientific political types. This requires special attention to the two terms involved, the "political" and the "types." Two ways of defining the "political" are current in social science. I will speak of them as the "institutional" and the "functional" methods of definition. Within any community there are many patterns of activity whose form and whose magnitude may be singled out for study. There is the production and distribution of material goods and services; the main patterns by which these operations proceed can be called the economic institutions of the community. There is the settlement of disputes, and the defense and extension of interests which are believed to be collective; these are the political or governmental institutions of the community. In the same way religious, charitable, and a host of other institutions may be discerned.

These institutionally derived categories fall short of clarity and comprehensiveness. Some social processes occur within the framework of every institutional process. Thus the settlement of disputes is a prominent characteristic of government as we know it; but it is not, and never has been, and cannot by the nature of things be, a monopoly of government when government is defined as an institutional division of social labor. No institution ever quite monopolizes the function which it most distinctively exercises. But this need not lead to confusion. When the settlement of disputes is a prominent function of one group in society, and there is no other group which participates in the same function in the same degree, there is no hesitation in deciding to call the first group the "governors" and to call the patterns according to which they are selected and operate the "political or governmental" institutions of the community. If there is a rival adjuster of differences, the distinction is by no means clear, as when the "church," "business," and the "state" are rivals. Perhaps the governors can be identified by finding who it is who handles the coercion employed in defending or extending communal enterprises, though this criterion may from time to time fail to differentiate. But, on the whole, these doubts are marginal doubts. Ordinarily it is possible to find a division of labor and a set of sentiments which can be called the "government of the state." The marginal instances call attention to the fact to which allusion has been made, the fact that no "institutional" process quite monopolizes the function which it most distinctively exercises. It is therefore advisable to describe communal processes by two sets of terms, one of which refers to "institutions" and the other to "functions" which are found within the various institutional frameworks. Much of the literature of social science consists in terminological quibbles about the "proper" words to use in this institutional or functional sense, often without appreciating the essential nature of the matter at issue. It is, of course, of the highest importance to understand the difference, and of minor importance to agree upon the words with which to describe the distinction.

From what has been said, it is clear that a word like "political" may be given an "institutional" or a "functional" meaning in a particular context, and that—and this is the most important consequence—any contribution to the understanding of the "institutional" process is a contribution to the understanding of the wider "functional" process, and the reverse. In this resides the unity of the social sciences. The apparent disunity arises from the differences in starting-point of particular inquiries. One begins with a series of phenomena which are selected from a single institutional process, and another begins with a series of phenomena which are selected from several institutional processes according to some functional conception.

This unity of destination and disunity of starting-point is abundantly manifested in the scientific study of human behavior. The specialist on some phase of the political process, institutionally conceived, who is asked to classify the types of political behavior, devises his categories on the basis of the institutional processes which he knew best. It would be possible, were it worth the effort, to pass in review the typologies which have been propounded from time to time by specialists in executive organization, public administration, judicial administration, legislation, political parties, propaganda and conspirative organizations, political revolution, nationalism, imperialism, interstate methods of adjustment (war, diplomacy, conference, adjudication, mediation, arbitration), and all the other topics in political science.

At first glance, the functional method of defining political types would seem to lead to even greater congeries of categories than the institutional method. From the functional standpoint politics is found wherever, to use the older terminology, "wills" are in conflict. This implies that intensely political manifestations in society are not con-fined to government officials and parties, but to banking houses, manufacturing enterprises, distributing services, ecclesiastical organizations, fraternal associations, and pro-fessional societies. It is probable that the most aggressive, power-lusting individuals in modern society find their way into business, and stay out of the legislature, the courts, the civil service, and the diplomatic service. If this be true, the student of political personalities will find the most in-teresting objects of study in J. P. Morgan and Company, in the United States Steel Corporation, and among the clerical or educational or medical politicians.

It follows from what has been said that the study of politicians who are chosen from a single institutional proc-ess makes a contribution to the general study of politicians in every institutional process, and that the conscious ab-straction of categories until they are comprehensive opens a wider range of exact comparison. This may eventuate in an actual simplification of some fundamental concep-tions. Of course, institutional processes differ in the scope which they give to certain human drives. Today the church offers less opportunity for the use of physical violence than it did in the sixteenth century, and very much less oppor-tunity than the police force, the private detective agency, or the political gang.

The advantages of comprehensiveness and possible sim-plification have been sacrificed by the political scientists of the schools because they have conceived their task in too narrow a spirit. They have been slow in studying the mani-festations of human nature in politics because they have been saturated with sectarian pride in legal and philosophi-cal distinctions; or they have checked their theories with their coats, and plunged into technical work. A body of theory which interacts fruitfully with philosophy, law, and technology is still very poorly developed. The formal sociological systems have been sacked for "premises" but neglected for hypotheses. (Witness the exploitation of the concept of "solidarity" in recent juridical theory.) The task of the hour is the development of a realistic analysis of the political in relation to the social process, and this depends upon the invention of abstract conceptions and upon the prosecution of empirical research. It is precisely this missing body of theory and practice which Graham Wallas undertook to supply in England and which Charles E. Merriam has been foremost in encouraging in the United States. It is the deficiency which led Catlin to propose to substitute what I would call the "functional" for the "institutional" definition of the field of political science.[7] This necessarily implies a new respect for the possibilities of using the ingenious suggestions to be found in the sociological systematists, a new curiosity about diverse ways of approaching events, and a new sympathy for parallels to institutional phenomena.

Various obscurities can be removed if we generalize our terms from the narrowly institutional to the broadly functional plane. Terms like "statesman" and "despot" were minted of the metal of political experience in communities where the high road to power was governmental. It is true that in Athens it was difficult to draw very sharp lines between governmental and other forms of communal activity, on account of the intimate interlacing of all institutional processes. Nevertheless, terms like "statesman" and "despot" came to refer to forms of political activity in a narrowly institutional sense, and such is their connotation today.

[7] *The Science and Method of Politics.*

But this connotation requires generalization and revi-sion. The road to power in our civilization is by no means an exclusively governmental highway, for technical imple-ments have scattered authority and created an industrial feudality. The directors of large corporations have to make decisions which are far more important for the daily happiness of mankind than most of the decisions of gov-ernments. Since government is so largely the agent of corporations, the government is hardly master in its own house.

The concept of the statesman has long carried the impli-cation that anyone who exercises social power outside the government is in hot pursuit of an exclusively private ad-vantage. Is this any longer tenable? Is there not such a thing as the "institutionalization of business" which arises when a given enterprise plans to operate indefinitely and is thus forced to calculate its interests over long periods of time? One of the major elements in this calculation is the necessity of taking precautions against a withdrawal of favor on the part of the community at large. This is the core of the political way of thinking, and assimilates the policy of aggregations of private power to that of the state which is guided by statesmen. It is timely, therefore, to disentangle the concept of statesmanship from its historical association with a single institution.

Some of the many senses in which the "politician" is used may be disposed of by drawing a clean distinction be-tween the "business man" and the "politician." The busi-ness man may be defined as one who pursues a private ad-vantage with little regard for conceptions of public right. The politician, in the here-selected "best" sense of the word, uses persuasion on behalf of his conception of public right. The politician pursues a genuine integration of interests in the community; the business man is satisfied with a compromise among competing private interests. The importance to political theory of the distinction between integration and compromise has quite properly been stressed by Mary P. Follett.[8] An integration of interests is the solution of a conflict in such a way that neither "party" recognizes that so much has been won and so much has been lost in the outcome. It represents a reinterpretation of the situation in a sense which renders the old line of battle, the older definition of interest, irrelevant. It is illustrated when a wage controversy is disposed of by the decision to try to divide the advantages of economies in production which may be brought about through new co-operative procedures. The essence of the contrast between integration and compromise is that between a synthesis and a trade. The politician is a discoverer of inclusive advantages, and the business man is a higgler for special advantages. Whether, as Adam Smith said, an invisible hand shapes a social synthesis from the general pursuit of private profit, we do not have to decide upon here. The contrast is between the conscious objectives of the individuals concerned. It should be observed that politicians are not limited to government and that business men are not limited to private ventures. The "boss" is one form of the business man in government; the director of a large private concern may be a politician in the sense used here.[9]

Having drawn a necessary distinction between the insti-

[8] *The New State.*

[9] It is not profitable to pursue these distinctions farther. I should prefer to distinguish the statesman from the politician by treating the latter as a function of a democratically organized community and as one who is limited to persuasion in the advancement of his conceptions of public right. The statesman may use force, and is not necessarily a function of democratically organized society.

tutional and the functional meaning of the "political," we are in a position to discuss the "type" concept. A "type" is a relation, and we may classify types according to the relations chosen. Political types may be set up on a three-fold basis: by specifying a nuclear relation, a co-relation, and a developmental relation.

What is meant by the choice of a nuclear relation may be illustrated by the concept of the *Machtmensch* as elaborated by Eduard Spranger in his *Lebensformen*. Spranger, the distinguished educational psychologist of the University of Berlin, has developed a morphology of personality on an original basis. Dilthey, it will be recalled, ushered in the modern era of typological inquiry in his famous address before the Berlin Academy of Science.[10] Dilthey selected forms of distinguished cultural activity and posited trait-constellations to fit. By the process of abstracting from many concrete fields of achievement, he finally built up his description of the sensual, heroic, and contemplative types. Most eminent political figures naturally fall in the second category. Spranger's approach has much in common with that of Dilthey. He proceeds on the hypothesis that all possible valuational dispositions are shared by all men. By inspecting human culture, Spranger comes to the conclusion that six distinctive cultural fields have materialized six valuational dispositions in man. Thus the cultural activities having to do with wealth production correspond to the economic value tendency. Science corresponds to the theoretical, art to the aesthetic, religion to the religious, the state to the power tendency, and society to the love tendency. Spranger goes on to deduce the at-

[10] His viewpoint is best expressed in "Die Typen der Weltanschauung," in *Weltanschauung-Philosophie und Religion in Darstellungen* (edited by M. Frischeisen-Kohler).

tributes of each personality in which one value tendency predominates, and traces out the implications for each field of activity of the predominance of this tendency. Thus the political man is the one whose principal value is the pursuit of power. The essence of power is understood to be the capacity, and usually the will, to impose one's own values as permanent or transitory motives upon others. The political man in science tends to substitute rhetoric for truth and to use ideas as forces (in the sense of Fouillée). In economics the political man tends to reach his ends by diplomacy and negotiation, by intimidation or violence, or by other political means. In art the political motive leads to efforts to impress by flamboyant decorative display. In social life the political motive, with its forcible urge toward self-aggrandizement, must usually disguise itself in fostering the interests of some collectivity. The god of the political man in religion is a god of might who requires mighty men to serve him.

In developing his image of the *homo politicus*, Spranger is fully aware that his "pure" type seldom exists. The bold, frank aggrandizement of self is rarely tolerated in society, for "the greatest power manifests itself as collective power," and the man who cherishes power must achieve some measure of socialization or he is outlawed. Although in principle no warm-hearted lover of his fellow-men, he must keep his contempt to himself or feign expansive sentiments of group loyalty. Indeed, self-deception is perhaps the rule, for the political personality with a strong artistic component possesses a florid imagination which dramatizes his personal history and subordinates all reality to ambitious plans. It seems to me that Spranger does not sufficiently stress this aspect of the political man, this large capacity for playing the impostor upon himself and others.

The gist of Spranger's generalization of the political man is schematically expressible in terms of desire-method-success. The political man desires to control the motives of others; his method may vary from violence to wheedling; his success in securing recognition in some community must be tangible. These are the nuclear relations which are essential to the type definition.

Naturally there are a number of necessary annotations to be made on this formula. Sometimes the man with a thirst for power is unable to indulge and quench his thirst, for his physical and social equipment may be too meager. And how are we to appraise results? *Wer regiert denn?* Power over others is partially exercised by every living being; but in any hierarchy of the powerful, some are on the lowest tier, if current social criteria be applied. The bedridden, complaining wreck may be of no significance except as a burden upon the care of a single nurse. Accepting the current values of society, such an individual would be on the very bottom of the heap. And yet, as Alfred Adler has so often insisted as to make the point peculiarly his own, the hysteric may use his symptoms to win a high degree of submission from his immediate environment, and this may be all that he cares about. And some of those who give up the visible struggle for social influence may retire to distil their bile into poisoned darts against the pursuit of external pomp, and secure reputation and eminence by embodying the results in sparkling rhetoric.

The man who runs his village may become more acutely aware that he does not run the county; and when he runs the county, that he does not run the province; and so on up the ladder. His appurtenances of power may be deferred to by those about him, yet his own soul may smart with the shackles of a larger slavery. Thus, Spranger is right in saying that, when one succeeds in penetrating the psychology of the search for power, it becomes comprehensible that he whose nature is bound up in the pursuit of authority is most keenly sensible to the limits of his own freedom, and consequently suffers so keenly from nothing else in life than his own subordination. Sensing this, the Stoics long ago contended that the essence of liberty is the self-sufficiency which makes no demands on others. Ascendancy involves dependence, a reciprocal relationship which has been exhaustively described by Simmel.[11] But there are some who combine easy success with indifference. These are no doubt recruited from among those who have natural suggestive power to certain groups—they possess the *charisma* of Max Weber.[12]

Allowing for these annotations, the nucleus of Spranger's thinking may be repeated. The *homo politicus* is characterized by the following relationship between desire, method, and success: desire to control the motives of others; methods varying from violence to wheedling; and success in securing communal recognition.

Spranger's subtle comments in elaborating this simple, central conception are among the most valuable in the literature of society. Starting from bold simplifications, he succeeds in formulating pictures which give richer meaning to the details of political life in all the institutional processes of culture. Of course the literature of political science is full of types which are described as Spranger has described the political man. Michels and Merriam have listed the qualities which they find in political leaders as a class. Conway has propounded his fa-

---

[11] *Soziologie*, chap. iii.

[12] *Grundriss der Sozialökonomik*, III, 1.

miliar trichotomy: crowd-compellers, crowd-exponents, and crowd-representatives. The possibility of defining types according to the reactionary, conservative, liberal, or radical nature of the opinions championed has often been discussed.[13]

The scheme which will be employed in presenting case materials stresses the capacity of political personalities to play rôles which are either specialized or composite. Hobbes was a theorist and an agitating pamphleteer; he is scarcely thinkable as an agitating orator and organizer like Garrison. The "pure-type" agitator is represented by the Old Testament prophets. Bodin combined a memorable contribution to political theory with the arduous duties of a successful administrator. Masaryk won his spurs in philosophy, sociology, cultural history, agitation, and organization. Numberless are those who have shown excellent organizing ability but who have been innocent of theoretical interests or of agitating power. Some political assassins and tyrants have enjoyed the use of violence as a *ding an sich*. The central point in deciding where to place a political figure is to discover the form of activity which means the most to him, and to modify the classification according to his success in combining this with other rôles. Marx wanted to impress himself upon mankind, certainly; and he craved the skill of a Lassalle, who could step on the platform and dominate the turbulent emotions of the crowd. But more: Marx wanted unreserved admiration for the products of his mind. He toiled through years of isolation and poverty to make his assertions impregnable.

[13] See Robert Michels, *Political Parties*; C. E. Merriam, *American Party System*, and *Introduction* to H. F. Gosnell's *Boss Platt and His New York Machine*; Martin Conway, *Instincts of the Herd in Peace and War*; Lowell, *Public Opinion in War and Peace*; Rohmer, *Die Vier Parteien*; A. Christensen, *Politics and Crowd Morality*; W. B. Munro, *Personality in Politics*.

It was more important to attain theoretical completeness than to modify his technique of social intercourse. Lassalle was the composite leader who could woo an audience, organize activities all over Germany, write excellent books, and win a place for himself in many circles of life. Marx was the limited specialist who had to exact submission to the assertions of his mind, come what may.

Table I brings out the distinction between specialized and composite types.

TABLE I

POLITICAL RÔLES

	Administrator	Agitator	Theorist
Specialized types:			
Hoover	*	....	....
Old Testament			
prophets	....	*	....
Marx	....	....	*
Composite types:			
Cobden	*	*	....
Bodin	*	....	*
Lenin	*	*	*

Other combinations may be indicated. By adding a fourth column for those who resort to violence, the schematic possibilities are enlarged. Most theorists have been agitators in some measure, and it is often a matter of taste whether emphasis is to be placed on one or the other feature of their activity. Characteristically, the theorists have sought to appeal to the sentiments of their contemporaries by pamphleteering or by the direction of their speculative interests to immediate ends. Hobbes and Rousseau were shut off from oratory and organization, but no small part of their writing was intended to add fuel to the flames around them. Such men as Tom Paine are able to strike

off excellent formulations of political theory in the heat
of the fray.

So far we have been discussing types which are distinguished according to some nuclear relation among a few
variables. The characteristic mode of elaborating such a
type is to imagine a host of situations in which the type
may be found, and to describe the resulting picture. This
is the elaboration of the preliminary sketch on the basis of
sophisticated experience with social life. For these im-
pressionist methods it is possible to substitute a more
formal procedure. Having chosen a central primary relation, is it possible to find, by reference to specific instances,
the relative frequency with which other traits are associated with the nuclear ones. The starting-point may be
either institutional or functional, of course: those who are
"judges," "legislators," or "bosses" may be investigated,
or those who are "statesmen," "conciliators," or "administrators." We have already had occasion to stress the
point that institutional definitions and functional definitions do not precisely coincide, although either is a valid
point of departure for research.

The result of the formal procedure outlined is to define
"co-relational" (correlational) types. A recent monograph
by Fritz Giese may be used to illustrate the possibilities.[14]
This is a statistical treatment of the data available in the
German *Who's Who* of 1914. After Giese had eliminated
those who were included on account of their hereditary
position only, he had over ten thousand names left. He
then distinguished thirty-three varieties of activity, which
were grouped into the five major categories of art, social
science, physical science, technology, and practical life.

---

[14] *Die öffentliche Persönlichkeit.* Beihefte zur *Zeitschrift für angewandte
Psychologie*, Vol. XLIV.

He also classified his subjects into those who were honored because of high-grade but essentially routine professional accomplishment, those who enriched their field of activity by some creative contribution, and those whose creativeness was unrestricted to their occupational field. The three types were the skilful, the productive, and the freely creative. Since the individual is not confined to one field of activity, the following scheme of connections was built up to show the relation between the person and the form of activity: (a) income source (the person regards a particular field as a "bread and butter" occupation); (b) successive activity field (the individual has deserted one field for another); (c) field of simultaneous double-production; (d) recreational activity. The relation of a person to a field of activity may show a splitting of his personality or a compensatory function. When a politician consciously decides to play golf or to collect pictures to relieve his mind from exclusive political preoccupations, he is realizing a compensatory value in this chosen field. When he finds himself impelled to try to live a double life of scientific investigation and political propaganda, he is exhibiting major, and contrasting, tendencies in his personality (splitting). Sometimes the tie between fields of activity which the same individual exploits is factual similarity, as when a politician becomes a literary man to the extent of writing the political history of a period. Sometimes the connection is a functional relationship, in that the same biopsychic dispositions are to be assumed to operate. Thus, business promotion and politics are intimately allied; sculpture and politics are not.

Giese's detailed analysis showed that those engaged in politics reveal the most heterogeneous affiliations and backgrounds. He raised the question whether it was proper to think of a distinctive functional gift which would characterize all those in political positions. When compared with art, especially architecture, and engineering, the heterogeneity of the political population is very evident. Indeed, the manifold connections of politically active persons with other fields suggest that political life depends upon very widely dispersed capacities of human nature, as does teaching, history writing, and journalism. But there is one important exception which is clearly brought out by the figures. This was a group of politicians who rose from humble circumstances and devoted themselves assiduously to organization and agitation. They offer a sharp contrast to those for whom political life was a sport, hobby, or honorary distinction. For the organizing and agitating group we may postulate a functional disposition of some kind.

The results show how the institutional approach to a problem may eventuate in the isolation of one group which very probably coincides closely with a functional group in other institutional activities. Some of the agitating and organizing people weren't yet in politics at the time the 1914 census was made, and some of them were so busy with private organizations that they never made the formal transition to politics in the institutional sense.

Another conclusion which bears on the same point is Giese's discovery that those who were freely creative in politics had much more in common with those who were freely creative in other fields than they had with those who were merely productive in their own. Giese's method of classifying his freely creative group is too ambiguous to justify one in considering his conclusion of more than suggestive value, but it is possible that he has isolated a functionally homogeneous group which cuts across all institutional lines.

Some of the studies of political personalities have carried the quantitative method far enough to substitute scales for rank orders at various points. Various reaction tests have been used in the hope of discovering constant differences among those who play different political rôles. Henry T. Moore undertook to decide whether there is such a thing as a temperamental predisposition toward conservatism or radicalism. He defined radicalism as "an attitude favorable to sweeping changes in social institutions, especially changes along lines opposed to class interest," and classified the opinion expressions of students according to the degree of radicalism or conservatism indicated. He then applied a series of reaction tests to the students and reached the following conclusion:

Our evidence so far as it goes points to some innate basis of difference. This basis does not seem to be the level of general intelligence or of emotional stability, nor in any general superiority or inferiority in learning or attention, but in such specific factors as greater speed of reaction, ease of breaking habits, readiness to make snap judgments, and independence in the face of majority influence. The last of these differences is the one most clearly indicated. . . . . If one man is by nature more keyed up for speed and flexibility, and the other is more designed for regularity of function, we can hardly expect that government of the hyperkinetic by the phlegmatic and for the phlegmatic can fail to develop periods of stress and strain.[15]

Floyd Allport classified students into typical and atypical members of the community, discovering whether they took up prevalent or minority positions on various political questions. He then applied a battery of tests to the

[15] "Innate Factors in Radicalism and Conservatism," *Journal of Abnormal and Social Psychology*, XX (1925–26), 234–44.

students and found that certain traits of the atypical (whether the opinions were "radical" or "conservative") proved to be homogeneous. Thus, not only do the "extremes" meet, but also those who hold minority positions along a hypothetical continuum of opinion distribution.[16]

W. H. Cowley, at the instigation of Charles E. Merriam and L. L. Thurstone, undertook to compare leaders in chosen situations. He used twenty-eight tests of such traits as aggressiveness, self-confidence, intelligence, emotional stability, and speed of reaction. While his tests were differentiating within the same group between leaders and followers, he reports that they did not distinguish between leaders as a class and followers as a class. He thus felt justified in denying that leadership is a universal trait of particular persons, and criticized efforts to itemize "traits of leadership."[17] Further applications of the blanket-test technique are under way.[18]

Gilbert J. Rich opened out a new field of investigation when he studied certain complex physiological and biochemical variables among leaders and followers. He measured the hydrogen-ion concentration of the saliva, the acidity of the urine, alkali reserve of the blood, and creatinine excretion of the urine. The least excitable subjects showed the most acid saliva and the most acid urine. The

[16] Allport really used a rank-order method of handling opinion expressions which he unjustifiably treated as marking definite positions along a base line. Thurstone has greatly improved the technique of opinion measurement. See Thurstone and Chave, *The Measurement of Attitude* (Chicago, 1929). For Allport's original paper (with D. A. Hartman), see "Measurement and Motivation of Atypical Opinion in a Certain Group," *American Political Science Review*, XIX (1925), 735–60.

[17] "Three Distinctions in the Study of Leaders," *Journal of Abnormal and Social Psychology*, Vol. XXIII (July–September, 1928).

[18] By Keith Sward, Social Science Research Council Fellow, and others. I discuss the problem of evaluating test results later on.

rating of the subjects was open to criticism, and was obviously much less refined than the biochemical techniques employed.[19]

The types which we have just been considering show more than a cross-sectional picture of the adult personality. They have made the transition from itemizing the instantaneous pictures to the selection of features of the immediate picture which show how the type has come to be. They are thus more than co-relational types; they have made some progress toward developmental types. When Giese found the group of political personalities of humble origin and persistent organizing and agitating activity, he postulated a common dynamic of development, a homogeneous functional disposition toward this sort of thing. Moore wanted to extricate the formative influence of temperamental reactive sets, and the other investigators have likewise sought to ascertain developmental factors in the production of the adult picture of traits and interests.

Almost every nuclear and co-relational type carries developmental implications. The terms which are used to characterize motives have dynamic, genetic, formative coronas of meaning which, vaguely though they may be sketched, are emphatically present. When Michels says that a "Catonian strength of conviction" is one mark of the political leader, it is implied that if one pushed his inquiry into the adolescence, childhood, and even infancy of the individual that this ruling characteristic would be visible. Of course, Michels does not himself develop these implications; it is doubtful if he has tried to find the early analogues of the trait which he called "Cantonian strength of conviction" on the adult level. But the dynamic penum-

[19] "A Biochemical Approach to the Study of Personality," *Journal of Abnormal and Social Psychology*, Vol. XXIII (July–September, 1928).

bra of the term can lead empirical investigators to scrutinize the behavior of children from a new point of view. Many of the terms which are used to describe adult traits are no doubt unpredictable from the less differentiated traits of infancy, childhood, and youth. But the growth of full-blown developmental types requires the sifting and refinement of terms until they are adequate to the description of sequences of growth. Developmental types will describe a set of terminal, adult reactions, and relate them to those critical experiences in the antecedent life of the individual which dispose him to set up such a mode of dealing with the world. Developmental types will not only include the subjective account of the history of the personality but will embrace the objective factors which were co-operating to produce the patterns described.

The notion of a developmental type may be illustrated by examining the place which is assigned to the political man in the chief modern characterological systems. Hans Apfelbach has used five dimensions for the description of characters. Each one is described as a gamut between two polar opposites, and a sixth pair of polar opposites is introduced into the system. The scheme is indicated in Table II.

This gives a formal range of sixty-four types of character formation without allowing for subtle variations in quantity. The first combination which Apfelbach specifies is, symbolically, ABCDEF. This is a very masculine, sadistic, hyperemotional, moral, intellectually keen, and upright character. Among men this is the type of the organizers, politicians, the great preachers, generals, dictators, and the like. Among women, this is the type of the organizer of every description, especially the political or patriotic enthusiast, like Joan of Arc. It should be observed that the terms "masculine" and "feminine" are not used in a mutually exclusive sense. Carrying on the tradition of Weininger and Fliess, these terms are employed to designate traits which may be present in different proportions in the same person.[20]

The political man appears in Jung's system at various intersections of his underlying scheme. The essential

TABLE II

Dimension	Polar Elements	
Sexuality	Masculine	A
	Feminine	a
Psychomotility	Psychosadistic	B
	Psychomasochistic	b
Emotionality	Hyperemotional	C
	Hypo-emotional	c
Morality	Moral	D
	Immoral	d
Intellectuality (specialized)	Superior	E
	Inferior	e
Accessory elements	Altruistic	F
	Egotistic	f

cleavage in Jung's classification is between those whose psychic energy (libido) flows outward toward objects (extraversion) and those whose libido flows inward (introversion). The former enter into full affective relations with the world around; the latter are mainly focused on their private interpretations of experience. In addition to these fundamental dynamic relationships, Jung subclassifies with reference to our fundamental psychological functions: thinking, feeling, sensation, intuition. These functions may operate against one another consciously or unconsciously. So, when thinking predominates in con-

[20] Hans Apfelbach, *Der Aufbau des Charakters*. Cf. Otto Weininger, *Geschlecht und Charakter*; Fliess, *Ablauf des Lebens*.

sciousness, feeling is repressed; and the reverse. Intuition is understood to be a kind of instinctive comprehension, a function peculiarly dependent upon the unconscious. According to the predominance of one or another of these basic functions, Jung constructs four special types of extraversion and introversion.

Certain conspicuous political types belong to Jung's category of extraverted thinkers. These individuals try to bring their whole life-activity into relation with intellectual conclusions, which in the last resort are always oriented by objective data, whether objective facts or generally valid ideas. By his formula are good and evil measured: all is wrong that contradicts it, and all is right that corresponds to it; all is accidental that is neutral toward it. Just as the extraverted thinking type subordinates himself to his formula, he seeks to subordinate all others to it, as a manifestation of a universal inspiration. His moral code forbids him to tolerate exceptions, and he would bend all to suit the scheme. "One really should" or "one must" figure largely in his program. If the formula is wide enough, Jung remarks that the extraverted thinker may figure as a reformer, a ventilator of public wrongs, and a propagandist. But the more rigid his formula, the more likely he is to grow into a grumbler, a crafty reasoner, and a self-righteous critic.

Many politicians answer to the general description which Jung gives of the extraverted, intuitive type. The intuitive is unattracted by the established values; he is drawn to the possible rather than to the actual. He seizes hold of new objects and ways of doing things with eager intensity, only to abandon them cold-bloodedly, when their implications become obvious. The irresistible magnet of the rising sun fires his imagination and guides his activity. For the risen sun and the setting sun there is no enthusiasm, no special hostility, only indifference. Here is the facile promoter, who senses the dawning future and speeds from project to project, bored with routine and detail after projects have been accepted and the blueprints finished.[21]

The types of Apfelbach and Jung are based upon a small number of reactive mechanisms which are supposed to influence in different degree the growth of the personality. These "mechanism" types may contain many useful leads, but the methodological problem in isolating these hypothetical mechanisms is unsettled. A "stable" reaction in adulthood may be far from stable when viewed at successive growth periods. These "mechanism" types seem to encourage endless classificatory ventures at the expense of detailed reporting of life-histories. For reasons which have been set forth, subjective histories are of the greatest importance to social science; and any excessive interest in "mechanism" which minimizes the importance of elaborate individual records is to be deplored. Jung and Apfelbach say very little about the principal epochs of individual development, and distract attention from the career as a whole, as this career is structuralized in successive phases.

Before outlining our developmental conception of the *homo politicus*, we return to the work of Freud, for his method has enabled him to keep close to the subjective sequence and to use classificatory terms in relation to the successive phases of impulse organization in the developing personality.

[21] C. G. Jung, *Psychological Types*, chap. x.

CHAPTER V

THEORIES OF PERSONALITY DEVELOPMENT

It will be remembered that Freud's search for signs of the traumatic situation led him to uncover the contemporaneous functioning of all sorts of unconscious motivations in both the diseased and the healthy personality. The quest led him farther. Freud felt impelled to set up a schematic representation of the typical genetic development of the human personality. This grew out of the comparative study of very thoroughly analyzed cases and was rooted in empirical observation. Freud has always kept close to his data; and no matter how far his imagination soared, actual clinical experience was the starting-place and the landing-field for the flight.

The energy of a developed personality can be treated as dispersed in three directions: in the affirmative expression of socialized impulses, in unsocialized impulses, and in the maintenance of resistance charges against unsocialized impulses. The original forms of energy expression which are available to the infant are in many ways incompatible with the demands of human intercourse. The infant must surrender many primitive forms of gratification, if he is to be loved, and to avoid discomfort and pain. He must build up a self which represents the demands of society. The surrounding adults coerce and wheedle him into taking their commands for his own laws. The conscience is the introjected environment which imposes limitations upon the antisocial impulses. As the infant and child grows, he avoids conflicts with the environment by removing the locus of the conflict within himself, and plays nurse, mother, and father to himself. He learns to control his own excretions and to chasten his own murderous rages. He achieves individuality of emphasis by accepting the socialization of his major impulses.

But this incorporation of the requirements of the social order into the personality does not proceed smoothly, nor does it abolish the primitive psychological structures which have been developed and apparently discarded at each step of the way toward adulthood. Much of the energy of the personality is spent in blocking the entry of the unadjusted impulses of the self into consciousness and into overt expression. Careful scrutiny of individual behavior over a twenty-four-hour period strikingly shows the extent to which the personality is controlled by very elementary psychological structures. Moments of fatigue, moments of deprivation, moments of irresponsible reverie, all betray the presence of tendencies which are unassimilated to the world of adult reality.

Freud began to build up his conception of personality development by the gradual universalization of phenomena which he encountered in actual clinical work, and which he first described in relatively modest and restricted terms. He began his original psychological contributions by stressing the rôle of sexuality in the etiology of certain neuroses. He found that all sorts of pathological conditions and developmental abnormalities were apparently due to some shortcoming in sexual integration. This emphasis upon sexual adjustment as a necessary prerequisite of healthy adulthood met with so much opposition that Freud's energies were taken up with defending and elaborating his position. Now the sexual function is essentially a species function and stresses the biological uniformities of man at the expense of individuality. A topic like "personality development" requires a comprehensive theory of individuality, and this Freud did not develop until the split with Adler, who insisted upon the rôle of a drive toward individualization and who denied that the much neglected "ego instincts" of Freud were enough to support a comprehensive theory.

The story of Freud's neurosis-sexuality-personality theories begins with his earliest independent psychological contributions. Many clinicians before Freud had been abundantly impressed by the frequency with which sexual troubles seemed to beget "nervous" troubles. In his hypnotic work, Freud was especially struck by the frequency with which specifically sexual episodes were involved in the pathogenic experiences. Freud now proceeded to generalize about the sexual element in neurosis, and announced that neurosis was a function of deviated sexual life.

Freud armed in defense of his generalization with two new weapons. The first was his experience in letting his patients talk it out and in treating most of their productions as symbolic of something else. He acquired facility in interpreting what other people took literally as being a disguised representation of something else. So, when Freud was confronted with cases which were not manifestly sexual, he felt able to treat the non-sexual elements as symbolic representations of sexuality and to justify himself by claiming that his more intensive research procedure supplied him with the sustaining facts. Needless to say, those who had not themselves experienced the shift in standpoint which Freud had achieved were alienated by his seeming arbitrariness.

Freud's second reliance was on an inclusive theory of

sexuality. Undaunted by the ridicule heaped upon his sexual theory of the neurosis, he carried the war into enemy territory by extending the whole concept of sexuality backward from puberty through the life of the growing child to infancy.

At first glance this might appear to be a cheap, dialectical trick to confound his critics by telling them that "sex" meant all the things they had called by other names. Freud's *Three Contributions to Sexual Theory* was saved from being a rhetorical quibble by the virtuosity of his imagination and by the apparent definiteness of the connections which he traced between the various features of childhood development and the patterns of healthy and perverse adult sexuality. Careful analysis of biologically efficacious intercourse shows that it is a complex integration of many acts. It involves a partner of the opposite sex. Its essential feature is an increasing tension until the point of explosive release, followed by perfect relaxation. The male must be sadistic enough to run the risk of hurting the female by injecting the penis in the vagina. The participants must be willing to indulge in all sorts of preliminary play for the sake of heightening the critical tension, involving tongue, lips, nipples, and all the erogenous zones of the body.

Comparing the details of this completed pattern of the unambiguously sexual act with the earlier activities of the infant and child, Freud drew a host of analogies. Children indulge in play in sexual postures, exhibit their sexual parts to one another, and take pleasure in sexual peeping; but Freud carried his analysis of the sexuality of children much farther. Child specialists had often remarked that the nursing male child frequently exhibits the phenomenon of an erect penis and a desire to suckle for some time after hunger contractions cease. The general pattern of the sequence hunger-nursing-peaceful relaxation follows the characteristic curve of the sexual act. Freud suggested that inspection of the nursing pattern reveals that the pleasure derived by the child goes far beyond immediate biological necessities. This excess gratification Freud treats as a primitive outcropping of the sexual instinct, which need not be supposed to appear suddenly with the maturation of the glandular apparatus, but may be thought of as growing like the usual biological process by integrating partial components into one complex synthesis.

Sexual differentiation arises gradually, for at first distinctions of sex are not recognized by the child. The human animal is bisexual, a concept which Freud took over with some reservations from Wilhelm Fliess. Distinctions are achieved within the world of family experience. The child is attracted sexually toward the parent of the opposite sex but is too weak to compete for the loved object. Thus the father, who is too mighty to be killed and put out of the way, is copied by the son, who seeks to absorb his power into his own personality. The repression of the father-hostility, mother-love sentiments produces the Oedipus complex. The child achieves a socialized self by playing the rôle of the father in relation to his own impulses. The "latency period" arises from four to six, according to Freud, when the early sexual struggle against the father is given up. The fear of the father (the "castration complex") leads to the passing of the Oedipus phase of growth.

Now Freud specified a variety of difficulties which arise whenever there is failure to achieve successful integration of the partial components of the sexual instinct. He con-

nected homosexuality, psychological frigidity and impotence, exhibitionism, sadism, masochism, voyeurism, and
a variety of other abnormalities with definite failures in
integration. Sometimes the individual becomes obsessed
by ideas which have a disguised sexual meaning, and sometimes he indulges in physical symptoms which possess a
similar unconscious significance. The first is an obsessional neurosis, and the second is hysteria.

The stress which Freud laid upon the sexuality of the
child, and upon socialization by intimidation, broke with
revolutionary violence in a culture which swaddled its
infants in sentimentality. The child of the poets was like
this:

> Not in entire forgetfulness,
> And not in utter nakedness,
> But trailing clouds of glory we do come
> From God, who is our home:
> Heaven lies about us in our infancy!
>
> —WILLIAM WORDSWORTH

The child of the Freudians was like this:

The child, at one time or another in its life, is, in a sense, auto-
erotic, narcissistic, exhibitionistic, inclined to play the rôle of
"Jack the Peeper," incestuous, patricidal, or matricidal, homosexual, fetichistic, masochistic and sadistic [G. V. Hamilton, *An
Introduction to Objective Psychopathology*, p. 301].

As early as 1898 Freud had begun to elaborate the
idea that sexuality begins at birth. But as late as 1900,
when the *Interpretation of Dreams* appeared, he wrote in
a footnote that "childhood knows nothing, as yet, of sexual desire." With the elaboration of his sexual theory,
Freud became less preoccupied in defending himself
against his psychiatric colleagues than in perfecting defenses against his friends. Freud began to build up a

circle in 1903. Of the original group, Alfred Adler and Wilhelm Stekel were the two who were destined to achieve the most subsequent attention. By 1906 Ferenczi of Budapest and the Zürich contingent—the eminent Bleuler and his assistants—became cordial and interested. In 1908 a conference was held at Salzburg, and in 1909 G. Stanley Hall invited Freud to lecture at Clark University. In 1910 an international society was organized at Nuremberg, and the institutionalization of the psychoanalytic trend was well launched.

The first cleavage came about when Freud and Adler finally broke in 1911. In and out of season Adler stressed the "masculine protest," the drive of the human being to master every situation in which he finds himself. The individual specializes in overcoming his short stature, his enuresis, his ugliness, and his other defects; his principal drive is to differentiate himself rather than to perform his species function.

Adler represented several other currents of dissent from Freud. Freud had felt compelled to stress the antisocial drives of human nature, and Adler held a less Hobbesian view. The "social-feeling" component of human nature was accorded a place in the Adlerian system; and when the "socially useful" norms of individual adjustment were violated by the individual, "inferiority feelings" ensued. Therapy consisted in bringing this interpretation home to the maladapted person, leading him to relinquish his socially useless means of mastery and to allow his "social feelings" to express themselves more freely. Adler's therapy showed that he represented a pedagogical-ethical reaction against Freud's denial of the training function of the scientific analyst. Freud said repeatedly that the business of the analyst is to expose the patient to himself, and to leave it to the patient to work out his particular modes of adaptation to reality. Adler wants to give the patient a general scheme of thinking and to let him have some practice in indulging the "social feelings" of his nature.

Adler likewise represented a protest against the complexities of Freud's style of thought. The distinction can be drawn best, perhaps, by saying that Freud proceeded from symptoms to meanings, and from meanings to other meanings, and from other meanings to conditions. The analysis consists in uncovering lifelong chains of meaning attached to particular objects. Janet never achieved this process, and Adler short-circuited it. Adler begins with the symptom and proceeds as directly as possible to the condition. His books abound in succinct characterizations of cases, and "symbolic" material is at a minimum. Employing his orienting principle, he directs attention to a sympathetic reconstruction of the social relationships of the patient and selects those problems which the individual has tried to master by antisocial or personally crippling devices. The "common-sense" simplicity of Adler's observations commends his doctrines in circles which are repelled by the alien terminology and the elaborate interpretative machinery of Freud.

Under the perpetual hammering of Adler, Freud undertook to expand upon his sketchy theory of the ego. At first Freud was inclined to say that Adler had nothing to add because he had himself spoken of the ego instincts as well as the sexual instincts. Such a solution was hardly satisfying, and the self did not find a suitable resting-place in Freud's theoretical system until the rôle of narcissism (love of the self) was taken up and set forth at length. This "saved" the sexual theory, and it made the analysis of ego processes a problem of major interest to psychoanalysis. Stress was laid upon the fact that when the individual's libido flows outward toward objects, and when obstacles or deprivations are imposed upon this outward reaching, the libido turns back upon the self. This excessive libidinization of the self rendered subsequent adjustment to reality very difficult, and many personality deformations and formations are traceable to this developmental warp.

The break between Freud and Jung in 1913 had less immediate importance for personality theory than the previous schism. Like Adler, Jung undertook to subordinate the rôle of sexuality; but Jung accomplished his purpose, less by postulating concurrent ego-instincts than by invoking an inclusive energy concept which would embrace sexuality, ego-drives, and many other accessory manifestations. Jung, paralleling Adler again, came to the rescue of human nature, postulating a moral trend in the unconscious. And Jung, like Adler, frankly advises and trains his patients. Jung's two distinctive lines of innovation were concerned with dream interpretations and ethnological applications. Jung expanded dream interpretations for the sake of laying bare the "racial unconscious." Using saga material and dream material, Jung undertook to deflate the claims of sexuality and to demonstrate the limited applicability of the Oedipus idea.

Freud was assailed at a vital spot and rallied to defend himself in *Totem and Taboo*. He scored a point over Jung, who had relied on saga material, by drawing heavily on the ethnological summaries of Frazer in the *Golden Bough* to justify the universality of the Oedipus complex. This was Freud's first contribution to systematic social theory, and will come up for consideration in that connection. From the standpoint of personality theory, perhaps the most valuable passages are those which describe the infant's overvaluation of thought—the "omnipotence of thought," as it was phrased by a patient.

Some years later Jung, now on his own for some time, devised his classification of personality types and vastly increased popular and technical interest in the subject. This in turn has stimulated the group around Freud to develop a formal psychoanalytic characterology. In this task they were assisted by some early communications of Freud, wherein he took note of some of the character types met with in his practice. This literature will be referred to in connection with the case histories which are to be discussed immediately.

The other schisms between Freud and his pupils (involving Stekel and Rank) have been less significant for personality theory thus far, although Rank's sociological interests may germinate now that he is away from the immediate presence of the master.

Freud, who had obstinately clung to the phraseology of sex, rejecting every proposal for an overmastering set of terms which would carry less restricted connotations, executed a brilliant maneuver in 1926 and proposed to regard human activity as manifestations of two principles, the life and the death instincts. Life consists in accumulation and the release of tension; and, generalizing this phenomenon, we have the life and death drives.[1]

Suppose we put aside further exposition of the analytical personality theories, and in the light of these conceptions set up a general formula which describes the developmental history of the political man. The most general formula would employ three terms. The first component, p, stands for the private motives of the individual as they

[1] *Beyond the Pleasure Principle.*

are nurtured and organized in relation to the family constellation and the early self. We shall have occasion to see that primitive psychological structures continue to function within the personality long after the epochs of infancy and childhood have been chronologically left behind. The prominence of hate in politics suggests that we may find that the most important private motive is a repressed and powerful hatred of authority, a hatred which has come to partial expression and repression in relation to the father, at least in patrilineal society, where the male combines the function of biological progenitor and sociological father.

The second term, d, in such a formula describes the displacement of private motives from family objects to public objects. The repressed father-hatred may be turned against kings or capitalists, which are social objects playing a rôle before and within the community. Harmonious relations with the father of the family may actually depend upon the successful deflection of hatred from private to public objects.

The third symbol, r, signifies the rationalization of the displacement in terms of public interests. The merciless exploitation of the toolless proletariat by the capitalists may be the rational justification of the attitude taken up by the individual toward capitalism.

The most general formula which expresses the developmental facts about the fully developed political man reads thus:

$$p \ \} \ d \ \} \ r = P,$$

where p equals private motives; d equals displacement onto a public object; r equals rationalization in terms of public interest; P equals the political man; and } equals transformed into.

The p is shared by the political man with every human being. Differentiation rises first in the displacement of affects on to public objects, and in the molding of the life in such a way as to give an opportunity for the expression of these affects. The non-political man may feel himself aggrieved against a brother and against every fellow-worker with whom he comes in contact. His mind may be taken up with personal fantasies of love or hate for specific people, and his ideological world (his attitudes toward the state, the church, the destiny of man) may be very poorly elaborated. He is a fly in the meshes of his immediate environment, and his struggles are fought in terms of the world of face-to-face reality. When such a man displaces his affects upon a person who happens to be a public object, this does not make him a political man. Impulsively killing a king who happens to insult one's sister does not make a politician of the regicide; there must be a secondary elaboration of the displacement in terms of general interest. It is the rationalization which finally transmutes the operation from the plane of private to the plane of public acts. Indeed, the private motives may be entirely lost from the consciousness of the political man, and he may succeed in achieving a high degree of objective validation for his point of view. In the "ideal" case this has gone so far that the private motives which led to the original commitment are of feeble current importance.

Upon what does the displacement and the rationalization depend? No doubt the general answer is that the selection of certain public objects depends upon the "historical" accident of the patterns offered by the personal environment of the individual at critical phases of growth. It is safe to predict that more politicians rise from families with political traditions than without them. But this very broad conclusion requires no technique of intensive investigation of individual instances to support it. If the psychopathological approach to the individual is worth the trouble, it must disclose a variety of relatively novel circumstances which dispose individuals to adopt, reject, or modify the patterns of act and phrase which are offered in the environment. Provisionally, we may assume that the puberty phase of biological growth, which coincides with increasing social demands, may be the period in which the attitudes toward the invisible environment most rapidly crystallize.

The details may be more hopefully dealt with if somewhat homogeneous groups of politicians are investigated for the purpose of bringing out significant differences in their developmental history. The agitators are the first to whom special attention will be paid.

CHAPTER VI

POLITICAL AGITATORS

The essential mark of the agitator is the high value which he places on the emotional response of the public. Whether he attacks or defends social institutions is a secondary matter. The agitator has come by his name honestly, for he is enough agitated about public policy to communicate his excitement to those about him. He idealizes the magnitude of the desirable social changes which are capable of being produced by a specific line of social action. From the standpoint of the administrative mind, we may say that an agitator is one who exaggerates the difference between one rather desirable social policy and another, much as the lover, according to Shaw, is one who grossly exaggerates the difference between one woman and another. Whether agitators behave like physicians or surgeons, as Munro would have it, they are united in expecting much good to come from single acts of innovation. The agitator easily infers that he who disagrees with him is in communion with the devil, and that opponents show bad faith or timidity. Agitators are notoriously contentious and undisciplined; many reforming ships are manned by mutineers. The agitator is willing to subordinate personal considerations to the superior claims of principle. Children may suffer while father and mother battle for the "cause." But the righteous will not cleave to their families when the field is ripe for the harvest. Ever on the alert for pernicious intrusions of private interest into public affairs, the agitator sees "unworthy" motives

where others see the just claims of friendship. Believing
in direct, emotional responses from the public, the agitator
trusts in mass appeals and general principles. Many of
his kind live to shout and write. Their consciences trouble
them unless they have periodic orgies of moral fervor.
Relying upon the magic of rhetoric, they conjure away
obstacles with the ritualistic repetition of principles. They
become frustrated and confused in the tangled mass of
technical detail upon which successful administration depends. Agitators of the "pure" type, when landed in
responsible posts, long to desert the official swivel for the
roving freedom of the platform and the press. They glo-
rify men of outspoken zeal, men who harry the dragons
and stir the public conscience by exhortation, reiteration,
and vituperation.

The first life-history to be excerpted here is that of
Mr. A. This is no "institutional" case. Mr. A is aware
of no mental pathology, and has never consulted a neurol-
ogist, psychiatrist, or "nerve doctor." He is one of those
who at first reluctantly, then whole-heartedly, allowed
himself to be studied with the same thoroughness, intimacy,
and detachment with which an obviously unstable person
would be scrutinized. Mr. A at once saw the advantage for
the progress of science of an accumulation of life-histories
taken from men who regard themselves as perfectly normal, since so much of our case material is from the ill.

A's claim to a place among the agitators is not open to
question. He was compelled to resign his position when
the United States went into the World War on account of
the tenacity with which he argued the pacifist position. He
had previously run for Congress on the socialist ticket. Suspected of unorthodoxy in the theological school, he steadily became more radical in his views, and was expelled

from one denomination. Previously he had been the secretary and principal spokesman for a civic reform organization which had vigorously attacked corruption in municipal affairs. He gradually became convinced that "white collar reforms" were futile as long as the capitalistic system prevailed in this country, and presently threw his energy into the propaganda of labor organization and socialism.

A leading characteristic as moralist, socialist, and pacifist has been his truculence in public on behalf of his cause. Mr. A speaks rapidly, with great fervor and earnestness, and his discourse is studded with abusive epithets, sarcastic jibes, and cutting insinuations. He confesses that he has taken an unmistakable pleasure in "rubbing the fur the wrong way." He enjoyed nothing better than accepting invitations to lecture on social and economic subjects before conservative audiences, and scandalizing them by declaring that "organized business and organized crime are hard to distinguish from one another," "corruption and capitalism are one and inseparable," and "capitalism depends on markets, markets ultimately depend on force, and force means war." Thus war was the logical result of the capitalistic system.

Mr. A prides himself on his ability to cut holes in the logical fabric spun by conspicuous men. He has engaged prominent preachers of the gospel in correspondence, arguing that something in their writings leads logically to the conclusion that any war, not excepting the last one, is wrong, and that they should confess this openly, declaring their sorrow for having been infected with un-Christian war-hysteria.

He believes that right reason is the hope of mankind,

and the name of science is exalted in his mind. He was glad to lay his own life-story on the altar of science, and in the name of science to endure the embarrassment of recalling private facts which most of us try to forget.

Mr. A's later convictions have been held with enough intensity to redefine many of his earlier opinions. Thus his pacifism brought him into sharp opposition to the government, which resented his expression of the truth as he understood it. Mr. A warmly champions the cause of the individual against official interference in matters of taste and conscience, and has modified his early enthusiasm for prohibition.

Although censorious, accusatory, didactic, and defiant in public address, he is cordial and winning in those face-to-face situations where he is unaware of hostility. His eyes twinkle with good humor, and he is gentle, responsive, and anxious to impress. His speech and gestures are quick, and his manner is alert and often tense.

A's physique inclines toward the asthenic end of a hypothetical pyknic-asthenic scale, such as Wertheimer and Hesketh have constructed from Kretschmer's observations on physical types.[1] He is noticeably lean, but strikes the impressionistic observer as being toward neither the tall nor the short end of the scale. The legs are somewhat longer than the length of the body warrants, and the bony structures of shoulder, hip, knee, and ankle are prominent. The thin face is rather delicately molded, and is given added dignity and distinction by a neat Van Dyke beard. The chest is flat, and the upper ribs fall inward. His erect carriage seems to be a compensation against a predilection toward a scholarly stoop. In middle and later

[1] "The Significance of Physical Constitution in Mental Disease," *Medicine*, V (1926), 375–451.

middle life he has been bothered by gastro-intestinal disorders.

The second son of an impecunious village parson, he grew up in straitened circumstances with a brother somewhat his senior. The mother died when A's youngest sister was born, and the children were cared for by the father and a succession of elderly housekeepers who left faint memories behind them. A and his brother went to an old-fashioned ungraded school, entering at the same time in spite of their disparity in years, so the younger one would not be left alone in the house.

From a very early age A had a certain sense of hostility toward his brother, and a feeling of his own superiority. For a reason that is not clear, the school children teased his brother as the preacher's son, but left him alone. A was more agile than his brother, and climbed trees and wriggled into tight places with ease. He prided himself in doing things which his brother hesitated to try, and seems to have awed him somewhat, for he remembers having heard his brother tell another schoolboy to let A alone, "because when he gets mad, he can lick me."

The older boy was held responsible by the father for pranks which were really joint enterprises. On one representative occasion, the father left the house to make a call, ordering the boys to stay indoors. They decided to go out, and their father, who discovered footprints in the snow outside the door, gave the older boy a sound whipping, but let A off scot-free. The younger son was unquestionably the favorite, and his father would frequently chide the older boy for being a dullard, and point with pride to the ease with which A could get his lessons.

Indeed, A got on famously at school. One of his teachers, who chanced to be a college man, told his father that

A was brilliant and promising. A also remembers a glow
of elation when a relative wrote to say that arrangements
must be made for him to have a college education, since
he had shown that he could be a worthy successor to his
uncle. This uncle was a famous professor, who had written well-known philosophical books, and remained a great
hero in the eyes of the family.

The father slept in the same bed with his two sons
until they were well along in the teens. For as long as he
can remember, A found the touch of his father very pleasant, though the touch of his brother was repugnant. A's
strong hostility against his brother, based on their rivalry
for the affections of the father, received a certain justification in the critical episode which occurred as his older
brother, who matured early, approached puberty and began to have emissions. The preacher was horrified, for
he took this as a sign of masturbation, and masturbation
was sinful and dangerous.[2] When he thought that A was
sound asleep, he would gravely lecture the older boy on
the evil consequences of self-abuse. Sometimes the son
would wake up in the morning and discover that an emission had taken place during the night. In a hushed and

[2] The popular superstition about the dangers of masturbation seems to
have become widespread in Western Europe in the eighteenth century.
Havelock Ellis dates it from the appearance of a sensational book by an
anonymous English doctor which was called *Onania: or the Heinous Sin
of Self-Pollution and All Its Frightful Consequences in Both Sexes, Considered, with Spiritual and Physical Advice, etc.* This is said to have
passed through eighty editions and to have been translated into German.
Tissot, a physician of Lausanne, contributed his *Traité* on the same subject
in Latin in 1760. This appeared in French four years later, and subsequently in nearly all European languages. His watchword was that masturbation was a crime, "an act of suicide." Voltaire popularized his viewpoint
in the *Dictionnaire philosophique,* and the tradition became firmly set. See
Havelock Ellis, *Studies in the Psychology of Sex,* I, 248–49. The cultural
relativity of this attitude toward masturbation is brought out in ethnological
reports.

contrite whisper he would say to his father, "I've gone and done it again!" at which the parent would exclaim reproachfully, "Oh!" The boy was presently taken to a physician who seems to have modified the excitement of the father and in some measure to have reassured the son that his manhood was not irreparably lost. Dark rumors about self-abuse were whispered through the village from time to time. The neighborhood idiot was supposed to have brought idiocy upon himself by self-abuse, and a bachelor in the village who went insane was supposed to have suffered from the same vice.

A listened to the rumors and to the nocturnal dialogues between his father and elder brother, and gathered that ominous things were connected with handling one's self. He felt ashamed of his brother, who brought so much suffering on his father, and silently determined never to be a disappointment to his father. The tag end of a biblical passage about bringing the gray hairs of his father to the grave in shame ran through his mind, and he resolved never to repeat his brother's weaknesses.

A's older brother surprised everybody about this time by suddenly changing from a phlegmatic lad into a fervent religious enthusiast. He became converted under dramatic circumstances and joined the church, thus propitiating the unknown powers which might visit horrible punishment upon him for his private iniquities. In this he was running true to the adolescent pattern. Adolescence is notoriously the time when the temptations of the "flesh" multiply and when many youths, oppressed by their "animal" impulses, seek to escape from the burden of guilt by adopting the ceremonial patterns provided in the religious observances of society. Adolescence is so often a period of high ideals, which are typically reaction formations to "low desires," that adolescence is the happy hunting ground for proselyters of every breed.

When A's own emissions began, he was terribly upset by worry and self-accusation. About fifteen he got an emission after a boy had fooled with his genitalia, thinking he was asleep. He was taut with sinful pleasure while the seduction was taking place, which added to his guilty feelings. This was the time when he, too, exhibited a fervent interest in the church. He quickly "overcame" masturbation, but until late in life there was always a "fight" to overcome his "wayward" impulses and his erotic imaginings. In his dreams he often saw roosters and hens performing sexual acts in the barnyard of his old home, and the reappearance of the old scenes is indicative of his early sexual curiosity. Many more of his dreams used common sexual language. Sometimes he was making his way across a valley of snakes, or he was naked and walking toward a goal he could never quite make out. The nude female figure was usually repressed, though it occasionally came through.

He was taken off the farm, on which his father eked out a supplement to his meager salary, by an aunt, who insisted that the boy must have better school facilities. This aunt had always taken a great interest in this promising motherless nephew, and tried to fill his life with the affection which would have been his had his mother lived. As a small boy he had often come on short visits to his aunt. He had slept in the same bed with her, and his lively curiosity about the female figure was partly satisfied by glimpses of his aunt at the morning bath. The aunt had a family with all of whose members he was on good terms, and he was supremely happy to live in town with them. Out on the farm he had been undernourished, but here he was filled out and flourished. He took an active part in the church and in the social activities of the neighborhood.

The early intellectual promise which A had displayed was no mere flash in the pan. He was one of the brilliant students in high school, and passed his college-entrance examinations with such distinction that he entered college with a mild intellectual halo. He resolved to make good scholastically, and this he did, finishing the four years at a first-rate institution at the top of his class.

As time passed, he began to dissent from many of the dogmas of his immediate social environment. During high-school days he had been assigned to act the devil's advocate and defend the free-trade side in a tariff debate. The more he read and thought about it, the more convinced he was that the free-trade position was sound. His relatives without exception were high-tariff Republicans, and his arguments were countered with sentimental rather than rational appeals. A's conversion to free trade led him to come out for the Democratic candidate for the presidency. He remembers that the first time he announced this heresy one of his aunts violently pushed her chair away from the table, exclaiming in vexed, incredulous, and reproachful tones, "And to think that my own sister's son could say such a thing!" His college course in biology converted him to evolution, and he argued this out at great length with one of his uncles, who was a traditionally minded preacher. A began to develop a feeling that intellectual brilliance meant dissenting from the convictions of middle-class people like his own relatives.

So far his nonconformity was strictly confined to a few theories. He was a member of the prayer-meeting group in college, and his fraternity consisted mainly of embryo doctors of theology who scrupulously upheld a rigorous code of personal abstinence from alcohol, tobacco, strong language, and women. One of the young men who had the temerity to enter the house with a lighted cigarette had it gently but firmly removed from his lips. It was in college that A took part in his first law-enforcement drive. The state prohibition law was poorly observed, as A had good reason to know, since he had a collection route which took him to "drug stores" and other equivocal establishments about town. "Tea" was openly ordered at the bar and drunk on the premises. A conceived the idea of leaving posters in these places to advertise the law-enforcement meetings, thus creating something of a stir.

Just before graduating from college A had a talk with a favorite professor. The professor asked him what he proposed to do, and was much interested when A said that he wanted to become a minister. The professor said that during his own active years in the pulpit, before he began to teach, he had learned at least one thing. Every man who was intellectually honest and independent would sooner or later discover that he questioned his own dogmas, and a period of bitter anguish would ensue. If a man were intellectually honest, he would never flinch from the truth, even for the sake of wife and family. But when the period of doubt arose he advised A not to abandon his work too abruptly. He had himself lived through six months of torture during which he had been on the verge of dropping everything and going into business. But finally he had arrived at a faith which he could defend, and stuck to it. "I would rather be drawn and quartered than preach anything I do not believe," he declared emphatically. This conversation made a deep impression upon A, leading him to anticipate doubts as a mark of intellectual keenness and honesty.

Thus far in his life he had never questioned the tenets of the strict and simple theology of his immediate surroundings. Indeed, he had never met anybody who questioned it. Only a single episode had slightly jarred his complacency and left a tiny scar behind. At one time his Sunday-school teacher had been a young professor of theology who was much more liberal than his contemporaries. A boy in the class had dared to ask something about the authority of the Bible, and the teacher, without the least trace of embarrassment, had replied that authority should not rest on blind faith but upon clear reason. "If the Bible told you to kill your father and your mother, you would not do it. You would not be bound to do it. The justification of the Bible is that its teachings prove to be sound in the experience of all reasonable men."

In the divinity school the first course which A attended was on the authority of the Bible. It was taught by a smug and full person of some eminence. A was accustomed to distinguish himself by bold opinions, and he undertook to challenge several of the propositions which were supposed to be accepted and repeated by rote. His main point was that authority rested on reason, not on faith. For his pains he got the reputation of being a smart and troublesome upstart of doubtful orthodoxy. His former Sunday-school teacher was a member of the faculty, and A wrote a thesis on the authority of the Bible, in which he elaborated the line of argument which had so much impressed him. Only the constant intercession of this professor kept A from being disciplined, or even expelled, at various times.

The young man was disposed to take rigid theology none too seriously on account of his increasing disrespect for his father. A and his brother both felt duty bound to return home every summer to help with the farm work. Their father was happy enough to have them rejoin him, but matters never ran smoothly. The father was quick to reassert his parental authority and to criticize freely. Most of the unpleasantness was as usual at the expense of the older son, but some of it was deflected against A. Both sons were uncomfortably aware of the uncouthness of their father in comparison with city preachers. He laughed too boisterously at his own stale witticisms. His ever present dignity was a little ludicrous when he wore an alpaca coat into the fields on the hottest midsummer day.

The social life at the divinity school was wholly satisfying. The students were warmly welcomed by the maidens of the local churches, and several became engaged. A proposed to two girls during his career there, and was turned down as often. He very quickly recovered his good spirits after a night or so of melancholy. The first girl was a relative whom he had known for many years, and the second was a close friend of the family. The double defeat was something of a bruise to his dignity and fed his determination to make a dent on the world.

A's first congregation was in one of the poorer quarters of a little city. A had no doubt of his towering intellectual superiority over his parishioners, and he found it exasperating when an uneducated housewife presumed to gossip about the dubious orthodoxy of his beliefs. At the end of three years he resigned in disgust at the peppering of criticism directed against his ideas. Looking back at the incident, he feels that he was too hasty.

It was at this first charge that A began to make good copy for the press, and to win a reputation as a sensationalist. He organized a Law and Order League to harry criminals and the police. His pulpit rang with stinging philippics against law-breakers and cowardly public officials. All this gave him a zestful sense of making a stir in the world of real affairs, so that he turned down an offer to join the faculty of a famous university where his old Sunday-school teacher was now located.

A's new pastorate was among working people in a large city. He at once began to hound the officials for non-enforcement of the law. He led raiding parties to visit the biggest gambling hells and put it up to the police to shut them. Renewed criticisms began to appear of his opinions, and the governing body of his denomination asked him to recant or resign. He refused to budge, and he was soon expelled. He was immediately called to lecture before an ethical society, where his comments on current religious and social problems won a wide hearing. Although attracting much attention, the society was exceedingly poor and A spent a little legacy which he had received upon it, indifferent to his own future.

During these exciting troubles he became a socialist and joined the socialist party. He had sympathized with the hard lot of the poor since he could remember, and had cast his vote for Bryan as a symbol of protest against the indifference of the privileged classes to the privileges of anyone but themselves. His favorite college professor had lost his job during the anarchist hysteria, when he came out against the "judicial murder" of the Haymarket suspects. A was profoundly moved by the spectacle of a man who backed his precepts of independence with sacrifice for their sake. The argument which finally won him for socialism was that political democracy is impossible until economic democracy is realized, and that socialism is simply democracy in industry. The principles of democratic brotherhood, once put to practice in the world of work, would soon govern public relationships of every kind.

His new convictions opened to A a new field of agitation and publicity. Ignoring or overcoming the coolness of certain "horny-handed" elements, he rushed into the little band of socialists, and was presently the congressional candidate. In this campaign he conducted a whirlwind tour of the district and enjoyed himself immensely.

A finally married a capable, motherly school-teacher whom he had known for several years, but whom he had been prevented from marrying until the death of her parents, who heartily disapproved of him. During his bachelor years in the ministry he had certain knowledge that various women were far from averse to becoming the preacher's wife or mistress. One married woman became the foremost worker in the church and passionately assured him, "I am at your service day or night." Another woman, whom he barely recognized, came to the pastor's study, declaring that they must be married at once and "end this awful agony for both of us." He had not been aware that any agony had begun, and was in no mood to begin it. He recognized that a wife would be a protection, but most of the women who threw themselves in his way were so homely that abstinence remained a pleasure as well as a principle.

For many years there had lurked in his mind the fear that he might not be potent, and he was humiliated to find that he was at first unable to consummate the sexual act. Since he first attempted sexual intercourse when nearly fifty, and had practically never masturbated, his troubles were not atypical, and they fortunately proved to be transitory. He regretted having failed to consult a physician before marriage, and was not at ease until the first of his children came.

Shortly after marrying, A came to the end of his financial resources, and found it necessary to relinquish his lecturing for other work until a suitable congregation should requisition his services. When a call finally came, the war broke out in Europe, and A denounced it with his customary ardor. He had read a book which popularized Prince Kropotkin's thesis that mutual aid and not struggle is the key to the evolutionary process. War was irrational because it contravened the principle of mutual aid, and it was un-Christian because it set the hand of man against his brethren. As the hour of America's participation drew nearer, A saw that his outspoken position would cause trouble. But he was accustomed to take a radical view and stick to it, and the idea of compromising his independence for the sake of family obligations was intolerable. His characteristic optimism also misled him into over-estimating the amount of pacifism which his congregation would put up with, and soon he was forced to resign.

A was left financially high and dry, and rather hoped that his wife would be willing to starve with him, if need be, as a gesture of sanity in a war-mad world. He was left financially dependent upon his family, and upon such support as was forthcoming from wealthy radical sympathizers. Since his own professional opportunities were curtailed, and he never applied for other types of work, he was left dependent upon others. He was somewhat embarrassed by this, but was never depressed by it, or by the social ostracism which was entailed by his unpopular stand. As he once expressed it, "melancholy is alien to a fighting nature."

Looking back over A's career, certain private motives appear which were well organized in his early family life, and continued to operate with considerable strength during his adult years.

A had a strongly repressed hatred for his brother. He

was consciously aware of his own coldness toward the brother, but succeeded in barring from consciousness any recognition of the emotional charge on this attitude. The older boy was his rival for the affection of his father, and A's quickness and boldness were cultivated in an effort to outstrip his brother. He showed many of the traits of the overactive younger child, as Adler has frequently described them. A felt rather ashamed of his brother, who went through school and college with no special distinction, and whose modest subsequent career was prosaically respectable. A struggled to keep hostile thoughts about his brother out of his mind, and sought to keep his attention away from the brother by corresponding or visiting with him infrequently.

Although A never frankly faced his own animosity toward this brother, he was plagued by a sense of guilt for his unfraternal attitude. This conflict was partially resolved by a reactive formation and by displacement. The reactive formation was the reverse of the anti-brother drive, but it was only supportable by displacing his affection upon remote social objects. He generalized his own prohibition against brother-hatred to all society, and identified himself with the workers and with humanity at large, serving a poverty-stricken congregation, spending his own money on the work of the church, adopting the socialist dream of a brotherly state, and demanding the abolition of fratricidal war.

His love for the downtrodden and for humanity (this reactive displacement of his own brother-hostility) was buttressed by the usual rationalizations. The democratic ideal in politics, the ideal of effective equality in political power, had his support, and he adopted socialism when it was presented to him as industrial democracy (brotherhood), the indispensable antecedent of genuine political democracy (brotherhood). His early prohibition appeals were cast in the form of an appeal to the brotherhood sentiments. He argued that every man was his brother's keeper, and therefore bound to refrain from an example which might lead his weaker brother to dash his foot against a stone. War meant the destruction of mutual (brotherly) aid among those who were brethren in Christ. A's brother-hatred, so manifest in his younger days, and so potent in arousing guilt feelings, created this disposition to choose generalized brother-substitutes to love, and to elaborate brotherly ideologies to defend his position. Then by keeping his distance from the physical brother, he could maintain a comfortable adjustment.

Another significant private motive, whose organization dates from early family days, but whose influence was prominent in adult behavior, was A's struggle to maintain his sexual repressions. He erected his very elaborate personal prohibitions into generalized prohibitions for all society, and just as he laid down the law against brother-hatred, he condemned deviations from the rigid puritanical code by which he lived. Individuals who possess super-ego structures of such rigor often try to protect themselves from the strain of sexual excitement by keeping away from "temptation," or by removing "temptation" from their environment. Thus Mr. A avoided exposing himself to "lewd speech" and "immoral suggestion." Consciences of such severity can often be traced back in deeply analyzed cases to unusually strong repressions at the time when infantile masturbatory activities are being curbed. And it often happens that the rôle of the intimidator is taken not only by the male but by the female imago. In another highly moralistic person, who was thoroughly psychoanalyzed, this came out distinctly. Thus for several days the subject dreamed of standing before a butcher shop where he had been sent by his mother, and where he saw his father sharpening long knives. Or he saw his mother, dressed as Brünnhilde, carrying a sword, while he cowered on a marble stairway. After many dreams of this kind, the original situations finally burst into view. They involved what were interpreted as direct threats to cut off a hand if the child didn't cease handling himself.

That A was never able to abolish his sexuality is sufficiently evident in his night dreams and daydreams. In spite of his efforts to "fight" these manifestations of his "antisocial impulses," they continued to appear. Among the direct and important consequences which they produced was a sense of sin, not only a sense of sexual sin, but a growing conviction of hypocrisy. His "battle" against "evil" impulses was only partially successful, and this produced a profound feeling of insecurity.

This self-punishing strain of insecurity might be alleviated, he found, by publicly reaffirming the creed of repression, and by distracting attention to other matters. A's rapid movements, dogmatic assertions, and diversified activities were means of escape from this gnawing sense of incapacity to cope with his own desires and to master himself. Uncertain of his power to control himself, he was very busy about controlling others, and engaged in endless committee sessions, personal conferences, and public meetings for the purpose. He always managed to submerge himself in a buzzing life of ceaseless activity; he could never stand privacy and solitude, since it drove him to a sense of futility; and he couldn't undertake prolonged and laborious study, since his feeling of insecurity demanded daily evidence of his importance in the world.

A's sexual drives continued to manifest themselves, and to challenge his resistances. He was continually alarmed by the lurking fear that he might be impotent. Although he proposed marriage to two girls when he was a theology student, it is significant that he chose girls from his immediate entourage, and effected an almost instantaneous recovery from his disappointments. This warrants the inference that he was considerably relieved to postpone the test of his potency, and this inference is strengthened by the long years during which he cheerfully acquiesced in the postponement of his marriage to the woman who finally became his wife. He lived with people who valued sexual potency, particularly in its conventional and biological demonstration in marriage and children, and his unmarried state was the object of good-natured comment. His pastoral duties required him to "make calls" on the sisters of the church, and in spite of the cheer which he was sometimes able to bring to the bedridden, there was the faint whisper of a doubt that this was really a man's job. And though preaching was a socially respectable occupation, there was something of the ridiculous in the fact that one who had experienced very little of life should pass for a privileged censor of all mankind.

He had long practice in the art of the impostor. From the plight of his older brother, A learned that he would lose the affection of his father if he was discovered to have indulged in certain practices like masturbation. He resolved never to do anything to cause his father to withdraw his affection, and when he was not entirely successful in living up to this ideal, he pretended to virtues which he did not possess. Never once was he found out, and his life was the life of a "model" boy and man. This reputation he owed in part to his abstinences, but likewise to his concealments. He learned to cultivate the mask of rectitude, and succeeded in carrying off the rôle so successfully that he was never found out during adolescence or adulthood.

Cut off by his impotence fears from loving others fully and completely, A loved himself the more. He had unbounded confidence in the brilliance of his mind, and this intellectual arrogance was nourished by the easy ascendance which he won over the poorly educated people among whom he worked. He was careful to keep in environments where his mind would not be put to the test of keen competition. A didn't compete with the clergymen who had the largest posts in his denomination, he struck out for himself in no hazardous business or professional enterprise, he took up and finished no piece of investigation; instead he cut a big figure among the workers, among whom he was the best-educated and the best-known leader. His chances of being elected to Congress when he was nominated were never good, and he had everything to gain and nothing to lose by making a campaign. After the days of his scholarly ascendance in high school and college, A fell out of competition in academic pursuits.

He valued his capacity to produce words. Ferenczi remarked in conversation with me that the revolutionary agitators who had come to his attention had been noticeably deficient in the intensity of their emotional attachment to objects. They were notably indifferent to the accumulation of property, and they were lacking in possessive jealousy in their sexual life. This deficiency in warmth of affective experience was sensed by the revolutionaries themselves, who felt that they were in some way estranged from others. Their orgiastic indulgence in language is to be interpreted as an effort to heighten the affective intensity of their own lives. Either because the emotional life is physiologically

defective or because the libido is too narcissistically fixated, this general description holds true of some obsessive
and many psychotic persons. It was no doubt a factor
in the history of A.

Before following out the full implications of this struggle of A's to repress his sexuality, we will take up another
topic of major and not unrelated importance. I refer to A's
ambivalence toward his father. A was not conscious of the
full force of his hatred and his love for his father, but his
personality history is full of evidence of the formative
influence of these bipolar attitudes. In the course of his
competition with his older brother, A accepted abstinence
from genital indulgence as the price of holding paternal
preference. Now psychoanalytic findings are unanimous in
showing that genital indulgence is not given up without a
continuous struggle, and that recurring waves of sexuality
break against the barrier of the introjected prohibition, and
reanimate hostile impulses against the sanctioning authority. It is of the utmost importance for A's development that
he fought to bar from consciousness any hostile thought
directed against his father, and that he succeeded in re-
pressing his father-hatred very deeply. He was able to
identify himself with the father, and to copy many of the
paternal standards and attributes. The strength of these
identifications is indicated by the tenacity with which A
held to certain paternal patterns. Although his much-
touted uncle had been a famous writer and professor, A
remained a preacher, even when tempted by a flattering
offer to leave his first humble parish for the faculty of a
great university. He cherished the paternal prejudice
against money-making and money-makers. His boyhood
home was where some wealthy people spent their summers,
and A's father would speak contemptuously of "the fash-

ionables" who loitered ostentatiously past the house. This was an additional determiner of A's subsequent devotion to the welfare of the poor, which manifested itself in financial sacrifice and socialist agitation. A was very susceptible to old men, and idealized not only his early teachers, but a venerable pacifist who approved of his wartime conduct.

The negative side of A's attitude toward authority came out in the choice of the abstract (remote) objects upon which to vent his hatred. The hostility which was denied conscious recognition and direct indulgence against the actual father was displaced against substitute symbols, such as the dogma which required the acceptance of the Scriptures by faith, of the capitalistic system, and of the militarists.

When A was introduced to a stranger, he was genial, talkative, and anxious to impress. When he was aware of opposition in his environment, he overreacted at once, hurling a vast repertory of jibes and flouts and sneers at the offender. This gives a clue to an important element in his makeup which will come out very distinctly in subsequent cases, namely, a strong latent homosexual trend. When the individual is not able to achieve full heterosexual adjustment, the sexual libido tends to work itself out in more primitive ways, and one of the phases of emotional development is the homosexual epoch. Earlier, however, than the adolescent homosexual period is the phase connected with the suppression of auto-erotic activities. The child characteristically uses its nutritional object (nurse-mother) for the sake of stimulating his own erogenous zones as much as possible. This "incestuous" drive is curbed, and the child is denied the pleasure of promiscuously fingering others, and of manually stimulating his own genitalia.

Though the nurse or mother, who is the target of the desires of the child, also administers the prohibitions, the
sanction which lurks most prominently in the background
is the strength of the father. Reduced to its ultimate expression, this sanction is the threat of depriving the child
of his much-valued organs unless he observes the "hands
off" prohibition. The "normal" development is for the
hostile protest at authoritarian interference to subside, and
for the child to copy the idealized father. The repression
of hostilities and the identification with the father do not
take place instantly. Identification is not achieved without a phase in which the child plays a femininely passive
rôle toward the father, and this is the passively homosexual reaction which may for one reason or another be
unusually strong. A's fantasies of his father's beautiful skin
are common screen fantasies for more primitive drives.

A's tendency to overreact to the stranger who is merely
polite, and to interpret the stranger's interest as a "personal" one, is characteristic of the one in whom this passive
"winning" rôle is of some importance. He tries to create
an overpersonal relationship in those somewhat formal
situations where ordinary conversational requirements are
such as to force conventional compliments.

The overreactive hostility toward those who merely differ from him is partially motivated by the desire to punish
those who have rejected the affection which he all too quickly volunteers. This wound to his narcissism demands that
wounds shall be inflicted on the offending objects. Now it
is commonly observed that repressed drives are likely to
secure partial gratification in the very activities which are
in part a protection against them. Sneers and jibes would
at first seem to free him from those who arouse and reject
him, but this is not the whole result. A exceeded the bounds

of convention and became recklessly provocative. His wild assaults and defiances tended to provoke the social environment into attacking him, and thus to gratify two powerful unconscious drives. He wanted to be forced into a passive, feminine, victimized rôle, and to inflict upon himself the punishment which he deserved for excessive hatred of others. Thus A felt quite happy, escaping moods of depression, as long as he was indulging his hostility against conspicuous conventional authorities in society, and as long as he was suffering from society's retaliatory measures. His romantic idea of starving to death as a gesture of sanity in a war-mad world is indicative of his pleasure in the "martyr rôle."

He could not endure "inharmonious" people, and built up a "soft" and overindulgent group around him. He had a small group of admirers who turned to him for advice and who looked up to his superior wisdom and moral courage. Nothing pained him more than the slightest jar in personal relations. This disparity between his demands for gentleness in the primary group, and his genius for creating a disturbance in a secondary group, suggests the tension produced within his personality by the struggle with the feminine component. He was careful to keep away from close-working subordination to a powerful personality. He stayed in environments where his authority was unchallenged. In the church he was both a financial pillar and the pastor, and among the socialists he was sustained by the halo of moral and cultural prestige.

It is noteworthy that though A was venomous when publicly opposed, he was capable of a wooing and persuasive strain which he could effectively use in his proselyting work. His humor was of the mock-modesty variety, and relieved the moral earnestness of his discourses. A showed much tenacity and skill in following people whom he once loved and respected, and in attempting to convert them to a community of views with him. He displayed a strong impulse to enter into and to cultivate personal interchanges by correspondence.

That A found the task of asserting himself in the world rather arduous is suggested by the desire for dependence upon women. He entered into a whole series of "platonic" friendships ("platonic" in the popular and not in the correct use of the word) with women, and he accepted economic support from his wife for several years. He was very "sensitive," and required a great deal of coddling in the home.

There are indications of the way in which his very early experiences influenced his trait formation. The infant takes pleasure in activities centering about the mouth, and this at first involves pleasurable sucking and later on, as the teeth begin to push through, this involves pleasurable biting. In our culture this leads to a withdrawal of the nipple, precipitating one of the major crises of growth. Weaning is the first substantial loss which is inflicted upon the individual after birth, and the way in which it is met establishes reaction patterns which may serve as important prototypes for subsequent behavior. About the time that the weaning deprivation occurs, the child is exposed to another set of conditions which demand sacrifice. He is supposed to control the elimination of his feces by giving up a part of his body at regular intervals. The growing child is also supposed to sacrifice another source of irresponsible pleasure by blocking his impulses to handle his genitalia. When the taboo on handling the genital organs for erotic purposes is set up with particular stringency by the methods adopted to curb early masturbation, some of the energy of the personality regresses to reanimate previous auto-erotic dispositions. This involves strengthening of the anal and oral components of the personality.

On the basis of the oral and anal origin of various traits, Karl Abraham has worked out a psychoanalytic theory of character formation.[3] The material which is available on A is too scanty to reveal the psychological mechanisms of infancy and early childhood. If a cross-section of his later character traits be tentatively interpreted in the light of Abraham's scheme, it may be said to show a predominance of traits from the oral phase of development. A striking characteristic of A has always been his optimism. He has never become despondent and passed through serious "blue spells," whether he lost his job, reached the end of his financial resources, lost a bride, or suffered social ostracism from all but a small though admiring circle. Disappointments and some illness have brought him comparatively little worry. Abraham traces this trait to the earliest level of character organization, saying that it indicates a child who, thanks to the abundance of nursing care, is accustomed to find the world responding copiously and quickly to his demands. A always felt an inner assurance that he would be cared for, and that all would come out for the best in the end "to those who serve the Lord, and are called according to his purpose." He accepted a position of economic dependence upon his wife, and upon the charity of radical ladies, without conflict. His nurse was still there to provide for him. A never showed any interest in

---

[3] *Psychoanalytische Studien zur Charakterbildung* (International Psychoanalytische Bibliothek, 1925), Nr. XVI. Freud's first contribution to the subject was published in 1908. His brief article, "Charakter and Analerotik," is reprinted in the fifth volume of the *Gesammelte Schriften*. Others who have written in the same field are Sadger, Ferenczi, Jones, and E. Glover.

accumulating money, and generously shared all that he possessed. His small legacy was eaten up by the society over which he presided, and he was always on the poverty line.

He not only gave bountifully of such money as he possessed, but copiously of his ideas. Automatically he took the lead in conversation, genially pouring forth streams of ideas. The savagery of his attack on those who disagreed with him, though an oral trait in part, stems, according to Abraham, not from the sucking phase of early development, but from the next succeeding or oral-sadistic phase.

Those individuals who have difficulty in accepting their heterosexuality are cut off from normal sex life, and seek to emphasize the acts preparatory to, and not consummatory of, copulation. An interest in sexual peeping was in some measure gratified by A's experiences in listening to the personal difficulties of those who came to him for counsel. The high value which he placed on appearing before the public, while perhaps adequately accounted for on the basis of his father-identification, probably had the additional advantage of gratifying his exhibitionistic drive. Since drink is in legend and life a frequent precursor of copulation, the reformer exaggerates its importance, and tries to stop it. Alcohol was early associated with sexual excesses in the mind of A, and his hostility to it was something more than a simple reflection of his milieu.[4]

A's intensity of manner betrayed the magnitude of the neurotic conflicts within his own personality. This intensity is not alone due to the insecurity arising from the failure to exterminate his own conscious awareness of sex, nor to

---

[4] Joel Rinaldo paraphrases Freud in his *Psychoanalysis of the "Reformer"* and without supporting cases argues that the reformer is always a meddling hysteric. This is not to be taken for granted, for he may more often prove to be an obsessive type, when he shows mental pathology. For the best picture of the two clinical types, see Janet, *Les névroses.*

his sense of sin for erotic impulses, nor to his fears of impotence, nor to the reaction organized when he was competing with his brother for the attention of the father. His sexual inhibitions removed from him one of the most dependable means of disposing of the tensions which arise from the miscellaneous frustrations met with in the course of daily life.[5]

We have traced A's demand for widespread emotional response to his difficulties of personal adjustment, especially in the field of early sexual development. We have followed through the displacement of the drives, which were originally organized with reference to the family circle, on to remote social objects, resulting in the espousal of ideals of social change. We have seen that A's particular technique for arousing emotional response was denunciatory oratory, and that such a technique expressed important underlying drives of his personality. Since A happened to be a socialist, it is natural to compare him with the socialist thinkers studied by Werner Sombart in *Der proletarische Sozialismus*. There is no doubt that A is numbered among the "artificial" rather than the "natural" men, since his relation to reality is less direct than with the "natural" type. But it cannot be said that social criticism was as deeply motivated in his life as among the men mentioned by Sombart. He expressed himself not only in radical agitation but in conservative, moralistic agitation. His career was not wrecked at any particular point in his history, and he possessed no mania for destruction, although showing much resentment against his family, and indulging in an active fantasy life. He was fundamentally an agitator, and secondarily a social radical.

[5] See Ferenczi, *Versuch einer Genitaltheorie* (Internationale Psychoanalytische Bibliothek, 1924), Band XV, esp. Sec. V. Also Wilhelm Reich, *Die Funktion des Orgasmus*.

CHAPTER VII

POLITICAL AGITATORS—*Continued*

B is an agitator who uses his pen instead of his tongue. He has achieved eminence in newspaper work, beginning as a news editor and editorial writer. At twenty, when he held his first newspaper job, B led a fight against the red-light district of the city, exposing the pimps, panderers, and prostitutes in sensational style. He has always responded quickly to the appeal of the underdog and revealed injustices wherever he found them, and he won great popularity among minority racial and national groups whose claims he championed before the American public. It is noteworthy that B has never been converted to "isms" and responds to the call of specific abuses. No one who knows B has ever questioned his sincerity, for the news value of his campaigns is often much less than the personal risks incurred.

B has a high reputation for absolute truthfulness and reliability, often carrying his scruples to what his fellow-newspapermen think are unwarranted extremes. On one occasion, he threw up an excellent job on a very well-known newspaper on a point of honor. The paper had divulged the source of a story which he had received in confidence, and which he communicated to the editor in confidence. Later he was made the editor of an important newspaper. For five months he produced brilliant results, when a misunderstanding arose with the proprietor over another point of honor. In a despondent moment he resigned, but the proprietor refused to let him leave, offering a substantial raise. He let himself be persuaded to go back, but refused to accept the raise. Before long, new points of honor arose, and he broke away for good. His passion for justice made him a favorite with his staff; and his quiet good sense and studiousness made him a name among older men and intellectuals.

Some of his reforming campaigns were very thinly veiled displacements of his own private motives. At the age of fourteen he was seduced by a colored woman, and he reacted to this experience with fright and disgust. He left a school which he attended after a series of boyish escapades which culminated in an argument over missing laundry. The laundryman was a negro. It was on his first newspaper job that he led the fight to clean up a red-light district, featuring the fact that both colored and white prostitutes were available.

B was one of the numerous family of a Civil War veteran on the Confederate side. His father carried himself like a soldier and expected his children to act like soldiers under all circumstances. He was spare, thin, and active, and his temper was short. He was boss in the house, ordering his wife about a great deal, and demanding implicit obedience from the children.

The mother of B was eleven years younger than her husband. She had ten children in quick succession, and she spoiled them, and was much beloved. She did all the cooking, washing, and ironing for the household, and slaved to allow the children to obtain an education. Everybody but her husband thought she worked too hard. She was herself eager for learning, but had no opportunity to continue her studies after marriage. Although poor, she was proud, and never asked alms or assistance of any kind. Though "obstinate as a mule," she was timid and shrinking in ordinary relations. Her routine was only broken by occasional headaches.

The father was a very suspicious man, and B bore the brunt of it. B was the sixth child and from an early age had trouble with his next older brother, who was three years his senior. On one memorable occasion the elder brother attacked him with a knife. B was able to take the knife away from him without being hurt. The affair was reported to the father by an aunt who was living in the house, and who always sided with the older boy. She said that B had been the aggressor, and in spite of his indignant assertions of innocence, B was soundly whipped. Such episodes aroused in him a deep protest against injustice, and an abiding hostility against his father. Years afterward the truth came out, and the father apologized, but animosities had grown too formidable to be ceremoniously brushed aside. B cherished a long list of grievances against his father. Once his father asked him to print some letters; he presently found that this was for the purpose of comparing them with an inscription on the lavatory wall.

Genital activities had their usual connotation of sinfulness. His father went so far with his prudery that B, who was once discovered naked in his own room, where he was slowly dressing, was severely reprimanded. Shortly after being seduced by the negro woman, his sense of guilt, combined with his ever present resentment against his father's unjust treatment, led him to run away from home. After staying away from home and working his way through school for about a year and a half, he returned home and went to work in the neighborhood, attracted chiefly by the prospect of being back with his mother.

It is noteworthy that in his career B was constantly finding pretexts to escape from a situation in which he was popular and successful. Salary increases, promotions, and social recognition came to him, but he managed to extricate himself from every such situation, often on a "point of honor." An excellent journalist, he always had a new door open. Thus he passed from one editorial desk to another, and even to a private news-service venture which turned out well in spite of the heavy handicaps on such an undertaking.

How can such behavior be accounted for? Let us suppose that friendly treatment on the part of superiors tends to activate a strong homosexual drive which has been repressed, but which continues to threaten to find expression. This unconscious drive urges him to intimacy with persons in the environment, whereupon his conscience, reacting blindly against the outlaw impulse, seeks to provoke a flight from the environment, and thus to escape from the exciting objects of desire. The outcome is a compromise formation in which the illicit hope of being attacked and violated by the environment is gratified by imagining that the environment has compromised his "honor." The conscience is gratified by the retreat from temptation. No sooner is B in a new environment than the tension begins to accumulate all over again. By throwing himself with zeal into a new and strange position, where the environment is impersonal, success comes, and with success and habituation to the milieu, there come familiarity and friendship. This produces the familiar strain by reactivating the unconscious homosexuality, and the defending conscience finds another retreat imperative.

What specific justification is there for the hypothesis just proposed? B finally came into a situation from which he could scarcely escape by the usual tactics. He scored one of the great successes of his career by being invited to accompany a government commission which investigated conditions abroad, and covered the assignment in brilliant style. He was shown all manner of courtesy. Working under high pressure, he plunged into another assignment, and once more had the journalistic world at his feet. But the strain of success was too much. This time he sought release, not by flight to a new job, which was difficult, but by developing a delusional system. In short, B went into a psychotic phase, and substituted for the world of reality a fantasy world of such sinister dimensions that he was justified in trying to escape from it. Unable to concentrate on his work, he moved restlessly from one town to another, and launched forth on long automobile tours with his wife.

The actual content of his delusional productions gives a clue to his mental conflict. He had ideas of reference, imagining that people on the street were looking at him mysteriously. He claimed that he was a party to the Teapot Dome scandal and that there was a dictaphone in the house. On the way to be examined at a sanitarium he claimed that he was being trailed by policemen. Upon admission he claimed that the orderlies were policemen, that he was being electrocuted, that his bed was wired to record all his movements, and that filthy songs were sung to him (with homosexual content). Discharged from the sanitarium, he was taken to a family reunion. He claimed to be treated as a negro, and declined to eat with family or sleep in the house. B claimed that a forest fire was caused by him and that books in the library were re-written on his account. On a motor trip he claimed that insulting remarks were made to him at every gas station. He turned against his wife (he had been sexually inactive in marriage), and finally called her a snake who ought to be killed, and proceeded to try it.

During the course of his psychosis it emerged that he recalls a sexual seduction by his older brother, and that he had been bothered by this fancy all his life. There was material to show that his father was likewise implicated in his homosexual fantasies, and that he had "eroticized" the injustices of his father and the physical attacks of his brother.[1]

The history of B belongs to a borderline group between agitators and administrators. His administrative ability is manifest in the managing editorships which he held, and in the special service which he organized and for a time conducted. His rôle as an agitator (in writing) began when he was twenty, and continued for more than another score of years. When this record is taken in juxtaposition to that of A, it shows how differences in displacement affect the growth of the personality. B was never able to displace his hatred and affections to remote, impersonal objects with the degree of success which characterized A. The campaigns of B against injustice were more concrete, more limited, and more personal than the agitations of A. It will be remembered that B's first crusade was against black-and-tan houses of prostitution, and this was in the nature of a revenge and a penance for his early experience with the colored woman. B was raised in a relatively inarticulate environment. His father made no public appearances, no member of the family achieved more than a rudimentary education, and no conversation was possible beyond the visible environment. Since B went to work at sixteen, he saw the world more from a concrete point of view while A was peering at the universe through the theoretical lenses of the schools. His history shows

[1] See Freud's discussion of paranoia in his "Psychoanalytische Bemerkungen über einen autobiographisch beschriebenen Fall von Paranoia," *Gesammelte Schriften*, Band VIII.

prolonged preoccupation with his own specific grievances against the original objects—against the father, brother, and aunt. This was a factor which disposed him to greater susceptibility to persons in the immediate environment than A. Although driven to become a rather seclusive child who read books more often than he played, no one took a special interest in his intellectual prospects. His maternal grandfather was said to have been a brilliant teacher, but not much was made of this model when B was a boy.[2]

Unlike A, B lacked the trick of dramatizing himself before a crowd. Inspection of his early history in the home shows that he lacked the practice in imposture which may be a prerequisite of this ability. B was never able to carry off a pose to impress his family with his own virtue and promise. Indeed, he had very early evidence of his own shortcomings, and his father not only accused him of sins he did commit, but padded the record with many that he had not contemplated. B was never able to get away with much.

The foregoing excerpts from the history of B illustrate how closely the behavior of the victim of a functional disorder may connect with the fundamental drives of the personality. Functional mental disorders are efforts at adjustment that fail, and the materials employed are those which the personality has available on the basis of its developmental history.

In the paranoid case just discussed, "grandiosity"—delusions of grandeur—was not as prominent as it often is.

---

[2] This grandfather committed suicide at an unreported age, and his youngest son is said to be "very nervous." B's oldest sister had a nervous breakdown in high school. The third sister is "neurotic." B is described as having been a frail infant, and a shy child. Bed-wetting continued until he was twelve or fourteen, and he occasionally had attacks of indigestion. Physical examination failed to disclose any significant physical factor in his difficulties.

Grandiose delusions seem to be linked with very strong impotence fears. This connection may be shown in gross clinical caricature in the case of C. This man belongs to the well-known group of verbose cranks who often surround themselves with admiring circles of disciples, and do nobody much harm. C went so far as to run for president of the United States on a minority ticket.

C came into medical hands quite by accident. He belongs to a very common type which preserves the personality sufficiently intact from deterioration to pass for well, though eccentric. C got into a dispute with a colored expressman over the charge for moving his goods to a new apartment, and the expressman called the police, who presently turned C over to a hospital. C imagined that the negro was plotting to ruin him by stealing his most valuable books and manuscripts. He announced that he was going to be the next president of the United States of America, since the reign of the present incumbent was to be short, and damned short at that. On the next inauguration day he will take charge by divine power, and after that his red-headed wife will be given full authority. He said that during the last presidential campaign he had a conference with the governor of New York concerning the leadership of American parties. At that time the governor told him that he was a wonderful man and a logical party leader. He declared that though as a rule he does not believe in prophets, one absolutely reliable prophet had testified that he would be president. This man had a vision in which a wedge was drawn between the Democrat and Republican parties, and an unknown man arose who was to rule the world. This man would have six letters in his name. He is "Six and Six," and this exactly fits C. C's real name is "Arabulah the Divine Guest." Using this name, he wrote a nine-thousand-word treatise on politics and world-peace which he said was thought to be supernaturally brilliant.

He was sure that he got into the hospital through a damnable trick of his enemies. "It is prophesied that I am to be the next president. To defeat this, they put me here. I'm just a martyr, but I'll come out on top in the end." He would be president in fulfilment of prophecy.

C more than hinted at the scientific secrets at his command. He had recently consulted Dr. A of the government about his process for the manufacture of diamonds. More pressure was all that was needed. He declared that he is a wonderful amateur chemist, and that he has a process for manufacturing coal that he learned confidentially from a shoemaker.

When a young man he was appointed a clerk in one of the government departments, but was thrown out of a job when the Democrats were elected in the late eighties. He then became what he called a promoter of inventions and an inventor.

A clue to the source of his delusional system is furnished by his sexual history and fantasies. At the age of fifty-nine he married a widow with two children. He describes his wife as of surpassing beauty, and as for himself, he declared that he possessed three testicles, and that he is a perfect specimen of a man, a most beautiful Apollo from the neck down, and asked to pose as a model. He refused, however, to be photographed, or to disclose anything further about his sexual history.

Impotence fear as the root of the luxurious tree of grandiose delusions is sometimes directly demonstrated by the obvious nature of the invention on which the individual

is engaged. The mysterious perpetual motion machine
turns out to be a crude version of the sexual organs.[3]

Shortly after C left the hospital, he was busy on the
stump, haranguing large audiences as a presidential candidate on a protest ticket.

C would not be taken seriously by many people of much
culture and discernment, but there are paranoid types who
are plausible enough in their accusations to win the support of discriminating men. Many of them are "litigious
paranoids," and, as implied by the term, they are characterized by the legal and agitational means which they exploit for the redress of grievances. They succeed in ration-
alizing their motives so adroitly that they are very dangerous troublemakers. Even when psychiatrists diagnose them
as psychotic, they are able to put up a front so successfully
that they are often released from custody by judge or
jury. Were the data available it would be interesting to
calculate how much this active and by no means uncommon
element in society costs in terms of litigation fees and
damaged reputations.

One of the smoothest customers of this description is D.
After leaving high school because of his ambition to earn
money, he presently became a traveling salesman for an
electrical company. He was very successful and soon accumulated enough to start himself in business, aided somewhat by the money of the woman whom he married. From
the beginning he was involved in numerous lawsuits with
big corporations. He was finally sent to the penitentiary
for having assumed the name of another company which
was already operating. Since the address of the new com-

---

[3] Examples are given in Kempf's *Psychopathology*, and in other textbooks
on the subject.

pany, as well as the name, was so similar to that of the older concern, he received mail and checks intended for the corporation. His own story is that he was persecuted by a certain big corporation, which tried consistently to ruin his business, even poisoning the mind of his wife against him (who soon divorced D). Whenever a suit was being tried against him, he claims always to have found a representative of the big corporation in town. These ideas of persecution extended through the trial, which he asserts was unfairly conducted, and to the penitentiary, where he claimed that officials were in league with the corporation to keep him imprisoned. His conduct was such that he was finally transferred from the prison to a mental hospital, where his attitude was that of contemptuous superiority. He collected evidence against the hospital, listening to all who complained of any sort of cruelty and incompetence, and constantly occupied himself with schemes to release prisoners and expose his persecutors.

D has an impressive, deliberate manner. There are no marks of the maniac about him to fit into the popular idea of a "crazy man." In conversation with strangers he puts his own case, and the case of others, with seeming moderation, emphasizing the obvious difficulties in the way of collecting conclusive evidence, and showing scrupulousness about affidavits and other documentary material. He has succeeded in establishing connections with prominent people in many walks of life, and is devoting himself to the cause of the underdog, with special reference to those unfortunates who are thrown into insane asylums and kept there by enemies who league themselves with doctors and superintendents.

He is associated with groups of people who band together in little agitational organizations with such unexceptionable names as Vigilantes of the Constitution, Foundation for Legal and Human Rights, American Equity Association. Their indictment of modern jurisprudence is pithily formulated in the slogan, "One Law for the Rich —Another Law for the Poor." The object of one of these associations is:

To secure to all persons the rights, privileges, and immunities which are theirs under the Constitution and laws of the United States, and to which they are justly entitled as members of the human family. . . . . Those aided are: worthy cases unable to hire legal counsel; victims of corrupt practices; friendless and unfortunates restrained in Institutions, who require assistance; ex-service men who have not been able to have legitimate claims considered, etc., etc.

One of the cases which is often referred to in the papers published by this group is that of William J. O'Brien. The headline of one article reads as follows: "Poor Private Wm. J. O'Brien, Sane Veteran of the Apache Indian Campaign, Railroaded to the Madhouse. Denied Justice—Denied His Day in Court—No Trial—No Lunacy Proceedings—Illegally Held 34 Years. . . . . " In the body of the article this statement occurs: "Mr. O'Brien indulged in some disorderly conduct in the office of the War Department. He was immediately arrested, charged with assault which he did not commit, and brought into the Supreme Court." I examined the record of the O'Brien case and found that "some disorderly conduct" consisted in visiting the War Department, shooting two clerks, and trying to shoot some more before his gun jammed.

The inference should not, of course, be hastily drawn that all the claims made by agitators, even of the psychotic stamp, are pure fabrications. That is to be determined in the individual instance. Thus the slogan about "One Law for the Rich—Another Law for the Poor" has very reputable support in the findings of such surveys of criminal justice as the one at Cleveland, in which Dean Pound of Harvard had a responsible share. But in the case of the litigious paranoids the underlying private motivation is so imperious that wholesale distortions of truth are inevitable. Sometimes reckless accusations bring cruel results, as when another psychotic, E, claimed that a certain Captain K was shot in the back while circling over a flying field. This fabrication got to the family of the soldier, who had been informed that the Captain had been killed in an aeroplane accident, and caused much unnecessary suffering.

The history of F affords some contrasts to what has gone before. F took up agitation in middle life. It will be remembered that A directed much of his agitational zeal against culture objects which were sanctioned by his family and the "substantial" elements in the nation. F was the reverse of a nonconformist. He was no pacifist, but a soldier-patriot. The enemies of his country were his enemies, and he denounced them up and down the land. The authority of revealed religion was not a debatable question; the enemies of Christianity were his enemies and he went on the platform to expose them.

Several of his patriotic and religious lectures became famous among the smaller communities of the land. He told the story of a renegade who impersonated Christ for the purpose of collecting funds to start an insurrection against the American government in one of our dependencies. He gave a thrilling account of how he sought out and apprehended this monster. A Y.M.C.A. worker, in a testimonial letter, declared, "Every man sat spellbound as the speaker bared the facts in the most sacrilegious undertaking of modern times to thwart the plans of the American government."

F was a moving spirit in the opposition to the Covenant of the League of Nations because the name of God was not mentioned in it. His argument on the point is said to have impressed President Harding. One of F's public pronouncements on the subject read as follows:

There might be no trespass in an "Association of Nations for Conference" coming together if they did nothing but *confer*, and did no acting or legislating whatever, *if* they beforehand and by common consent did the following before the whole world:

1st, Acknowledge Almighty God before the world, with a promise to serve *Him!*

2nd, Acknowledge allegiance to God's Peace Plan—the Kingdom of the Prince of Peace—for world peace, which the Bible provides for!

3rd, Ignore all man-made plans for peace, such as World Federations, Hague Tribunals, World Leagues, World Courts and all forms of *Human* world-governments, which the Bible provides against!

4th, Refrain absolutely from everything that has the slightest tinge of world-alliance, world-control, or world-domination influence or world concert of civil action, the human instrumentalities that Holy Writ severely prohibits.

5th, Especially for the United States. Refrain absolutely from everything that contravenes our U. S. Constitution and the Declaration of Independence! (And every nation should alike protect their Constitution!)

When thru centuries of trial the world failed to keep *the Covenant* written at Sinai by the Hand of Almighty God Himself and *He* promised that *He* would give the world "A New Covenant" for peace, which *He* did, then how can the world, except anything whatsoever from *The League of Nation's Covenant* written at Paris by the mortal hands of just mere men like Wilson, Lloyd George, Clemenceau & Co.?

After serving in the army as a young man, F joined the secret service, and spent several years in pursuit of the enemies of law and order. His record was excellent, and when the World War came he was put in charge of secret military police. He became overzealous in the performance of his duties, spending an altogether disproportionate amount of time investigating two Mennonite ministers who were alleged to have letters in their possession written in German criticizing the Liberty Loan. He claimed to have found ground glass in the bread served to men in camp. When the laboratory did not confirm his findings, he said that he mixed ground glass with flour and submitted a sample to the laboratory, which reported no ground glass, thus confirming his suspicions that the laboratory staff was composed of aliens—a German, an Austrian, and a Turk. He began to make direct accusations that some of the camp officers were in league with the enemy. One of them he accused of using a German private in his office for translation work, and intrusting him with a key to the iron safe where the United States secret codes were kept. Presently F was referred to a psychiatrist for examination, to whom he complained that he was the victim of a persecution by a little clique of officers. He managed to publish an interview in the press asserting that ground glass in the food had made fifty men ill at a certain training camp, and this led to much unnecessary anxiety among the folks at home.

F's anxiety to "do his bit" in the suspicion-ladened atmosphere which surrounded America's entry into the war led his suspicious nature to overdo the matter. When some of his efforts were blocked by fellow officers, he began to develop persecutory ideas. But he was soon able to dispense with them by reinforcing his identification with the interests of the nation and God, and displacing his suspicions upon more generalized foes. When his secret-service work was blocked, he was able to make a transition to agitation, where he balanced the lost gratification of cherishing secret knowledge with the pleasure of exhibiting it in public. The record does not contain enough early childhood material to justify one in venturing to select the determiner of his capacity to make such an adjustment. The history simply furnishes a striking example of how a flight into agitation may perform the function of keeping the personality in some sort of passable relation to reality, when it has met a serious setback. It gives another instance to the sum of those which show the difficulties which may be created in society by those whose personality is influenced by strong paranoidal trends.

The histories so far abstracted have had to do with male agitators of various kinds. Miss G, when thirty-five years of age, came to the physician complaining that she was constantly bothered by blushing, stage fright, uncertainty, palpitations of the heart, and weeping spells. She is known to be forceful, ambitious, and aggressive. Her contentiousness is notorious. She is active in the support of all kinds of measures, particularly for the emancipation of women from the domination of men. She rose to her present distinction from a very humble position as a handworker, and she champions the radical cause.

An early reminiscence was recovered during analysis which had been completely buried before. Sometime between the ages of five and three she had been asked by a nurse to touch her nurse's genitals, and threatened with dire things if she told. When she was in bed with her mother, she had to fight against a powerful compulsion to touch her mother's genitalia. This early assumption of the male rôle was strengthened by her father-identification. In the analysis she reported that she and her father possessed many common traits, such as stubbornness. As sometimes happens with children showing traits of the opposite sex, their brothers or sisters reveal cross-traits. Thus her younger brother cooked and sewed. Her father took her side in family altercations with the mother (the father was an artist). The mother was religious, and on the death of her mother the patient was religious for six months from a sense of possible guilt for having precipitated her death. Everybody said that she ought to have been a boy since she showed so much physical dash and hardihood. Between six and ten she often stole money from her parents, and was caught reading other people's letters.

As a child she suffered seriously from vague worries. At the age of seventeen she was unable to read her own compositions before the class. She talked rather badly in groups and before strangers, but was very effective in face-to-face conversations. In public she spoke best when attacked. She had a constant fear of being subordinated to a man, and was constantly on the alert to assert herself. She had a horror of marriage, which she thought of as gross subordination to the crude physical desires of men. One budding love affair broke up when the man went insane and died.

For a long time she longed to have a child, but only one child. She wished that there were some other means of impregnation than by using a man, but finally decided to bend to the inevitable. Several years before analysis she looked around to select a man to be the father of her child. It was a year after she became acquainted with the man before she could bring herself to coitus, and she felt befouled. After the birth of the child she became utterly indifferent to the man, and broke off their relationship. She was, of course, sexually frigid.

What is the meaning of this demand for a child, and for but a single child? It was essentially a subconscious demand for the penis to finish her assumption of the male rôle. The psychoanalytical study of the growth of the female personality stresses the importance which this motive assumes.[4] Gregory Zilboorg has analyzed certain post-pregnancy psychoses from this point of view, and in so doing has thoroughly surveyed the theoretical field.[5]

Castration dreams appeared in the guise of losing muffs and keys. Homosexual dreams took the usual shape of a nude homosexual figure. Horrified by dreams of sexual intercourse with her father, she began the analytical process. Her narcissism expressed itself in both simple and disguised form. She dreamed of being the mayor and of humiliating men in all manner of ways. She dreamed of influencing the whole world (telepathic dreams). Incidentally, she credits dreams with some prophetic significance. Once she dreamed of a clay field over which she was passing which changed to plowed land, signifying work, and, sure enough, she found a job the next day. Another time she was crossing a brook and saw an ugly body in the stream, and developed laryngitis the next day.

The narcissistic component was strong. She felt the universal rule of the analytical situation to say everything that crosses the mind to be a personal command from the doctor. She bitterly resented this subordination to a man, and finally broke off the analysis. She showed a record of having been quite rebellious against those in authority over her—shop foremen and party leaders.

Miss G had an enormous masculine complex. She chose

[4] See Helene Deutsch, *Psychoanalyse der weiblichen Sexualfunction.*

[5] See "The Dynamics of Schizophrenic Reactions Related to Pregnancy and Childbirth," *American Journal of Psychiatry*, VIII (1929), 733–66.

masculine goals, and ruled out the female rôle as far as she could. Her narcissism brought her from obscurity to distinction, though at the cost of several neurotic difficulties in which her repressed drives found crippling expression. She swings between vanity and inferiority feelings. She blushes when praised, she blushes in public because of the dependence of her sex on men, and she is timid in the presence of academic people. She always feels ill at ease with strangers, and lives in isolation from society.

In theory and in practice Miss G is for free love, and for the complete equality of the sexes. She sought out politics as a career as a means of expressing the male rôle of dominance, a drive which was powerfully organized in her early childhood experiences.[6]

What has been said about the agitator may be brought together at this point in a provisional summary. Our general theory of the political man stressed three terms, the private motives, their displacement on to public objects, and their rationalization in terms of public interests. The agitator values mass-responses. Broadly speaking, this requires an extension of the theory to make it possible to divide politicians among themselves according to the means which they value in expressing the drives of their personalities. Now what is there about the agitator's developmental history which predisposes him to work out his affects toward social objects by seeking to arouse the public directly? Why, to state it another way, is he the slave of the sentiments of the community at large? Why is he not able to work quietly without regard to the shifts of mood which distinguish the fickle masses? Why is he not able to cultivate interests in the manipulation of objective materi-

---

[6] The physician in charge of this case comments that there may be a homosexual *anlage* on the physical level, but that this is not certain.

als, in the achievement of aesthetic patterns, or in the technical development of abstractions? Why is he not principally concerned with the emotional responses of a single person, or a few persons in his intimate circle? Why is he not willing to wait for belated recognition by the many or by the specialized and competent few?

Agitators as a class are strongly narcissistic types. Narcissism is encouraged by obstacles in the early love relationships, or by overindulgence and admiration in the family circle. Libido which is blocked in moving outward toward objects settles back upon the self. Sexual objects like the self are preferred, and a strong homosexual component is thus characteristic. Among the agitators this yearning for emotional response of the homosexual kind is displaced upon generalized objects, and high value is placed on arousing emotional responses from the community at large. The tremendous urge for expression in written or spoken language is a roundabout method of gratifying these underlying emotional drives. Agitators show many traits which are characteristic of primitive narcissism in the exaggerated value which they put on the efficacy of formulas and gestures in producing results in the world of objective reality. The family history shows much repression of the direct manifestation of hatred. There is often a record of a "model boy" during the early years, or of a shy and sensitive child who swallowed his resentments. Repressed sadism is partly vented upon objects remote from the immediately given environment, and favors the cultivation of general social interests. The youth has usually learned to control by suppression and by repression the full amplitude of his affects, and this is a discipline in deceit. The narcissistic reactions prevent the developing individual from entering into full and warm emotional relationships during his puberty period, and sexual adjustments show varying degrees of frigidity or impotence, and other forms of maladjustment.[7] Speaking in terms of early growth phases, the agitators as a group show marked predominance of oral traits.

Distinctions within the agitating class itself may be drawn along several lines. The oratorical agitator, in contradistinction to the publicist, seems to show a long history of successful impostorship in dealing with his environment. Mr. A, it will be recalled, was able to pass for a model, and became skilled in the arts of putting up a virtuous front. Agitators differ appreciably in the specificity or the generality of the social objects upon which they succeed in displacing their affects. Those who have been consciously attached to their parents, and who have been successful impostors, are disposed to choose remote and general objects. Those who have been conscious of suppressing serious grievances against the early intimate circle, and who have been unable to carry off the impostor's rôle, are inclined to pick more immediate and personal substitutes. The rational structure tends toward theoretical completeness in the former case. Displacement choices depend on the models available when the early identifications are made. When the homosexual attitude is particularly important, the assaultive, provocative relation to the environment is likely to display itself; when the impotence fear is active, grandiose reaction patterns appear more prominently.

[7] Harry Stack Sullivan has stressed the critical importance for personality growth of the adolescent phase in which the individual is impelled to enter into intimate emotional relations with one or two other persons of his own age. Those who partially fail in this show various warps in their subsequent development.

CHAPTER VIII
POLITICAL ADMINISTRATORS

Some administrators are full of ideas and others are seldom attracted by novelty. Some do their best work under a rather indulgent chief; others fall to pieces unless there is strong pressure from above. There are administrators who derive their influence over subordinates from the authority of their positions rather than from the authority of their personalities. There are some who may be depended upon for the conscientious performance of detailed tasks, while others neglect details and think in terms of general policy.

Viewed developmentally, it appears that one group of administrators is remarkably akin to the agitators, differing only in the fact that they are bound to particular individuals more closely, and thus displace their affects upon less generalized objects. This gives a certain independence to the administrator from the compulsion to "get a rise out of" large numbers of the population. It ties him more securely, however, to the members of his own environment, whose relations he seeks to co-ordinate. The administrator is a co-ordinator of effort in continuing activity.

The group which is allied to the agitators includes those who show imagination and promoting drive. The history of H belongs in this class, and has the incidental interest of showing how H behaved in war time.

While it is accurate to say that H is diplomatic and seemingly open and frank in dealing with his superiors, it should be added that in situations which involve the fate of his own projects, he is noticeably overtense, and likely to evaluate himself much higher than others. He becomes slightly accusatory if his demands are rejected. The elderly executive with whom H did his best work sometimes complained that a conference with H was as fatiguing as a whole day's work. The older man felt that H might be entirely broken up if his projects were rudely rejected, and he also believed the young man to be too valuable to damage. H recognizes that he has often found himself shirking when his superiors let him alone, and wonders why this attitude, which is contrary to his own interests, should take hold of him. H displays a tendency to behave arrogantly toward subordinates, and when he was in the army it was obvious that he could maintain discipline only through the formal authority vested in him.

H is an only child. His father was a big, overpowering person, who was a strict disciplinarian. The parents were very prudish in sexual matters, and one of his embarrassing memories is the confusion and vexation of his mother when he asked her about babies. Left to his own resources, and stimulated by a variety of incidents to explore sexual problems on his own initiative, the boy became involved in a set of episodes and reveries which he tried to keep from the family, and thus met every family situation with some anxiety lest his sins should find him out. H grew into a hyperactive and seemingly light-hearted youngster, who obeyed his parents implicitly and met strangers with ingratiating charm. H was constantly occupied with the task of adopting a manner toward authority which would conceal his secret preoccupations.

About the age of four, H surprised his parents in a sexual embrace, and vividly recalled his own mixture of burning curiosity and embarrassment. Some of his early dream fragments indicate that he repressed a powerful hostility toward his father, who he thought was hurting his mother, and likewise repressed hatred of his mother, who he felt was disloyal to him.

His experiences continued through a long chain of incidents. There was mutual exposure of sexual parts between him and a playmate of his own age. A deeply repressed episode was a seduction in which he played the principal part. He was meanwhile completely successful in playing the rôle of model boy.

When H was ten years of age, however, there transpired an incident which for a time branded him in the neighborhood as a nasty little renegade, and which had many subsequent repercussions. He touched the exposed sexual parts of a neighbor girl, who was somewhat his junior. The sister and brother of the girl were interested spectators. The children told the cooks, and the news finally got around to the mother of the girl. She took it calmly enough, but thought she ought to tell the boy's mother. H's mother passed the story to his father, which was the worst thing that could happen, from H's point of view. His father administered a sharp dressing-down, and forbade him to play outside the yard for a fortnight. H's father was very angry, and lectured him about his sins every night for a while. Presently the father went over to see the neighbor, and seems to have taken the line that the girl was as much to blame as his son if not more so. This tactless behavior completely alienated the neighbor.

Now this neighbor happened to edit an important newspaper, and ever afterward this newspaper lost no opportunity to assail the efficiency of the department in the city government headed by H's father. These attacks continued over many years, and H's father occasionally threw it up to him that he had been responsible for the original quarrel.

As it was, the boy was ostracized in the neighborhood for a year or more, and was not invited to go to parties, although he could play with the children. But H was self-conscious, and sought companionship farther away. The brother of the girl thought that he ought to turn against H, and there were some fights.

At fourteen H began to go to high school. He kept away from the swimming pool during the first year or two because he was much embarrassed by the lack of hair around his genitals. This supposed retardation, about which he worried a great deal, lasted but a short time, when a new set of worries came up. He now believed that his penis was abnormally large, and that his testicles were too low-hanging and perhaps deformed. In college he was nicknamed "Cocky," on account of his jauntiness, but he secretly suspected that this was an allusion to his penis.

A chum taught him how to masturbate, and he continued to do so for about six months, when his emissions became so frequent that his mother told his father. For once, H's father handled the situation with good sense, and after a kindly interview in which the father explained that it was not a good idea to indulge excessively, H quit. But even this matter was not terminated, for the disturbing reverie remained that perhaps his excessive masturbation had permanently impaired his manhood.

H had a lively curiosity about his mother's body of which he was intensely ashamed. He recalls loitering in his mother's room while she made ready to change her clothes, hoping that she would forget to send him out. He found himself speculating about the shape of her body, and was several times on the verge of spying through the keyhole. But his impulse was inhibited when he remembered the story told by his father in which a "peeper" was spoken of with the greatest contempt. H dreamed of sexual intercourse with his mother on several occasions, nearly always during periods of unusual strain. These dreams were deeply buried and came out into the clear with great difficulty.

His sexual curiosity extended to animals, and he stimulated the sexual parts of his dog. This further associated sex with the bestial and unclean, and convinced him of his own guilt for so much as wondering about it.

H's first sexual intercourse cost him much worry. It occurred during his second year in high school. He had been sent with the family automobile to drive home a guest, and noticed a girl of about his own age who was gay and flirtatious. On the way home he picked up the girl with two boys whom he knew slightly. All of them had sexual intercourse with the girl. He was terribly worried that he might reach home too late. His strict father had laid down the rule that if he got home at any hour of the night, he was to wake up the family and give an account of himself. In his haste he neglected to inspect the car and his father found some hairpins in the tonneau. H denied that he knew anything about them. The incident, however, was not closed. He saw an item in the newspaper about several men who were arrested for rape, and wondered whether he had committed a horrible crime himself with his companions. Before long the girl became pregnant and was brought before the juvenile court. She named another gang of boys, and this gang accused H and his two companions of being to blame. He was horrified at the prospect of going into court and dragging his family to disgrace. H was afraid that his partners in wrongdoing would confess, but he denied everything to his father, and his father's political influence kept him from being haled into court. But for at least a year the black cloud of possible exposure hung on the horizon of his mind.

All during his high-school days he had occasional sex intercourse, but every episode was marred by some disagreeable features. While there were such experiences with girls of low social standing, he had many friendships with girls of good social position whom he idealized as above sexuality. He attended a private school which was patronized almost exclusively by children from very wealthy families, and H, who was handsome, well dressed, quick, and agreeable, found his friends among them. He was often in their homes and admired the signs of wealth and culture. He became sensitive of the cultural limitations of his own parents, and was afraid to entertain his school friends at home, but fortunately from his point of view his father was willing to furnish enough money to make it possible to hold up his end of the social bargain at exclusive clubs and restaurants.

In college H continued to draw a sharp line between those who could be petted, but who were too rich and refined to be approached for intercourse, and those who could be petted, and who were poor enough to be asked for intercourse. He continued to associate with a smart and wealthy set, and finally concentrated his attention on the daughter of a rich business man whom he wanted to marry. His left-handed affairs continued at irregular intervals, and he felt remorseful when he had the perversions performed on him.

Enough has been reported to convey an impression of H's inner state. His unsatisfied sexual curiosity had been whetted by his prudish parents. His father defended his own ascendancy in the home by ordering the boy about a great deal, and H responded to authority by a system of reactions which became characteristic of him. He was tactful, deferential, and acquiescent, qualified by inner resentment and rare gestures of defiance. The father was not a friend but a barrier to be circumvented, and the father's hegemony was protected by the sense of guilty inferiority which he had created in his son. Family differences, such as arose when the father objected to housekeeping details, or when the boy wanted more freedom to use the car, always showed the same balance of forces —mother and son versus the father. The mother did not defend herself by robust contradiction but by weak complaints. There were only two instances in which the boy flared up enough to resist his father openly.

If H had been more successful in winning applause outside the family, it is quite possible that his position would have been made much easier inside it. His social charm brought him into the most influential circles, and this gratified his parents, but his father was a man of action who felt that while wealthy friends were an asset, his son ought to show more positive achievements. Though he never nagged H, the father's sternness, suspiciousness and absence of praise made a deep impression on the boy, and gave him a sense of insecurity and inadequacy. Although H scored no great successes, he went along without academic catastrophe until college. He was suspended at the end of his Freshman year for poor work, but came back after six months, during which he pretended to his father that he was still in school. The suspension was partly due to the advice given to the dean by his fraternity brothers, who had found him very hard to manage, and wanted to "bring him to his senses." H was having a fling, since he was away from home for the first time, and away from the intimidating father. Presently he steadied down enough to get along.

Reminiscences of his guilty sexual experiments, deeply charged with guilt-feeling, were continually bobbing up to interfere with his progress. Once he was assigned to debate in high-school public-speaking class. His opponent proved to be the brother of the girl with whom he had the notorious incident several years before. The brother was a prominent school leader who had no doubt forgotten the affair, but it continued to weigh on H. He always had felt uncomfortable in the other boy's presence, and on this occasion, being poorly prepared, the situation became so unbearable that he fainted.

He began to study agriculture at college, but soon found that he had made a mistake. His family owned a ranch which he often visited during vacations, and very much enjoyed. Farming was an avocation of his father, and H had the idea that ranching was a genteel occupation without much work, and with much ordering of other people about. He vaguely thought of himself as a country gentleman of cultivated leisure. The war saved H from agriculture. He took up aviation, without losing "credits," partly because the snobbish mother of his favorite girl was bowled over by the uniform, and partly because he thought it would be better to go into the war, if he had to go, as an officer than as a private. His father's influence secured a deferred classification for him in the draft, and H, though feeling quite small about it, said to himself that it was better for people to die who were without his own advantages and achievements.

His career as an officer in the camp brought out the traits to which reference has previously been made. His engaging deference toward his superiors won them all, but he had trouble with the men. His own insecurity led to an arrogant pose on his part that offended every man in the company. He also discovered that the moment discipline was relaxed he became very careless in performing his own duties.

The same constellation of traits reappeared in his administrative career, modified by the fact that he learned to assume a less provocative attitude toward his subordinates. He made a very good record, and proposed a number of changes that were adopted for the improvement of the service.

Looking back over H's history, the striking thing is his prolonged worry about his adjustment to specific persons. H was never able to make the hurdle into abstract interests. Even his administrative ideas were closely tied to the immediate context of the service. H's life was very much dominated by his relationship to definite people, and this meant a prolonged carry-over of early attitudes to these individuals. Unlike B, who could rightly feel that his father and brother and aunt were treating him unjustly, H was all too aware that he "deserved" more than he got. His success as an impostor was rudely interrupted in some early episodes.

Another "marginal" history shows what happens to some men with agitating aspirations who are not able to disentangle themselves from a place inside an organization and to give themselves up wholly to agitational work. Mr. I is a type occasionally met with inside administrative staffs who makes a serious problem for himself and others. He radiates plans that he neglects to execute, and he is supercilious and defiant toward superiors. He lacks the drive, however, to move over into agitational work entirely by identifying himself with a sufficiently dramatic cause. Sometimes this is due, as in I's own case, to powerful early identifications with particular projects, and with administrative work as such. When such a person can be pried loose from certain of these early fixations, he often proves capable of fulfilling the expectations which he is able to arouse.

The father of I was a man whose extraordinary talents won him great distinction, but who never quite managed to come through as brilliantly as people had a right to expect from one so richly endowed. I's father could talk five or six languages and read many more. He was educated in England, France, and Italy, and after serving as a professor of modern languages, his interest in educational problems led him to become the head of a famous preparatory school, and later of a public school. He spent most of his time reading, and during the last decade of his life drank heavily, but without impairing the quality of his work. Someone who knew him pronounced the man "a self-centered intellectual who died without a friend." The mother of I was an adopted daughter of a member of the British aristocracy, and was brought up in distinguished social and intellectual circles. The mother was exceptionally active in all sorts of humanitarian enterprises but lavished much time and love on the boy, who was "dreadfully spoiled," and accepted everybody's judgment that he was a budding genius.

True to anticipations, the boy shot through school like a meteor, ranking first in his subjects, and taking every available honor with ease. In college he branched out into social and political life on a large scale, and joined about twenty organizations, managing to have himself put on every important committee.

Like his father, the son took up public-school work. Becoming interested in psychology, he did some graduate work, and quickly published a book that received very favorable comment among those best qualified to judge it. The idea of educational reform fired his imagination, and he lectured far and wide, engaging in agitations to secure legislation which would authorize a number of experimental schools.

The part of his history which is especially interesting to the student of administration is this: He was continually at outs with his superiors and colleagues. His first teaching position began with a feud, and lasted but a little while. He was invited to resign his next post. He was asked to resign the next position. He was asked to resign the next position. These entries appear monotonously through his record.

Everybody conceded the brilliance and fertility of his mind, and did homage to the originality of his plans. He began work but failed to carry it far, seeming to think that work planned was work done. His methods were always aggressive. Seized of an administrative idea, he went to his superiors. When they criticized the scheme, or rejected his suggestion, he often took the bit in his teeth and tried to run the ship in his own way.

More than once financial irregularities have been discovered in connection with his work. He has given out checks when no funds were available, and run unduly large expense accounts. Whenever he has been in financial jams, he has turned to other people for aid as a matter of course, seeming to feel that he has a claim on the world for support.

He has always been childishly dependent on his wife for praise. He resented his wife's motherhood, but has been overindulgent with the two children, who, his wife says, have no respect for him. He likes to be the center of attention, and is a clever showman, and a great deal of a bluffer. He is usually not high tempered but affectionate. He is inclined to be accusatory toward his wife—"a vixen" —but his wife appears to be a keen person, who was enough impressed by his precocious brilliance to marry and to pamper him, but who in later years has delivered herself of pointed comments on his character.

It seems that he has gone through several periods of alternating exhilaration and despondency. The exhilarations came when he had a position and when life became a little monotonous or a little hard. At least one of these swings was sufficiently pronounced to lead to a period of retirement in a sanitarium. During this time he was asked what kind of work he liked best, and replied, "Reforming the world—my first choice; second, exploiting the world."

The strength of his narcissism is self-evident, and the feminine marks in his character are numerous. He expects to be nurtured and supported by the world as a matter of right. He demands constant "mothering" from his wife, and coddles the children. His father-hatred, which was thoroughly repressed in the family, comes out in his difficulty with father-surrogates, and in his determination to change the educational system at points where the father took it for granted or overtly defended it. The selection of the pedagogical rôle is itself indicative of the strength of his father-identification. What seems to have happened in his development is a fixation of interests in a relatively narrow sphere in which the affects are so powerful and at the same time so contradictory that difficulties are assured. He finds it impossible to shake off his managerial aspirations sufficiently to devote all his time to the propagation of ideas. Although his affects are displaced upon abstract problems, they are not displaced upon objects sufficiently removed from his father, and the displacement does not succeed in making it possible for him to achieve an impersonal attitude toward his superiors and colleagues in educational administration. The exaggerated praise heaped upon him as a boy had much to do with the narcissism. His incapacity to follow through is no doubt related to his early conflicts over genital activity. The chief point of significant contrast with A is that the narcissistic component interfered more seriously with H's development, since it led him to insist upon playing an administrative rôle. A's environment was less prostrate before him, and he was able to avoid assuming administrative obligations where he would be cramped and subordinated.

The history of J, which has been reported by Alexander,[1] shows what lies behind a powerful administrator's thirst for responsibility, and reveals how changes in the working relations inside an organization may disorganize the individual.

J was a driving executive whose superiors deferred to his judgment and accepted his plans. His abounding energy sought an outlet through the assumption of heavier and heavier responsibilities inside the organization. Finally, a change in the chief executive brought J under the immediate control of a man who handled him with cool assurance, holding him firmly but considerately to his own formal sphere of action. Confronted for the first time in his life by a more powerful personality who knew how to regulate him, J took the wife of another man for his mistress, and in spite of the remonstrances of those

[1] "Der neurotische Charakter," *Internationale Zeitschrift für Psychoanalyse*, XIV (1928), 26–44.

who knew him, he held tenaciously to both the mistress and the wife.

An analysis showed that J was characterized from early childhood by a notable split in his personality. Side by side with his aggressive, masculine drive there existed a strongly repressed, though powerful, feminine tendency. His personality is to be rendered intelligible only as a compromise formation between those two incompatible motives. The repression of the passive component produced a regressive fixation upon the wife, who was compelled to play a markedly maternal rôle, and to humor his every whim. He resented it if his every wish was not defined and fulfilled before he had to go to the trouble of putting it into words. J has delicate aesthetic sensibilities, and is a cultivated amateur in the arts.

In sharpest imaginable contrast to his behavior at home was his insatiable thirst for authority and responsibility in his professional life. One of his dreams acutely symbolized him as a giant automobile of untold horse-power, whose body was a light French coach of the rococo period.

As Alexander comments, J's life-problem was to indulge his passive demands without doing violence to his masculine ideal. But this was not accomplished without strain. He could earn periods of indulgence in aesthetics by exaggerated aggressiveness in his work, but as his feminine tendencies were gratified, his masculine ideal was endangered, and he would be driven back to high-pressure management. The psychological significance of his work was symbolized in the following dream: He was penetrating a thick sheet of cardboard with a needle, and continually asking for new sheets to bore through. He succeeded in going through several thicknesses. The cardboard represented his occupational problems, and the needle his penis.

His professional activity was largely a sublimation of his aggressive, active sexuality.

The equilibrium between his aggressiveness in work and his passivity in marital life was upset by the new chief executive, who skilfully hemmed in his activity. Alexander remarks that it is impossible for a man who has struggled all his life against very strong unconscious homosexuality to serve under a strong man. The dominating personality arouses the latent attitude, and the subordinate must resort to special means of maintaining his repression. In the case of B, which we have previously considered, the means of restoring some sort of equilibrium was escape (by resigning), but when that became very difficult, he fled into a world of fantasy (a psychosis). J met the crisis by breaking through the sublimation of his heterosexuality, and taking a mistress as an outlet for his thwarted drives. Further than that, he vindicated his masculinity in a very dramatic way. He not only took a mistress, but he took the wife of another.

From now on, he was dependent on both women to preserve the equilibrium of his personality. Previously the equilibrium had been maintained between wife and work; now it depended on wife, mistress, and work, for the aggressive, masculine component required the mistress to make up for the limitations imposed upon his working sphere.

Alexander reports that in the course of a long analysis this remarkable split in the personality was traced back to early childhood. "At the age of four he was already the same person." At the age of four he continued to drink milk out of a bottle, stubbornly resisting every effort to break him of the practice. But—and it was with an emphatic "but" that J produced the reminiscence—at the same time the boy was especially adventurous and independent, riding all by himself out on the highway. Here was the same antithesis that later expressed itself in his peculiar relation to wife and work. The child won the right to indulge his infantile, oral tendencies in one particular by exaggerated boldness in other respects. This solution was the prototype for his later life.

The rôle of the bottle was later taken by his wife, whom he often treated like an inanimate object whose only function was to minister to his needs, while his work, and later his mistress, were the successors to the bicycle, by means of which he was able to prove his independence and his masculinity to himself and the world.

The castration fear, which was aroused by the means adopted to break up his infantile masturbation, favored the oral fixation, and came into conflict with his strong masculine genital drive, laying the basis for this notable character split.

The records so far discussed have had to do with inventive or driving administrators. A type often met with in the public service is the conscientious, overscrupulous official, whose touchiness, fondness for detail, delight in routine, and passion for accuracy at once preserve the integrity of the service and alienate the affections of anybody who has to do business with the government. K was such a man. For some years he was in the forestry service, where part of his duties was to mark the trees that might be cut by private lumbermen. The lumbermen naturally argued that the straight, sound trees should be cut and the damaged ones left for seed. K took a variety of other factors into account, and spent days measuring and estimating position, growth rates, and shade area, exasperating the lumbermen with his everlasting and often superfluous scrupulousness. He keenly felt his responsibilities as a public servant, and disliked the very appearance of succumbing to private pressure. At one time K resigned the service in disgust because of "uncivil" treatment by a superior, but his "touchiness" was much more deeply rooted in his nature than he had any idea.

The record of K is not only the story of a pedantic official but of an ardent patriot. One of the highest forms of patriotism is supposed to be volunteering for posts of conspicuous danger in war. K pulled all the wires within reach to get a place on the front line, and only the point-blank refusal of his superiors to allow him to squander his technical ability prevented him from achieving his desire. From a close examination of his intimate history we learn how one variety of superpatriot comes to be.

K was the youngest of four children. His next brother was eight years his senior, his sister was five years older than this brother, and his oldest brother was eighteen years ahead of him.

He never remembered a time when his mother and father, who were divorced when he was eight, were on good terms with each other. They seldom spoke, except to quarrel. This family background was reflected in the mental life of the growing child. K was notoriously nervous and timid. From a very early day he began to be preoccupied with why he was different from everybody else in the world. His sense of isolation and strangeness led him to believe that perhaps he was the only real person in the world and that everybody else was an illusion. He would sometimes come up wonderingly to touch his mother, and then himself, to see if she, too, were real. He speculated on how he could get away from the human shadows around him, and became convinced that he could fly. Several times he laboriously climbed up on the seat of a kitchen chair, spread his arms like a bird, and leaped into space. Every time he crashed to the floor, his frightened mother rescued him, but he always felt surprised and rather aggrieved that he should fall, and secretly believed that he could fly after all. This type of reaction characteristically appears where emotional conflicts in the home create an acute problem of emotional orientation for the child.

As a small boy he was sent by his mother to follow his father when he left the house, and to report where he went. K developed a strong sense of guilt for this, and after the divorce was afraid that his father would return and take revenge on him in some unknown and horrible way. His father did occasionally reappear, and once invited the boy to spend the night with him, but K was too frightened to accept.

The family often lived in the country, and the self-consciousness of K in the presence of strangers was heightened by frequent removals into new and often isolated places. One of the towns near which he lived when about nine was on a frontier. Gun-play was frequent, and K remembers having seen the corpses of men who had been shot down in street brawls. There were ominous-looking fellows around town, and the boy gave them a wide berth.

The death of his mother when he was twelve robbed K of his main emotional support in a dangerous world. She died after two years of suffering from an infected limb. She would also spit into bits of papers and burn them in the stove. K wondered why she did this, and later developed a reverie the importance of which will soon appear.

The older members of the family were left with K on their hands, and they decided to club together and put all thought of marrying out of their heads until he was able to stand alone. The boy did not then realize the sacrifices they made for him, but he later discovered that his older brother put off marrying the girl of his choice until she broke off the engagement and married someone else. It was not until about the time that he graduated from high school and the home was broken up that he became aware of what he owed them, and ever after he was plagued by the thought of his unworthiness, and his incapacity to repay his brothers and sister for their care. Up to that time he had experienced no particular sense of gratitude, and although his older brother once or twice referred to his dependent position, his private feelings were mainly of resentment against the restrictions imposed upon him.

And these restrictions were not inconsiderable. The family ran a greenhouse, and the drudgery involved in such an occupation was incessant. There were slips to transplant, beds to weed, and loads to pull and carry. There were long hours of boredom over routine occupations. K was expected to dash home from school at the earliest possible moment, and to lend a hand with the endless chores about the place.

Occasionally he succeeded in evading his duties. He stopped to play on the way home from deliveries, and he stayed at school on some pretext or other to join the drill squad. But he was always haunted by fear and guilt. His older brother was a strict disciplinarian, and beat him several times. His sister occasionally let him have some spending money, but as a rule he was tightly cramped financially. When his gang organized into a drill squad, and chose their uniforms, he was humiliated when the necessary dollars were not forthcoming from home.

K was worried by what appeared to be a lack of physical stamina and endurance. This idea (which had no basis in fact) in part grew out of his efforts to do what his brothers did. They occasionally broad-jumped or pulled weights, and of course K made a poor showing beside them. But for the unconscious hostility against them, such unequal results would not have disturbed him. His morbid worries about his strength led him to submit to a great deal of bullying by town toughs.

His adolescent years were marred by perpetual anxieties about his social adequacy. He had been the victim of an explosion which left his face marked with powder stains, and this repugnant tattooing, which disappeared very gradually, embarrassed him for years.

K's older brothers and sister sometimes took him with them to parties because there was nobody to leave him with, and an annoying sense of being in the way added to his growing sense of social inadequacy. During high-school days he fell in love with the daughter of the most influential man in the locality, but as her social standards became more exacting, his lack of money, leisure, and prestige made it impossible for him to travel with her set. One of the most humiliating episodes in his life was the one which broke up their relations. K had arranged to meet her at a dancing class. Another girl called up to see if he would take her, but he said he wasn't going. His oldest brother had listened in on the telephone extension, and was astonished to see K appear all dressed up and on the way out. He launched forth on a tirade, declaring that K gallivanted around throwing money away and shirking his job, though he was absolutely dependent on others for his daily bread. K was cut to the quick, and went back to his room churning with too many emotions to call up and offer explanations to the girl.

K had taken it for granted ever since he was a small boy that he would go to college. He traced back his determination to an incident when he was driving across the plains one magnificent starry night. He sat in the bottom of the rig, rapt in contemplation of the sparkling sky, while his mother chatted with her neighbor. Suddenly he asked how he could find out about the stars, and she replied that people could study all about them in college. He then and there resolved to go to college, and never had a moment's doubt about it, although the members of his immediate family went no farther than the common school.

In spite of his inferiority feelings, K was not cut off from some measure of recognition in high school. His dependable and sympathetic qualities impressed themselves upon those who came into close daily contact with him, and he was made an officer of his high-school class. He was respectful toward his teachers and good in his studies.

College was an entirely different affair. His personal worries multiplied during the transition period. Lacking funds, he sought a scholarship. The only one tenable from his district to the state university was in ceramic engineering, and after looking up "ceramic" in the dictionary, he applied and was selected for admission. The work proved to have no particular interest for him, and his social life was even less satisfying. He was met at the college town by the members of a church group who lived together in a dormitory (some friend had written them), and he, though never devout, stopped with them during the first term. This marked him as a non-fraternity man. He waited tables in a fraternity house, and as bad luck would have it, a former teacher wrote highly recommending him to the consideration of this particular fraternity. When a committee broke the news to him, he was utterly confused and made such a lamentable impression that it was not possible to extend him the bid. One of his odd jobs was beating carpets at a sorority house, and this turned out to be the sorority that had pledged the girl with whom he had been (and still felt) in love.

For relaxation K was forced into the domain of the kitchen maids. A servant girl struck up a friendship with him, and he had sexual relations with her. He had tried intercourse once during high-school days, and had a premature emission, a practice which often bothered him later, providing a permanent source of humiliation.

Transferring to another college, he began his work in forestry, in which he had acquired some interest during hikes with a friendly high-school teacher. Handicapped by lack of money and worried by a mounting sense of social inadequacy, his life was no more successful than before. In high-school days he envied a talkative lad who astonished the company by glibly recounting anecdotes about Napoleon. One of his relatives whom he had known as a boy left an ideal of social charm which never was attained.

K's inner uncertainties finally reached a point which led him to resolve that he ought to discover once for all whether forestry would prove to be a proper vocation. He left college and joined the government service. This was to be the great test of his ability to master himself.

So keen was his preoccupation with self-mastery that he resented every effort to influence him, and acted with unnecessary strictness in dealing with private lumbermen. He was often deprived of human relationships during his days in the field, and gradually his mind became more and more enmeshed in morbid reflections about himself.

His mind simply refused to concentrate on the technical volumes which he had brought with him to improve the solitude. Reveries which had been slowly germinating on the periphery of his attention now began to foliate. K had always wondered why his mother burned those little bits of paper. It dawned on him one day that she might really have died of tuberculosis, and that he must therefore be predisposed toward that disease. Early in his high-school days, he had begun deep-breathing exercises, though he had never freely admitted to himself or anybody else what lay behind it. He always gave the usual account of his mother's death to insurance examiners, smothering his doubts in affirmation.

This was his state of mind when America entered the war. He found himself saying that since he was going to die anyhow from a loathsome disease, he might as well die at once and get it over with. Enlisting without delay, he sought to reach an exposed position as rapidly as he could. But the government had different ideas, and assigned him to a branch of the service where his technical skill would prove useful. In his disappointment, all the old feelings of inadequacy returned. Interviewed by an officer he floundered and stumbled, neglecting to report essential facts about his training and experience. The accidental intervention of an acquaintance straightened out the matter, and secured the authority to which his record entitled him. At first he was very much embarrassed in the company of lumberjacks, but his behavior never showed his confusion. His actual record was, as usual, excellent, and his conscientious efficiency won the indorsement of everybody who knew him.

K married a rather dominating school-teacher whom he had known for some time. When things went badly, as they often did, he was partially impotent, and also showed the phenomenon which has been christened "Sunday neurosis." Every Sunday afternoon when he was at home he would find himself assailed by deep depression, and would weep quietly to himself.[2] In spite of these neurotic troubles, K was able to make an important place for himself inside a bureaucracy, when he came back from the army.

From one point of view, K's character may be summed up by saying that his overscrupulous performance of duty was an elaborate effort to demonstrate his potency, and that his longing for danger came at a time when he was willing to surrender the struggle. K's morbid moods and persistent feelings of inadequacy are self-imposed penalties for his hostilities against the environment. He possessed very powerful aggressive drives which were partly expressed in the adoption of a self-ideal which was far more ambitious than anything deemed feasible by the family. His narcissism was such that he was prevented from viewing himself as an object, and from modifying his demands upon the world for recognition, and upon himself for production, until these demands bore a closer relationship to his own skills and opportunities. The basis for his obsessive scrupulousness was laid during early childhood, when he was torn between father and mother-loyalties, and acted out within his own nature the clashes that occurred between them. His strong mother-identification is shown by his belief that he suffered from her diseases, and would die from tuberculosis as she had died. He preferred death to a reduction in his demands upon himself and the world. Such a reaction has in it the primitive demand of the child to treat the world as controllable at will by the omnipotent

[2] Abraham and Ferenczi have reported cases of this kind.

fantasy. His genital difficulties testify to the intensity of the castration conflict, and show the passive-oral regression. K deeply resented having to adjust to the world at all. His capacity for hard work was achieved against high resistance, and in part had the value of a penance. Thus when workless days came around, he was always ill at ease, and sometimes showed the spells of weeping on Sunday afternoons. To work was to prove his potency, and to supply a ritual substitute for and defense against his antisocial impulses. He was unable to emancipate himself very far from the reactions of the people in his immediate environment.

As a class the administrators differ from the agitators by the displacement of their affects upon less remote and abstract objects. In the case of one important group this failure to achieve abstract objects is due to excessive preoccupation with specific individuals in the family circle, and to the correlative difficulty of defining the rôle of the self. Putting agitator A at one end of the scale, we may place administrator K or H′ near the other. Agitator B was less able to displace than A, as shown by the more personal character of the reforms which interested him. K or H were so concerned about definite people, and about their own failures in relation to many of them, that emancipation was unattainable.

As a hypothetical construction from these "marginal" cases, we may suggest that another group of administrators is recruited from among those who have passed smoothly through their developmental crises. They have not overrepressed powerful hostilities, but either sublimated these drives, or expressed them boldly in the intimate circle. They display an impersonal interest in the task of organization itself, and assert themselves with firmness, though not with overemphasis, in professional and in intimate life. Their lack of interest in abstractions is due to the fact that they have never needed them as a means of dealing with their emotional problems. They can take or leave general ideas without using them to arouse widespread affective responses from the public. Tied neither to abstractions nor to particular people, they are able to deal with both in a context of human relations, impersonally conceived. Their affects flow freely; they are not affectless, but affectively adjusted. Very original and overdriving administrators seem to show a fundamental pattern which coincides with that of the agitators; the differences in specific development are principally due to the cultural patterns available for identification at critical phases of growth.

CHAPTER IX
POLITICAL CONVICTIONS

Political prejudices, preferences, and creeds are often formulated in highly rational form, but they are grown in highly irrational ways. When they are seen against the developmental history of the person, they take on meanings which are quite different from the phrases in which they are put.

To begin, almost at random, with L. He believes that the United States ought to join the League of Nations and that our government ought to lead the world toward conciliation and peace. He is a Republican in party preference, and possesses well-rationalized judgments on a number of public questions. It is for none of these reasons that his history is of special value to the political scientist. What his intimate history does disclose is an exact parallelism between his political opinions and those of his father and mother, and, besides that, a conscious anxiety on his part to conform to the parental pattern of belief and occupation. He has a strange premonition that if he goes his own way something terrible will happen. Thus L is not only a simple conformer, but a compulsive conformer.

He is the youngest of four children. The next older member was a brother who was killed when L was eight and the brother was seventeen. Since L was so much younger than the other children, he was at first petted and spoiled. He slept around with all the members of the family, but mostly with his mother. A cousin of his own age with whom he visited provided the immediate point of departure for much exaggerated sexual fantasy. The cousin initiated him into various sexual practices when L was seven. He began very early to masturbate, and the habit stayed with him as a problem until he was through college. A certain masochistic element appeared when he got erections at an early age upon being spanked by a girl playmate. He was sexually stimulated when attending to the natural wants of small children.

L developed his guilty fantasies about his sinful impulses until he began to fear that grave retribution would be visited upon him or his family on account of his secret crimes. It was at this time that his brother, who was his favorite in the family next to the mother, was killed while out on a boyish escapade. L was profoundly stirred by this. His forebodings of disaster seemed to have direct confirmation, and he soon developed whole congeries of compulsive rituals.

When L went to the bathtub, he felt that something terrible would happen to his family, and especially to his mother, unless he plunged his head under water and held it there just as long as he had the breath. He became afraid of taking a bath because of this compulsive drive to duck his head under the water. Often in the bathroom he had the same feeling that disaster could be prevented only if he succeeded in drinking all the water that gushed out of a faucet. At night he would be seized by the sudden conviction that he must bury his face in the pillow and keep it there just as long as he possibly could without suffocating. Once he swallowed a pin after long inner debate over the efficacy of this measure. Several times he hung over the edge of the roof on top of the house until he barely had strength enough to swing back to safety on top of the porch. He felt that he could permit no one to pass him on the street. Later he thought he must outstare people, and calculated that if he kept staring until seven out of ten people dropped their eyes, that all would be well.

His mother was the central figure in L's anxieties. He evolved quite independently a theory which had been anticipated many centuries before by some primitive people and philosophers. He believed that his mother had a spirit which left her body the moment any member of the family left her alone, and that this spirit was forced to undergo all sorts of trials and tests. The spirit would always come back to his mother's body before any member of the family spoke to her. In some magical fashion his own acts relieved the burden which was laid upon his mother's spirit. Even in adulthood, he found an occasional fantasy which was reminiscent of the preoccupations of those years. Not long ago he was floating on the water in a swimming pool and found himself thinking that his mother could never hold her head under water as long as he could hold his foot under water.

With all his timidity, removal to a strange environment was a severe trial. Just before high-school days his family moved to a new community, and he never quite overcame his sense of strangeness. He had always been a coward, shrinking from physical combat. One of his first memories is of sitting on a curb with an older brother, who suddenly proposed that he should fight the little brother of another boy. L began to fight, but was overcome by fear and ran away. Later he was the center of a small clique of children in his block, all of whom were very much his junior. One of his group bragged about L's physical prowess to the leader of another group, but when the challenge was issued L backed down. He was worried by his own timidity, but seemed unable to do anything about it.

He made a handful of friends in the new environment, but was on intimate terms with no one. With one boy he was able to talk somewhat freely about sexual fantasies, and L once proposed a sexual experiment to a neighbor girl. When he was repulsed, his guilt was enormously increased.

About this time L began to think seriously of entering the ministry, so that he might always think "pure" thoughts and do "pure" things. When he went to college he at first roomed with boys from his high school, but they talked so openly about sex that he felt the atmosphere was deplorable and demoralizing. Before the month expired, he sought a new room and went into a solitary retreat. During the first year of his college life he was acutely religious and besought church services regularly. He sought guidance from the sermons upon personal and political questions.

Having developed the idea that he must live up to the family ideal at any price, L felt that he could never depart from the opinions and customs of his parents. In politics he was a stout Republican, and later, when in a religious mood, he heard his preacher espouse the League. He felt that he ought to support the League, but was plunged into a serious conflict, because he thought his parents were against it. Greatly to his relief he discovered that his father and mother had also been won over to the League by a preacher, and that his lapse from orthodox Republicanism would not bring dishonor on the family.

His father-hatred fantasies were very oppressive. They took the form of believing that if only his father were dead, his mother would have a much easier time of it. L's father was suffering from a steadily advancing paralysis. At nine he dreamed that his father was in the bathtub and that around him were fat, red snakes that were bound to devour him. L who was standing by in the dream, awoke in a fright. He often dreamed that his father was away and that his mother was happy with him.

L still shows many signs of his early neurosis in some of his ceremonial acts, and in the timid conservatism of his character. The private meaning of his political convictions is clear enough, for they are self-imposed obligations to lift his load of guilt for the murderous and incestuous fantasies which he long struggled to repress. The opinions of the family were sanctioned as a kind of religion. It is interesting to see how at first he invented a large array of ceremonial practices to substitute for his own illicit impulses, and later worked off his guilt feelings through the religious patterns which were provided by society, and which were revalidated on the basis of his private meanings. The acceptance of the political convictions of the family was on a par with the acceptance of theological dogma.

Among the nonconformists to the family pattern we may choose M, whose history was taken by Stekel. M was a prominent socialist who agitated for an economic brotherhood of man, and whose most important private motive in this particular was a bitter hatred of his own brother. Most of this hatred was displaced from his brother on to capitalistic autocracy, and overreacted against by a social ideal of fraternal equality. His hatred of his own brother was not entirely disposed of by this displacement, and it was necessary to keep at a distance from him, and from many of his traits. Thus M despised music because his brother liked it, followed a style of dress at the opposite pole from his brother, and nearly walked out on the physician when he discovered that the physician had treated his own brother.

M spent the years agitating at home and abroad, spending a year and a half in prison. Thus he succeeded in gratifying his masochistic desire to be punished for his hatred by provoking society to avenge itself on him. The motivation in this personality is notably similar to that which has been more elaborately sketched in the history of A.

Another nonconformist appears in the history of an anarchist who was once a patient of Stekel. N carried his social doctrine beyond the sharing of property, insisting that wives should be in common. He took the initiative by urging his wife to cohabit with the male members of his anarchistic society, while he demanded access to the wives of others. His own wife finally fell in love with another man, and asked N for a divorce. But before arrangements could be made, she became pregnant by her new partner, who was poor, and asked N to acknowledge the new child as his own, since this child would fall heir to some money from its supposed grandfather, the father of N. He consented to this, as he had to the divorce, but his self-esteem was hurt by his wife's desertion. He had always felt elated when his wife came back to him after each of her erotic adventures, and now he was all broken up. Stekel believes that N's espousal of communal principles in theory and practice was powerfully motivated by an irrational desire to humiliate his father by playing a generous rôle with his sexual partner, and substituting the morality of generosity for his father's possessive monopoly of the mother. When his wife-mother deserted him, N's brilliant career was ruined, and he resorted to opium, and finally secured a revenge on his father by blocking his ambitions for a successful son.

A father-hatred (due to unrequited love) of remarkable intensity was the basis of another career which Stekel examined. O was the young leader of an anarchist band whose anarchism went beyond precept to dramatic practice. O had his companions conduct some holdups to get money to start an anarchist paper. O was an illegitimate child who was brought up and spoiled by an over-indulgent mother. When he realized that he had a father who was still living, but whose identity was never divulged, his anger boiled up against his mother upon whose affections he no longer had monopolistic claim, and against his unknown father, who refused him love and distinction. For he had no doubt that his father was a rich and important personage. O displaced much of his animosity on to remote, abstract symbols of authority, like kings and capitalists, and devoted himself to destroying them. Much of his affection was likewise displaced upon abstract ideals of a fatherless fraternal society, living together without coercion. His sadistic impulses were by no means entirely sublimated upon remote goals and harmonious means, for he led his companions on common robberies. O threw a thick mantle of rationalization over his murderous impulses and his criminal acts, seeking to justify coercion in the name of a coercionless ideal which could only be laboriously achieved in the world.

It is the history of such cases, in which the emotions are peculiarly intense, which leads one to conclude that political assassins have hated their fathers with unusual bitterness. E. J. Kempf remarks in his psychopathology, after reviewing the historical evidence in the cases of

Guiteau, the assassin of President Garfield, and of Booth, the assassin of President Lincoln, as follows:

The writer does not hold that every case of severe affective repression in youth, due to the father's hatred or a father equivalent's, will lead finally to a parricidal or treasonable compulsion. It is only held that such affective repressions produce a revolutionary character which, if given an appropriate repressive setting during maturity, will then converge upon the parricidal act. Without the rather specific type of affective repression in his youth, he would be invulnerable to parricidal suggestions later on.[1]

Illegitimate children, especially when the identity of their father is undisclosed, carry with them the perpetual query, "Who is my father?" Indeed, the fantasy of belonging to other parents than those physically in the family is sufficiently widespread as a disguised hostile reverie against the actual parents to enable everyone to appreciate in some measure the mental state of the illegitimate child. "My father may be rich and powerful." "My father may be an aristocrat of distinguished lineage, and he is denying me all my just privileges." Such fantasies are taken up and spun out in the reveries of the victim. There is a presumption that those who suffer from this kind of social inferiority are especially numerous among those who commit acts of political violence, as Lombroso held.

P accepted violence, but of a different kind. P is a patriot who proved his patriotism by volunteering in the late war during the course of which he was distinguished for bravery in action. His deepest longing is for war to come again. He is in favor of an aggressive foreign policy since it increases the chances of war, and war he would welcome again as he welcomed it before.

P has a younger brother and an older sister. His mother

[1] *Op. cit.*, p. 448.

died when he was six and his relations have been strained with his stepmother, who entered the family shortly afterward. His father was a very successful professional man.

P began to fall behind in his schoolwork when he was about seven years old. This brought him into disrepute at home, for his previous promise led everyone to expect much from him, and the change seemed to prove that he was "lazy." The family has nagged him ever after, hoping to stimulate him to work harder. Just why he failed to continue to cope successfully with the demands of school becomes fairly clear when his reminiscences of the period are recovered. He had loved his second-grade teacher and had been her special favorite, and both his marks and his enthusiasm were high. The third-grade teacher impressed him as stern and cruel, and he soon began to despise the sight of her. The boy's work began to crumble, for his mind was full of hostile fancies about his new teacher, and of yearning fancies for the teacher whom he had just lost.

His emotional life was further disturbed about this time by the loss of his nurse. P's stepmother discharged her as soon as she came. Now the nurse was the lad's main love, for his own mother had been ill for some years before her death. The nurse's presence gave the child that stable reassurance which is so necessary if the mind of the child is to be kept free from morbid fears. In P's case, there were strong reasons why this reassurance was necessary. An insane man lived across the street and terrified the passers-by by screaming at everyone who passed. Shortly after his mother's death P went under ether for a minor operation and was terrified that he would die. The fear of suffocation reappeared in dreams and nightmares, and he was very timid about learning to swim.

The stepmother was a disturbing element as a strange and unknown quantity in the environment, and a competitor for the affection of the father. When she discharged the nurse, P thought of her as a malignant influence. His troubles at school were exaggerated by his home changes, and his mind became preoccupied with fantasies directed against his stepmother, or some substitute.

P's father was ambitious for the boy. P remembers him as quick to reprove and slow to praise. He dreamed of his father's death, and of seeing his father in an accident. But his manifest attitude was one of respectful affection. No matter what happened in the home, he excused his father by reflecting that the stepmother was to blame. However, on the deeper level, it appeared that he held his father accountable for the death of his mother and the disappearance of his nurse.

At school P was popular because of his good physique and his docile nature. But his studies came hard. Having failed on college-entrance tests, P bolted and joined the army. The war came along just in time to give him a dignified retreat from an unbearable personal situation. He hoped that his father would think about him with pride. He was bitterly self-accusatory because of his failure to "make good," and felt a strong unconscious need of punishment. Under these conditions he entered army life with enthusiasm, and made a fine record for personal courage.

Once the war was over, his troubles began again. He succeeded in entering college, but college felt like a nursery. He felt that his army experience sophisticated him above schoolboy tasks and chatter. All his old worries returned, complicated by his longing for a new war. He had a long series of difficulties in his occupational life.

Seen against this background, his militarism is perfectly intelligible. War gave him a chance to destroy, wildly and extensively, and also a chance to work off his guilt feelings by exposing himself to death. His repressed hatreds were partly turned against himself. An interesting feature of his ideology is that his longing for personal participation in war is combined with indignation against the exploitation of backward peoples by the imperialist powers. He identifies with the "underdog."

Q, a contrast to P, is a pacifist and a socialist. His intimate history shows that relatively simple association of ideas upon which this depends. From an early age Q showed a morbid fear of blood. Later on, when he heard that western capitalism meant war and bloodshed, he experienced a profound emotional revulsion against "capitalism," "imperialism," and their associated concepts, and called himself a "socialist," "pacifist," and "internationalist."

The blood-phobia itself was a powerful factor in developing his character. By slow degrees, he was able to push the screened memories back until he recovered a simple incident which was heavily ladened with affect, and whose recollection disposed of the blood-phobia, even though it was not completely analyzed. Q's father was accustomed to shave in the kitchen on Saturday afternoon, and Q as a small child took a great interest in the proceedings. Occasionally the father cut a pimple on his face with the big razor he was using, and flinched as the blood spurted out. He immediately swabbed the cut, and presumably forgot it. But Q did not forget so quickly. He found himself much engaged in speculating about it, drawing the inference that all the reddish projections on the body are full of blood, that, indeed, the body is a reservoir of blood; and that the reddish formations are in danger of being punctured, so the blood will spurt out and run off.

Q had previously seen his father naked in the bathtub, and he thought that his father had rubbed soap over his nipples with the palm of his hand and not with the fingers, from which he concluded that the nipples must be especially tender, and whenever he washed himself, Q carefully avoided his own nipples and massaged them most delicately with the palm of his hand.

His brother had the habit of biting his finger nails until the blood came, and the family reproached him for it, prophesying that all sorts of infections might set in. Q began to expect that something disastrous would happen, and he was not altogether averse to having it happen because of his jealousy of the brother. But it came with a great shock when his brother did actually develop an infection, thus confirming his own suspicions about the necessity for stopping outflows of blood.

About this time Q was playing with his older sister, and in the course of a scuffle his hand slid down his sister's body and over her breast. Q distinctly felt a nipple catch for a moment beneath his fingers, and he was instantly terrified for fear that his sister would bleed to death. The breasts, he thought, must be partly filled reservoirs of blood, since they were soft and yielding.

During his fourth year Q's grandmother died, and he was horrified to think of what would happen to one he loved. He had seen a photograph of a reclining nude with a beatific smile and the caption "Death" beneath. From this he surmised that people were undressed when they died, and lowered naked into the ground. But he had seen worms in the ground, and the worms would attack the body. Since the nipples were prominent and therefore easy to reach, the nipples would be eaten through first.

He shuddered to think of the worms gnawing away at his grandmother's nipples, and sometimes woke up in a fright, having dreamed that the worms were biting off his own nipples.

Once Q came running into his aunt's house and discovered a small infant cousin nursing at the breast. His aunt hastily readjusted her dress. Because of the care with which the breasts were guarded from exposure by his mother, sister, and aunt, he leaped to the conclusion that they had something to do with the secret relations of men and women.

He had all sorts of trouble trying to figure out how these relations were conducted, but when he was about eight he originated a theory that temporarily solved the problem. Q figured that a man and woman must lie on the bed with their faces close together. The male would then squeeze the breasts, alternately pressing and releasing them, as if they were balloons. Then they turned over and rubbed their anuses together. Not long after, he completed his theory of procreation by imagining that children must be born through a hole in the stomach from which the blood gushed copiously. The cutting must be very painful and bloody.

Haunted by the fearful prospect of a world which might at any time knock a hole in his body and deprive him of blood, Q was a bundle of excessive timidities. He was afraid of his grandmother's cat, he ran to his mother if he saw a dog, and he was afraid that a horse would bite off his hand if he fed it. He hated to watch a ball game for fear a foul tip would hit him, and he avoided bugs, worms, and lizards like the plague. Q never put up a fight outside the house, and cried when the other boys of the neighborhood bullied him. Sometimes he was taunted as a Jew but he never fought back, much to the disgust of his father. His forebodings spread to thunder, lightning, fire, redness, and numerous articles of food.

In marked contrast to his cringing demeanor abroad was his attitude toward the older brother, ten years his senior. Time after time he would pick a quarrel and pummel the older youth, until the brother tired of the situation and gave him a sharp blow. Thereupon he went to someone for comfort. Q's father felt that the older boy might be a little rough, but that the little fellow had something coming to him. The mother was uniformly comforting, although she reproved both boys for not behaving as brothers should.

The boys were profoundly hostile to each other, although usually cordial. The older brother made himself conspicuous for his tenderness during a serious illness of Q, running errands with alacrity, and watching constantly by the bedside. When it became clear that Q would live, the older boy's devotion stopped abruptly, indicating the unconscious basis of the exaggerated reaction. He was over-reacting against a death wish against his brother as an intruder between him and the mother.

Q envied the achievements of his older brother, and often compared himself unfavorably with him. The older boy not only stood at the head of his classes, but earned his way by playing the violin. Although Q stayed at the head of his classes, he was by no means as self-supporting as his brother. The brother-hatred appeared in such dreams as:

Dream 1.—My brother is getting married. He is in a dress suit. A long line of young men in dress suits are coming up to congratulate him. As the first one reaches out his hand, he falls backward and all the others fall over one another like tenpins.

Dream 2.—My brother and I are walking down the street near home. I hear a scream. An Italian is chasing a woman with a baby who seeks refuge in a store. The Italian knocks her down. Then my brother goes into the store and tries to deal with the Italian, but is knocked down. I enter and knock down the Italian.

The brother-jealousy is of secondary significance in Q's history. The crux of the blood-phobia was a critical experience whose traumatic effects were due to the strength of the affects which were mobilized and repressed. Q slept with his father, and the blood-letting incident aroused his slumbering desire for the death of his father and his own active fear of suffering mutilation (castration). Blood derived its significance because it involved a reinstatement of the most acute phase of the conflict. To escape from it, Q fainted unless he succeeded in getting out of the sight of blood at once. It is noteworthy that Q did not at once faint when the razor cut the pimple; it was not until the elaboration of the fantasy had continued, and the affects had become greatly concentrated, that the blood came to signalize an instant and overwhelming emergency from which a kind of suicide (fainting) was the only escape.

The following terse dream expresses something of the underlying situation:

Dream 3.—I am looking down a city street which is covered with snow and lighted by street lights. The President of the United States is walking along the street and suddenly slips and falls. My attention is then called to a place farther down the street where two tumblers are leaping over a rope stretched across the street. They are leaping backward and forward with a curious mechanical motion.

The rhythmic leaping is a pictorial symbol for the pulsations of genital excitement. The President is an authority substitute for the father. When the father is out of the way, genital activity will become safe. Since the father prescribes sexual abstinence (abstinence from handling the genitals), this expresses a desire to give greater freedom to the repressed impulses of the subject's character. The repressed positive identification with the brother shows itself in opposing two tumblers instead of one to the father.

Dream 4.—A goose or ducklike creature is being chased back and forth across the road by two dogs. The creature has a red bill and head, a blue back and wing feathers, and a white breast. The white, fuzzy dogs chase the animal back and forth but do not reach it because of their overanxiety. After two round-trips the animal, which moved with a curiously mechanical motion, runs toward a man who has come to the door and jumps between his legs. The man is middle-aged and his hair is white. He is in white pajamas. He says, "My leg is the leg of weakness; my health is hell. . . . ." I am in a winter coat standing outside the house of a friend of my sister's in whom I remember having had a mild interest, but which led to nothing since she was older than I, and not very attractive. I had just delivered a valentine. The scene is illuminated by a street light, and is especially clear because snow is on the ground. The man in the picture is unknown.

The odd creature with the red bill and head symbolizes the penis. The two dogs (brothers) try to capture it, but the father protects it. However, the hope of achieving masculinity is not wholly dashed because the old man is growing weaker.

For some time the productions of Q showed that sexuality was powerfully linked with death, and that the death was to be his own rather than that of his father, or simultaneously with the death of his father. As the castration anxiety lifted, the blood fear abated, and dreams, word-associations, posture, and other significant reactions altered toward greater ease and assertiveness.

We have seen that well-rationalized theories and preferences are not alien fungi on the personality, but an important expression of the essential trends of the personality. Thus theories are at least as indicative of the individual who espouses them as of the ostensible subjects of speculation. Pessimism, for example, is common in old age, when the sexual powers decline and the individual projects upon the world the sinfulness which he feels for wanting to indulge beyond his powers, and defy his inadequacy. The mechanism of this sort of thing stands out most clearly in extreme cases, such as R. R believed that the world was going from bad to worse and that wars and rumors of wars were devastating the earth. He spent so many hours over a plan to secure the peace of the world forevermore that he developed a confusion state. He would go out in a park, find a secluded spot and weep over the troubles of the world as Jesus wept over Jerusalem. One day in passing a market he saw some chickens in a coop without any water. The cruelty of this was more than he could bear, so he went home and went to bed. His ideas were that he had been chosen to work out the salvation of the world, and that he had been endowed with unusual, indeed supernatural, understanding of men's motives, and special power to heal insanity.

R elaborated a private form of religion. He said that he was worshiping the sun as God, as a symbol of Christ and truth (actually, of masculine virility). When it became necessary for him to commune with his spirit, he was in the habit of facing the sun and repeating a litany of his invention, which ran:

To the sun, the heart of the world! It warmeth the earth with its loveliness. Glory to God! It riseth in the east, lighting the dark corners of ignorance and wickedness. Glory to God! It chaseth the darkness before it like the host of Syria before the children of Israel. Glory to God! It chaseth the darkness before it like the host of Syria before the children of Israel. Glory to God! etc., etc.

He began to chant, and then assumed an exalted, heroic pose, with his arms and head thrown back. Presently he felt that a big storm was coming that would ruin the world. The world is like a giant serpent, a serpent asleep.

R's story is not sufficiently detailed to show much about the development of those reaction patterns which disposed him to meet old age in such a way. He was the only child of a poverty-stricken family who played by himself and got on well with his books. Some local lawyers took an interest in him and helped him through school. He read law and was admitted to the bar. After making a precarious living for a number of years, he was elected to various local offices, and then to Congress. He was reputed to be an impractical dreamer, and enjoyed making rather fanciful speeches. His legislative career as recorded in the *Congressional Record* was undistinguished, containing the usual quota of pension bills and "extensions of remarks" during tariff debates. He was opposed to the annexation of the Philippines, and hostile to imperialism; in this he went along with his party, and likewise indulged a personal conviction. He practiced law desultorily, after having been defeated for the legislature, and devoted himself to study and writing. His one published volume is a vague disquisition on human affairs, which accurately reflects the indeterminate, rhetorical, and meliorative quality of his thinking. He married a woman of his own age when he was a young man. There were no children.

When the paranoid rather than the manic-depressive strain runs through the character, nebulous and all-embracing pessimism about the world is sharpened to specific accusations. Everyone who is prominent in public life is a potential object of such attacks. One might hazard the conjecture that the importance of an individual in the community's estimation may be measured by the number of "crank" letters to him and about him. One such crank, S, wrote a trunkful of letters accusing public men of graft, of being dominated by "Big Biz," and offering suggestions to government officials. He complained of being persecuted and victimized by prominent people, especially by Harry F. Sinclair, the oil man. This was attributed by him to the fact that he had written a letter to the Chief Justice of the Supreme Court calling His Honor's attention to the Teapot Dome scandal which was being ventilated in the press, and naming Mr. Sinclair as the responsible party. Since then Mr. Sinclair had prevented him from getting a job, and paid his own sister to throw him out on the street. During his divorce proceedings he wrote to the American Bar Association to protest against the "shyster lawyers" who were representing his wife, and claims that Mr. Taft and Mr. Root answered him in the papers the following day. When Mr. John W. Davis was a presidential candidate he wrote to him, describing the various attacks to which he, S, had been subjected. Mr. Davis neglected to reply and did nothing about it, so S prevented his election, and feels that Mr. Coolidge owes him something for being elected. "I wrote to Hearst and I believe that turned the trick." In this letter he divulged the fact that Mr. Davis was connected with Wall Street, and this hint was enough to arouse Mr. Hearst. In reply to the routine question, "What is going on in the world?" he answered, "More deviltry than there ever was before."

Unfortunately the history is too meager to explain S's development, except by analogy with others who have displayed the same behavior. Certainly his life-story would, if accessible, reveal the effects of a disorganizing family environment. We do know that his father was drunk much of the time, and that the children had an unhappy lot. At five S went to live with his grandparents who wanted to take him away from his drunken father. At about fifteen he came back for a while. Shortly afterward he saved his sister from being strangled to death by their father, who in a drunken tantrum had her by the neck against the wall. S became a good mechanic, but disintegrated in later life.

Another "crank" devised an ingenious theory to explain President Wilson's conduct. T says that he discovered that Mr. Wilson was not a citizen of the United States. He first made this revelation on his draft questionnaire, and when this became generally known, Mr. Wilson went to France to escape the anger of the enraged citizenry of the United States; later Mr. Wilson fell ill of a guilty conscience at new revelations that he made. Mr. Wilson was part of the Masonic conspiracy which had been hatched against him when he was very young. T's stepfather, who was a Shriner, probably furnishes the material for this delusion. As for T himself, he believed that he descended directly from Mary, Queen of Scots, and that he had fore-knowledge of the approaching end of the world. The members of the millennium are "a creed and not a denomination," and only twenty million people will be saved, over whom T will rule.

From the excerpts included, it appears that the significance of political opinions is not to be grasped apart from the private motives which they symbolize. The degree of insight into objective relationships is one thing; the extent to which "private meanings" are accreted to the "public" or "manifest" meanings is another. When we see the private meaning of public acts, the problem of interpreting the full significance of political behavior presses itself upon our attention. Are there any implications for the general theory of the political process which follow from the intensive scrutiny of individual subjective (and objective) histories? This is the question to which we next turn.

CHAPTER X

THE POLITICS OF PREVENTION

Political movements derive their vitality from the displacement of private affects upon public objects. The intensive scrutiny of the individual by psychopathological methods discloses the prime importance of hitherto-neglected motives in the determination of political traits and beliefs. The adult who is studied at any given cross-section of his career is the product of a long and gradual development in the course of which many of his motivations fail to modify according to the demands of unfolding reality. The adult is left with an impulse life which is but partially integrated to adulthood. Primitive psychological structures continue in more or less disguised form to control his thought and effort.

The state is a symbol of authority, and as such is the legatee of attitudes which have been organized in the life of the individual within the intimate interpersonal sphere of the home and friendship group. At one phase of childhood development the wisdom and might of the physical symbol of authority, typically the father, is enormously exaggerated by the child. Eder traces the significance of this for the state in the following words:

What occurs as we come more in touch with the external world, when the principle of reality develops, is the finding of surrogates for this ideal father. We discover that the parent is not all-wise, all-powerful, all-good, but we still need to find persons or abstractions upon which we can distribute these and similar attributes. By a process of fission these feelings are displaced on to and may be distributed among a number of surrogates. The

173

surrogates may be persons, animals, things or abstract ideas; the headmaster, the dog, the rabbit, the Empire, the Aryan race, or any particular "ism."

He comments that it is upon this self-ideal that is formed the possibility of leadership, of leaders, and of the supreme leader, who is the one capable of doing all that the child once thought the physical father could do. The unconscious motivation is reflected in the sober formula of Blackstone, "The sovereign is not only incapable of doing wrong, but even of thinking wrong: he can never mean to do an improper thing; in him is no folly or weakness."[1]

There is very deep meaning in the phrase of Paley's that "a family contains the rudiments of an empire." The family experience organizes very powerful drives in successive levels of integration, and these primitive attitudes are often called into play as the unobserved partners of rational reactions. To choose another extract from Eder:

The behaviour of the elected or representative politician betrays many characteristics derived from the family. For example, during the time I filled a political job in Palestine I noticed in myself (and in my colleagues) the satisfaction it gave me to have secret information, knowledge which must on no account be imparted to others. Of course good reasons were always to be found: the people would misuse the information or it would depress them unduly and so on—pretty exactly the parent's attitude about imparting information, especially of a sexual nature, to the children. . . . .

At the back of secret diplomacy, and indeed the whole relationship of the official to the non-official, there rests this father-child affect. This also serves to explain the passion aroused in former days by any proposed extension of the franchise.

[1] See the chapter on "Psycho-analysis in Relation to Politics" in *Social Aspects of Psycho-Analysis* (London, 1924).

In the sphere of political dogma, unconscious conflicts play the same rôle which Theodor Reik discussed
when he drew a parallel between religious dogma and
obsessive ideas.[2] Dogma is a defensive reaction against
doubt in the mind of the theorist, but of doubt of which
he is unaware. The unconscious hatred of authority discloses itself in the endless capacity of the theorist to
imagine new reasons for disbelief, and in his capacity
to labor over trivialities, and to reduce his whole intellectual scheme to a logical absurdity. Sometimes this appears in a cryptic formula to which some sort of mysterious potency is ascribed, but which is hopelessly contradictory in so far as it possesses any manifest meaning.
The celebrated doctrine of the unity of the trinity is an
instance of such culminating nonsense. Words lose their
rational reference points and become packed with unconscious symbolism of the ambivalent variety. The description of sovereignty found in Blackstone refers to nothing
palpable, and functions principally as an incantation.
Much solemn juridical speculation, since so much of it
is elaborated by obsessive thinkers, ends thus. Deep doubts
about the self are displaced on to doubts about the world
outside, and these doubts are sought to be allayed by
ostentatious preoccupation with truth.

Defiance of authority is defiance of the introjected conscience, and involves a measure of self-punishment. We
have seen how a powerful need for self-punishment is the
stuff out of which martyrs and sensational failures are
made; but of more general importance is the rôle of the
sense of guilt in supporting the *status quo*. Deviation from
accepted patterns becomes equivalent to sin, and the con-

[2] "Dogma und Zwangsidee," *Imago*, XIII (1927), 247–382.

science visits discomforts upon those who dare to innovate. Radical ideas become "sacrilegious" and "disloyal" in the view of the primitive conscience, for they tend to represent more than a limited defiance of authority. They put the whole structure of the personality under strain. The childish conscience is easily intimidated into preserving order on slight provocation; it knows little of the capacity to consider the piecemeal reconstruction of values. "Radicalism" is felt as a challenge to the whole system of resistances which are binding down the illicit impulses of the personality, rather than as an opportunity for detached consideration of the relation of the self to the rest of reality. There is little boldness in political thinking which is not accompanied by an overdose of defiance, for even those who succeed in breaking through the intimidations of their infantile consciences must often succumb in some measure and "pay out." Much of the struggle, the fearful *Sturm und Drang* of the emancipated thinker, is his unconscious tribute to the exactions of the tribunal which he erected within himself at an early age, and which continues to treat innovation as *ipso facto* dangerous. The non-obsessive thinker is one who can coolly contemplate revisions in the relations of man to reality unperturbed by his antiquated conscience. Often readjustments of human affairs which are proposed are driven to absurdity because the original mind is compelled to transform his mere departure from the conventional into a defiance of conventionality. When one perceives the operation of this powerful self-punishment drive, and the secondary efforts to free one's self from feelings of guilt for defying the authorized order, it is possible to remain understandingly tolerant of the eccentricities of creative minds. To put the point a bit sharply, it is safe to say that the adult mind is only partly adult; the conscience may be four years old. The conscience, the introjected nursemaid, reacts undiscriminatingly to change, and construes it as rebellion.

The organization of motives which occurs in adolescence possesses direct significance for the interpretation of political interests.

The physical and mental storm of puberty and adolescence often culminates in the displacement of loves upon all humanity or a selected part of it, and in acts of devotion to the whole. It is here that the fundamental processes of loyalty are most clearly evident as they relate to public life. S. Bernfeld has written extensively on the psychology of the German youth movement. He comments on the very different lengths of puberty, and distinguishes between the physical and the psychological processes. When the psychological processes outlive the physical ones, certain characteristic reaction types arise. Dr. Bernfeld believes that the discrepant type prevails most characteristically in the youth movement, and he enumerates its characteristics. The interests of this group are turned toward "ideal" objects like politics, humanity, and art. The relation to these objects is productive, since the youth tries to produce a new form of politics or art. There is always a great deal of self-confidence present, or many symptoms of a repression that has failed. This is expressed in the high opinion of one's self and the low opinion one holds of his companions. An outstanding individual, the friend or master, is loved and revered. Often this love for a friend is extended to the whole group. The sexual components of the personality do not concentrate on finding objects, but in creating a new narcissistic situation. Bernfeld distinguishes this secondary narcissism from infantile narcissism on the ground that it is accompanied by deep depression reminiscent of melancholia. The reason lies in the formation of an ideal self that attracts a great part of the libido and enters into contrast with the real ego, a process which is particularly characteristic of the complex or discrepant type which he found in the youth movement.[3]

Political life seems to sublimate many homosexual trends. Politicians characteristically work together in little cliques and clubs, and many of them show marked difficulties in reaching a stable heterosexual adjustment. In military life, when men are thrown together under intimate conditions, the sublimations often break down and the homosexual drives find direct expression. A German general has gone so far as to declare that one reason why Germany lost the war was that the command was shot through with jealousies growing out of homosexual rivalry. Dr. K. G. Heimsoth has prepared a manuscript describing the rôle of homosexuality in the volunteer forces which continued to operate against the Poles and the communists after the war. In the case of certain leaders, at least, the reputation for overt homosexuality was no handicap; indeed, the reverse seemed to be true. Franz Alexander has suggested that one reason why homosexuality is viewed with contempt in modern life is the vague sense that complex cultural achievement depends on an inhibited sexuality, and that direct gratification tends to dissolve society into self-satisfied pairs and cliques. The observations of Heimsoth throw some doubt

[3] Succinctly described in "Über eine typische Form der männlichen pubertät," *Imago*, IX (1923), 169 ff. On the homoerotic elements see Hans Blüher, *Die deutsche Wandervogelbewegung als erotisches Phänomen*, and his more elaborate volume cited in the Bibliography.

on the wisdom of this "vague sense."[4] The prominence
of alcoholism and promiscuity among like-sex groups has
often been observed, and both indulgences appear to be
closely connected with homosexual impulses.[5]

Political crises are complicated by the concurrent reactivation of specific primitive impulses. War is the classical situation in which the elementary psychological
structures are no longer held in subordination to complex
reactions. The acts of cruelty and lust which are insepa-
rably connected with war have disclosed vividly to all
who care to see the narrow margin which separates the
social from the asocial nature of man. The excesses of
heroism and abnegation are alike primitive in their manifestations, and show that all the primitive psychological
structures are not antisocial, but asocial, and may often
function on behalf of human solidarity.[6]

Why does society become demoralized in the process
of revolution? Why should a change in the political procedures of the community unleash such excesses in behavior? Reflection might lead one to suppose that since
important decisions are in process of being made, calm
deliberation would characterize society. Evidently a reactivating process is at work here; there is a regressive
tendency to reawaken primitive sadism and lust. The conspicuous disproportionality between the problem and the

[4] I was kindly permitted to see this manuscript which is not yet published.

[5] See Sandor Rado, "Die psychischen Wirkungen der Rauschgifte," *Internationale Zeitschrift für Psychoanalyse*, XII (1926), 540–56; A. Keil-
holz, "Analyseversuch bei Delirium Tremens," *ibid.*, pp. 478–92; and
Stekel's volumes.

[6] For a sketch of the unconscious processes involved in warfare see S.
Freud, "'Zeitgemässes über Krieg und Tod," *Imago*, IV (1915–16), 1–21;
Ernest Jones, *Essays in Psycho-Analysis*; William A. White, *Thoughts of
a Psychiatrist on the War and After*.

behavior necessitates an explanation in such terms. Federn published a sketch of the psychology of revolution in his pamphlet *Die vaterlose Gesellschaft* in 1919. When the ruler falls, the unconscious triumphantly interprets this as a release from all constraint, and the individuals in the community who possess the least solidified personality structures are compulsively driven to acts of theft and violence. An interview which Federn gave to Edgar Ansel Mowrer in 1927 on the occasion of the Vienna riots reviews in somewhat popular form some of his conceptions.

VIENNA, AUSTRIA, July 20.—"Distrust of father was the chief cause of the Vienna riot," said Paul Federn, onetime president of the Psychoanalytical Society. From a psychoanalytical standpoint all authority is the father, and this formerly for Austria was incorporated in the imposing figure of Emperor Franz Josef. But during the war the father deceived and maltreated his children, and only the material preoccupations of life and the joyous outburst when at the close of the war the old authority broke asunder prevented Austria from having a revolution then.

The state again built up the old ruling caste and began to hope for restoration, and therefore an abyss opened between Vienna, which under socialist leadership is trying to replace the traditional father principle by a new brotherhood, and the Austrian federal state, which had returned to a modified father idea. Trust in father is the child's deepest instinct. Vienna first respected the Austrian republic, but gradually this belief was undermined by the continual misery, by newspapers preaching fanaticism and by legal decisions which virtually destroyed the people's belief in the new father's justice.

Accordingly there occurred a spontaneous manifestation which unconsciously drove the disillusioned and furious children to destroy precisely those things on which the paternal authority seems to rest—namely, records and legal documents.

Why the peaceful Viennese should suddenly be transformed temporarily into mad beasts is also clear to the psychoanalysts. Had the police offered no resistance the crowd would soon have dispersed and no harm would have been done. But once the police fired blood flowed and the mob reacted savagely, responding to the ancient fear of castration by the father which is present in all of us unconsciously in the face of the punishing authority. Therefore, fear grew along with the violence, each increase leading to new violence and greater fear, as appeasement can only follow a complete outbreak and as the inhabitants were widely scattered in their houses it took three days before the last hatred could fully get out.

One further point can only be explained by psychoanalysis. The social democratic leaders are at heart revolutionary, but they did not wish this demonstration. They realized that revolution in little Austria today would be suicidal, and, therefore, at a given moment called out the republican guard with orders to interfere and prevent violence. The guard arrived much too late.

Why did not the leaders send out the guard at 6 a.m. when they knew the demonstration was beginning? They say they "forgot." This is a flagrant example of unconscious forgetfulness. The socialists forgot to take the only step which could have prevented something which they consciously disapproved, but unconsciously desired.

The Vienna riots were in the deepest sense a family row.[7]

Eder speculates about the unconscious factors in the well-known tendency of certain political alternatives to succeed one another in crude pendulum fashion.

I think it was Mr. Zangwill who once said that it is a principle of the British Constitution that the King can do no wrong and his ministers no right. That is to say, the ambivalency originally experienced toward the father is now split; the sentiment of disloyalty, etc., is displaced on to the King's ministers, or on to some of them, or on to the opposition. . . . . Modern society has discovered the principle of election, and the vote to give expression to the hostile feelings toward their rulers. Psychoanalytically an election may be regarded as the sublimation of regicide (primary parricide) with the object of placing oneself on the throne; the vote is like a repeating decimal; the father is killed

[7] *Chicago Daily News*, July 20, 1927.

but never dies. The ministers are our substitutes for ourselves. Hence the political maxim of the swing of the pendulum.

Alexander and Staub have undertaken to explain the unconscious basis of the crisis which is produced in the community when criminals are permitted to go with no punishment or with light punishment. The study of personality genesis shows that the sublimation of primitive impulses is possible on the basis of a kind of primitive "social contract." The individual foregoes direct indulgences (which have the disadvantage of bringing him into conflict with authority), and substitutes more complex patterns of behavior on the tacit understanding that love and safety will thereby be insured. When another individual breaks over and gratifies his illicit impulses directly on a primitive level, the equilibrium of every personality is threatened. The conscious self perceives that it is possible to "get by," and this threatens the whole structure of sublimation. The superego tries to maintain order by directing energy against the ego, perhaps subjecting it to "pricks of conscience," for so much as entertaining the possibility of illicit gratification, and seeks to turn the ego toward activities which reduce temptation. This may involve the reconstruction of the environment by seeking to eliminate the "non-ideal" elements in it, and may be exemplified in the panicky demand for the annihilation of the outsider (who is a criminal) for the sake of keeping the chains on the insider (who is a criminal). Every criminal is a threat to the whole social order since he reinstates with more or less success an acute conflict within the lives of all members of society. The success of the superego depends upon imposing certain ways of interpreting reality upon the self. When reality grossly refuses to conform to the "ideal," the energies of the self are divided, and an acute crisis supervenes. The superego undertakes to reinforce its side of the contradictory ego trends by punishing the ego, and by forcing the projection of this situation upon the outer world. Certain aspects of the outer world become "bad" because they are connected in private experience with the pangs inflicted by the taskmaster within, the conscience. A strong conscience may enforce this "distortion" of reality upon the self to such a degree that the self acts on quite fantastic assumptions about reality. These are most acutely manifested in such phenomena as confusion states, hallucinations, and delusions, all of which are forms of deformed reality. When reality becomes "ominous," violent efforts to change may appear futile, and safety is sought in physical flight, or in physical passivity and autistic preoccupation. Since our conceptions of reality are based upon little "first-hand" experience of the world about us, the superego usually has a rather easy time of it.

Political movements, then, derive their vitality from the displacement of private affects upon public objects, and political crises are complicated by the concurrent reactivation of specific primitive motives. Just how does it happen that the private and primitive drives find their way to political symbols? What are the circumstances which favor the selection of political targets of displacement?

Political life is carried on with symbols of the whole. Politics has to do with collective processes and public acts, and so intricate are these processes that with the best of intentions, it is extremely difficult to establish an unambiguous relationship between the symbols of the whole and the processes which they are presumed to designate. To the common run of mankind the reference points of political symbols are remote from daily experience, though they are rendered familiar through constant reiteration. This ambiguity of reference, combined with universality of use, renders the words which signify parties, classes, nations, institutions, policies, and modes of political participation readily available for the displacement of private affects. The manifest, rational differences of opinion become complicated by the play of private motives until the symbol is nothing but a focus for the cumulation of irrelevancies. Since the dialectic of politics is conducted in terms of the whole, the private motives are readily rationalized in terms of collective advantage.

Politics, moreover, is the sphere of conflict, and brings out all the vanity and venom, the narcissism and aggression, of the contending parties. It is becoming something of a commonplace that politics is the arena of the irrational. But a more accurate description would be that politics is the process by which the irrational bases of society are brought out into the open. So long as the moral order functions with spontaneous smoothness, there is no questioning the justification of prevailing values. But when the moral order has been devalued and called into question, a sincere and general effort may be made to find a reflectively defensible solution of the resulting conflict. Politics seems to be irrational because it is the only phase of collective life in which society tries to be rational. Its very existence shows that the moral order, with all its irrational and non-rational sanctions, is no longer accepted without a challenge. A political difference is the outcome of a moral crisis, and it terminates in a new moral consensus. Politics is the transition between one unchallenged consensus and the next. It begins in conflict and eventuates in a solution. But the solution is not the "rationally best" solution, but the emotionally satisfactory one. The rational and dialectical phases of politics are subsidiary to the process of redefining an emotional consensus.

Although the dynamic of politics is to be sought in the tension level of the individuals in society, it is to be taken for granted that all individual tensions are not removed by political symbolization and exertion. When Y hits a foreman in the jaw whom he imagines has insulted him, Y is relieving his tensions. But if the act is construed by him as a personal affair with the foreman, the act is not political. Political acts are joint acts; they depend upon emotional bonds.

Now people who act together get emotionally bound together. This process of becoming emotionally bound is dependent on no conscious process. Freud said that he was made clearly aware of the emotional factor in human relations by observing that those who work together extend their contact to dining and relaxing together. Those with whom we work are endowed with rich meanings on the basis of our past experience with human beings. Since all of our motives are going concerns within the personality, our libido is more or less concentrated upon those with whom we come in touch. This reinforces the perception of similarities, and supplies the dynamic for the identification process. Even the negative identification is a tribute to the extent to which the affective resources of the personality become mobilized in human contact.

People who are emotionally bound together are not yet involved in a political movement. Politics begins when they achieve a symbolic definition of themselves in relation to demands upon the world. The pre-political phase of the labor movement as sketched by Nexo in his *Pelle the Conqueror* is an able characterization of what the facts may be. The workers had plenty of grievances against their employers, but individuals took it out in sporadic acts of violence, and in frequent debauchery. It was not until a new "set" of mind was achieved with the appearance of socialist symbols, and their adoption, that the tension found an outlet in political form. When J hits a foreman on the jaw because the foreman swore at him, J is not acting for the working classes; but after J becomes a socialist, his acts are symbolically significant of the expanded personality which he possesses. Acts cease to be merely private acts; they have become related to remote social objects. The conception of the self has new points of reference, and points of reference which interlock with those of others.

It is of the utmost importance to political science to examine in detail, not only the factors which contribute to the raising and lowering of the tension level, but the processes of symbolization. In regard to the former aspect of the problem, data will have to be taken from specialists of many kinds, but in regard to the latter problem, the student can come into ready contact with the raw material. The stock in trade of realistic politics is the analysis of the history of "pressure groups," ranging from such associations as the Fabian Society through political parties to conspirative organizations. What are the conditions under which the idea is itself invented, and what are the conditions of its propagation? That is to say: What are the laws of symbolization in political activity?

I wish to call attention to certain possibilities. Several social movements will be found which represent a desire on the part of an intimate circle to perpetuate their relationship at the expense of society. It is worth remembering that Loyola and the other young men who founded the Jesuits were in long friendly relationship before they hit upon their famous project. Not only that: they were anxious to remain in some sort of personal relation through life, and they invented many expedients before they hit on the final one. What we had here was a friendly group which desired to preserve their personal connections before they knew how they could actually do it. It is less true to say that institutions are the lengthened shadow of a great man than that they are the residue of a friendly few.

Other social movements will be found to have adopted their project from a lone thinker with whom they have no direct connection. The process here is that one member of the group, with whom the others are identified, is impressed by the scheme, and interprets and defends it to the others. He gets a hearing because of his emotional claim on the others, and he may whip the doubters and waverers into line by wheedling or by threatening to withdraw affection.

The formation of a radiating nucleus for an idea is especially common among adolescents, and among those who function best in single-sex groups. Thrasher has described gangs which had a mission in his book on *The Gang*, and the literature of youth study is full of instances of two's, three's and quartettes which have sworn undying fealty to one another, and to a project of social reform. When the idea is embraced later in life it not infrequently appears among those who have shown pronounced evidence of emotional maladjustment. Much social and political life is a symptom of the delayed adolescence of its propagators, which is, of course, no necessary criticism of its content.

The psychology of personal, oratorical, and printed persuasion by means of which support is won for particular symbols has yet to be written. William I. Thomas long ago commented on the quasi-sexual approach of the revivalist to the audience. Some orators are of an intimate, sympathetic, pleading type, and resemble the attempts made by some males to overcome the shyness of the female. Other orators fit into the feared yet revered father-pattern; others are clowns who amuse by releasing much repressed material; others address the socially adjusted and disciplined level of the personality. Thus the relationship between the speaker and the audience has its powerful emotional aspects, which are not yet adequately explored. There are some who excel in face-to-face relations, but who make a poor showing out on the platform.

The processes of symbolization can be studied with particular ease when widespread and disturbing changes occur in the life-situation of many members of society. Famine, pestilence, unemployment, high living costs, and a catalogue of other disturbances may simultaneously produce adjustment problems for many people. One of the first results is to release affects from their previous objects, and to create a state of susceptibility to proposals. All sorts of symbols are ready, or readily invented, to refix the mobile affects. "Take it to the Lord in prayer," "Vote socialist," "Down with the Jews," "Restore pep with pepsin," "Try your luck on the horses"—all sorts of alternatives become available. The prescriptions are tied up with diagnoses, and the diagnoses in turn imply prescriptions. "A sinful world," "Wall Street," "a collapse in the foreign market"—all sorts of diagnoses float about, steadily defining and redefining the situation for the individuals affected. Political symbols must compete with symbols from every sphere of life, and an interesting inquiry could be made into the relative polarizing power of political and other forms of social symbolism. Certainly the modern world expects to fire the health commissioner rather than burn a witch when the plague breaks out.

The competition among symbols to serve as foci of concentration for the aroused emotions of the community leads to the survival of a small number of master-symbols. The mobilization of the community for action demands economy in the terms in which objectives are put. The agitation for the control of the liquor traffic passed through many phases in America until finally legal prohibition became the chief dividing-line. To prohibit or not to prohibit grew into the overmastering dichotomy of public thought.

Symbolization thus necessitates dichotomization. The program of social action must be couched in "yes" and "no" form if decision is to be possible. The problem of he who would manipulate the concentration of affect about a particular symbol is to reinforce its competitive power by leading as many elements as possible in society to read their private meanings into it. This reinforcement and facilitation of the symbol involves the use of men of prestige in its advocacy, the assimilation of special economic and other group aims, and the invention of appeals to unconscious drives. Propaganda on behalf of a symbol can become a powerful factor in social development because of the flexibility in the displacement of emotion from one set of symbols to another. There is always a rather considerable reservoir of unrest and discontent in society, and there is nothing absolutely fixed and predestined about the particular symbol which will have attracting power.

The analysis of motives which are unconscious for most people, though widespread, gives the propagandist a clue to certain nearly universal forms of appeal. The moving pictures which have been produced by the communist government in Russia are often remarkable examples of the use of symbols which not only have their conscious affective dimension, but which mobilize deep unconscious impulses. In one film, for instance, it is the mother who suffers under tsarism and fans the flames of revolt. Analysis has disclosed the general, and presumably universal, meaning of the attachment to the land. The boy-child's wish for union with the mother, for all-embracing care and protection, undergoes some measure of sublimation in social life. Eder remarks that it finds expression in attachment to the earth, the land, the mother-country, home. The *Heimweh* of the Swiss, the pious Jew's desire for burial in Palestine, and a host of similar manifestations are instances of this emotional tie whose significance for state loyalty is large.

At first sight it might appear questionable that political science can ever profit from the disclosure of motives which are supposed to operate in the unconscious of every human being. If these motives are equally operative, how can they throw any light on differences in political behavior? And are we not able to point to conditions of a more localized and definite nature which suitably explain why the Republican party loses out when the farmer loses his crops? Or why there is revolution in 1918 and not in 1925?

The mere fact that motives are more or less universal does not mean that they are always activated with the same intensity. They may block one another, until some exciting condition disturbs the adjustment and releases stores of energy. Indeed, the exploration of unconscious motivation lays the basis for the understanding of the well-known disproportionality between responses and immediate stimuli, a disproportionality which has been the subject of much puzzled and satiric comment. Farmers do vote against the Republicans when the crops fail through adverse weather conditions, although reflection would tend to minimize the possibility that the party in power exercises much authority over the weather. Oversights in personal relations which seem very slight do actually give rise to huge affective reactions. The clue to the magnitude of this notorious disproportionality is to be found in the nature of the deeper (earlier) psychological structures of the individual. By the intensive analysis of representative people, it is possible to obtain clues to the nature of these "unseen forces," and to devise ways and means of dealing with them for the accomplishment of social purposes.

Modern democratic society is accustomed to the settlement of differences in discussion and in voting. This is a special form of politics, for differences may also be settled with a minimum of discussion and a maximum of coercion. In its modern manifestation, democracy and representative government have enthroned "government by discussion," that is, "government by public opinion." President Lowell some time ago pointed out that public opinion could only be said to exist where constitutional principles were agreed upon. Differences must be treated as defined within an area of agreement. Democratic and representative institutions presuppose the existence of the public which is made up of all those who follow affairs and expect to determine policy in discussion and by measures short of coercion. The public has a common focus of attention, a consensus on constitutional principles, and a zone of tolerance for conflicting demands respecting social policy.

When debate is admissible, some standards of right are tacitly admitted to be uncertain. The zone of the debatable is not fixed and immutable, but flexible and shifting. Questions rise and debate proceeds; and presently the resulting solution is no longer discussible. It has become sanctified by all the sentiments which buttress the moral order, and any challenge is met by the unanimous and spontaneous action of the community in its defense. In the presence of a challenge, the public may be dissolved into a crowd, by which is meant a group whose members are emotionally aroused and intolerant of dissent.

What light does the study of the genesis of personality throw on the factors which determine which symbols are debatable? What is the mechanism of the process by which the moral patterns are broken up, discussed, and eventually reincorporated in more or less modified form into the moral consensus of the community?

The growth of emotional bonds among individuals of diverse cultural and personal traits is the most powerful solvent of the moral order. A valuable treatise could be constructed on the theme, "Friendship versus Morality." It is well-known that governments are continually handicapped in the impersonal application of a rule by the play of personal loyalties. Robert E. Park has stressed the importance of curiosity in the field of interracial relations. In no small measure this is very primitive curiosity about the sexual structure and behavior of odd-looking folks. When personal ties are built up, exceptions are made in favor of the friend; what, indeed, is the constitution among friends?

The mechanism is clear by which issues once settled are presently non-debatable. Growing individuals incorporate the end result into their own personalities through the process of identification and introjection. Once a part of the superego of the rising generation, the moral consensus is complete. Where no dissent is tolerated and dialectic is impossible, we are dealing with a superego phenomenon. Certain symbols are sacrosanct, and aspersions upon them produce the crowd mind and not the public.[8]

Even this brief sketch of political symbolization has shown ample grounds for concluding that political demands probably bear but a limited relevance to social needs. The political symbol becomes ladened with the residue of successive positive and negative identifications, and with the emotional charge of displaced private motives. This accumulation of irrelevancy usually signifies that tension exists in the lives of many people, and it may possess a diagnostic value to the objective investigator. The individual who is sorely divided against himself may

[8] The distinction between the crowd and the public is best developed in the writings of Robert E. Park. Freud undertook to explain the crowd on the theory that an emotional bond was forged by identification of the individual with a leader, and by a process of partial identification through the perception of this similar relationship to the leader. He set out from the observation that when people are interacting upon one another they behave differently than when they are alone. The loss of individuality represents a relinquishment of narcissistic gratification which can only come when libido is directed outward toward objects. Freud's theory applies strictly to a special case of crowd behavior only. Crowd states may also arise when interlocking partial identifications occur on the perception of a common threat. Crowd behavior often arises before anybody assumes a "leading" rôle, and rival leaders are "selected" by the crowd.

seek peace by unifying himself against an outsider. This is the well-known "peacefulness of being at war." But the permanent removal of the tensions of the personality may depend upon the reconstruction of the individual's view of the world, and not upon belligerent crusades to change the world.

The democratic state depends upon the technique of discussion to relieve the strains of adjustment to a changing world. If the analysis of the individual discloses the probable irrelevance of what the person demands to what he needs (i.e., to that which will produce a permanent relief of strain), serious doubt is cast upon the efficacy of the technique of discussion as a means of handling social problems.

The premise of democracy is that each man is the best judge of his own interest, and that all whose interests are affected should be consulted in the determination of policy. Thus the procedure of a democratic society is to clear the way to the presentation of various demands by interested parties, leaving the coast clear for bargain and compromise, or for creative invention and integration.

The findings of personality research show that the individual is a poor judge of his own interest. The individual who chooses a political policy as a symbol of his wants is usually trying to relieve his own disorders by irrelevant palliatives. An examination of the total state of the person will frequently show that his theory of his own interests is far removed from the course of procedure which will give him a happy and well-adjusted life. Human behavior toward remote social objects, familiarity with which is beyond the personal experience of but a few, is especially likely to be a symptomatic rather than a healthy and reflective adjustment.

In a sense politics proceeds by the creation of fictitious values. The person who is solicited to testify to his own interest is stimulated by the problem put to him to commit himself. The terms in which he couches his own interest vary according to a multitude of factors, but whatever the conditioning influences may be, the resulting theory of his interest becomes invested with his own narcissism. The political symbol is presumably an instrumental makeshift toward the advancement of the other values of the personality; but it very quickly ceases to be an instrumental value, and becomes a terminal value, no longer the servant but the coequal, or indeed the master. Thus the human animal distinguishes himself by his infinite capacity for making ends of his means.

It should not be hastily assumed that because a particular set of controversies passes out of the public mind that the implied problems were solved in any fundamental sense. Quite often the solution is a magical solution which changes nothing in the conditions affecting the tension level of the community, and which merely permits the community to distract its attention to another set of equally irrelevant symbols. The number of statutes which pass the legislature, or the number of decrees which are handed down by the executive, but which change nothing in the permanent practices of society, is a rough index of the rôle of magic in politics.

In some measure, of course, discontent is relieved in the very process of agitating, discussing, and legislating about social changes which in the end are not substantially affected. Political symbolization has its catharsis function, and consumes the energies which are released by the maladaptations of individuals to one another.

But discussion often leads to modifications in social

practice which complicate social problems. About all that can be said for various punitive measures resorted to by the community is that they have presently broken down and ceased to continue the damage which they began to inflict on society.

Generalizing broadly, political methods have involved the manipulation of symbols, goods, and violence, as in propaganda, bribery, and assassination. It is common to act on the assumption that they are to be applied in the settlement of conflicting demands, and not in the obviation of conflict. In so far as they rest upon a philosophy, they identify the problem of politics with the problem of coping with differences which are sharply drawn.

The identification of the field of politics with the field of battle, whether the theater be the frontier or the forum, has produced an unfortunate warp in the minds of those who manage affairs, or those who simply think about the management of affairs. The contribution of politics has been thought to be in the elaboration of the methods by which conflicts are resolved. This has produced a vast diversion of energy toward the study of the formal etiquette of government. In some vague way, the problem of politics is the advancement of the good life, but this is at once assumed to depend upon the modification of the mechanisms of government. Democratic theorists in particular have hastily assumed that social harmony depends upon discussion, and that discussion depends upon the formal consultation of all those affected by social policies.

The time has come to abandon the assumption that the problem of politics is the problem of promoting discussion among all the interests concerned in a given problem. Discussion frequently complicates social difficulties, for the discussion by far-flung interests arouses a psychology of conflict which produces obstructive, fictitious, and irrelevant values. The problem of politics is less to solve conflicts than to prevent them; less to serve as a safety valve for social protest than to apply social energy to the abolition of recurrent sources of strain in society.

This redefinition of the problem of politics may be called the idea of preventive politics. The politics of prevention draws attention squarely to the central problem of reducing the level of strain and maladaptation in society. In some measure it will proceed by encouraging discussion among all those who are affected by social policy, but this will be no iron-clad rule. In some measure it will proceed by improving the machinery of settling disputes, but this will be subordinated to a comprehensive program, and no longer treated as an especially desirable mode of handling the situation.

The recognition that people are poor judges of their own interest is often supposed to lead to the conclusion that a dictator is essential. But no student of individual psychology can fail to share the conviction of Kempf that "Society is *not* safe . . . . when it is forced to follow the dictations of one individual, of one autonomic apparatus, no matter how splendidly and altruistically it may be conditioned." Our thinking has too long been misled by the threadbare terminology of democracy versus dictatorship, of democracy versus aristocracy. Our problem is to be ruled by the truth about the conditions of harmonious human relations, and the discovery of the truth is an object of specialized research; it is no monopoly of people as people, or of the ruler as ruler. As our devices of accurate ascertainment are invented and spread, they are explained and applied by many individuals inside the social order. Knowledge of this kind is a slow and laborious accumulation.

The politics of prevention does not depend upon a series of changes in the organization of government. It depends upon a reorientation in the minds of those who think about society around the central problems: What are the principal factors which modify the tension level of the community? What is the specific relevance of a proposed line of action to the temporary and permanent modification of the tension level?

The politics of prevention will insist upon a rigorous audit of the human consequences of prevailing political practices. How does politics affect politicians? One way to consider the human value of social action is to see what that form of social action does to the actors. When a judge has been on the bench thirty years, what manner of man has he become? When an agitator has been agitating for thirty years, what has happened to him? How do different kinds of political administrators compare with doctors, musicians, and scientists? Such a set of inquiries would presuppose that we were able to ascertain the traits with which the various individuals began to practice their rôle in society. Were we able to show what certain lines of human endeavor did to the same reactive type, we would lay the foundation for a profound change in society's esteem for various occupations.

Any audit of the human significance of politics would have to press far beyond the narrow circle of professional politicians. Crises like wars, revolutions, and elections enter the lives of people in far-reaching ways. The effect of crises on mental attitude is an important and uncertain field. Thus it is reported that during the rebellion of

1745–46 in Scotland there was little hysteria (in the technical pathological sense). The same was true of the French Revolution and of the Irish Rebellion. Rush reported in his book *On the Influence of the American Revolution on the Human Body* that many hysterical women were "restored to perfect health by the events of the time." Havelock Ellis, who cites these instances, comments that "in such cases the emotional tension is given an opportunity for explosion in new and impersonal channels, and the chain of morbid personal emotions is broken."[9]

The physical consequences of political symbolism may be made the topic of investigation from this point of view:

When the affect can not acquire what it needs, uncomfortable tensions or anxiety (fear) are felt, and the use of the symbol or fetish, relieving this anxiety, has a marked physiological value in that it prevents the adrenal, thyroid, circulatory, hepatic and pulmonic compensatory strivings from becoming excessive.[10]

Political programs will continually demand reconsideration in the light of the factors which current research discloses as bearing upon the tension level. Franz Alexander recently drew attention to the strains produced in modern civilization by the growing sphere of purposive action. He summed up the facts in the process of civilized development in the following way: "Human expressions of instinct are subject to a continual tendency to rationalization, that is, they develop more and more from playful, uncoordinated, purely pleasure efforts into purposive actions." The "discomfort of civilization" of which Freud recently wrote in the *Unbehagen der Kultur* is characteristic of the rationalized cultures with which we are acquainted. Life is poor in libidinal gratifications of the primitive kind

[9] *Studies in the Psychology of Sex*, I, 231.
[10] Kempf, *Psychopathology*, p. 704.

which the peasant, who is in close touch with elementary things, is in a position to enjoy.[11] Modern life furnishes irrational outlets in the moving picture and in sensational crime news. But it may be that other means of relieving the strain of modern living can be invented which will have fewer drawbacks.

Preventive politics will search for the definite assessment, then, of cultural patterns in terms of their human consequences. Some of these human results will be deplored as "pathological," while others will be welcomed as "healthy." One complicating factor is that valuable contributions to culture are often made by men who are in other respects pathological. Many pathological persons are constrained by their personal difficulties to displace more or less successfully upon remote problems, and to achieve valuable contributions to knowledge and social policy.[12] Of course the notion of the pathological is itself full of ambiguities. The individual who is subject to epileptic seizures may be considered in one culture not a subnormal and diseased person, but a supernormal person. Indeed, it may be said that society depends upon a certain amount of pathology, in the sense that society does not encourage the free criticism of social life, but establishes taboos upon reflective thinking about its own presuppositions. If the individual is pathological to the extent that he is unable to contemplate any fact with equanimity, and to elaborate impulse through the processes of thought, it is obvious that society does much to nurture disease. This leads to the apparent paradox that successful social adjustment consists in contracting the

[11] Franz Alexander, "Mental Hygiene and Criminology," *First International Congress on Mental Hygiene.*

[12] For an appreciation of the rôle of the pathological person in society see Wilhelm Lange-Eichbaum, *Genie-Irrsinn, und Ruhm,* and Karl Birnbaum, *Grundzüge der Kulturpsychopathologie.*

current diseases. If "health" merely means a statistical report upon the "average," the scrutiny of the individual ceases to carry much meaning for the modification of social patterns. But if "health" means something more than "average," the intensive study of individuals gives us a vantage ground for the revaluation of the human consequences of cultural patterns, and the criticism of these patterns.[13]

If the politics of prevention spreads in society, a different type of education will become necessary for those who administer society or think about it. This education will start from the proposition that it takes longer to train a good social scientist than it takes to train a good physical scientist.[14] The social administrator and social scientist must be brought into direct contact with his material in its most varied manifestations. He must mix with rich and poor, with savage and civilized, with sick and well, with old and young. His contacts must be primary and not exclusively secondary. He must have an opportunity for prolonged self-scrutiny by the best-developed methods of personality study, and he must laboriously achieve a capacity to deal objectively with himself and with all others in human society.

This complicated experience is necessary since our scale of values is less the outcome of our dialectical than of our other experiences in life. Values change more by the unconscious redefinition of meaning than by rational analysis. Every contact and every procedure which discloses new facts has its repercussions upon the matrix of partially

[13] Something like this is no doubt the thought in Trigant Burrow's very obscure book on *The Social Basis of Consciousness*.

[14] This point was forcibly made by Beardsley Ruml in his speech at the dedication of the Social Science Research Building at the University of Chicago. See *The New Social Science*, edited by Leonard D. White, pp. 99–111.

verbalized experience, which is the seeding ground of conscious ideas.

One peculiarity of the problem of the social scientist is that he must establish personal contact with his material. The physical scientist who works in a laboratory spends more time adjusting his machinery than in making his observations, and the social scientist who works in the field must spend more time establishing contacts than in noting and reporting observations. What the instrumentation technique is to the physicist, the cultivation of favorable human points of vantage is for most social scientists. This means that the student of society, as well as the manager of social relations, must acquire the technique of social intercourse in unusual degree, unless he is to suffer from serious handicaps, and his training must be directed with this in mind.

The experience of the administrator-investigator must include some definite familiarity with all the elements which bear importantly upon the traits and interests of the individual. This means that he must have the most relevant material brought to his attention from the fields of psychology, psychopathology, physiology, medicine, and social science. Since our institutions of higher learning are poorly organized at the present time to handle this program, thorough curricular reconstructions will be indispensable.[15]

What has been said in this chapter may be passed in brief review. Political movements derive their vitality from the displacement of private affects upon public objects. Political crises are complicated by the concurrent reactivation of specific primitive motives which were or-

[15] I have suggested that those who write human biography should be included among those who require this comprehensive training. See "The Scientific Study of Human Biography," *Scientific Monthly*, January, 1930.

ganized in the early experience of the individuals concerned. Political symbols are particularly adapted to serve as targets for displaced affect because of their ambiguity of reference, in relation to individual experience, and because of their general circulation. Although the dynamic of politics is the tension level of individuals, all tension does not produce political acts. Nor do all emotional bonds lead to political action. Political acts depend upon the symbolization of the discontent of the individual in terms of a more inclusive self which champions a set of demands for social action.

Political demands are of limited relevance to the changes which will produce permanent reductions in the tension level of society. The political methods of coercion, exhortation, and discussion assume that the rôle of politics is to solve conflicts when they have happened. The ideal of a politics of prevention is to obviate conflict by the definite reduction of the tension level of society by effective methods, of which discussion will be but one. The preventive point of view insists upon a continuing audit of the human consequences of social acts, and especially of political acts. The achievement of the ideal of preventive politics depends less upon changes in social organization than upon improving the methods and the education of social administrators and social scientists.

The preventive politics of the future will be intimately allied to general medicine, psychopathology, physiological psychology, and related disciplines. Its practitioners will gradually win respect in society among puzzled people who feel their responsibilities and who respect objective findings. A comprehensive functional conception of political life will state problems of investigation, and keep receptive the minds of those who reflect at length upon the state.

CHAPTER XI[1]

THE PROLONGED INTERVIEW AND ITS OBJECTIFICATION

The empirical material assembled in this book has appeared in the course of prolonged interviews with individuals under unusually intimate conditions. This method of the prolonged interview has now had a history of some thirty years in the form devised by Freud, but so far there are very few efforts to objectify the events which transpire there. Otto Rank has written a series of studies of the "interview situation" which is the most important effort so far made to characterize the distinctive features of the method. But the empirical material which is so far reported does not rest upon the verbatim recording of what happens, except in a few specimen instances of highly pathological cases, and attempts are only now being made to record some of the principal physiological changes in the subject.

It will be remembered that Freud learned to predict the future course of reminiscence by watching word slips, random movements, and many other acts which were formerly dismissed as chance occurrences. He also found that he could abbreviate the laborious efforts of the patient to recall the traumatic (the original) episode by proposing various interpretations. It is at this point that the cautious physician and psychologist have picked serious quarrels with psychoanalytical findings. They allege

[1] Modified and expanded from "The Psychoanalytic Interview as a Method of Research on Personalities," in *The Child's Emotions*, pp. 136–59.

that the patient produces the kind of material which the analyst suggests is to be brought forth, and that the whole process is one of putting a rabbit in the hat which you triumphantly extricate later on. They have seized upon the schisms in the analytical fold, and declare that you eventually dream about anima figures if you are analyzed by Jung, that you relive birth traumas if you are analyzed by Rank, and that you welter in a galaxy of anal, oral, and urethral symbols if you are deeply analyzed by Freud. You talk about inferiority feeling if you work with Adler, and about castrative anxiety if you work with Freud.

One might suppose that after thirty years of labor there would be in existence a body of documents which could be consulted by a group of competent specialists who were trying to reconcile their differences and doubts about what actually goes on in the analytical interview.[2] At the present time the interview situation is poorly reflected in the notes taken by the analyst at the expiration of each period (if and when he takes them). Nobody knows what processes distort the reporting practices of different listeners, and nobody knows the value of the published scraps. Since one of the avowed purposes of therapeutic analyses is to bring the person to stand on his own feet and to stop leaning on others, or upon symptom indulgences, personal relations are usually broken off at the end of the interview. This obviously impedes the possibility of following up the subsequent history of the personality, and of ascertaining the stability of the supposed therapeutic results. The case-history documents available

[2] See Harold D. Lasswell, "The Problem of Adequate Personality Records: A Proposal," *American Journal of Psychiatry*, May 1929. Also Appendix B of *The Proceedings of the First Colloquium on Personality Investigation*.

in good institutions have the advantage of representing the combined product of several people who are in touch with the subject, and who may be supposed to operate as a check upon one another. But these documents are usually short, and betray the psychopathological slant of the ones chiefly responsible. And these documents are typically incomplete in reporting the whole personality of the subject on account of the clinician's interest in the more circumscribed disease phenomena displayed.

When John Brown reports an episode in which he was told that his nose would be cut off if he didn't quit handling himself, how do we know what importance to assign to the alleged reminiscence? Are we to accept this as a historical statement? Are we to construe it as a fabrication which, however, shows what he wanted to have happen, or supposed would happen, if he disobeyed orders? Are we to interpret it as a sign of his fear of the interviewer, couched in the language of the past, because this mode of exercising the imagination has been trained into him? Are we to interpret this as a sign of his hatred of the interviewer, on the theory that a self-punishing fantasy is a defense of the conscience against a murderous impulse of the unadjusted portion of the self? Are we to accept it as an effort to win the approval of the interviewer by reporting the kinds of things which he has learned to suppose the interviewer wants to hear, a supposition which is based upon a private study of psychoanalytical literature? Are we to accept it as an "original trauma" and to expect an immediate or eventual decrease in the neurotic anxiety which the individual shows? Are we to look upon it as a screen reminiscence for a genuinely traumatic episode in which the threat was made, not against his nose, but against his penis? Or is it a screen for a prohibited impulse which was once activated, and which seized upon a past episode and gave it the significance of a threat?

These are a few of the specific questions which can be raised about the proffered material, and the scientific problem is to devise more convincing demonstrations of the available theories, or more conclusive refutations, than we now have. What are some of the criteria of a "traumatic episode"? If the reminiscence is accompanied by much affect (excitement), there is a presumption of its authenticity. And how is affect measured? We depend at the present time upon the observer's judgment of the variations in the voice, and shifts in posture, or the twitches and jerks of the body. This can be augmented under experimental conditions by taking a continuous record of variations in blood pressure, respiration, galvanic reflex, etc.—all of which offer some indication of excitement.[3] We are thus able to improve our assessment of the possible significance of the reports, speculations, and general fantasies of the subject. It may be that in due course we shall be able to differentiate on a physical basis between "suppressions" and "repressions," and that we shall be able to follow through the transformations from beginning to end of the interviewing process.

Our judgment of the "traumatic episode" is also influenced by the subject's certainty. If the subject reports that he believes what he remembers, this has some value in raising a presumption. This is especially true if the subject has fought against the idea, but it has spontaneously continued to appear and plague his associations. But a re-

[3] We are now engaged upon studies of this kind at the Personality Laboratory in the Social Science Research Building at the University of Chicago. Harry Stack Sullivan is conducting a series of researches on expression changes, with particular reference to schizophrenia, which are of the greatest importance.

ported sense of certainty is flimsy stuff, unless this certainty survives for some time. We know that individuals try to escape from anxiety feelings by a flight into explanations, and that they are ready to volunteer or to accept all kinds of interpretations of their behavior rather than to continue to endure anxiety. This is the basis for the credulity of the neurotic, and explains why everything from mysterious "glandular unbalances" to "astral perturbations" are accepted from time to time as completely adequate explanations of personal troubles. So the subject's reported certainty must survive even disparaging suggestions and prolonged self-scrutiny, and become emancipated from affect, if it is to be taken very literally.

Another criterion is the consistency of the reported episode with all the other relevant facts. There must be something wrong about the report that K was brutally punished by his father at a time which was some years after the parent's death.[4]

The obstacles which lie in the path of a research program which calls for objective records of as much as possible of what transpires in the interview situation are not to be minimized. The bulk of a verbatim report of an hour's conversation per day over several months is almost overwhelming. But historians are accustomed to plow through whole libraries of pages about Napoleon or Bismarck, and from the standpoint of a comprehensive theory of personality development any personality is almost as good as any other, although high elaboration and distinguished achievement are advantages.

There are some points in favor of applying this technique of personality study to people who are normal, at least in the sense that they are suspected of normality by

[4] The topic of reliable criteria will be dealt with in detail in the reports upon experiments in progress.

themselves and others. There is a moral to be learned from some of Freud's early mistakes when he assigned critical significance to certain childhood experiences which later investigation showed were very common. The clinical caricature is invaluable for the high relief in which certain tendencies of the normal are revealed. Indeed, "normality" is more difficult to understand than disease, from one point of view, since it involves a complicated integration of many tendencies, a flexible capacity to snap from one mood, preoccupation, and overt activity to another, as the changing demands of reality require. Normality is complexity and integration, and it ought to be approached as directly as possible as a control on the pathological.

The main advantage which the normal subject hopes to glean from the analytical interview is a judgment of the importance of this, in comparison with other, psychological methods. Records being as they are today, only one who has been through the mill can talk with much assurance about what happens, and if he has a critical mind, he isn't too sure then. The analytical interview is a discipline in self-scrutiny. The subject learns to exploit a new method of using the mind, which he tries to cultivate and to correlate with the logical methods to which he is partly accustomed in ordinary adult life. The new technique of using the mind is the free-fantasy technique, whose chief function is to produce new material for logical consideration.

The interview necessitates the reactivation of the individual's struggle with his antisocial impulses. This happens be the subject sick or well, for every individual possesses more or less active and powerful antisocial drives. Every personality displays some pathology in the form of remainders of the Oedipus phase of growth. The socially adjusted portion of the personality takes up the battle again against the unsublimated drives, and a considerable amount of neurotic anxiety is generated in the process. The problem is to encourage the subject to face these unadjusted remnants frankly, to bring them to the full focus of waking consciousness, and to discharge their bound energy. This comes to pass in the roundabout way of recapturing the original episodes in which the neurotic solution was invented. The work of reminiscence is the preliminary to liberation and understanding.

The interview substitutes the talking-out for the acting-out of personality drives. One learns to recover the critical points in one's past history by watching the present for clues to the full meaning of the present situation, and this includes the inspection of reminiscences. A reminiscence is always relevant to a present situation, and serves the double rôle of annotating the present and reporting the past. The interview experience is long and arduous, and the subject learns very slowly to deal with himself as an object in a world of objects, and to free his judgment more and more from the distorting effects of primitive psychological structures.

The analytical situation is so arranged as to facilitate this process of self-inspection. The provocations to act out rather than think out are reduced by simplifying the sensory present. The subject lies in a relaxed position, and is better able to observe those stiffenings of the body, those variations in respiration, those oscillations of visceral tension, those impulses to scratch and finger which escape ordinary attention, but which are indicative of the meanings put in the current situation. The sensory environment remains substantially constant, and the interviewer handles the situation on a rather fixed routine. The subject is temporarily encysted from the demands of professional and conventional tasks, but the interviewer is present to prevent the individual from dissipating his energy in musings which are quickly forgotten. The interviewer is a prod to associate freely, and a spur to the critical consideration of the material supplied by the freely moving fancy. The necessity for verbalization brings the acts of fantasy into clearer focus than usual, which is a necessary preliminary to moments of sustained logical reflection. Since the interviewer permits the subject to disregard the usual amenities of society, and to let his fantasies fly for the sake of finding where they land, regressive responses are permitted to appear. That is, the individual is not required to adjust to a conventional world of adult reality, but is permitted to reactivate earlier forms of dealing with the world. In the world of adult reality, the multiple tendencies of the individual are canalized into conventionally acceptable forms, and the most maladapted drives may display themselves in unobtrusive variations on the pattern. When conventional reality is no longer present, and the individual is encouraged to watch his partly forming responses, rather than to co-ordinate, condense, ignore, or suppress them, these tendencies spread forth diffusely in imagination and reminiscence. When this process continues far enough, the individual achieves a high degree of insight into the genetic development of his current preoccupations and traits.

Since the analytical process is a period of strain for the subject, it may be wondered why it is bearable. Fortunately for the investigator, there are many advantages to the participant which sustain and fortify his conscious purpose to persevere until understanding has been substantially deepened. The analyst treats every manifestation of the personality, no matter how trivial, with respectful interest. This is exaggerated unconsciously by the subject, who greatly overestimates the personal affection which the interviewer has for him. Some of the energy of the personality is always free to begin new object attachments, and this energy is concentrated upon the interviewer. The subject is permitted to talk at length about himself, and when the interviewer listens attentively and patiently, the subject identifies himself with the listener on the basis of a common attitude of interest in a beloved object. The interviewer's ascendancy in technical knowledge (his authority) resembles the authority of the adults who were once supposed to possess unlimited knowledge. The day-by-day solicitude tends to reinstate the emotions of the early family situation in which the child could play irresponsibly, under the watchful, responsible care of the adult. The subject relaxes the effort to keep baudy, disloyal, mean, and revengeful thoughts from welling into this mind. The frank expression of these thoughts in ordinary social life would bring down punishment upon his head, or mark him out as a victim of mental disorder. The subject is enabled to welter in unsocial or antisocial ravings and imaginings, and the process of developing these symptoms in the presence of another person becomes an absorbing part of his daily, weekly, and monthly existence. The subject intensifies his warm emotional interest in the one who exempts him from society's code of reticence. This is a mark of the analyst's tremendous power, and also of the analyst's special interest in the subject. The free-fantasy procedure even exempts the individual from abiding by the ordinary forms of logic and grammar. He is also able to enjoy the pleasure of impressing someone else with the brilliance of his language. From time to time, new insight comes into old habits and worries, and the zest of intellectual comprehension is added to the other pleasures.

At first sight the teaching or research interview might seem to sacrifice the most powerful motive upon which the interviewing procedure has relied, namely, that of securing relief from disturbing symptoms. The individual who is suffering from some crude pathological disturbance, like a functional gastro-intestinal disorder, psychological impotence, obsessive ideas and compulsions, comes to the interviewer as a weak person seeking aid of a stronger. If he has been shuttled from one internist to another perhaps receiving derisive looks and contemptuous preachments, the objective interest with which the psychotherapist treats his symptoms produces a keen conscious and unconscious gratification. Even the symptoms are beloved parts of the self, and like the ugly ducklings, they are sometimes treated with special affection (Ferenczi). The hope of being relieved of the annoying symptoms, which is consciously present in many pathological cases, is supported on the unconscious level by an old infantile attitude which expects the interviewer to work miracles. Even some of the antisocial impulses of the personality may welcome the therapeutic situation. These antisocial tendencies are themselves not entirely gratified in the symptoms, for the nature of a symptom is a compromise between these antisocial tendencies and the socialized impulses of the self. Nunberg has pointed out that the unsocialized portions of the personality may support the misguided hope that the outcome of therapy will be the boundless and unlimited gratification of their demands. There is also evidence of the existence of a compulsion to confess (Reik) to antisocial tendencies, which are rejected by the socialized self, and thus to gratify an unconscious need of punishment.

Now the sense of being sick and the desire to get well are not entirely absent from any normal person. No one is entirely free from remnants of his adjustive problems, and no one is entirely satisfied with himself. At the beginning of the interview, this motive may appear in consciousness as nothing more substantial than the innocuous belief that any increase in self-knowledge will enable one to deal even more satisfactorily with personal problems as they arise.

Among the other motives which play into the analytical situation, and enable the subject to go through with it, may be mentioned a few very primitive ones. Life has meant the blocking of many impulses by authorities whose power cannot be successfully defied on the spot. Hatreds can only express themselves under these conditions with some prospects of success when they seek to overcome the superior by trying to take his power into one's own personality by copying him. That is to say, the individual seeks to identify himself with the one who possesses superior knowledge in the analytical situation, and by becoming like him, to secure independence, and thus to annihilate him as an intimidating and obstructive external object. There may be a desire to secure a weapon by means of which other people may be eviscerated, and deprived of their power to outstrip the individual. On the conscious level, these motives are partly visible in excessive aspirations for self-mastery and control. This taking-in and biting-off of the analyst's power is also rooted in some of the earliest reaction patterns which the infant displays toward objects. The sheer pleasure of talking, and giving and withholding information is also present.

As the subject withdraws attention from the original symptoms or motives, concentrates on the game of dilating upon the past, and indulges in prohibited delights, the analytical situation becomes an orgy of illicit pleasure.

Emotions are released from old channels and find new objects of crystallization, especially in the person of the analyst. The interviewer who permits this "transference" is now in a position to aid the subject in coming to grips with the underlying unsocialized impulses of the personality. The behavior of the subject has by this time given a host of clues to the history of his emotional growth. The analyst continues to stimulate the individual to scrutinize his associations, to state honestly the wayward wishes flit across his mind, or which lurk half-seen in the marginal recesses of attention. Back and forth, bit by bit, there is reconstructed the subjective history of a life. To put it metaphorically, old sores run anew, smoldering embers of jealousy and lust flame once more, and ancient wounds yawn again. Reminiscence reguilds the faded tapestries of the past, and restores to the full glare of consciousness the cobwebs of the mind which house the spiders of malevolence and lechery. Primitive meanings, once appropriate to a situation, and later projected unintentionally into the adult world, are recovered and criticized in the light of their appropriateness to society. Regressive reliving, which is powerfully supported by narcissism and the repetitive compulsion, is observed and overcome.

It should not be supposed that the secrets of the mind are exposed for the asking. The method of repression is a primitive means by which the feeble, nascent self seeks protection from impulses which, if tolerated, if not shut out with unreflecting violence, would overrun it (Alexander). When the self becomes strong and stable, primitive impulses can be permitted to develop farther in consciousness without imminent danger that they will pass over into action by controlling the motor apparatus. Now the critical, reflecting, deciding self must not be crippled by an unduly strong conscience. The structure which we know as the conscience is begun in early childhood, and is formed by the incorporation into the self of the orders and commands which are administered by authority. When the self is weak, as during these formative years, the conscience relies on crude methods to protect its hard-won ascendancy over the antisocial drives in the personality. It visits penalties of anxiety upon the self whenever there are any signs of leniency toward these impulses. The conscience keeps its summary, sadistic quality long after, and neurotics are properly said to suffer from an excess of conscience. Blind denial of the existence of fundamental trends in the personality must be supplanted, and the *obiter dicta* of the conscience subjected to the criticism of the more mature and experienced self. An obstacle to this procedure is furnished by those energies of the personality which are specialized in resisting the antisocial impulses which have been repressed and denied direct and undisguised access to consciousness. Any lowering of resistance subjects the individual to acute anxiety, as the conflict between the socialized and the unsocialized drives is reinstated. All sorts of subterfuges are hit upon to obviate the necessity for enduring this anxiety and bringing the hidden into consciousness, where it can lose its charge. The overcoming of this resistance to taking up the battle again is a major process in the prolonged analysis.

The recapitulation of the drives which the individual has experienced throughout his life is the process which lends unique value to the psychoanalytic interview record. The literature of psychoanalysis is full of sample fantasies which are assigned to places in the hypothetical sequence of personality growth. Over twenty years ago Freud wrote some preliminary remarks on character types, especially stressing the rôle of certain excretory pleasures in the development of some psychological structures. The sucking, biting and anal retention interests of the infant and young child have been the subject of theoretical treatment by several analysts, among whom Abraham is the most important. Ferenczi has sketched a comprehensive theory of the rise of genital interests on the part of the child, and this has been amplified in various directions by Reich. The differences between male and female development have been sketched by Sachs, Deutsch, and Horney.

It is not within the necessary limits of this discussion to go farther into the nature of the hypotheses which have been proposed by these various investigators. We will be able to formulate them more precisely when we have succeeded in objectifying what happens in the course of the interview, and this is to be achieved along the lines previously sketched. Some day we can state hypotheses more definitely which can be taken and tested by non-analytical methods. Some of these conceptions can be confirmed or eliminated by the direct observation of children of all age groups. It is quite possible, however, paradoxical though it may sound, that the best way to study some phases of infancy and childhood will be to study the adult. There is some reason to believe that the superior expressive power of the adult, whether in words or in drawing, may render explicit many states which are beyond the scope of one who merely looks at movements. If we find that the subjective reconstructions during the adult analysis check closely with the results secured by modified analytical and behavioristic procedures applied directly to older children, we will have more confidence in the material which purports to relate to very early experience. We may also test out as far as possible the "historicity" of the reminiscences produced at different phases of the analysis. It should be said in passing that the analysis of children requires important revisions in the externals of the technique, as Anna Freud has shown.

I want to stop at this point to comment upon the significance of the fact there should be such a thing as the psychoanalytic method of dealing with the genesis of personality. How does it happen that at the end of the nineteenth century there appeared in Western European civilization this remarkably intricate procedure? Why do we regard it as worth while to spend months or even years in constant introspection?

Viewed in the large, I suppose this is the most spectacular sign of the value crisis in our civilization. Here is an effort to stimulate the individual to the reconstruction of values, not on the basis of imposed authority, but through prolonged scrutiny of the self as a process. The processes of the human personality are subjected to the same patient, arduous, and minute inspection which has proved so successful when applied to the objects of the physical world by the naturalist, astronomer, and microscopic specialist. The end result of a long and successful analysis is an individual who is able to interpret his relation to the world in terms of a few master-symbols. These symbols take on meaning because they have been acquired in the course of a long apprenticeship under the exacting eye of another. These symbols define for the individual in comprehensive terms his relation to unfolding reality. They permit in favorable instances added smoothness of adjustment, and offer a means of relief from disproportionate feelings of futility, despondency, persecution, and omniscience.

The appearance of a system of communicable master-symbols for the definition of one's relation to the universe is anything but a novel phenomenon in the culture history of mankind. At one time a leading question was, "What is God's will for me?" The belief was that this could be made manifest after the reading of Holy Writ, reverent supplication, and sudden revelation. Our Western civilization has sapped at the pillars of this structure of thinking. We are committed to the persistent querying of the world of change, and the problem is always *"How* does it change?" How do the routines of the seeable, smellable, touchable, audible, tasteable universe actually work? In what characteristic order do the subjective events of the mind follow one another? In what order do subjective and objective events occur? And no matter how many intermediate links in the sequence have been named there always remain new intermediate and new all-embracing frames of reference to be identified and placed in orderly relationship.

Values are sought to be defined, not on the authority of another, but in the act of scrutinizing processes. We place enormous value upon the quest for sequences, and discover our new values in the act of broadening or deepening our understanding of change. If you tell a sophisticated carrier of Western culture that God reveals his wisdom after the reading of a printed passage, he will be less impressed by what is put in than by what is left out of the account. What relation is there between what is read and what is decided? Can you set up controlled repetitions for the sake of testing the predictive value of these generalizations? Are there other words which can be read but which will result in the same decisions when the reader has the same pecuniary stake in acting a certain way? And so on and on.

It is worth noticing that the symbols supplied by analysis are not "ought" words but "process" words. You are not told to die for your country; you are told to face all the values which you can find in the situation. This does not, however, eliminate the "arbitrary" character of decisions actually reached. The decision comes with all the shock of revelation, of inevitability, of unexpectedness; the individual may only control decisions by rehearsing the pertinent values until he finds himself in the clutches of a judgment. This willingness to accept uncertainty, to scrutinize intermediate terms and pertinent values, is an outcome of the analytical discipline.

Such a procedure grew up in a civilization whose values have been in confusion since the medieval cosmology broke down. President Masaryk, serious thinker and scholarly writer, began his sociological work with a study of suicide, which he found to be a rough index of the value strains in culture. When emotional bonds are forged with exponents of life-patterns of different design, the mental stage is set for both creative originality and destructive disintegration. The individual must assume the load of working out his own scheme of values, and many are disorganized in the attempt.

The validation of the prolonged interview as a contributor to our dependable knowledge about life depends upon objectifying its processes; the achievement of its implications for the reconstruction of the hierarchy of individual values is an impressionistic and often turbulent experience.[5]

---

[5] The best technical discussions of the nature of the analytical situation are in the writings of Freud, Rank, Ferenczi, Nunberg, and Alexander.

CHAPTER XII[1]

THE PERSONALITY SYSTEM AND ITS SUBSTITUTIVE REACTIONS

So far in this book human behavior has been interpreted in terms of various "tendencies" which such behavior is supposed to manifest. Suppose we call into question this type of psychological explanation. What, after all, is a "tendency"? It postulates a relationship between events, one of which is taken as the terminal situation, and others of which are treated as relative approximations to the type situation. Terms like "wishes," "desires," "instincts," "impulses," "drives," and "motives" are all employed in this sense.

For purposes of analysis, tendency interpretations may be divided into five main classes, depending on the nature of the relationship which is postulated between the approximate and the terminal situation. First, personality events may be interpreted as approximations toward, or realizations of, goals (terminals) which are communicated by the subject. We may believe a man who tells us that he is running for a train when we see him dashing along the street toward the railway station.

Second, personality events may be interpreted as degrees of approximation to subsequent events which are actually observed. Mr. C's solicitude for the health and welfare of the needy ones of the district may be construed in the light of his subsequent campaign for Congress.

[1] Expanded from an article with the same title which appeared in the *Journal of Abnormal and Social Psychology*, January, 1930.

Third, personality events may be treated as degrees of resumption of terminal situations of a type which have already been observed. Lying in bed after waking up in the morning, whenever there are difficulties to cope with, may be interpreted as a reactivation of an earlier psychological impulse to lie still and be waited on.

Fourth, personality events may be construed as approximations to "normal" terminal events which are observed for the biological or cultural category of the individual. Thus heterosexuality may be postulated as a tendency of a human being, although he consummates no heterosexual adjustments.

Fifth, personality events may be interpreted in terms of end situations which are "extreme" for the members of the species or the culture. Thus the acts of man may be viewed as degrees of approximation to murder, suicide, and incest.

Each sense in which the tendency conception is used is valid and useful for certain purposes, and is exposed to characteristic liabilities to error. Thus if we accept the man's statement that he is running to catch a train, we may be wrong; he may be running to the woods beyond to escape the constable.

The reactive type of statement is an alternative (I should prefer to say a supplement) to tendency generalizations. When we make a reactive statement, we specify quite definitely the antecedent-consequent relation to which reference is made. The specific stimulus-response description of the events which elicit the knee jerk, or call out an avoidance reaction to yellow cloth, illustrates what is meant here. Of course the stimulus-response style of thinking is not nearly as exhaustive, and the tendency style of thinking is not nearly as ambiguous in actual application, as might appear at first glance. The stimulus-response statement of how to elicit the knee jerk which is usually given may be predictively valid in eight cases out of ten; but there are "exceptions" which show how wide is the context of factors which it would be necessary to include in the picture, were it nearly complete. And when the stimulus-response mode of thinking is extended from such relatively stable and touchable situations to those which involve complex central (subjective) events in the sequence, it becomes in reality a disguised form of tendency interpretation.

The chief possible virtue of tendency conceptions is in introducing some sort of order in complex phenomena. If the observer tries to enumerate all the body movements, all the electronic gyrations, all the nuances of social adjustment which are thinkable in a given constellation of personality events, he is likely to become lost in aimless classification, and to prove barren in the invention of procedures which are calculated to elicit particular aspects of the whole which may be of high predictive value. The human mind is able to operate with a very small number of categories with which to introduce order into events, particularly when these are, for the most part, still defined qualitatively. Clarity of thought demands economy in the orienting frames of thought.

How a tendency simplification may lead to fruitful research for predictively valuable particulars is shown in the case of Freud, in contrast to Janet. Janet made remarkably clear classifications of the psychopathological facts as he saw them, and although his terms and categories were abundant, his work was comparatively sterile of novel procedures for the modification of human personalities. Even his classificatory pursuits were hampered by his little-criticized assumptions. His notion that dreams were passing confusions which were traceable to diminished psychological tension in sleep deprived dream material of all significance as classifiable data, and he almost completely ignored it. Freud, who tended to operate with a few bold tendency simplifications, brought into the range of observation whole categories of data which have high predictive value.

When tendency simplifications are used until vast numbers of instances accumulate of their supposed operation, "subtendencies" (such as the variations of the manifestations of the Oedipus constellation) multiply apace until the problems of rendering one tendency consistent with the expressions of another one carry scientific speculations into the logical molds of legalism and dogmatic theology. If the subtendencies are not modified, and long lists of special tendencies are added, terminological difficulties likewise arise in applying the unwieldy list. The long inventories of supposed instincts are less at fault because they imply an unwarranted assurance about the innate propensities of man than because they are "too numerous to mention," and introduce confusion rather than orienting principles in the field of study.

Although the prediction of one set of tangible reactions from another is the aim of scientific formulation, this by no means implies, then, that the reactive style of thinking is the one best calculated to guide the attention of the thinker to the selection of the most fruitful hypotheses ("if" predictions). Indeed, especially valuable results have been secured in the personality field by the pattern of thinking which views a cross-section of facts as an expression of a few tendencies.

But a reactive style of thinking which operates with a few simplifications might prove useful in the study of human personality at the present time, since both the psycho-analytical and the "itemistic" psychologies have a plethora of particulars with which they are familiar, but suffer from certain crippling viewpoints inherent in their early starting-points. Psychoanalysis is well accustomed to the use of a few orienting terms, but since these are stated in "tendency" form, there is much lack of emphasis upon rendering the objective marks of their manifestation precise. The inventory psychologies though accustomed to precision are accustomed to overlooking the woods for the trees.

Can the personality be viewed as a system, and can we think of it in a few terms which can be gradually objectified, and which indicate the principal varieties of personality manifestation? If the personality is a true system, interferences which are introduced at various points ought often to produce substitutive reactions at many remote parts of the personality. Personalities may be compared from one cross-section to another, and from one personality to another, by exposing them to similar interferences, and by examining the substitutive reaction sequences which emerge.

For the purpose of summing up the personality at any given period, we may consider it to be a constellation of the following action patterns: object orientations, adjustive thinking, autistic reveries, somatic reactions.

The object orientations of the individual are describable as various degrees of assertiveness, provocativeness, or submissiveness toward sexual and non-specifically sexual objects in the environment. In extreme instances the individual may be abusive, insulting, domineering toward superiors, colleagues, clients, and subordinates in his profession, and toward his wife or mistress in intimate life;

or he may be cowed in his work and timid in his sexuality; or he may show extreme variations between his professional and private levels of behavior. These are the differentiating reactions upon which it is hoped to throw some light by the examination of the personality system in its principal manifestations.

Adjustive thinking has to do with the relationship of the individual to reality. It issues in socially relevant acts, which on the creative level mean contributions to science, art, administration, and philosophy. Autistic thinking is highly egocentric, but adjustive thinking when it dwells upon the relationship of the self to its surroundings is able to treat the self as an object among objects.

Autistic reveries are non-adjustive to reality. They may be divided into several classes of which morbid-suicidal, pessimistic, megalomanic, denunciatory, and persecutory reveries are particularly common. In exaggerated form they become the most conspicuous feature of the personality, and various clinical names are used to distinguish them. Common, and representative, themes are suggested by these quotations: "I'm a hopeless sinner"; "The world's going to the dogs"; "I'm the slickest guy in the world"; "The President is the Judas of mankind"; "The President is using death-rays on me." Autistic thinking flourishes in greater or less abundance in every personality whose history is taken for any length of time.

The somatic reactions at any given cross-section of the personality are striped muscle movements and tensions; heart and circulatory reactions; gastro-intestinal responses; skin adjustments; organic sexual behavior; respiratory, pupillary, and urogenital adaptations; inner glandular action on the biochemical balance of the blood; heat production (fever and certain metabolic alterations not included before); electrical conductivity; and immunological responses. Under the same environing conditions individuals show wide variations in physical behavior, and when these manifestations show certain gross deviations from norms, though no organic lesion can be shown to be present, the presumption is that the energy of some mental process has been converted into somatic form. This notion of hysteria (and what may be called hysteroid reactions) was classically formulated by Freud. Every individual who is closely scrutinized shows, from time to time, tendencies to urinate excessively (though no adequate physical explanation is apparent), to refrain from passing feces, or to suffer pains in the back or neck.

The comparisons which may be made among personalities on the basis of the nature of the substitutive reactions which arise when they are subjected to similar conditions may be illustrated on the gross level by citing some "experiments" which society has tried. Mr. A is a member of the city council in one of our large cities. On two occasions, when he was defeated for re-election, he developed autistic reveries to such an extent that he was confined in a sanitarium under the care of a psychiatrist. Thus Mr. A met a deprivation in the sphere of his orientation to social objects (political activity) by developing exaggerated autistic reveries (depressive preoccupations). The case of A may be thrown up against that of Mr. B. When Mr. B lost out in his campaign for re-election to the legislature, he began to worry about his health, and although the physicians could find no adequate physical basis for his trouble, he developed a host of gastro-intestinal disturbances which incapacitated him from regular professional life. His substitutive reaction was somatic. Another man, a Mr. C, was defeated and spent most of his time writing a subsequently well-recognized book on political theory. His substitutive reaction was in the sphere of consecutive, theoretical, adjustive thinking. It will be remembered that one of our driving administrators, J, had his administrative duties curtailed and immediately took the wife of another for his mistress showing that his object orientation in the world of affairs was a substitute for his object orientation in the sexual field.

From this point of view, we are able to examine the relative function which political activities and preoccupations play in the personality integration of the individual. For one it is an alternative to mental disorder, for another it is an alternative to physical disease, for another an alternative to aggressive sexuality.

Now it is of interest and importance to observe that the study of the life-histories of these men showed that their mode of meeting the world had become organized rather early. The man who developed somatic symptoms had shown a physical upset after losing a contest for the presidency of his class in college, and also in adolescent and preadolescent deprivation situations. Alexander traced the basis for the personality splitting in J to very early childhood.

I want now to indicate how the prolonged interview throws much light on personality development, and lends itself to consideration from the point of view outlined here. If the analyst is "insulted" by the subject in the course of a day's interview, the subject may the next day report somatic trouble, or morbid reveries, or unusual kindliness toward an annoying person, or a burst of creative work. The interviewer, taking such facts in juxtaposition to others, may be able to predict the kind of substitutive reactions which this person is likely to show in a whole range of social situations, and to predict retrospectively the form of reaction which was manifested at different levels of development. The trained psychoanalyst watches the subject like a hawk for clues of this kind; the possibility of removing his "hunches" from the realm of art into the area of dependable knowledge depends upon the objectification of his observations, and upon the development of specifically experimental methods.

A method by which some certainty is to be introduced in personality records is by testing the coincidence of observations taken through time by observers who occupy specified positions in relation to the subject. Very important applications of this procedure have been made to child study by several child psychologists, more particularly by Florence Goodenough and Dorothy Thomas. A set of categories were set up to describe various acts, such as "smiling," "physical contact with other child," and "physical contact with object." The definiteness of each term was then tested by having two independent observers make the same number of observations at fixed intervals during a prescribed period. The results showed which categories were ambiguous, and which categories were sufficiently clear to justify their inclusion in behavior studies. It was discovered, for example, that "smiling" behavior showed much less definiteness than "physical contact with another child." This procedure makes it possible to measure the error of a measuring procedure and is strictly comparable to the calibrating process common to the physical sciences in determining the relative reliability of measurements made by a particular instrument. The social scientist is compelled to rely on the use of his eyes, and the problem is to standardize the use so that objective results can be secured.[2]

[2] Dorothy Swaine Thomas and Associates, *Some New Techniques for Studying Social Behavior.*

Such methods of devising and testing categories for the observation of behavior need urgently to be developed for the study of courtroom, legislative, committee, mass meeting, and other types of behavior in situations of immediate political interest. It is possible to record the differential reactions of participants, and to distinguish that which is inherent in the rôle performed (chairman), and that which is the individualized penumbra of the act (individual gesture).

These objective categories and recording practices can be extended to the study of behavior wherever dominating and submissive behavior is found. The gap between the studies of children and the study of personalities in complicated adult political situations can be filled in with the idea of finding reliable criteria of the stability of political reactions. Some early studies have been made which suggest that types of dominating behavior are isolable at very early ages. Charlotte Bühler detected children who dominated through pressure of activity, despotic behavior, and "leadership" behavior. Her monograph reproduces photographic illustrations of what she means by the terms employed.[3] An outgrowth of her work is the experimental study by Marjorie Walker at the Minneapolis Institute of Child Welfare (under direction of Anderson and Goodenough). An observational study by Mildred Parten at the same place showed that in uncontrolled play activities the dominating or submissive rôles might be strikingly monopolized by individual children.[4]

[3] "Die ersten sozialen Verhaltungsweisen des Kindes," *Quellen und Studien zur Jugendkunde*, Heft 5.

[4] Referred to by John E. Anderson, "The Genesis of Social Reactions in the Young Child," *The Unconscious: A Symposium*. These researches are abstracted in William I. Thomas and Dorothy S. Thomas, *The Child in America*.

By methods which are less objective but much better than simple impressionism, there have been a number of "political types" observed in later development. Karl Reininger kept a careful record of the behavior of his pre-puberty schoolboys, and brought out very clearly the functional distinction between the "leader" and the "specialist." The specialist might temporarily guide the group in some activity for which he was particularly competent, but the leader kept him within limits and reassumed the direction as soon as the special activity was over. Reininger has many shrewd observations to offer about the bearing of what he saw on the whole range of social psychological theory, and his monograph is a beautiful example of how a circumscribed empirical study can be given meaning and distinction against a broad theoretical background.[5] Hildegard Hetzer watched the spontaneous groupings of children in play groups, and shrewdly distinguished organizers, specialists, and social leaders from one another.[6]

At a still later level is the study which Viktor Winkler-Hermaden made of the psychology of youth-movement leaders. These leaders are recruited from youths who are not much ahead of their groups in age, and in a well-balanced and penetrating chapter he contrasted the "ruler," "teacher," and "apostle."[7]

Special studies of dominating and submissive types in various situations ought to be made with some reference to the reaction-type classifications for the age period which are made by competent students. Since puberty-adoles-

[5] *Über soziale Verhaltungsweisen in der Vorpubertät,* "Wiener Arbeiten zur pädogogischen Psychologie" (herausgegeben von Charlotte Bühler and Viktor Fadrus), Heft 2.

[6] *Das volkstümliche Kinderspiel,* Heft 6, in the same series as the above.

[7] "Psychologie des Jugendführers," *Quellen und Studien zur Jugendkunde* (herausgegeben von Dr. Charlotte Bühler).

cence is of so much importance, the categories which are proposed in the literature ought to be examined by the special investigator. H. Hoffman gives a modified list of the puberty types described by Spranger and Croner in one section of his general book on character formation.[8] Suggestions on various distortions of development which lie behind certain forms of dominating and submissive behavior are to be found in August Aichhorn's lectures on *Verwahrloste Jugend*.[9] This is the most valuable book to a student of youth which has yet been explicitly devoted to the subject by an analyst. Aichhorn reports in his eighth lecture the results of an extremely important experiment which he made with the most aggressive and uncontrollable boys under his supervision (he has served for many years as the head of a home for homeless boys). The whole group was put together, and the staff members were instructed never to interfere with them, short of stopping permanent injury. These "hard-boiled" youths broke up the furniture, mauled one another, and wore out several attendants before they gradually tamed down. After having learned that they could not taunt the environment into punishing them, and into justifying their own suspicions of it, they went through a process of character re-education. The behavior of the group is reported in graphical form, and representative instances of what occurred are recited in the text of the lecture. Several specific genetic hypotheses are set up to explain particular

[8] *Das Problem des Charakteraufbaus*, pp. 68–80. See E. Spranger, *Psychologie des Jugendalters*, and Else Croner, "Die Psyche der weiblichen Jugend," *Schriften zur Frauenbildung*, Heft 6.

[9] *Internationale Psychoanalytische Bibliothek*, Band XIX.

kinds of behavior on the part of the boys with whom Aichhorn has had intimate touch.[10]

Will we be able to predict from objective studies made of preadolescent boys who dominate their play groups that one set of them will stand a high chance of dominating play and work groups in adolescence? Can we thus isolate rather stable developmental sequences for various trait constellations which are of direct importance to the student of politics? Can we achieve a composite picture for a given culture by studying overlapping age groups for a two-year period? Certainly the way is becoming clearer to an effective relationship between political science and the disciplines associated with the study of the growing individual.

One of the difficulties which lie in the path of successful collaboration with psychiatrists and child psychologists is that the political scientists have not themselves made it entirely clear just what the adult differentials are whose genetic history they would like to understand. What are the questions about the specifically political life of the individual which the political scientist would like to have included in any master-inventory of possible facts about the intensively studied individual?

The following classification of political attitudes is intended to have suggestive value rather than formal completeness. The first section of this classification refers to the political preferences and expectations or forebodings of the individual investigated. Some individuals cherish a fraternal and some a paternal ideal. The anarchist, so-

---

[10] See especially p. 278. Harry Stack Sullivan is tracing out the developmental history of various forms of personality in his forthcoming volume on *Personal Psychopathology*.

cialist, and democrat talk the language of equality among a family of brothers; the monarchists preserve a father.[11] A series of other ideological distinctions are perhaps sufficiently clear from the terms used.

CLASSIFICATION OF POLITICAL ATTITUDES

SECTION A. POLITICAL VIEWS

I. Preferences

　　Paternal ideal
　　Fraternal ideal

　　Strong central authority
　　Weak central authority

　　Revolutionary ideal
　　Counter-revolutionary or reactionary ideal

　　Cataclysmic change
　　Evolutionary change

　　Indulgent toward coercion, secrecy, ruthlessness
　　Insistent upon persuasion, openness, scrupulousness

　　Emancipatory, defensive, expansive ideal for group
　　World-unity ideal

II. Expectations and forebodings

　　Small political change can have great results
　　Small political change can have some results of value
　　Little of value can be accomplished by politics
　　Revolutionary changes imminent, eventual, contingent

It is probably in relation to political practices, as distinguished from political views, that the intensive study of the individual has the most to offer. I have included a list of questions in Appendix B which are intended to suggest the sort of thing which is directly pertinent to the interest of the political scientist in this regard. How has the individual acted as a subordinate when confronted by superiors of various kinds (in the army, in school, in frater-

---

[11] Paul Federn commented in his pamphlet that a democratic state must depend upon a democratic family life.

nity organizations, in business, in party clubs, in propaganda organizations, in administrative hierarchies, and the like)? How has the individual acted as a superior when confronted by subordinates of various kinds? Besides considering the behavior of the person as subordinate or superior, we may inquire into his attitude toward individuals who have not been members of his various organizations, but who have been possible helpers or obstacles. Thus he may have approached strangers for money, or sought to win diplomatic support from another organization against a common menace. His tactics may be classified according to the means employed and the measure of success attained. Special attention may likewise be devoted to the behavior of the individual, not toward particular persons, but toward publics, which are necessarily anonymous. Summarizing:

SECTION B. POLITICAL PRACTICES

I. As subordinate

Confronted by superiors who are

A. Strong, brutal
B. Masterful but rather objective
C. Weak

Reaction (conscious)

1. Does not assume a friendly mask (exterior) even though he sees it would be an advantage (seeks to escape, becomes stubborn, surly, assaultive, joins anti-authoration acts engaged in by associates, continues to contemplate revenge long after)
2. Does not see or press up own individual advantage because of attachment or intimidation (deference without conscious hostility, pronounced affection, intimidated sacrifice of associates to curry favor, overgratitude)
3. Combines friendly mask with conscious acts of hostility (plays up qualities admired by chief, whether imitative of chief or expressive of the chief's repressions)
4. Irrational elements in adaptation at a minimum

II. As authority
Confronted by subordinates who are
A. Strong, hostile, dangerous rivals
B. Strong and objective
C. Weak
Reaction
1. Does not refrain from taking up a hostile front even when it is recognized to be inappropriate
2. Takes apparently friendly line while pursuing hostile purposes
3. Does not take strong-enough measures to secure efficiency or respect (too indulgent of mirrors of self or of those who work out frustrations)
4. Objective (inflicts narcissistic wound when advantageous, reassures when useful, develops abilities of subordinates, thwarts when dangerous)

III. In dealing with possible helper or obstructor who is outside organization (most effective tactics chosen and range of tactics)
Appeals to logical standards
Appeals to sentiment
Non-violent and violent coercion
Inducement (tangible advantage)

IV. In dealing with public
Types of tactics chosen, success

Forms of expression, thought, and interest may be singled out for special consideration. What is intended here is sufficiently apparent from the captions:

SECTION C. FORMS OF EXPRESSION, THOUGHT, INTEREST

I. Forms of expression
(Includes all symbolizing forms: political editorials, novels, poems, paintings, cartoons, plastic media, plays, acting)
Most effective style
Analytical and dialectical
Persecutory (sarcastic, denunciatory)
Enthusiastic

Humorous
Commanding
Range of style wide or limited

II. Mode of thought

Quick or slow to suggest policies or tactics
Almost totally uninventive
Systematically collects data prior to judgment
Impressionistic improvisation
Welcomes suggestion and criticism before decision
Impatient of suggestion and criticism before decision
Anxious to justify decision to those about or to world
Indifferent about justifying decision
Stubbornly holds to decision
Oscillates in decision
Much influenced by facts and arguments (or little)
Much influenced by appeals to sentiments (or little)
Much influenced by personal inducements (or little)
Much influenced by coercion (or little) (note that influence may be negative as to direction)
Genuine pursuit of general interest in exercise of discretion, or not
Elated by victory or depressed
Genuine or narrow in sharing credit
Deeply depressed by defeat or satisfied in defeat
Interested in programs and values
Interested in processes and methods
Long-run or short-run objectives
Aims at immediate or eventual political action
Presses through to a decision capable of being tested
Conclusions or decisions vague
Ideal of responsible personal participation
Consistency between opinion and practices
Self-consciousness of own techniques
Conforms or not to family pattern (exaggerated, adoption of opposite, ...)

III. Political interest

Formulated early and persists through life
Formulated early, lies dormant, reawakened

Aroused early, disillusioned
Aroused late

By this time it is perhaps superfluous to comment that every fact is defined from the point of view of an observer, and that the problem is to specify as definitely as possible the angle of observation of the recorder. Trait lists are meaningless unless they can be filled in by a fact-collecting process which surveys the various situations with respect to which it is of possible relevance. It is very obvious to the psychopathologist that the man who is "aggressive" at work may be "timid" in sexuality. All too frequently personalities are supposed to be "aggressive" when a certain number of raters have agreed on it, without stopping to consider whether the raters have a chance to become acquainted with the behavior of the individual in many situations. The multiplication of ratings by persons who are in a poor position to judge the subject (even by "intimate" friends who do not, however, act as sexual partners) adds nothing but a spurious specificity to the data. The interviewer who listens to the intimate life of the individual through many weeks and months is in a very strategic position to become acquainted with details of individual reactions which even intimates have not seen. A "rating" must be taken with special reference to the history of the relations of the rater and the rated. It may be that we shall presently find that the ratings of analysts in dealing with certain types of people who can be easily identified do not substantially deviate from those of "intimates" or even rather casual acquaintances of certain kinds. Such knowledge will enable research to proceed with more certain pace toward the time when we shall know what to look for and how to elicit what we want with the maximum of economy. The specialist who interviews a man for an hour may be able, during the course of what appears to be an ordinary social relation, to find the tell-tale signs which detailed research has shown to be invariably, or almost invariably, connected with particular impulse systems and developmental histories. As Bjerre so well put it:

As soon as our intercourse with a certain person is no longer governed by common interests, but by a desire to acquire a knowledge of his inmost being, we immediately abandon the formal content of his utterance and begin unconsciously to seek for whatever indication of his inner life appears in his speech independently of, or even in spite of, his conscious will.[12]

What is achieved is a correlation of the results of "casual" contact and "intensive" study, a correlation which is the common target of a converging attack upon the understanding of the human personality.

Some day we shall know how to validate the saying of the old physician which is on the title-page of this book: "From him who has eyes to see and ears to hear no mortal can hide his secret; he whose lips are silent chatters with his fingertips and betrays himself through all his pores."

[12] See his excellent methodological chapter in *The Psychology of Murder*.

CHAPTER XIII

THE STATE AS A MANIFOLD OF EVENTS

Implications have continually been drawn in the foregoing pages about the bearing of the intensive study of individual personalities upon the meaning of the political process as a whole. Since the psychopathological approach to the individual is the most elaborate procedure yet devised for the study of human personality, it would appear to raise in the most acute form the thorny problem of the relation between research on the individual and research upon society. We are therefore justified in devoting more extended attention to the theoretical problem involved than we have yet taken occasion to do.

It may be asserted at the outset that our thinking is vitiated unless we dispose of the fictitious cleavage which is sometimes supposed to separate the study of the "individual" from the study of "society." There is no cleavage; there is but a gradual gradation of reference points. Some events have their locus in but a single individual, and are unsuitable for comparative investigation. Some events are widely distributed among individuals, like breathing, but have no special importance for interpersonal relations. Our starting-point as social scientists is the statement of a distinctive event which is widely spread among human beings who occupy a particular time-space manifold.

Subjective events occupy definite positions in the flow of events, and the problem of explanation is the problem of locating stable relations. Since subjective events are

not open to direct observation, but are inferred from movements, the observer, O, must infer the existence of subjective terms in the sequence by imagining what he would
experience under all the similar circumstances which he
can survey and compare to his own experience. Reduced
to its simplest terms, the observer's procedure is that of
isolating a subjective event which he wishes to investigate,
and of searching for the "externals" which will make the
conditions of its occurrence clearly communicable to others.
These externals are sometimes fairly clear, and can readily
be stated in precise, "touchable" form. The sensation of
"roughness" can be predicted to follow the application of
certain objects to specified parts of the skin. A transition
from a rough to a smooth object may also produce "flinch-
ing," which can be somewhat definitely described, and
which accompanies and (perhaps) initiates some of the
subjective events.

When any observer undertakes to talk about the state,
he may choose specific subjective experiences, such as a
sense of loyalty to a community, and say that all who have
this experience (and/or certain others) under specified
conditions make up the state. Such specified conditions
may include the act of testifying to it when asked by an
intimate friend, or when warned that the community is
in danger. The concept of the state may be amplified by
searching for the external circumstances which precipi-
tate the appearance of the subjective events which are
characteristic of stateness.

Such a method of defining the state absolves us from
"superindividual" constructs. The locus of the subjective
events is still individual. The group is not a superindividual phenomenon but a many-individual phenomenon. The
time-space abstraction of the "group" is just as "real"

or "unreal" as the time-space abstraction called the "individual." They are both equally real or unreal, and they stand and fall together.

The state has duration. It is a time-space frame of reference for individual events. Particular individuals may pass on, but if the overwhelming majority of those who occupy a certain geographical area continue to experience the subjective events of the type chosen as critical for the state, the state endures. The state is thus independent of any one individual, but it ceases to exist when enough individuals change their minds or die without procreating.

I have not yet defined the particular events which are to be treated as the marks of the state. In the sea of subjective events we must choose certain typical ones. Now definitions of this kind can be developed most advantageously when we proceed, not by a method of rigorous exclusion, but of relative emphasis. Suppose we tentatively begin by saying that the distinguishing experience is that of communal unity, when it is manifested by the use of coercion against outside and inside disturbers of the communal order. Imagine an observer is overlooking a primitive village. He sees a band of young men whose behavior he interprets thus: They are wearing painted stripes, brandishing spears, and having left the village, they engage in fighting a band of young men from a neighboring village. Is this evidence of the existence of the state? The facts are insufficient to justify a decision. Closer observation may show that these young men all live in one quarter of the village and that other young men are idling about. When the "warriors" come back, they are only cheered by those who live in one section. Those who live there may prove to be members of one family, some of whose young men have avenged a private wrong in which the village as a whole has no part. The system of claims and expectations which is the essence of the communal order is not at stake. The communal order must be involved if the state is involved.

Robert H. Lowie[1] has shown that the term "state" may properly be used to designate even the most primitive communities, and that the common distinction between a prestate and a state period of cultural development is a distortion of the facts. The simplest peoples known, the Yurok of northwestern California, the Angami of Assam, and the Ifugao of northern Luzon, all have a sense of belonging to a social unit larger than a kin group, and act in overt defense of this order. The theft of property of one kin group, when committed by a fellow-villager, is mulcted by a traditional fine, but the theft, when committed by a marauding outsider, is punished by death. In the case of adultery, warring families inside the village are merely engaged in adjusting the size of the penalty; it is universally assumed that some penalty is due.

The marginal cases notoriously play havoc with definitions. The statement made before that the distinguishing mark of the state is the experience of communal unity, when it is manifested by the use of coercion against outside and inside disturbers of a communal order, is too narrow to cover a small but extremely interesting series of facts. There may be no use of coercion against outsiders, for the war pattern may be entirely absent from the community, although violence against insiders who threaten the communal system of claims and expectations appears to be universal.

The view so far proposed rests upon a frank acceptance of social "parallelism."[2] Hans Kelsen has subjected

---

[1] *The Origin of the State.*

[2] Not to be confused with mind-body parallelism, which is not accepted.

the theories of parallelism of psychological states (common emotion and the like) to a sharp, and in many ways devastating, criticism. He says that "common emotion, common volition and common idea can never mean anything more than a description of the coincidence in consciousness of a number of individuals." But

if one really wished to consider the state as consisting of a community of consciousness such as this, and as a matter of fact, such a realistic, empirical psychological meaning is often attributed to what is called the collective will or the collective interest of the state, then, in order to avoid inadmissible fictions, one would have only to be consistent enough really to consider the state as formed only by the contents of those whose consciousness had shown the necessary agreement. One would be bound to realize that community of will, feeling or thought, as a psychological group manifestation, fluctuates tremendously at different times and places. In the ocean of psychic happenings, such communities may rise like waves in the sea and after a brief space be lost again in an ever-changing ebb and flow.[2a]

In this keen dialectic Kelsen has been led astray by a failure to recognize the time dimension of the events referred to by such a concept as the state. Subjective facts are located in time in relation to one another when viewed from the standpoint of any observer. The concept of the state involves similar events in relation to one another within a duration. The concept of the state includes this idea of a temporal frame, and can best be grasped as a relational system (a manifold) in which a certain frequency of subjective events is maintained. Thus the state is not abolished when some individuals sleep or occupy themselves with the banalities of existence, unless

[2a] Cf. Kelsen, *Der Soziologische und der juristische Staatsbegriff*; "Der Begriff des Staates und die Sozialpsychologie," *Imago*, VIII (1922), 97–141; "The Conception of the State and Social Psychology," *International Journal of Psycho-Analysis*, V (1924), 1–38.

the state is defined with reference to a duration of a few seconds or hours or days. But there is no reason whatever for choosing such a transitory frame of reference. It is just as valid to use a year as a minute, or a decade as a year, for the time dimension. Thus the state can be treated in what Kelsen speaks of as an "empirical psychological" sense. It is a durable empirical fact just so long as a certain frequency of subjective events occurs. If Kelsen agrees that contents of consciousness are "empirical," he is bound to see them in a world of duration, and he has no authority to prescribe that the state must refer to subjective events as a "knife-edge instant."

The state, then, is a time-space manifold of similar subjective events. Kelsen is incorrect in alleging that the acceptance of the parallelism of psychological phenomena as a fundamental fact destroys the state as a permanent institution.

Mere parallelism of psychological events does not give us the state, for a distinguishing type of subjective event must be selected if we are to characterize the state, the family, and other social groups. Kelsen is entirely correct in criticizing those theories of the state which invoke parallelism but neglect to specify the particular "contents of consciousness," "since not every and any group manifestations formed upon the parallelism of psychic processes is able to constitute that community."

That subjective event which is the unique mark of the state is the recognition that one belongs to a community with a system of paramount claims and expectations. This recognition of belonging does not necessarily imply an indorsement of this state of things. The essence of the state is this recognition, and the individual may indorse or deplore the fact without abolishing it. One need not be sentimentally bound to the order; it is enough if the order is noted.

This unique experience is never found unassociated with other subjective events. The recognition is usually amplified by pride in belonging to the state, and by a determination to enforce the order upon one's self and others. One's recognition of the order is usually accompanied by an idealization of one's participation in it, by an idealization of the order itself, and by a condemnation of deviations from it. All this is frequently expressed as the "sense of justice" which is the foundation of certain theories of law and the state.

The subjective event which marks the state is usually manifested in various "externals." Thus the use of coercion is well-nigh universal. The externals may be broadened to include behavior which may be treated as a substitute for coercion. Ordering and obeying relationships which function in a coercive crisis may continue when peace comes. There may be an apparent "elaboration backward" of processes antecedent to coercion in foreign and domestic affairs, and this may obviate a resort to the *ultima ratio*. The regulation of the use of coercion, and the maintenance of a certain degree of mobilization during non-crisis periods, devolves upon "leaders," who may preside over initiations, goods distribution, and general ceremonials. The process by which "heads" are selected may involve electoral colleges, elections, and agitations.

It is worth observing that in the description of political processes terms are employed which often carry no "subjective" connotations on their face. But in fact every term unavoidably carries subjective implications, and if these be ignored, there is danger that social theory will hypostatize "patterns" or "traditions" as extra-subjective entities, endowed with distinctive energies and amenable to special laws.

Often the subjective "burr" on the pattern is so dim that the subjective need scarcely ever be made explicit. Many generalizations can be made by disregarding the subjective element and focusing attention upon the transformations through which the associated patterns pass. Linguistics has achieved notable success by this method. Phonetic arrangements are named as objects of investigation and the fact discovered that those sounds which occur in certain relationships presently alter in regular ways.

It is theoretically possible to make a rough scale of descriptive conceptions according to the relative fulness or thinness of the subjective element in the pattern. To express this symbolically, the complexity of the S to the E (subjective to external) varies between nearly 100 and nearly 0. The contemporary prominence of what is called "social psychology" is due to the effort to draw attention to the consideration of patterns in which the S factor is large.

The failure to stress the subjective dimensions of the events referred to as "processes," "patterns," or "customs" is not only due to the circumstance that the S is often negligible, but that the objective element may often appear with other subjective elements. John B may rise when the national anthem is played, but he may do so "automatically" with his mind mostly preoccupied with the sore on his heel. The particular S which is meant when the full pattern of patriotic ceremonialism is discussed may thus be supplanted by another S with the same E. Thus the act becomes an entirely different phenomenon, and may erroneously be classed with patriotic ceremonialism in the full sense.

This point has far-reaching consequences for political science. The accurate comparison of behavior patterns depends upon comparison of the whole pattern. It must not be automatically inferred that S exists where E is found. The nature of the subjective factor can be inferred from extending the observation in several directions. It may be lengthened (John B may complain of a sore heel after the anthem). It may be more intensively scrutinized within the same period (John B may be seen to shift his weight from one foot to another, and to frown when one heel touches the floor).

Descriptive political conceptions are undergoing a continuous redefinition in the life of society, and unless the student of political processes is on the alert to test his descriptive conceptions in the light of changing reality, he will operate with falsifications and not with simplifications. "Voting," to choose an instance, is a concept of the greatest complexity. It does not alone consist in the dropping of ballots into urns or boxes or hats, or in the punching of buttons on a machine. These external elements, the E's, in the concept of voting are not the heart of the matter. What count especially are the subjective terms in the constellation of which these externals are a part, and a highly variable part at that. How seriously do people take the responsibility of collecting information about the personalities and issues with which they are confronted and judging these matters in the light of a conception of the public interest? Voting is an entirely different matter when individuals are coerced into casting ballots a certain way and when they are free, leisured, and interested. To call the casting of ballots under all circumstances "voting" is to deprive the term of most of its significance.

It is highly probable that the phenomenon which is loosely called voting in Chicago is today quite different from what is was fifty years ago; it is radically true that the phenomenon called voting in London is something different from voting in Cook County.[4] How are we to decide what meaning to assign to particular aspects of the political process as we observe them at different times and places? The ocean of subjective happenings which are related to external movements of a kind often associated with politics is ever changing, and it cannot be described by inventory methods. Not inventory but sampling is essential if empirical definiteness is to be attached to a term.

Speaking very generally, two modes of procedure are possible. The first is to begin with the externalities which are a rather fixed feature of a pattern of social behavior with which the investigator is familiar, and to proceed to find out how the subjective features of this pattern change. One may study "balloting" or "modes of punishment" and the like from this point of view. Throughout Western European culture there prevails such relative homogeneity of pattern that research may proceed directly from this starting-point.

The field ethnologist, who deals with cultures of a drastically different kind, must often use another avenue of approach. A set of external movements like "balloting" may not be sufficiently widespread to permit comparison. The ethnologist must proceed by stating to himself the subjective fact whose presence he would like to detect (such as a desire to participate earnestly in deciding com-

[3] Perhaps the most important part of the Merriam and Gosnell study of *Non-Voting* is the symposium of conversational scraps which suggest what balloting actually means to various classes and sections of a modern metropolitan community.

munal problems), and participate as fully in the daily life of the people as he can, in the hope that presently he will divine such a subjective viewpoint and its characteristic modes of expression. It is true that there are some movements of man whose significance is practically universal, but these are too few to enable the utter alien to dispense with a long period of participation in the day-to-day life of the people. What happens is that the observer presently begins to recognize the subjective fact behind the movements of the body, but this primitive judgment of his is a diffused judgment, based upon a mass of subtle particulars which he may long be unable to isolate in his own thinking and to point out to others; indeed, this process is never complete, or we should have a complete understanding of human life.

Obviously both points of departure for research have their advantages. The American student of social patterns in Western Europe has thousands of subtle meanings established in common with Frenchmen, Germans, or British. This is an enormous time-saving asset. If anyone undertakes to use the ethnologist's approach to a familiar culture, the results are likely to strike the participant in that culture as perfectly obvious and hardly worth the effort.[4]

The whole aim of the scientific student of society is to make the obvious unescapable, if one wishes to put the truth paradoxically. The task is to bring into the center of rational attention the movements which are critically significant in determining our judgment of subjective events, and to discover the essential antecedents of those patterns of subjectivity and of movement. For all the

[4] Such criticism has been directed against the pioneer venture of the Lynds, *Middletown*.

people who are startled to find that they have spoken
prose all their lives, there are many to emulate the rustic
who "know'd it all the time" when scientific facts are
stated about human nature. That which is known implicitly and based upon diffused, unverbalized experience
must be made explicit if new ways of dealing with the
world are to be invented.

The work of investigation may eventuate in statements
of the subjective constellations which find expression in
particular cultural forms, or in the description of the
subjective constellations which are connected with forms
which are universal for all men. The frame of reference
of the social scientist is the culture; the frame of reference of the human psychologist is the species.

What is known as the "quantitative method" provides
a valuable discipline for the student of culture because it
directs his attention toward the discovery of events which
are often enough repeated to raise a strong presumption
that a particular sequence does actually exist. These
events must be so defined that similar events can be identified by other workers. This necessitates an operational
definition of the concept, which is to say, terms must be
used to specify the position of the observer in relation to
the configuration which it is proposed to describe.[5]

The impatience among students of culture with the slow-
footed quantitative approach is partly due to the diffuse,
implicit nature of the experiences upon which is based
the judgment about a subjective event outside one's self,
and the resulting bias of the student of culture against
exaggerating the significance of items in the pattern. The
statement that "his life-experience has been hued with

[5] An able discussion of the operational concept is in P. W. Bridgman,
The Logic of Modern Physics.

melancholy" is a generalization which presupposes a knowledge of a prodigious number of facts. Or the statement that "the prestige of public office is greater in Germany than in any country" depends upon possible observations as numerous as the sands of the sea. Any proposition in Bryce's *Modern Democracies* or in Masaryk's analysis of Russian civilization refers to tremendous ranges of data. Of course, the experience of any observer is puny beside the Gargantuan proportions of the facts, and able inquirers always proceed upon a sampling basis. They get in touch with men of every income group, every religious, every racial, and every provincial group; they study the manifestations of the culture in painting, literature, mathematics, legislation, administration, and physical science.

The procedure of a Bryce was quantitative in the sense that many observations were accumulated before inferences were fixed, but it was not quantitative in the special mathematical sense of the word. The student of culture is often alienated by the quantitative approach, because the quantitative method necessitates the simplification of the number of facts taken into account; the impressionistic-quantitative approach of the student of culture gets an undivided reaction to the whole and makes simplification afterward, perhaps revising and indeed oscillating at frequent intervals.

There is more in common between the student of culture, and especially of alien culture, and the student of the individual by prolonged-interview methods than might appear at first sight. The ethnologist confronting the manifestations of an alien culture and the psychopathologist confronting the alien manifestations of the unconscious secure unique training in their research for meanings in details which escape the attention of the naïve man. Both form their idea of the subjective events from a multitude of signs, which may be spread over months of intimacy, and both are somewhat inclined to disparage the search for simple external facts which can be relied upon to indicate a specific subjective content.

The psychopathologist possesses the most elaborate known means of exploring the manifold subjective events which may be associated with external movements. Besides the conscious subjective experience there is a rich unconscious life which he is especially proficient in exposing. Thus our movements are not alone the outcome of simple conscious processes; they are said to be "overdetermined" by a variety of factors.

This concept of overdetermination is not unknown to popular common sense. We know that John B is proud of being an American, and that he wants to fight for his country; we comment slyly that John B's best girl likes the uniform, and this is one reason why he volunteers. And more than that. We know that action is not always the outcome of experiences that point in the same direction. We may know that John B. is anxious to stay on the job a month longer and to get a promotion, and that going into the army at a given moment means sacrifice. Thus his mind is partly divided against itself. What psychopathological methods do is to disclose yet wider vistas, and to expose the operation of factors which cannot be readily seen. Thus a deep longing for death may be a contributing factor to heroism.

The psychopathological approach is embarrassing less in the specific content of its revelations than in the wealth of meaning which it discovers behind what is at first glance but a simple pattern. The rôle of a particular subjective experience and of a movement cannot be fully appraised apart from the total context at which it functions, and this method discloses a wider context than common sense is aware of.

Now the multiplicity of human motives has always been a source of embarrassment to people who wanted to manage men or merely to understand them. The clumsy machinery of judicial administration has been worked out along certain lines in the hope of introducing some degree of uniformity into adjudication by limiting the consideration of the motives which operate in a particular case. The judge is thus supposed to limit himself to the determination of the existence of a particular state of facts, and to act in a particular way if these facts can be established according to a prescribed procedure. The movement toward the standardization of the discretion of public officers expresses itself in this general pattern of thought:

An act is prohibited by the state.

Certain prescribed "externals" shall establish the fact of the act having been committed.

The actor shall be dealt with in certain specified ways.

This crusade against the subjective element in the mind of the public officer is in some measure determined by the desire of the judge or civil servant to avoid responsibility.[6]

The psychopathological approach precipitates something very like a panic among those who have tried to box the manifestations of human life into conventional common-sense categories. A dozen motives seem to bloom where but one was found to bud before.

Let us see what this does for political theory. The prolonged study of individuals enables us to discern the de-

[6] Alexander and Staub have commented on this in *Der Verbrecher und seine Richter*. But it is principally due to the suspicion of the public officer.

tails of the process by which the political pattern, as we meet it in adult life, comes to be achieved by individuals.

When X runs for office or passes judgment, his behavior is overdetermined by motives, conscious and unconscious, which were organized in successive patterns during infancy, childhood and youth. The recognition of belonging to a communal order never functions in isolation, and the comparison of life-histories shows that this is implanted in the child on the basis of meanings which he has elaborated in his struggle, first against inhibitory factors in the environment, and presently, when he has introjected the demands of the environment, against his own anti-social impulses.

The early restrictions which the environment imposes upon a child are important in that they are met by reactions on his part which predispose him to meet subsequent limitations in certain ways. These early restrictions are imposed upon the child by inflicting pain or by distracting attention to pleasurable stimuli. Inhibition is thus established in the organism by *force majeur* on the part of the environment, since the infant is simply overpowered or outgeneraled by the environment.

Thus far in his development the growing individual has not become socialized in the sense that he has become self-regulating in relation to objects in the environment. The infant learns "sphincter morality" (in the phrase of Ferenczi), but this involves no emotional relationship to objects. His pleasures remain on his own body (auto-plastic), and the environment is an instrument for removing bodily tensions in the simplest manner. Gradually the child begins to look for gratification by lively erogenous activities upon the body of another. This outward push of activity is again limited and frequently blocked by *force majeur.* In the place of sexual relations to objects there now appears a new form of relation, and the child socializes himself by incorporating the practices of those about him.

It will be remembered that emotional bonds are established in two ways: by object choice (for sexual acts) and by identification. Identification, Freud writes, is the original form of emotional tie with an object. It can become a substitute for a libidinal object tie, and it may arise with every new perception of a common quality shared with some other person who is not an object of the sexual instinct. This latter is partial identification. The qualities of the object are copied (introjected). The energy for the identification is said to be supplied by aim-inhibited sexual instincts. The name of the state, the ceremonial acts of deference toward ceremonial symbols— all this and much more is characteristically a feature of the child's growth.

Characteristic, that is to say, frequent, but not invariable. Children are always brought in relation to a system of interferences and indulgences (ways of raising children), and they always perceive an order of some kind. But in some cases when a nation lives subjected to a state, the recognition of the state relation may be accompanied by resentment.

The state pattern itself prevails when many people take it as more than a mere state of affairs, and the idea is reinforced by "irrelevant meanings." Some individuals impose motivations upon others through the state pattern. These individuals, whether despots or enthusiasts, may be termed "radicles," the active ones who serve as radiating centers for the preservation and amplification of the state pattern.

Freud treats the state as an emotional unity.[7] The members of the state identify themselves with an abstract object (the idea of the state) and are bound emotionally by the partial identification which arises in perceiving an analogous relationship to the object. Kelsen has objected to this conception of the state as a real subjective unity by arguing that identification is a process between individuals, and that each member of a state cannot be thought of as having entered into personal relationships with every other member. Even if his narrow construction of identification were well founded, the state could still be treated as a real subjective unity on the basis of interlocking identifications. A has identified with B and B with C, and one of the features of B which the child A would typically take over (introject) would be the name and other symbols of the state.

Indeed, it is the interlocking character of identifications which reasonably insures the incorporation of the state symbol into the child's conception of himself. There is such a process as negative identification, the rejection of patterns which are connected with hated persons. The child is usually exposed to many adults and contemporaries, and if they all associate themselves with the state, the child is almost certain to reject only those patterns which pertain exclusively to the hated individuals. This is the fundamental reason for the staying power of patterns once accepted in a group.

It has been customary in the psychoanalytical literature on social and political processes to describe the state as a universal father-substitute. We are at length in a position to discuss the problems raised by such a generalization.

[7] See his sketch of social psychology in *Massenpsychologie und Ich-Analyse.*

The distinctive contribution of the psychopathological approach is the plurality of individual meanings which it discloses. It is an anticlimax to discover that the appearance of diversity is, after all, spurious, and that those who insist upon the strenuous simplification of human motives are justified. The point which I wish to insist upon is that the data revealed by the psychopathological procedure are far more significant for political and social science than this single-track generalization would lead one to suppose.

The special value of the psychopathological approach is that it represents a supermicroscopic method of utilizing individual instances for the study of culture patterns. If we begin with a political pattern and view it against the private histories of actual people, we find that this pattern takes on variable meaning from one individual to another, but that broad groupings of associated meanings are possible of ascertainment. Any subjective event which is frequently associated with a political pattern is important. Valid generalizations depend upon multiplying cases which are selected from different groups in the culture, and which are studied by methods capable of disclosing subjective contexts. This is the point where quantitative procedures can be made profitable to the student of culture, whose attention is riveted on patterns whose subjective element is important.

But are these studies likely to lead to anything valuable if subjective events are so variable that any subjective event may be associated with any other subjective event? Why not terminate the investigation at the outset by saying that the general law of probabilities can be relied upon to predict the frequency with which any two of a number of specified subjective events may be expected to occur together? Is not our empirical inquiry likely to terminate in an inventory of subjective states and their frequently accompanying movements, thus foredooming any effort to discover more-frequent-than-chance simultaneities, antecedents, and successions? If you look long enough, won't you find every subjective event associated with every other one?

A great many facts tend to substantiate this point of view. It is true that many imposing psychological schools of thought have arisen, run swiftly for a time in narrow channels, and then stagnated in a shallow pool of "faculties" or "instincts," mere inventories of patterns which are abstracted from all concrete events and which are therefore capable of being combined in any event in nearly infinite combinations. The search for specific connections slacks down, and the psychological mill pond is only stirred when somebody throws a stone in the pool in the form of a new theory of specific causation, which troubles the waters until it is found that the specific event is found to occur with only chance frequency. In this sense the only contributors to psychology are those who are sufficiently naïve, or sufficiently unscrupulous, to exaggerate the rôle of a specific type of experience. So we have psychologies based on "fear" or "love" or "imitation," or we have a long string of separate terms, "subfears," which multiply as the range of concrete observation widens, and the failure of the selected factor to explain everything is made manifest, or disguised.

Thus a history of psychology could be written by taking "completed" systems, analyzing the functional equivalence of the categories applied, and reducing every new system to a collection of synonyms for the terms of preceding systems. This hypothetical history of psychological theories would show how an inquirer, much impressed by certain experiences, would seize upon certain terms to describe them, and how, confronted by more and more empirical realities, he would modify the distinctive meaning of his explanatory conceptions out of existence. A history of psychoanalytic terminology, such as Rank has sketched in his treatment of genetic psychology, might be raw material for such a comparison.

Would nothing remain but dictionaries of synonyms, all rather dubious contributions to the grist of linguistic research? It might be that our projected history would show that each psychological system left a permanent legacy behind it in the form of a significant "mechanism" which had not previously been stressed. Now the whole world of "causation" is implicated in any event, and the whole number of significant mechanisms which may be discerned in the "mind at a moment" is infinite. So our hypothetical volume might conclude by accepting the assumption that some events can be brought about by more than chance frequency, subject to the reservation that experimental confirmation is never reliable as to the future. The critical configurations may never "reappear." We commonly say that the probability of an event's future repetition is greater if it has been oft repeated in the past. But there is no means of demonstrating that the future contains analogous configurations to the elapsed. The probability of the future repetition of an event is "no probability." If events appear to be predictable, this is so because our knowledge of contingencies is limited, and our sequences of similar configurations may still be treated as special instances of "no sequence." The stable is a special case of the unstable, to put the ultimate paradox. The discovery of aggregates of mechanisms whose rearrangement in short periods would enrich the apparatus of social control is the dream (the mirage?) of psychology.

Whether these objections will be well founded depends on the outcome of the test, and are incapable of dialectical resolution. It may be pointed out that the search for generalized mechanisms rests on no firmer logical foundations than the search for subjective sequences, since mechanisms are likewise aspects of the world of events, and as such are subject to the same "no probability" laws of recurrence.

It should be repeated that the aim of life-history investigation is not to arrive at such thin generalizations as the statement that the state is a universal father-imago (symbol). What matters to the student of culture is not the subjective similarities of the species, but the subjective differences among members of the same and similar cultures. The life-history configuration is precisely the one which has special meaning for the study of culture, and has its own valid place as an object of investigation in the world of events.

We may at this point briefly retrace the steps which have been taken in this monograph. The psychopathological approach has been examined in its historical setting, and the distinctive value of the free-fantasy method of using the mind has been illustrated. Its importance, likewise, for the understanding of political types has been shown with special reference to the agitators and the administrators.

The general formula for the developmental history of the political man employs three terms:

$$p \ \Big\} \ d \ \Big\} \ r = P$$

p equals private motives, *d* equals displacement on to public objects, *r* equals rationalization in terms of public interest. *P* signifies the political man, and $\Big\}$ means "transformed into."

The political man shares the *p*, the private motives which are organized in the early life of the individual, with every man, and the *d*, the displacement on to public objects, with some men. The distinctive mark of the *homo politicus* is the rationalization of the displacement in terms of public interests. Political types may be distinguished according to the specialized or the composite character of the functions which they perform and which they are desirous of performing. There are political agitators, administrators, theorists, and various combinations thereof. There are significant differences in the developmental history of each political type.

The hallmark of the agitator is the high value which he places on the response of the public. As a class the agitators are strongly narcissistic types. Narcissism is encouraged by obstacles encountered in the early love relationships, or by overindulgence and admiration in the family circle. Libido is blocked in moving outward toward objects and settles back upon the self. Sexual objects which are like the self are preferred, and a strong homoerotic component is thus characteristic. Among the agitators yearning for emotional response of the homoerotic kind is displaced upon generalized objects, and high value is put on arousing emotional responses from the community at large. The oratorical agitator, in contradistinction to the publicist, seems to show a long history of successful impostorship in dealing with his environment. Agitators differ appreciably in the specificity or in the generality of the social objects upon which they succeed in displacing their affects. Those who have been consciously attached to their parents and who have been successful impostors ("model children") are disposed to choose remote and general objects. Those who have been conscious of suppressing serious grievances against the intimate circle, and who have been unable to carry off the impostor's rôle successfully, are inclined to pick more immediate and personal substitutes. The rational structure tends toward theoretical completeness in the former case. The object choices for displaced affects depend on the models which are offered when the early identifications are being made. When the homoerotic attitude is the important one, the assaultive, provocative relation to the environment is likely to display itself; when the impotence fear is active, grandiose reactions figure more prominently.

As a group the administrators are distinguished by the value which they place upon the co-ordination of effort in continuing activity. They differ from the agitators in that their affects are displaced on less remote and abstract objects. In the case of one important group this failure to achieve abstract objects is due to excessive preoccupation with specific individuals in the family circle, and to the correlative difficulty of defining the rôle of the self. Very original and overdriving administrators show a fundamental pattern which coincides with that of the agitators. The differences in specific development are principally due to the culture patterns available for identification at critical phases of growth. Another group of administrators is recruited from among those who have passed smoothly through their developmental crises. They have not overrepressed powerful hostilities, but either sublimated these drives, or expressed them boldly in the intimate circle. They display an impersonal interest in the task of organization itself, and assert themselves with firmness, though not with overemphasis, in professional and intimate life. Their lack of interest in abstractions is due to the fact that they have never needed them as a means of dealing with their emotional problems. They can take or leave general ideas without using them to arouse widespread affective responses from the public. Tied neither to abstractions nor to particular people, they are able to deal with both in a context of human relations, impersonally conceived. Their affects flow freely; they are not affectless, but affectively adjusted.

The psychopathological method was also employed to discover the significance of political convictions, for it is evident that beliefs are expressive of a rational and logical "manifest" content, and that they symbolize a host of private motives. In this connection there was passed in review the history of a compulsive conformist to the pattern of the family, and the histories of several nonconformists. The private meaning of militarism and pacifism, and of the pessimism and censoriousness of old age, were explored.

Attention was then turned from the case-history fragments to the problem of drawing out the implications of intensive personality study for the theory of the collective political process.

Political movements derive their vitality from the displacement of private affects upon public objects. The affects which are organized in the family are redistributed upon various social objects, such as the state. Political crises are complicated by the concurrent reactivation of specific primitive impulses. One might suppose that when important decisions are in process of being made society would deliberate very calmly; but the disproportionality between the behavior of man during wars, revolutions, and elections, and the requirements of rational thinking is notorious. Evidently a reactivating process is at work here; there is a regressive tendency to reawaken primitive sadism and lust.

Political symbols are particularly adapted to serve as targets for displaced affect because of their ambiguity of reference, in relation to individual experience, and because of their general circulation. Although the dynamic of politics is the tension of individuals, all tension does not produce political acts. Nor do all emotional bonds lead to political action. Political acts depend upon the symbolization of the discontent of the individual in terms of a more inclusive self which champions a set of demands for social action.

Political demands are of only a limited relevance to the changes which will produce permanent reductions in the tension level of society. The political methods of coercion, exhortation, and discussion assume that the rôle of politics is to solve conflicts when they have happened. The ideal of a politics of prevention is to obviate conflict by the definite reduction of the tension level of society by effective methods, of which discussion will be but one. The preventive point of view insists upon a continuing audit of the human consequences of social acts, and especially of political acts. The achievement of the ideal of preventive politics depends less upon changes in social organization than upon improving the methods and the education of the social administrators and the social scientists.

The empirical material utilized in the book was brought together in the course of prolonged interviews with individuals under unusually intimate conditions. At the present time there are no satisfactory records of what actually happens under these interview conditions, and it is important for the future of personality study to improve the methodology of these procedures. The objectification of what transpires in the interview can be secured by arranging for a verbatim transcript of what goes on, and by recording the physical changes which occur.

Effective personality research depends upon viewing the personality reactions as a system, and upon perfecting the procedures by which the substitutive reactions of this system may be exposed. Broadly speaking, the personality may be treated as a system of object orientations, adjustive thought, autistic reveries, and somatic reactions. The problem is to introduce interferences into the system, and to reveal the substitutive reactions for comparison and further analysis. Every "fact" about personality events is to be defined from the standpoint of a specified observer, and a major problem for the future is to check the "facts" of the observer in the prolonged interview against the "facts" of observers in other situations. Personality research can be made more valuable for political science when the adult reactions are clearly seen which chiefly interest the political scientist (see Appendix B).

What, in general terms, is the relationship between research upon the individual and upon society? There is no cleavage; there is but a gradation of reference points. Events which are of collective interest always have an individual locus, and these events may be studied in their relation to the sequence of events "within the individual" or in relation to the events "among individuals." The distinctive event which serves as the orienting frame for political research is the recognition of belonging to a community with a system of paramount claims and expectations. This event, when distributed with sufficient frequency among the individuals who occupy a given territory during a specified time period, define the state, which is thus a manifold of events. Research which studies the order of events "within the individual" or "among individuals" is equally relevant to the understanding of the state; the difference is a difference of starting-point and not of final result.

When the state is seen as a manifold of events the conditions of whose occurrence are to be understood, the theoretical foundation is laid for both the intensive and the distributive inquiries upon which the politics of prevention can be built. In particular will it be possible to profit as the years pass, and as psychopathology widens the range of its investigations, and increases the dependability of its methods.

APPENDIX A

SELECT BIBLIOGRAPHY

The literature of psychoanalysis from its inception to 1926 is conveniently available in John Rickman's *Index Psychoanalyticus, 1893–1926*. The *Gesammelte Schriften* of Sigmund Freud have been published by the Internationaler Psychoanalytischer Verlag, Vienna, in eleven volumes. This publishing house puts out most of the literature of the circle around Freud. Of Freud's books the beginner may be referred to his *General Introduction to Psychoanalysis, The Interpretation of Dreams,* and *Three Contributions to Sexual Theory*. An English edition of Freud's collected papers is in process of publication. The most important technical journal is the *Internationale Zeitschrift für arztliche Psychoanalyse*. There is an English journal, *the International Journal of Psycho-Analysis,* and an American one, *The Psychoanalytic Review*. (A French periodical has recently appeared.)

Among the "orthodox" psychoanalytical treatises the following are of particular importance:

FERENCZI, S. *Bausteine zur Psychoanalyse*. Leipzig, 1926.

———. *Versuch einer Genitaltheorie*. Leipzig, 1924.

FERENCZI, S., and HOLLOS, S. *Psychoanalysis and the Psychic Disorder of General Paresis,* "Nervous and Mental Disease Monograph Series," No. 42. New York and Washington, 1925.

The psychological manifestations of a physical disease are predicted on the basis of the psychoanalytical theory of personality development. Of great methodological importance.

ABRAHAM, K. *Klinische Beitrage zur Psychoanalyse aus den Jahren 1907–20*. Leipzig, etc., 1921.

———. *Psychoanalytische Studien zur Charakterbildung*. Leipzig, etc., 1925.

The most influential approach to the problem of character formation. Amplified in many directions by Jones, Glover, etc.

ALEXANDER, F. *Psychoanalyse der Gesamtpersönlichkeit.* Leipzig, etc., 1927.

A notably lucid presentation of the general theory. Recently translated as *The Psychoanalysis of the Total Personality* and published in the "Nervous and Mental Disease Monograph Series."

HARTMANN, H. *Die Gründlagen der Psychoanalyse.* Leipzig, 1927.

A very important book which views analytical concepts in relation to the data of experimental psychology.

DEUTSCH, FELIX. "Experimentelle Studien zur Psychoanalyse," *Internationale Zeitschrift*, IX (1923), 484–96.

Reports the demonstration of the mechanism of repression by the use of post-hypnotic suggestion.

KEMPF, E. *Psychopathology.* St. Louis, 1921.

Stresses the function of the autonomic functions, and undertakes to amplify psychoanalytical theory in this direction.

Among those who have broken off from Freud, after having been associated with him, are Stekel, Jung, and Adler. Stekel has published ten volumes of case histories which are valuable for the beginner who needs to acquire a sense of what sort of thing the human mind is capable. The other two are of more theoretical importance. Jung's *Psychological Types* is of the most immediate interest to social scientists, although his speculations about the "racial unconscious" are suggestive. Alfred Adler's standpoint is set out in his *Individual Psychology*. His circle in Vienna publishes a journal.

An excellent manual is *The Structure and Meaning of Psychoanalysis* (New York, 1930), by William Healy, Augusta F. Bronner, and Anna Mae Bowers.

The psychoanalytical movement can be placed in the general perspective of medical psychology by referring to such a manual as William A. White's *Outlines of Psychiatry* or Bernard Hart's *Psychopathology*. There are excellent books in German on medical psychology by Kronfeld, Birnbaum, Schilder, Kretschmer, and many others. The general movements in the field can be followed in the *American Journal of Psychiatry* or the *Journal of Nervous and Mental Diseases,* the latter of which is edited by William A. White and Smith Ely Jelliffe, who also supervise the well-known series of books, usually translations, called the "Nervous and Mental Disease Monograph Series." Pierre Janet's *Psychological Healing* reviews the general history of psychopathology. Among the innumerable articles and books which undertake to appraise the clinical and normal implications of psychoanalysis, the symposium edited by Hans Prinzhorn may be chosen, *Krisis der Psychoanalyse* (Leipzig, 1928), Band I (the projected second volume will not appear). Otto Rank, who has likewise broken with Freud, is publishing a series of books on the psychoanalytical interview which promises to serve as a bridge between the general theory and the objective studies of the interview situation which are in progress in America.

On the special problem of personality and character types, the volume by A. A. Roback, *The Psychology of Character*, may be instanced as a very comprehensive guide to the literature. His *A Bibliography on Personality* is also available. An acute analysis of typologies was offered by O. Selz before the German experimental psychologists in 1923. See the following:

SELZ, O. "Über die Personlichkeitstypen und die Methoden ihrer Bestimmung," *Bericht über den VIII. Kongress für experimentelle Psychologie*. Jena, 1924.

KLÜVER, H. "An Analysis of Recent Work on the Problem of Psychological Types," *Journal of Nervous and Mental Diseases*, LXII, No. 6 (December, 1925).

The current output is reviewed from time to time in relation to tests by Mark A. May, Gordon W. Allport, and certain other psychologists who are especially interested in the field. The *Psychological Index* can be consulted for the purpose of keeping abreast of the large quantity of published material.

The most influential recent book is Kretschmer's *Physique and Character*. The somatic factors in personality are stated with charm and brevity by E. Miller, *Types of Mind and Body*. Useful summary and critical volumes are by William I. Thomas and Dorothy S. Thomas, *The Child in America* (New York, 1928), chapters viii–xiii inclusive, and by R. G. Gordon, *Personality* (New York, 1926).

The psychoanalytical literature which has undertaken to deal with politics or politicians explicitly may be appended here:

PFISTER, OSKAR. "Analytische Untersuchungen über die Psychologie des Hasses und der Versöhnung," *Jahrbuch der Psychoanalyse*, II (1910), 134–78.

————. "Die Bedeutung der Psychoanalyse für die Staats- und Gesellschaftslehre" (Vortrag an VI. Int. Psa. Kong., Hague, September 8–11, 1920), abstract in *Internationale Zeitschrift*, VI, 400.

————. "Die menschlichen Einigungsbestrebungen im Lichte der Psychoanalyse," *Imago*, XII (1926), 126–35.

The *Imago* is the psychoanalytical journal which is devoted to applications of psychoanalytical theory to the interpretation of culture.

SACHS, HANNS. "Die Bedeutung der Psychoanalyse für Probleme der Soziologie" (Vortrag), abstract in *Centralblatt für Psychoanalyse*, II (1911), 464–69.

————. "Ein Traum Bismarcks," *Internationale Zeitschrift*, I (1913), 80–83.

SACHS, HANNS, and RANK, OTTO. *Die Bedeutung der Psychoanalyse für die Geisteswissenschaften*. Wiesbaden, 1913.

This was published in the "Grenzfragen des Nerven und Seelenlebens," No. 93, a series which contains many volumes of great interest to social scientists. Kretschmer now is the responsible editor. The book also appears as No. 23 in the "Nervous and Mental Disease Monograph Series."

RANK, OTTO. "Der 'Familienroman' in der Psychologie des Attentaters," *Der Künstler* (virte vermehrte Auflage; Leipzig, etc., 1925), pp. 142–48.

This fragment first appeared in 1911.

STORFER, A. J. "Zur Sonderstellung des Vatermordes." Leipzig, etc., 1911.

Parricide and regicide are punished with unusual severity in different legal systems.

ABRAHAM, KARL. "Amenhotep IV (Echnaton)," *Imago*, I (1912), 334–60.

One of the earliest applications of analytical concepts to a historical personage.

FREUD, SIGMUND. *Totem und Taboo.* Leipzig, etc., 1913.

Outlines his hypothesis of the origin of culture in an original parricide by a band of revolting brothers, who resented the monopoly of the females by the old man of the tribe, and who undertook to repress memories of the crime. See the discussion by Malinowski of this hypothesis in *Sex and Repression in Savage Society* (New York, 1927).

――――. "Zeitgemasses über Krieg und Tod," *Imago,* IV (1915–16), 1–21.

――――. *Massenpsychologie und Ich-Analyse.* Leipzig, etc., 1921.

An application of Freud's theories to the psychology of crowds and social institutions. See William McDougall, "Professor Freud's Group Psychology and His Theory of Suggestion," chapter xvii of *Problems of Personality* (ed. Campbell and others; New York, 1925).

――――. *Unbehagen der Kultur.* Leipzig, etc., 1929.

JEKELS, LUDWIG. "Der Wendepunkt im Leben Napoleons I," *Imago,* III (1914), 313–81.

KAPLAN, LEO. "Der tragische Held und der Verbrecher," *ibid.,* IV (1915), 96–124.

JONES, ERNEST. "War and Sublimation." Read before the British Association for the Advancement of Science, Section of Physiology, September 10, 1915; published in *Reports* of the Association, LXXXV, 699 ff.

――――. (ed.). *The Social Aspects of Psychoanalysis.* London, 1923.

TAUSK, VIKTOR. "Zur Psychologie des Deserteurs," *Zeitschrift,* IV (1916–17), 193–204, 228–40.

BLÜHER, HANS. *Die Rolle der Erotik in der männlichen Gesellschaft.* 2 vols. Jena, 1917.

BERNFELD, SIEGFRIED. "Die Psychoanalyse in der Jugendbewegung," *Imago,* V (1919), 283–89.

――――. "Über eine typische Form der männlichen Pubertät," *ibid.,* IX (1923), 169–188.

FEDERN, PAUL. *Die Vaterlose Gesellschaft.* Leipzig, etc., 1919.

CLARK, L. PIERCE. "A Psychologic Study of Abraham Lincoln," *ibid.,* VIII (1921), 1–21.

————. "A Psycho-historical Study of the Epileptic Personality in the Genius," *ibid.*, IX (1922), 367–401.

————. "The Narcism of Alexander the Great," *Ibid.*, X (1923), 156–69.

————. *Napoleon: Self-Destroyed*. New York, 1929.

KOLNAI, AUREL. *Psychoanalyse und Soziologie*. Leipzig, etc., 1920.

LAZELL, EDWARD W. "Psychology of War and Schizophrenia," *Psychoanalytic Review*, VII (1920), 224–45.

RINALDO, JOEL. *The Psychoanalysis of the Reformer*. New York, 1921.

WHITE, WILLIAM A. *Thoughts of a Psychiatrist on the War and After*. New York, 1919.

LOW, BARBARA. "Civic Ideals: Some Psycho-analytical Considerations," *Sociological Review*, 1922.

BOVEN, WILLIAM. "Alexander der Grosse," *Imago*, VIII (1922), 418–39.

BERGER, G. "Zur Theorie der menschlichen Feindseligkeit," *ibid.*, IX (1923), 344–67.

LORENZ, EMIL. *Der politische mythus, Beitrage zur mythologie der Kultur*. Leipzig, etc., 1923.

Illustrates the state-father relationship from the lore and literature of many cultures.

REIK, THEODOR. *Geständniszwang und Strafbedürfnis: Probleme der Psychoanalyse und der Kriminologie*. Leipzig, etc., 1925.

Outlines in masterly fashion the implications of the need for punishment and the compulsion to confess for criminology. Reik has also published extensively on religion from the psychoanalytical standpoint.

KOHN, ERWIN, *Lasalle der Führer*. Leipzig, etc., 1926.

ALEXANDER, FRANZ, and STAUB, HUGO. *Der Verbrecher und seine Richter*. Vienna, 1929.

A sketch of criminology from the psychoanalytical standpoint, drawing heavily on Alexander's conception of the neurotic character, as distinguished from the neurotics who show hysteric or compulsive symptoms.

FRIEDJUNG, JOSEF K. "Zur Psychologie des kleinen Politikers,"
Imago, XIV (1928), 498–501.

Among those who have undertaken from allied fields to apply
psychoanalytic viewpoints may be mentioned William F. Ogburn,
who read a paper before the economists in 1918; Thomas D.
Eliot, sociologist; Harry Elmer Barnes, historical sociologist;
E. D. Martin, social psychologist; Preserved Smith, historian;
R. V. Harlow, historian; W. H. R. Rivers, ethnologist; and Theodore Schroeder, lawyer. See especially:

BARNES, HARRY ELMER. *The New History and the Social Studies*, chap. iii. New York, 1925.

Discusses the bibliography in English.

SWOBODA, HERMANN. "Zur Psychologie des Parlamentarismus,"
Oesterreichische Rundschau, Band XIV, Heft 1, January 1,
1908.

————. "Die Kunst des Regierens," *ibid.*, Band XVII, December 15, 1908.

————. "Der Volksvertreter," *ibid.*, Band XXXII, Heft 3, August 1, 1912.

These articles of Swoboda are the first well-considered applications of
psychoanalysis to politics by a non-specialist. The first article treats the
rôle of parliamentarism as "catharsis," and specifically refers to the work
of Breuer and Freud.

Aside from specifically psychoanalytical efforts to interpret
individuals and collective trends, there have been many efforts on
the part of other psychiatrists and physicians, or their followers,
to offer such interpretations. The whole literature of "pathography" is abstracted and discussed here:

LANGE-EICHBAUM, WILHELM. *Genie-Irrsinn, und Ruhm*. Leipzig,
1928.

Students of politics will be most interested in the references
and abstracts concerning Rousseau, Alexander the Great, Amenhotep IV, Bismarck, Blücher, emperors and princes, Frederick
the Great, Lincoln, Loyola, Ludwig II of Bavaria, Napoleon, and

Robespierre. Möbius put "pathography" on a scientific basis. The following is one of the best of the "pathographies," since it stresses the diseased aspects of the personality in the perspective of the total development of the subject's career:

HEIDENHAIN, ADOLF, *J.-J. Rousseau, Persönlichkeit, Philosophie und Psychose* "Grenzfragen des Nerven- und Seelenlebens," Heft 117. Munich, 1924.

The study of the effect of individual pathology on culture, and of culture upon individual pathology, is envisaged as a program in the following:

BIRNBAUM, KARL. *Grundzüge der Kulturpsychopathologie,* "Grenzfragen des Nerven- und Seelenlebens," Heft 116. Munich, 1924.

The reckless extension of individual pathological terms to the state of society as a whole has caused much confusion, but a case can be made out for a valid use of the concept of the pathological. Thus:

SCHNEERSOHN, F. "Zur Grundlegung einer Völker-und Massen-psychopathologie (Soziopsychopathologie)," *Ethos,* I (1925–26), 81–120.

This includes an exhaustive bibliography of the efforts of psychiatrists to extend their conceptions to society, and a detailed consideration of the methodological issues involved.

Special attention should be called to the forthcoming volume by Harry Stack Sullivan on *Personal Psychopathology* in which a systematic treatment of the whole field of psychiatry and sociology is presented. Dr. Sullivan has vastly stimulated a *rapprochement* between physician and social scientist in the United States. See the *Proceedings* of the two colloquiums on personality investigation, held under the auspices of the American Psychiatric Association, first published in the *American Journal of Psychiatry* for May, 1929, and May, 1930, and separately obtainable.

APPENDIX B

QUESTION LIST ON POLITICAL PRACTICES

This question list refers directly to the organized political life of the subject. Questions which are designed to elicit preferences are not included. For general personality questions and trait lists, the usual sources may be consulted for suggestions.[1]

The question list here must, of course, be modified if used orally or with naïve subjects. An effort is always to be made to elicit specific incidents which arise in the mind. "Reminiscences" and not theories about the self are desired.

1. List the various associations and organizations of which you have been a member and in which you enjoyed rights which were approximately equal to those exercised by everyone else. Specify in each case whether you were almost inactive, moderately active, quite active. State when you became a

[1] More specifically, Kretschmer's *Psychobiogramm*, published in H. Hoffmann, *Das Problem des Charakteraufbaus*, as an appendix; Heyman's trait list (republished in *Gesammelte Kleinere Schriften*, Dritter Teil); the psychograms of W. Stern (in *Die differentielle Psychologie in ihren methodischen Grundlagen*), of Baade, Lipman, and Stern (*Zeitschrift für angewandete Psychologie*, Band III), of P. Margis (Breslau dissertation, 1911, *Das Problem und die Methoden der Psychographie mit einer Individualanalyse von E. T. A. Hoffmann*), of L. Lewin (*Friedrich Hebbel: Beitrag zu einem Psychogramm* [Berlin, 1913]), of E. Stern ("Patho-psychographische Untersuchungen," *Archiv für Psychiatrie und Nervenkrankheiten*, Band LXI), of F. Kehrer and S. Fischer, ("Modell einer klinisch-experimentellen Pathographie," *Zeitschrift für die gesamte Neurologie und Psychiatrie*, Band LXXXV); the outlines of Dr. Paul Federn (*Schema der Libidoaufnahme*, MSS in my possession), of F. L. Wells (MSS in my possession), of G. V. Hamilton, of Adolf Meyer (mimeographed MSS in my possession), of Amsden and Hoch, of Floyd Allport, and the lists of Woodworth, Laird, House, Freyd and Thurstone.

member and how your subsequent activity fluctuated. Give
dates when possible. Remember that you have been a member of various democratically organized political units. Mention also the prep-school class organizations, school and college organizations, alumni associations, profession organizations, civic associations, parties, and elective public offices. Organizations which were autocratically organized
(that is, which exercised authority over those who had no
formal right to choose the officials) should not be included.
Do not omit associations of war veterans, Daughters or Sons
of the Revolution, pacifists, anarchists, reform agitators, constitutional defense leagues, etc.

2. List the various organizations with which you have been associated either as one in autocratic authority or as one subject to autocratic authority. This should include schools
which you have attended, appointive offices in the government, most business connections, trusteeships, etc.

3. List your various free-lance activities which have involved
scarcely any organization but which have been a source of
income. Partnerships which have involved practically no
staff, private secretaryships, and such are meant to be listed
here.

The following questions are intended to bring out the
salient facts in connection with your relationship to each
democratically organized and autocratically organized association or institution with which you were affiliated.
Answer for each organization which you have listed in so
far as applicable.

4. Just how did you become a member of this organization?
What steps did you take? Who helped you? Why were
you taken in? If you organized this body, why did you do
it? When did you first entertain the idea? How did your
plans develop? What assistance did you get and by what
means? What was your reputation inside the organization
when you first came in? Were you, for instance, ignored or

regarded as promising or accepted and given responsibility immediately?

5. What friends or enemies did you have inside the organization when you first came into it?

6. To what offices or positions of authority in the organization were you elected or appointed?

7. In each case explain how it came about. When did you first entertain the idea that selection was possible? How much did you hesitate and ponder before deciding to try for the position or before accepting it if it was thrust upon you? What alternatives did you consider? With whom did you talk over the matter? What was urged on you? What were the disadvantages which deterred you or the advantages which lured you? Just what did you do to get the office or position? Who were your chief aids? Who were your chief competitors? What were the points in your favor and in favor of the others? How did the various cliques, groups, and other components of the organization line up? Sketch your strategy and practices in dealing with each one before selection. Did any issues of policy figure and how?

8. What were the cases in which you ran or were considered at one stage or another for selection? Answer the questions as before for each instance.

9. What appointive power or influence did you exercise in office? Whom did you consult in making or influencing these appointments? To what extent did you consider competence? The rewarding of friends? The division or elimination of your opponents?

10. What objectives, if any, had you thought out when you assumed responsibility?

11. What were the chief issues on which you took a position? How did your influence make itself felt in each instance (in public speaking, interviewing, appointive pressure, etc.)? How did each major issue happen to emerge? How did you arrive at your position? Whom did you consult? What considerations were balanced on both sides of the question? To what extent did you make issues by interjecting specific proposals into the situation? How did you happen to do this? What were the elements in the organization which were lined up on either side of the question? What concessions

did you make in order to achieve your ends? Do you regard your concessions as too cheaply bought as you look
back upon them? What results did you secure which satisfy you?

12. During your tenure were there personal misunderstandings,
quarrels, and hatreds between you and anybody? How did
they come about? What did you do and what was the relation of what you did to what happened?

13. Were there personal misunderstandings, quarrels, and antip-
athies among others inside the organization which you were
asked to settle or which you tried to settle? What did you
do and what relation did it bear to what finally happened?

14. Were there personal misunderstandings, quarrels, and antip-
athies between members of your own organization and people in other organizations which you were asked to settle or
which you tried to settle? What did you do and what relation did it bear to what finally happened?

15. Did your organization have any ill feelings as a body for
other organizations or groups when you came into office?
What did you do to inflame or reduce it? What effect? Why?

16. Did your organization have any friendly feelings as a body
for other organizations or groups? What did you do to
cement or to disrupt these relations? Why? With what effect on the course of events?

17. Did your organization develop any friendly or unfriendly
relations with organizations or groups to which they had
been previously indifferent during your term in office?
What did you do that had anything to do with this result?
Why?

18. Did your organization use physical, legal, or other forms of
pressure upon any other organization or group during your
term? What was your rôle in suggesting, supporting, directing, or obstructing the adoption of these tactics? Why?
What resulted?

19. Did your organization use physical, legal, economic, or
other forms of pressure upon any of its own members during
your term? What was your rôle in suggesting, supporting,
directing, or obstructing the adoption of these tactics? Why?
With what effect?

20. By whom were you praised during and after your term of office for your record? How were you praised or recognized and honored and for what? Effect on you?

21. By whom were you adversely criticized during and after your term in office for your record? How were you censured and for what? Effect on you?

22. Were you re-elected or reappointed, promoted or demoted, after serving your term or before? Why?

23. How did you get along with your immediate superiors, collaborators, and assistants? To what extent did you manipulate them? What different tactics did you employ with each? What success?

24. What were your formal and ceremonial duties in the organization as an officer? Did you enjoy them?

25. How did you enjoy your other official activities?

26. As a non-official, or non-position-holding member of the organization, what did you enjoy about it? The ceremonies? The routine operations? The uncertain features?

27. As a member of the rank and file, what policies and activities did you initiate, support, or oppose? Why? How much did you do and to what effect? How did the elements of the organization line up? Were you usually in the minority or the majority? What elements were usually with you?

28. How did your reputation change during your years in the organizations?

29. What particular friends and enemies did you acquire?

30. As a member of the rank and file, did you have personal misunderstandings, quarrels, and hatreds between you and other members? Why? What did you do? Results?

31. Did you arbitrate any grievances or try to smooth them out? Success? Why?

32. What was your attitude toward other organizations or groups with which your organization either competed or had some relations? As a member of the rank and file, what did you do to change or intensify prevailing attitudes? Influence?

33. Did your organization use physical or other means of pressure against outside organizations and other members of your organization? As a member of the rank and file, what did you do and with what effect? Did you think your organization was the best of its kind?

34. Have you severed your connection or become inactive? Why?

35. If you are still active, what are your plans and hopes?

36. How did this particular organization touch the administrative, legislative, and judicial branches of the government? The political parties? How? What methods were used to bring pressure to bear? What was your part in them?

37. As you look back on your life in the organization do you think of practices which you indulged in or tolerated which you regard as perhaps questionable? Instances? Did you so regard them at the time? What would have happened if you had not indulged in them? Should an organization be run on a different basis now?

38. What effect did life in the organization have upon your activity in the politics of the community at large? Did you have impulses to express yourself publicly or privately upon matters which you felt it expedient to follow? Or were you driven to such expression and activity?

39. If you were to judge entirely in terms of your experience as a member of this organization, what would be your judgment of the honesty and efficiency of the public service and the party machine?

40. What political prejudices or philosophies were current among various elements inside the organization?

41. Think of various members of this organization who were rather typical. How did you act toward them when you met them? What topics of conversation, of anecdote, etc., did you indulge in? What activities in common were there?

42. Did you think that you were imposed upon by any members as you look back upon it now? Did you estimate some of them too highly? Who? Why?

43. Did you underestimate some? Who? Why?

44. Were you estimated too high or too low? By whom? Why?

45. What things apart from common dishonesty would have caused you to lose standing in the organization? What opinions and activities would have compromised you?

46. Did you risk loss of standing at any time by word or deed? Were you tempted to? Why did you refrain?

47. When you tried to add others to the organization, whom did you seek? What type of people, in general, were you interested in?

48. Did the organization live up to your ideal? Why?
49. Who were the most powerful ones in the organization at different periods? What were your relations with them? What did you do consciously to win them? Success? What did you do to antagonize them? How did they take it? What, in short, was the attitude of the leaders toward you?
50. Did you ever have a sense of frustration arising from your failure to participate in discussions of policy, either because you hesitated to express yourself or because you expressed yourself badly?
51. What is your matured judgment of the utility of this organization in society?
52. How did your organization connections help or hurt you socially or any other way?
53. How did your outside connections help or hurt you in the organization?
54. What, generally speaking, were your advantages and disadvantages with reference to securing and holding a prominent position in the organization?
55. In general, what place did this organization play in your life?
56. With respect to each one of your so-called free-lance or very personal activities, answer such questions as these: How did you happen to take it up? Upon what factors would your success and failure depend? What did you do to manage the persons upon whom success or failure depended? With what result? What reaction did your experience have upon your outlook upon political life generally?

POLITICS: Who Gets What, When, How

POLITICS

Who Gets What, When, How

BY HAROLD D. LASSWELL

☆ ☆

THE FREE PRESS · GLENCOE · ILLINOIS

PREFACE

The interpretation of politics found in this book under-
lies the working attitude of practicing politicians. One
skill of the politician is calculating probable changes in
influence and the influential.

This version of politics is not novel to all students of
social development. Yet it is constantly in danger of at-
tenuation. Even now there is no brief book in English
which states this standpoint for student, teacher, scholar,
citizen, and politician, and which sees it in relation to
passing time.

Certain practical and theoretical consequences follow
from the lack of opportune reminders of this fundamental
standpoint. That practicing politicians, caught in the immediate, lose sight of the remote, is to be expected. That
systematic students, exempted from instant and overwhelming necessity, often grow precise about the trivial, need
occasion no surprise.

Concepts for the study of influence must be changed or
invented when influence is sought by novel means or under
changed conditions. In epochs of rapid development, there
is need to reassess the relevance of intellectual effort. Of
the need for orientation in our day nearly everyone is convinced. A society newly devoted to planning may (as Karl
Mannheim contends) require new styles of thought.

The spirit of critical discontent is rife in the world outside the Soviet Union. Well-built highroads of intellectual achievement are traveled with reluctance, not in protest against the engineering, but in skepticism of starting point and destination. Much of the literature of comparative government, law, and administration is devoted to the taxonomy of institutional practice, with little reference to the living forms which are thereby helped or hurt. The rude glare of political analysis is dimmed in the literature of political quietism.

British, Austrian, and American economics are not impervious to the intellectual weather. Classical economics, if we are to believe Ricardo, was concerned with the distribution of wealth, one of the principal means of influence. The conditions of wealth distribution under conditions of free competition have been carefully phrased. Distribution under other conditions was understressed in classical analysis. Modern events have sharply reminded us that distribution depends on myth and violence (on faith and brigandage) as well as bargaining.

Little more has been done in this book than to state and illustrate the standpoint. The connection between what is written here and what has been written elsewhere is to some extent shown in the bibliographic notes to the separate chapters which are printed at the end of the book. Specialists will be at no loss to distinguish between the original and the large body of derivative material. Those who accept the frame of reference here proposed will share common standards to guide future intellectual effort.

There are many practical implications which follow from various aspects of this analysis. My findings are in many respects parallel to the concluding chapters of *The Promise of American Politics* by my friend, colleague, and representative, Professor and State Senator T. V. Smith. This is most gratifying to me in every one of my capacities as friend, colleague, and constituent.

The quotation from *An Experiment in Autobiography*, published by The Macmillan Company, is by kind permission of H. G. Wells. The sentences from Eugene O'Neill's *Mourning Becomes Electra* are reprinted by courtesy of Random House.

CHICAGO, ILLINOIS
June, 1936.

H. D. L.

CONTENTS

PART I

ELITE

PART II

METHODS

PART III

RESULTS

PART IV

RÉSUMÉ

CHAPTER I

ELITE

The study of politics is the study of influence and the influential. The science of politics states conditions; the philosophy of politics justifies preferences. This book, restricted to political analysis, declares no preferences. It states conditions.

The influential are those who get the most of what there is to get. Available values may be classified as *deference, income, safety*. Those who get the most are *elite;* the rest are *mass*.

The distribution of deference is relatively clear in a formal hierarchy. The peak of the Roman Catholic pyramid is occupied by a comparatively small number of officials. There are one Pope, 55 cardinals, 22 apostolic delegates, 256 vicars apostolic, 245 archbishops, 1,578 bishops. The Communist party in the Soviet Union comes to a sharp head in the Political Committee of nine or ten members. The looser structure of government in the United States none the less confers special influence upon the Supreme Court of nine, the Presidency of one, and the Congress of a few hundred. Although any bright and talkative lad in the United States may be told that one day he may be president, only eight boys made it in the last generation. The potent American Senate, though comparatively large, would provide a place for only 480 senators each generation were none reelected. Deference pyramids, in form and in fact, are steep.

The distribution of safety is usually less inequitable than the distribution of deference, and may often show a negative relationship to it. Thus one study showed that 31.9 per cent of a series of 423 monarchs of different countries and different periods died by violence. Forty per cent of the presidents of the Republic of Bolivia came to a violent end. Such figures may be put in rough perspective by recalling that deaths by violence (including suicide) in the United States were 7.2 per cent of the whole number of deaths in 1921; 12.1 per cent of the presidents of the United States and of France, and 9 per cent of the Catholic popes, died by violence. The relative safety of whole populations varies from epoch to epoch. Five of every thousand Frenchmen who died in the seventeenth century were killed or wounded in battle. The number rose to twelve in the eighteenth century, thirteen in the nineteenth, and fourteen in the twentieth.

In countries of Western European civilization wealth and income are inequitably distributed. In 1928, a year of great business and speculative activity, the national income of the United States was $541 per capita, which was two and a half times the figure for France or Germany (the dollar is quoted in terms of the purchasing power of 1913). In 1913, just before the World War, the figure had been $368 per capita in the United States. In the interim the United States showed the largest absolute increase among the major powers, but the sharpest relative advance was made by Japan, whose per capita rose from $22 in 1913 to $53 in 1925. The United Kingdom, next to the United States in absolute numbers, stood at $250 in 1911 and $293 in 1928. Russia rose from $52 in 1914 to $96 in 1928, which was greater than the relative gain of France or Germany. Italy dropped from $108 in 1914 to $96 in 1928.

There are sharp differences in the apportionment of income within given communities. Ten per cent of the population of the United States took one-third of the money income of the nation in the years between 1918 and 1926.

The values of deference, safety, and income which have just been singled out are representative and not exclusive values. Political analysis could make use of other combinations, and the resulting elite comparisons would differ. The findings of political analysis also vary when different characteristics of the influential are chosen for emphasis. One form of analysis considers the division of values according to *skill*.

Fighting skill is plainly one of the most direct ways by which men have come to the top, whether the fighting be done in the name of god, nation, or class. Mustafa Kemal Pasha fought in the Turco-Italian War in 1911, and commanded the northern section of the Turkish army in Gallipoli in 1915, and elsewhere. Mussolini and Hitler got their baptism of fire in the World War. Several men at the helm in the Soviet Union made their way mainly by illegal, rather than legal, violence. Josef Stalin was first arrested in 1901 by the authorities, and thereafter went into hiding, worked in the revolutionary movement, and ran constant risks. Joseph Pilsudski, former dictator of Poland, banished to Siberia for his connection with the Polish national movement in 1888, joined the Socialist party in 1892, and organized secret military units.

Hermann Göring was the last commander of the "Freiherr von Richthofen" squadron, which made distinguished history in the last years of the World War. Rudolf Hess, National Socialist party secretary, and close associate of Hitler, was a former member of the German scouting flight "35." Dr. Robert Ley, leader of the National Social-

ist trades unions, was a military airman, as was Gregor
Strasser, who was so closely connected with Hitler until
shortly before the Nazi's assumption of power. The same
active role in partisan politics has often been assumed by
naval officers, and particularly by submarine officers.

In connection with civil posts intimately associated with
violence may be recalled the prescriptive right of the
Roosevelt family to an assistant-secretaryship of the navy.
Once there was Theodore Roosevelt; later Franklin D.
Roosevelt served from 1913 to 1920, and was in charge
of the inspection of United States naval forces in European waters, July-September, 1918.

Skill in political organization is traditionally represented in the American Cabinet by the postmaster general. Skill in organization was indispensable to the elimination of Trotsky by Communist party secretary Stalin.
Hitler is a notable combination of oratory and organization; Mussolini, of oratory, journalism, and organization; Masaryk, of oratory, journalism, scholarship, and
organization. It is noteworthy that the political committee
of the Communist party has gradually altered its composition, substituting more skill in organization for skill
in oratory, journalism, and scholarship.

Skill in handling persons by means of significant symbols involves the use of such media as the oration, the
polemical article, the news story, the legal brief, the
theological argument, the novel with a purpose, and the
philosophical system. The opportunities for men to live
by manipulating symbols have grown apace with the
complication of our material environment through the
expansion of technology. Since 1870, for example, professional authors in America have jumped from an in-
consequential number to between 12,000 and 13,000.
There are 60,000 artists where formerly there were

4,000; 40,000 actors instead of 2,000; 165,000 musicians in place of 16,000. There has been a tenfold increase in the teaching profession. There are ten newspapermen where there was one in 1870. There are 300,000 lawyers today; and it is common knowledge how much influence is exercised by lawyers in courts, legislatures, commissions, and on boards of directors. Half of the President's Cabinet are lawyers.

Specialists on the handling of things, as well as persons, have spectacularly increased in modern times. In the United States technical engineers (excluding electricians) have risen from 7,000 in 1870 to over 226,000 in 1930 (the gainfully employed as a whole expanded only 300 per cent). Yet those who specialize in engineering receive less deference than those who specialize in symbols which sway the masses.

It was skill in bargaining that was the road to eminence as modern industry expanded during the nineteenth and twentieth centuries.

Elites may be compared in terms of *class* as well as skill. A class is a major social group of similar function, status, and outlook. The principal class formations in recent world politics have been aristocracy, plutocracy, middle class, and manual toilers.

In 1925 the landed aristocracy of Germany owned most of the large estates which occupied 20.2 per cent of the arable land of the country. They had 40 per cent of the land east of the Elbe River. All told, these large estates constituted but 0.4 per cent of the total number of landholdings in Germany. At the base of the pyramid were those who occupied small holdings: 59.4 per cent of the total holdings of Germany accounted for only 6.2 per cent of the arable land.

The concentration of landownership in the hands of a

small aristocratic coterie is especially noteworthy in Chile,
where it has been officially estimated that 2,500 individuals hold 50,000,000 acres of the 57,000,000 acres in
private possession. In prewar Hungary properties of 1,300
acres or more, comprising only one-tenth of one per cent
of the total number of holdings in the country, included
17.5 per cent of the total area. So large were the holdings
of the aristocracy in the Baltic provinces of the former
Russian Empire that a new state like Estonia found at the
beginning of its national life that 1,149 large estates occupied 58 per cent of its total area. In Latvia, where one-half
of the country was in 1,300 baronical estates, land reforms
created 43,000 new peasant holdings by 1922.

Great plutocracies have arisen from commerce, industry, and finance, as capitalistic society developed through
its several phases. Typical of the merchant capitalist period
was the fortune of John Jacob Astor, which aggregated
$20,000,000 and was derived from the oriental and fur
trade, and from speculation in New York real estate. Industrial fortunes rose later. Cornelius Vanderbilt left
$100,000,000 from speculations in railroads. Cyrus Mc-
Cormick built on the basis of agricultural machinery, An-
drew Carnegie on steel, John D. Rockefeller on oil, and
J. Pierpont Morgan on investment banking. By 1929 there
were 504 persons in America whose incomes were in excess of $1,000,000, and whose wealth was $35,000,000,-
000. As a rule these great fortunes were highly diversified,
representing paper control over remote operations.

At the end of the eighteenth century the rising bourgeoisie clashed sharply with the French aristocracy, but
elsewhere the new bourgeoisie fused more readily with
the declining aristocracy. Although the largest fortune in
Germany in 1913 was the Krupp fortune of $70,000,000,
representing the new industrial capitalists, the second

largest fortune was owned by the aristocrat Prince Henc-
kel von Donnersmarck. The Kaiser was fifth. Most of the
aristocratic fortunes had become diversified and depended
upon typically capitalistic undertakings.

The gradualness of the eclipse of the aristocracy by
new social formations is indicated by the analysis of British Cabinet ministers since the beginning of the nineteenth century. Harold J. Laski has shown that between
1801 and 1831 no less than 52 of the 71 ministers of
Cabinet rank were sons of nobility. Between 1906 and
1916 the sons of nobility sank to parity with other social
classes, contributing 25 of the 51 ministers. From 1917
to 1924 but 14 of the 53 ministers were from the nobility.

In Japan the transition to modern industrialism and
finance was managed by parceling the new enterprises
among the great feudal families.

The lesser middle class is composed of those who exercise skills which are requited by modest money returns.
Hence the class comprises small farmers, small businessmen, low-salaried professional people, skilled workers
and craftsmen. The manual workers are those who have
acquired little skill; they are the true proletariat. The
line between plutocracy, lesser bourgeoisie, and proletariat is a matter of acrimonious debate in practical politics, and of great uncertainty among scientists. Socialist
propagandists have sometimes sought to include skilled
workers, and even low-income professional people, among
the proletariat. Propagandists of plutocracy have sought
to obscure the demarcation between big business and big
finance, on the one hand, and lesser business and lesser
finance, on the other, by speaking of "business" as a unit.

Arthur N. Holcombe applied the terms defined by Bukharin to the United States with these results: by assigning
24,800,000 of the gainfully employed and 14,000,000

female homemakers to the "proletariat," he arrived at a figure for the "proletariat" which was 51.7 per cent of the gainfully employed; 1.6 per cent were "capitalists"; 8 per cent were "landlords"; the rest were "intermediate," "transitional," "mixed," and "unclassified." W. I. King estimated the average income of each person gainfully employed in the United States during 1924-1927 at $1,885. A substantial, though undetermined proportion, of the "proletariat" received more than this average amount.

There is an inner psychological attitude in common among those who make sacrifices to acquire skill, and this bond tends to keep the lesser bourgeoisie identified with the plutocracy rather than with the skill-less proletariat. Common resentment against a social order which does not invariably apportion high rewards to skill draws the small professional man, businessman, farmer, and skilled worker away from the social forms which preserve plutocracy. Those who are classed as "proletariat" in the Holcombe analysis are skilled as well as semiskilled and unskilled; hence many of them belong to the lesser bourgeoisie as here understood. There is evidence that the white-collar worker and the professional man have been supplanting the muscle man in American life. It is estimated that the machine revolution has released about 25 per cent of all the working population of the United States from arduous toil, and labor-saving machinery has lightened the physical burdens of those who remain on farms and in mines and factories. In 1870 there were 52.8 per cent of the gainfully employed in agriculture. By 1930 this had declined to 21.3 per cent. Most of the change occurred in trade and transportation (rising from 9.1 to 20.7 per cent), clerical service (1.7 to 8.2 per cent), and professional service (2.7 to 6.5 per cent).

The distribution of values may be considered with reference to *personality* in addition to skill and class. What is the relative success of all the forms of personality known to clinical and cultural psychologists? What is the varying fortune of the masochists, the sadists, the detached, the hysterical, the obsessive, the compulsive? From this standpoint the march of time ceases to pivot exclusively around the cavalcade of classes and skills; it becomes a succession of personality forms.

Special interest attaches to personality forms which are predisposed by nature and by early nurture to find satisfaction in playing particular roles on the stage of politics. The agitator is such a type: he is set off from his fellows by the intensity of his craving for prompt and excited deference from his contemporaries. Hence he is emotionally disposed to cultivate such skills of mass appeal as oratory and polemical journalism. Men with less need for emotional responsiveness may be less spectacular organizers. The agitator comes into his own during the fiery intensity of crises; the organizer is favored by the intercrisis periods. As crises intensify, Asquith gives way to Lloyd George; von Hindenburg to Hitler. As crises relax, the stage is set for Stanley Baldwin or Warren Harding.

During the initial phases of crisis, personalities may forge ahead who are benevolent as well as firm, and more considerate than ruthless. The stern cloud of approaching war or revolution generates profound anxieties among the masses. The need for reassurance may favor the gentle Lincoln over the flaming Seward on the very eve of disaster.

There are forms of personality easily addicted to imperious violence. They have often learned to cow their environment by the sheer intensity of their willfulness.

They have succeeded in control by externalizing their rages against deprivation. Such are the men of Napoleonic mold, prone to break themselves or others.

Whatever the special form of political expression, the common trait of the political personality type is emphatic demand for deference. When such a motive is associated with skill in manipulation, and with timely circumstances, an effective politician is the result. The fully developed political type works out his destiny in the world of public objects in the name of public good. He displaces private motives on public objects in the name of collective advantage.

The true political personality is a complex achievement. When infants are born, they are unequipped with language of reference to environment, immediate or remote. Their impulses are first organized toward an immediate intimate circle. The symbols of reference to the world of affairs are endowed with meaning in this primary situation, and the true politician learns to use the world of public objects as a means of alleviating the stresses of his intimate environment. Cravings for deference, frustrated or overindulged in the intimate circle, find expression in the secondary environment. This displacement is legitimized in the name of plausible symbols. He does not act for the sake of action; he implies that he strives for the glory of God, the sanctity of the Home, the independence of the Nation, the emancipation of the Class. In the extreme case, the politician is bound to no specific objects in his environment. He is not preoccupied with the routines of nature, discernible in science, art, technology; he is concerned only with the deference meaning of objects for his ego.

Besides skill, classes, and personality groups, we may

examine the distribution of values among *attitude groups*. The world is divided among those who are influential on the basis of shared symbols of loyalty to nation, class, occupation, person. Some rise to eminence in the name of militant or conciliatory methods; in the name of demands for a vast gamut of policies; in the name of optimistic visions of the future. Quite different personality types may be united in loyalty to nation or class, method, policy, outlook. Thus attitude groups cut across personality classifications, even as they cut across skill or class. At any given time the members of a skill or class group may not have risen to full skill or class consciousness. Although an objective observer may be able to consider the meaning of events for their relative success or failure, the members of the skill or class group may talk the language of patriotism, and have no common symbol of class or skill.

At this point it may be convenient to cast a glance backward over the ground which has been covered. The term politics has been used to mean the study of influence and the influential. It is plain, however, that no simple index can be profitably used to measure influence and the influential. One aspect of influence is the relative sharing of values. Different results can be obtained by using different values. *An* elite of deference is not necessarily *an* elite of safety. More values may be added to the present list of three (deference, safety, income). Whatever the list, the items may be differently combined, thus reaching different results to correspond to varying judgments of *the* elite. New results may be obtained by defining influence in other terms than relative share of values. The term may be used to indicate a judgment of how values *might* be influenced if there were conflicts about them. Thus financial capitalists may be judged to be stronger or weaker than industrial capitalists in case of a hypothetical collision.

From analysis, then, we can expect no static certainty. It is a constant process of reexamination which brings new aspects of the world into the focus of critical attention. The unifying frame of reference for the special student of politics is the rich and variable meaning of "influence and the influential," "power and the powerful."

Perhaps the reader may find himself pausing to consider his own position in the world from the standpoints thus far developed. What is my principal skill? What is my class? What is my type of personality? What are my loyalties and my preferences about collective policy and attitude? Where do these skill, class, and personality formations stand with reference to the distribution of such values as deference, safety, and income in my locality, my region, my state, my continent, my world? How has my position altered so far during my life, and what are the probable alterations before I die?

Plainly the last question poses the most crucial problem in the sharpest possible way. One purpose of thought is to help in locating the self as an object among objects in the march of time. The goal is to view the self correctly in the context of events which include the future as well as the past. In this case, the objective is orientation in the succession of skill, class, personality, and attitude forms through time.

This is the *contemplative* approach to political events. But there is a *manipulative* approach as well. It views events in order to discover ways and means of gaining goals. Such a standpoint does not necessarily call for overt participation in revolutionary or counterrevolutionary, reformist or counterreformist movements, although it does bring the attitude of the analyst much closer to that of the agitator-organizer. If events are viewed in this perspective, a new sense of personal involvement may have a vitalizing effect upon the thinker when he resumes the contemplative attitude.

How may elites be attacked or defended? How may specific objectives be reached by means of symbols, violence, goods, practices? Such are the major problems of the manipulative approach to politics as here understood; such are the questions to be broached in the next four chapters. The contemplative approach is then resumed, and the meaning of events is construed with reference to skill, class, personality, attitude.

It may be serviceable to put the present interpretation of politics in the perspective of recent specialized thought on the subject. Not until 1906 were there enough political scientists in the United States to organize a national organization (although the American Economic Association was founded in 1885). The original members of the association were recruited from the faculties or departments of government or political science, and from some departments of history and philosophy, and from some schools of law. Although these political scientists had different technical skills at their command, they were united by common interest in what was understood to be the institution of government. As distinguished from law and philosophy, political science was chiefly comparative government, emphasizing the broad historical transformations which ushered in modern institutions, especially in Western Europe and in English-speaking countries.

In recent years, academic political science has enlarged its descriptive content by concentrating attention upon public administration, political parties, promotional groups, and political personalities. Political scientists have become more preoccupied with the recent past and the impending future than with the remote past. One result of this shift in focus of attention has been the use of methods of investigation which were not included in the traditional equipment of historians, philosophers, and lawyers.

The study of the recent past and the impending future drew attention to the techniques of the interview and of field observation. This brought more political scientists into contact with specialists who were skilled in interviewing primitive people (cultural anthropologists), in eliciting life history documents (social psychologists, sociologists), in prolonged and technical interviewing (clinical psychology, notably psychoanalysis), and in controlled observation (behavioristic psychology, child psychology, applied psychology).

Preoccupied with the recent past and the impending future, political scientists have studied classes of recurring events (like voting). This made it possible to compare results by the use of quantitative procedures, and brought political scientists into more intimate contact with statisticians.

Thus it was not to the historian, the lawyer, or the philosopher that the political scientist was able to turn for aid in the solution of his problems, but to the new and growing skill groups in the academic division of labor.

Plainly such changes in outlook were likely to work changes in the concepts, as well as in the techniques, of political scientists. Some became discontented with the identification of their field with "government" or the "state." They found that the traditional vocabulary of political science was not easily adapted to the statement of relative changes. The traditional distinctions were between "sovereign" and "not sovereign," "state" and "not state," "centralized" and "decentralized." But most events seemed to fall somewhere between these "either-or" words, and to demand language capable of distinguishing between "more or less." Prolonged research might result in classifying the states of the world into "dictatorships" or "nondictatorships," but the two-term classification did not seem to be particularly important. Hence the growing interest in varying degrees of "power" or "influence," and in the use of tentative and partial indicators of influence.

That political science concentrates upon the influential does not imply the neglect of the total distribution of values throughout the community. It is impossible to locate the few without considering the many. And the emphasis upon the probability that the few will get the most does not imply that the many do not profit from some political changes.

Moreover, the analysis of political results in terms of certain values (like deference, safety, income) does not imply that the results or the values are consciously sought. It is a matter of investigation to determine the influence of self-conscious striving. "Class consequences" and "skill consequences" may, in some circumstances, come to pass with a mere modicum of "class consciousness" and "skill consciousness." The subjective attitudes actually found may damage rather than improve the relative influence of class or skill groups. Such attitudes would be "false class (or skill) consciousness," rather than "true class (or skill) consciousness."

Political science, then, is the study of influence and the influential. Influence is determined on the basis of shares in the values which are chosen for purposes of the analysis. Representative values are deference, safety, and income. No single index is wholly satisfactory as a gauge of influence, but situations may be clarified by the successive application of specific standards. Whatever the measures utilized, attention is centered upon the characteristics of the influential which may be described in selected terms, like class, skill, personality, and attitude. The fate of an elite is profoundly affected by the ways it manipulates the environment; that is to say, by the use of violence, goods, symbols, practices.

This book will begin with the methods *of* the influential, and conclude with the consequences *for* the influential.

CHAPTER II

SYMBOLS

Any elite defends and asserts itself in the name of symbols of the common destiny. Such symbols are the "ideology" of the established order, the "utopia" of counter-elites. By the use of sanctioned words and gestures the elite elicits blood, work, taxes, applause, from the masses. When the political order works smoothly, the masses venerate the symbols; the elite, self-righteous and unafraid, suffers from no withering sense of immorality. "God's in his heaven—all's right with the world." "In union there is strength"—not exploitation.

A well-established ideology perpetuates itself with little planned propaganda by those whom it benefits most. When thought is taken about ways and means of sowing conviction, conviction has already languished, the basic outlook of society has decayed, or a new, triumphant outlook has not yet gripped the automatic loyalties of old and young. Happy indeed is that nation that has no thought of itself; or happy at least are the few who procure the principal benefits of universal acquiescence. Systems of life which confer special benefits on the other fellow need no plots or conspiracies when the masses are moved by faith and the elites are inspired by self-confidence.

Any well-knit way of life molds human behavior into its own design. The individualism of bourgeois society like the communism of a socialized state must be inculcated from the nursery to the grave. In the United States, as one

among the bourgeois nations, the life of personal achievement and personal responsibility is extolled in song and
story from the very beginning of consciousness. Penny
banks instill the habit of thrift; trading in the schoolyard
propagates the bourgeois scale of values. Individual marks
at school set the person at rivalrous odds with his fellows.
"Success and failure depend on you." "Strive and succeed" means "If you strive, success comes; if success does
not come, you have not striven hard enough."

"The almighty dollar": money is scarce and "it is not
wise to buy the bicycle now"; "we must be economical and
keep the old car another season"; "they're headed for the
poorhouse; have you seen how she dresses!"; "they were
worthy people, but she's a shame and a disgrace to her
parents"; "they had a falling out over the will"; "she
really married him for his money"; "some say he poisoned
her so he could collect the insurance"; "he was a brilliant
man but he took to drink and went to the dogs"; "he was a
good provider until he went running around spending his
money on loose women"; "I hear Harry is making a good
thing of it in real estate"; "how much did that cost you?";
"how much is the tuition at that college?"

The rich and successful uncle, the rich and successful
deacon, the rich and successful alumnus, the rich and successful banker are there at the focus of adulation. Their
portraits ornament the walls; their busts adorn the halls;
their presences dignify occasions. Epithets are passed
around the dinner table or the nursery or the street corner when "failures" beg for charity, or resort to theft
or worse.

Gossip, fiction, motion pictures sustain the thesis of
personal responsibility for failure or success. He failed
because he lacked tact or had halitosis or didn't finish his
education by correspondence or didn't go to the right col-

lege or forgot to slick down his hair. She was successful
because she got the right shade of lipstick, took French
lessons at home on the phonograph, kept the skin you love
to touch, and bought soft and subtle kinds of lingerie. If
she took up typewriting and shorthand, she would marry
the boss. Not untypical of the sudden success motifs are
the following motion pictures seen in succession by a
movie addict: In "I'm No Angel" the ex-carnival girl
marries a society man. In "Morning Glory" a stage-struck
country girl is shoved into the star part on the opening
night of a play and makes a hit. In "My Weakness" a
servant girl made into a lady wins a society man. In "Emperor Jones" a negro porter rises to kingly heights before
he fails. In "Footlight Parade" a young producer makes
good with one night of strenuous work.

Social and industrial difficulties are automatically
traced to personal equations. If conditions are wretched
at the X Company coal mine, it is because the owners back
in New York didn't know about it. Meanwhile trouble may
be made by radical agitators or by racketeers, who stir up
the men in order to get themselves employed as strike
leaders or as strikebreakers.

The focus of attention is thus absorbed by personal
problems. The newspapers report that he killed her because he found her with another man, or because she could
not see him go to another woman. The newspapers report
that he won an election because he made a smart speech.
The newspapers report that he got killed because he forgot
to look to see if the train was coming. The newspapers report that she got hurt because she did not read the instructions on the package. The particular incident is not written
about as representative of a context of relationships. Not
desperation through unemployment, not insecurity through
crop failure, not diminished administrative efficiency be-

cause of greater burdens of prohibitory regulation, but personal motives and struggles are the subject matter of the secondary means of communication in the bourgeois world.

When such an ideology impregnates life from start to finish, the thesis of collective responsibility runs against a wall of noncomprehension. In any collective society, the whole texture of life experience would need to be respun. In the Soviet Union, for instance, there have been efforts to remodel the psychological environment of the rising generation. This has meant collective houses, where community laundries and similar services replace the private unit. Group tasks supplant individual tasks in order to keep collective enterprises rather than ambitious persons at the center of attention. Theatricals emphasize the play and not the star, and treat the fate of movements rather than the problems of the individual person.

The emblems and words of the organized community are also part of the precious haze of early experience. In the United States the memories of all are entwined with the flag, snapping in the breeze on Memorial Day; "The Star-Spangled Banner," sung in uncertain unison on special holidays; the oath of allegiance to the flag, repeated before hours of study and recitation; the pageant of the Pilgrim Fathers, rehearsed at school, at church, at club. There are memories of stiff, embarrassed silence at the name of the slacker relative; tales of travel and adventure with the fleet, the army, the air force; solemn requiem for the dead; marching columns of the gray, blue, khaki.

On occasions like the inauguration of the President, the unifying symbols of the nation rise again to the threshold of attention. The identifying term has changed from time to time. Before the Civil War, this was the "Union," but the bloody and contentious associations of that word led to its practical elimination in presidential rhetoric after the

Civil War. The term "United States" has been dropping out to the advantage of "America" or "American," notably since the World War. Inaugural oratory has invariably contained reference to the deity, and usually to words like "freedom," "liberty," "independence," "economy," "self-government." Even George Washington made an allusion to the common past, and after Franklin Pierce "our glorious past" or "our memories" were duly celebrated. Such expressions as "our fathers, our forefathers, the framers, the founders, our sages, heroes" were seldom left out. "Confidence in the future" was omitted by James Monroe and Grover Cleveland only. Adverse references were made to "partisanship" in most of the addresses. Usually there were self-adulatory words like "intelligence of our people, our righteous people, our great nation."

In the picture language of the public, reflected in cartoons, foreign nations have often played a sorry role, except when public sympathy moved more or less episodically in their favor. For many years the "Mexican" stereotype included a bolero coat, a large sombrero, spurs, revolver, and rifle. The clothes were often torn and ragged, with patched shoes or bare feet. The dark hair, slightly upturned mustache, dark eyes, clenched fist, defiant face aroused annoyance rather than hatred. The "Mexican" was often shown as a small, thin urchin who should be soundly spanked and put to bed. Sometimes he was depicted as playing with fire, or sticking his tongue out at Uncle Sam, or being caught in a juvenile prank by his policeman neighbor to the north.

Before 1915 there was some uncertainty about the stereotype of the "Japanese." He figured as a little boy or as a tiny man wearing a kimono. As late as May, 1915, the cartoonist Bowers drew the "Japanese" with a kimono reaching to the knees, big bow tie at the back, bare arms and legs, shaven head, row of white teeth, and spear in hand. But in 1915 the tendency was to discard the kimono and array the "Jap" in a military outfit, usually a short plain coat (minus decorations), trousers, tight-fitting military boots, military cap, sword, and often a revolver or bayonet. Occasionally, especially at the era of the Washington Conference, the "Jap" was portrayed in an ordinary business suit; but by 1925 he was back in full military regalia.

The bias against government is strikingly indicated by the absence of a cartoon stereotype for the public as a recipient of benefits from public expenditures. The emphasis is all on the "Taxpayer." Often arrayed in a dark suit with a white collar, four-in-hand tie, sometimes with a white vest, often with light trousers, the taxpayer is one of those pathetic souls who always get it in the neck. Formerly equipped with straw hat, derby, or large cowboy hat, he is now more commonly shown in a soft felt hat of varying size, sometimes perched on top of his head, sometimes plopped down over his ears. Shoes may be ragged and patched, but the white collar of respectability remains. The frail little fellow has thinning hair, a long nose, a slight mustache, and glasses. The nosepinchers were replaced by horn-rims about 1921. The "Taxpayer," unlike the "Public," is always being acted upon. He may be an Isaac about to be sacrificed; a bandaged cripple leaving the office of Doc. Democrat to get relief from Doc. G.O.P.; a rower, trying to row five large cruisers to the scrap heap; a sawhorse, on which governmental extravagances and waste are teeter-tottering.

Singularly enough, the stereotype of the "Capitalist" has remained uncomplimentary for many years. The checkered trousers with dark coat and checkered suit tended to give way in 1910 and 1911 to the dark suit or a dark coat and striped trousers. The white vest, winged collar, bow tie (or four-in-hand), stovepipe hat, varying in size and height, have long been consistently included within the stereotype. The amount of jewelry varies. At times he is bedecked with diamond studs, or a stickpin, cuff links, and diamond rings, even on thumb and first finger. Spats were added to his attire around 1912 and 1913, and his shiny patent leather shoes have been fixtures. Big cigars and a big cane are sometimes added. The "Capitalist" is fat necked, round bellied, and bald. The hands at times are excessively large to emphasize the grasping habits of the owner. Most of the time the "Capitalist" has been grinning, or smiling, at the expense of "Laborer" or "Public." But in the years 1919-1921 the negative symbol was that of "Labor" who was decked out with silk shirts and arrogance.

When elites resort to propaganda, the tactical problem is to select symbols and channels capable of eliciting the desired concerted acts. There is incessant resort to repetition or distraction. The changing emotional requirements of the community, moods of submissiveness, moods of self-assertion, all complicate the task of managing men in the mass. After periods of discipline for the common cause, the mass trend is toward individualism and variety; after periods of self-assertion, the mass trend is toward disciplined fundamentalism. This means that when the mores are observed, the countermores are suppressed; that when countermores are indulged, mores are suppressed. The inhibited is not extinct; hence the sudden change in direction which distinguishes the variable moods of men.

Propaganda, when successful, is astute in handling:

> Aggressiveness
> Guilt
> Weakness
> Affection.

The organization of the community for war takes advantage of the concentrated aggressiveness which accumulates in any crisis. When another nation is presented as a threat, retaliatory impulses to destroy it are promptly evoked; but such impulses cannot find direct expression. They are partially suppressed, partially repressed, but they contribute to the trend and tone of mental life. The energy of frustrated impulses may be discharged in many paths, but men in the mass are likely to use the most primitive. One of the rudimentary modes of coping with internal stress is projection. This mechanism resolves the inner emotional difficulties by treating an impulse of the self as an attribute of the environment. Instead of recognizing the simple intensity of one's retaliatory destructiveness, one feels that the outside world is more destructive than in reality it is. This "moralizes" the murderous impulse by imputing destructiveness to the other fellow. The symbol of the "other" is elaborated into a scheming, treacherous, malevolent "influence."

Deep-seated guilt feelings can also be projected upon the world outside. Hostile impulses arouse guilt feelings because society has taught the individual during infancy, childhood, and juvenility to chasten his rages. The initial tendency to hold the destructive tendencies in check by raging against the self can be dealt with by projecting the accusation away from the self, and raging at the "immorality" of the enemy.

Intense inner rage arouses deep fears of death and mutilation. (In part these are the "castration anxieties" spoken of in technical psychoanalysis.) Such fears of being hopelessly weakened, of enduring the humiliation of inferiority now and in the future, may also be assuaged by projection. Not ourselves, but our enemies, face defeat; our victory is sure.

As crisis grows, the "nation" is constantly kept at the focus of attention. The recurring preoccupations of everyday life are modified by news and rumors of international friction. All eyes focus upon the fate of the national "we" symbol in relation to the surrounding "they" symbols. Love and respect for the symbols of the foreigner are withdrawn and become attached to symbols of the collective "we." The sense of being threatened increases the need for love; hence the symbol of the nation is redefined as infinitely protective and indulgent, powerful and wise.

When war propaganda is addressed to the neutrals, the task is to lead influential elements in the neutral state to identify our enemy as their enemy, our cause as their cause. This can be accomplished by affording active opportunities for observers to become participants. Thus the cause of the Entente in the United States benefited from the charity drives to "adopt an orphan" from the devastated regions of "bleeding Belgium." British propaganda in America, 1914-1917, was wise in that so much of it was secretly or privately managed. It used the personal touch, and depended on American personnel and material wherever possible. Some of the German agents permitted themselves to become conspicuous; hence they were discredited. As a reminder of the ancient history of propaganda, it may be remarked that one of the plays of Euripides was probably a propaganda drama written to influence Argos against Sparta. The play was first produced, not at Athens, but at Argos; Peleus, it will be recalled, indulges in disparaging remarks about the Lacedaemonian women.

When the propaganda problem is to deal with allies, the cardinal themes are our strenuous exertions in the war and our hearty support of the cherished war aims of our allies.

The principal goal of propaganda in enemy countries is to deflect animosity against another foe, or to turn this animosity inward, thus fomenting civil war or revolution. The connection between fluctuating levels of insecurity and the effectiveness of propaganda is shown in the history of German morale during the World War. After the check on the Marne and the immobile war of the trenches, the bubbling self-confidence and enthusiasm at the front and at home began to subside. The glorious march to Paris had not come off. The simpler soldiers yearned to get out of the trenches by Christmas. But it was not until the food shortage pinched the population at home that waves of discontent assumed significant proportions. In October, 1915, the chief of the Foreign Office press section noticed that complaints from wives at home were affecting morale at the front. In the summer of 1916, the letters home began to reflect the impact of the terrific losses around Verdun. The word *Schwindel* began to be used to refer to the war. The Somme created the impression that Allied resources of men and material were inexhaustible. A critical, carping spirit began to show itself, and the gap between officers and men began visibly to widen. The privations of the "turnip winter" of 1916-1917 augmented the depression at home. In the summer of 1917 war aims were much discussed, and the blatant demands of the *Vaterlandspartei* for great annexations undermined the impression that the war was solely for defense. The soldiers at the front resented the high wages of the workers in the munitions factories, and the high profits of the munitions makers.

After three months of incessant struggle in Flanders, there was an appreciable increase in the number of losses by capture. This telltale indication of sagging morale spread apace as the war drew to an end. Disciplinary difficulties were sometimes extreme when troops were transferred from the eastern theater to the western "graveyard." Partly as a result of such evidence, the High Command decided to stake everything on the great offensive of 1918. As early as June, however, the troops were plainly disintegrating. By July difficulties were flagrant, as shown by leaves without permission, crimes of cowardice, and open defiance of orders. August was a month of general apathy, hopelessness, indifference. During the last months of the war from three-quarters of a million to a million men succeeded in withdrawing themselves from active combat, and many of those who stayed at the front engaged in passive resistance. Willing soldiers began to be called "strikebreakers" and "warprolongers" by their comrades.

Ludendorff first took note of the effects of enemy propaganda in the summer of 1917. During 1918 the menace of enemy propaganda was betrayed by the phrases of enemy origin which appeared in letters home from the front, and in conversations overheard on troop trains and reported by intelligence officers to the high command. Such words as "Prussian militarism," "Pan-German," "bloodthirsty Kaiser," and "Junker" were employed in the sense intended by Allied propagandists. Soldiers learned the word "Republic" because the French promised to give special consideration to all captives or deserters who shouted the word and surrendered. Radical socialist propaganda had revived at home, after some of the socialist leadership recovered from the abandonment of internationalism in 1914. In 1918 troops transferred from the eastern theater of war to the western front had often fraternized with the Bolshevik soldiers, and spread a revolutionary interpretation of the war.

Entente propaganda was hammering home the thesis of the ultimate defeat of Germany, and inciting a governmental, as distinguished from a social, revolution. In the famous "war without weapons" the use of leaflets reached spectacular proportions. All told, 65,595,000 leaflets were snowed over the German lines. The French distributed 43,-300,000, the British, 19,295,000, and the Americans 3,000,000. The German high command tried to defend itself by offering a bounty to soldiers who would turn in these leaflets. One-sixteenth of the leaflets dropped by the Allies were actually handed to their officers by the German soldiers. The Germans also tried to coordinate special propaganda at home with a strong counteroffensive against the Allies. They spread 2,253,000 copies of the *Gazette des Ardennes* on the western front.

The object of revolution, like war, is to attain coercive predominance over the enemy as a means of working one's will with him. Revolutionary propaganda selects symbols which are calculated to detach the affections of the masses from the existing symbols of authority, to attach these affections to challenging symbols, and to direct hostilities toward existing symbols of authority. This is infinitely more complex than the psychological problem of war propaganda, since in war the destructive energies of the community are drained along familiar channels. Most of those who have a hand in revolution must face a crisis of conscience. Constituted authority perpetuates itself by shaping the consciences of those who are born within its sphere of control. Hence the great revolutions are in defiance of emotions which have been directed by nurses, teachers, guardians, and parents along "accredited" channels of expression. Revolutions are ruptures of conscience.

The psychological function of revolutionary propaganda, like war propaganda, is to control aggressiveness, guilt, weakness, affection. Marxism, for example, fosters the projection of aggressiveness by denouncing "capitalism" as predatory. Marxism fosters the projection of guilt by indicting capitalism as the root of the ills of war, poverty, misery, disease. Marxism favors the projection of

love upon "socialism" and the "proletariat." Marxism
facilitates the projection of weakness by asserting that capitalistic society is bound to decay, for it bears the seed of
revolution in its bosom. Hence, as was said by this writer
in another context, "Dialectical materialism is the reading
of private preferences into universal history, the elevating
of personal aspirations into cosmic necessities, the re-
moulding of the universe in the pattern of desire, the completion of the crippled self by the incorporation of the
symbol of the whole. No competing symbolism rose to such
heights of compulsive formulation."

Partial revolutionary movements are led by an elite
which fights to exterminate those who are associated with
the latest world revolutionary movement. Such movements,
like Italian Fascism and German National Socialism, are
belligerently antialien and pronational. Regardless of how
much they borrow in symbol or practice from the latest
world revolutionary pattern, they conceal the theft, abomi-
nate the source.

The use of the "non-Aryan" as the unifying devil behind all the lesser devils of Marxism, Versailles, Weimar,
Dawes Plan, is easy to understand. The same type of mass
movement in Italy had not utilized the Jew; but several
circumstances conspired to heighten the availability of the
Jew as a target of demagoguery in Germany. An analysis
of these factors will illustrate the function of symbols in
relation to context.

There were few Jews in Germany: they were bankers,
merchants, and professional people who were inclined to
treat Jew-baiting with disdain. There was no proletarian
bloc of Jews to create a pro-Jewish backfire among the
working masses. In short, the Jews were so numerous that
they could conveniently be hated; not so numerous that
they could effectively retaliate. The solid background of

traditional anti-Semitism could be retouched and exploited with impunity.

Anti-Semitism gave an opportunity to discharge hatred against the rich and successful without espousing the proletarian socialists. Not "capitalism" but "Jewish profiteering" was the festering sore. Some German Jews were well-known international bankers, affording a solid basis of common knowledge for the tissue of exaggeration built about their influence. Smaller business and professional men, and petty officials, could attack the "system" without "degrading" themselves to the level of the "proletariat."

Even middle-class hatred of the proletariat could be split by means of the Jewish symbol. Thus the workers who were sufficiently German to renounce "Jewish doctrine" could be tolerated; those who remained Jewish and "Red" and "Marxist" could be destroyed.

Aristocratic hatred of the consequences of modern industrialism could be split by having recourse to the Jew. The undesirable features exhibited the effect of international Jewish finance, not the inherent traits of the system. Hence it became possible to cooperate with capitalistic elements, and to turn the rage generated by recent economic changes against the irrelevant scapegoat.

Anti-Semitism was a means of crippling professional competitors, especially in the relatively congested fields of medicine, law, philosophy, science, and journalism.

Anti-Semitism was also an important means of discharging the hatred of the villager against the urbanite. Smoldering conflicts between rural, lesser urban, and metropolitan communities persist in every culture. Cities are the home of the new and hence of the shocking, for the new is ever threatening the older codes of morals and manners and tastes. City types are prominent among the enemies of the mores, and the Jews were city types. Had not Freud

invented psychoanalysis, scandalizing the bourgeoisie?
Had not Magnus Hirschfeld come to the defense of devia-
tional sexual types? Had not Jewish writers, actors, painters contributed to the subversive fads of "cultural Bol-
shevism"?

The stresses of war, blockade, inflation, and deflation
had exacted a tremendous moral toll in Germany. Multi-
tudes had succumbed to sexual and property "temptations"; hence they were predisposed toward "purification"
to remove the heavy hand of conscience. For them the Jew
was the sacrificial Isaac. Indeed, the whole nineteenth century had witnessed the growth of the secular cult of nationalism, furnishing a substitute for the fading appeal of
established religion. This decline of piety, however, left
legacies of guilt which could be expiated by attacking the
Jew, traditional enemy of Christianity.

Plainly the Jew was available as the symbol which more
than any other could be utilized as a target of irrelevant
emotional drives. The hatred of the country for the city, of
the aristocracy for the plutocracy, of the middle class for
the manual toilers and the aristocracy and the plutocracy
could be displaced upon the Jew. The frustrations of economic adversity and international humiliation, guilt from
immorality, guilt from diminishing piety—these stresses
within the lives of Germans were available to be exploited
in political action.

Propaganda, then, is conducted with symbols which are
utilized as far as possible by elite and counter-elite; but
the intensity of collective emotions and the broad direction
and distribution of collective acts are matters of the
changing total context.

CHAPTER III

VIOLENCE

Violence, a major means of elite attack and defense, takes many forms. The number of men who have been permanently included in the armed forces of the world gives some indication of the place of violence in politics.

In the early Roman Empire the standing army had about 300,000 men, or three in every thousand persons. Undoubtedly this was the largest standing army of ancient times. In the thirteenth century, Europe is estimated to have had the same proportion of its population under arms, though dispersed in a swarm of tiny principalities. By the early seventeenth century, Europe regained a population equal to that of the Roman Empire, and expanded both in numbers and in proportion in the army. During the Napoleonic period France sometimes had ten in every thousand persons under arms, and before the end of the nineteenth century all peacetime establishments of the great powers had climbed to this Napoleonic peak. During the World War no less than one hundred in every thousand of population were in arms. By 1934 the standing armies of Europe were twice the relative size of the Roman armies under Augustus.

The length of wars has declined, however, and so has the proportion of war years to peace years, if expeditions against peoples of inferior technique are excluded from the count. In the seventeenth century the great European states were at war about 75 per cent of the time. In the eighteenth century the per cent is 50; in the nineteenth century, 25. Counting the lesser acts of hostility, the great powers have been fighting most of the time. "Even the United States," says Quincy Wright, "which has perhaps somewhat unjustifiably prided itself on its peacefulness, has had only twenty years during its entire history of 158 years when it has not had the army or navy in active operations during some days, somewhere."

Such impressive reminders cover but a fraction of acts of collective violence. A balance sheet of violence would add those killed in revolution and counterrevolution, in uprisings, in the administration of criminal justice. Specialists in violence include watchmen, guardsmen, and policemen, besides members of the naval, military, and aerial forces. It may be noted that in some communities, like Chicago, the number of policemen in private employ is estimated to outnumber the policemen in government service. A prisoner is deprived of liberty by means of legal action sanctioned by the coercive authority of the community, and the prison population of the United States rose faster than population increased, jumping from 67,000 in 1890 to 140,000 in 1930.

If we include those who practice the use of firearms and explosives, and who learn the manual of arms, the function of violence seems to be even more extensive than shown by the foregoing indices. And if we add the frequency with which violence is resorted to in private relationships which do not come to the cognizance of officials, we would arrive at stupendous figures.

Plainly the rational application of violence as an instrument of influence depends upon the clear appraisal of the act of violence as a detail of the total context. It is seldom an instrument of total destruction. It is a means to an end and not an end in itself. Yet so potent is the love of cruelty, whether in the form of direct gratification or in the indirect form of overreactive weakness, that the rational use of violence is beset by serious difficulties. As a precaution against the joys of wanton destructiveness, classical commentators on violence have emphasized its instrumental function and its peculiar dangers.

The military classic of the Chinese, the *Book of War*, dates from the fifth century B.C., and warns of the limits of violence.

"Now, of the fighting races below heaven; those who gained five victories have been worn out; those who have won four victories have been impoverished; three victories have given dominion; two victories have founded a kingdom; and upon one victory an empire has been established.

"For those who have gained power on earth by many victories are few; and those who have lost it, many."

For modern specialists the political view of war was formulated by Clausewitz when he enunciated the famous theory that "war is a mere continuation of policy by other means." Clausewitz had experience as a Prussian staff officer, and he was impressed by the fact that hostile relations were never a question of purely military effort aiming at the extreme of all that was possible. Available energy was conditioned by expedient calculations of all kinds, especially by the intensity of collective interest in the undertaking at hand. Hence war was rarely, if ever, "absolute war"; it was a detail in a changing context of loyalties, hopes, and expectations.

The dependence of military objectives upon general political circumstances was shown in the American War of Secession. The political object of the Federal States was to prevent Confederate States from leaving the Union. The political object of the South was independence. The North was greatly superior in numbers and in resources, and the South never thought of conquering the North. The general strategy was to prolong resistance, in the twofold hope that the North would be convinced that it was not worth the cost to compel the South to stay in the Union, and that foreign intervention would come to the support of the South.

General Robert E. Lee sought to obtain both of these political objectives by carrying the war to the North, and his strategy from 1862 until the summer of 1863 was offensive. When he was defeated at Gettysburg in July, 1863, he no longer possessed the means to continue an offensive policy, and it became plain that foreign aid was not forthcoming. His strategy was now defensive, with the object of exhausting the power and patience of the North. The North, like the British in relation to the Boers in the South African War, could reach its objective only by defeating the armies of the enemy and by occupying most of the enemy's territory.

Many of the principles of war which are generalized in books on strategy emphasize the connection between the act of violence and its context. The "principle of security" stresses the importance of making sure that the attitudes of those upon whom the operation depends are carefully conserved throughout the enterprise.

Major General Sir F. Maurice shows how the opening campaign of 1862 in the American Civil War failed partly through neglect of this principle of security. McClellan, commander of the Federal forces, had 180,000 men on the frontiers of Virginia. The Confederates had 71,000 men available for the defense of Virginia and their capital, Richmond. The Federal forces had failed the year before in their advance on Richmond, when they had sustained the defeat of Bull Run. During the spring months the few roads were bad. McClellan conceived the plan of utilizing the command of the sea, and transferring the greater part of his army secretly to the Yorktown peninsula, where it would be within sixty miles of Richmond. President Lincoln approved of this plan of campaign on the express condition that adequate provision was to be made for the security of Washington, which is separated from Virginia only by the width of the Potomac River.

General McClellan embarked his troops for the peninsula without taking the President into his confidence, or explaining the measures taken for the protection of Washington. Nor did he ascertain whether General Wadsworth, appointed to command the defenses of Washington, was satisfied that he had enough troops. He simply sent the War Office a list of troops left behind.

President Lincoln ordered a military committee to inquire whether his instructions for the security of the Capital had been complied with. General Wadsworth said that the troops at his disposal were insufficient in numbers and quality, and the President ordered the 1st Corps of McClellan's army, commanded by General McDowell, to remain in northern Virginia and cover Washington. McClellan's attitude had created suspicion in the mind of the President, and lack of confidence soon gave way to alarm when on May 25 General Stonewall Jackson with 16,000 men defeated the defender Banks in the Shenandoah Valley. Panic in Washington led to the diversion of further troops from McClellan and to a wild-goose chase after Jackson.

McClellan and his friends believed that the President was guilty of a breach of faith and of excessive timidity. But the President felt the great weight of his responsibility for the protection of the citadel of the national government, and was quite justified in doubting the reliability of the reticent and seemingly evasive general. McClellan had failed to consider the operation in its entirety; he had neglected to solidify certain attitudes of cooperative confidence indispensable to the execution of the plan.

The effective use of violence implies a preponderance of destructive power at vital places through the entire operation. Many of the principles of war remind generals and rulers of the importance of considering the entire course of the undertaking, selecting points of specific application with a view to all pertinent contingencies. Hence the emphasis upon "economy," "cooperation," "offensive," "movement," "surprise," and "concentration" as means to the general end. Hence, also, the importance of gauging the probability that outside intervention will produce defeat or remove the fruits of victory. In retrospect it is plain that the German high command failed to see the full potentialities of the United States in relation to the European war. Great Britain, on the other hand, adopted contraband rules and practices which were designed to soften American anger.

In the quest for preponderance, the dream of every alert strategist is the development of an offensive so surprising and so destructive that the enemy is rendered incapable of effective resistance. This is aptly called the dream of Cannae. The original Cannae was fought between Romans and Carthaginians at Apulia in 216 B.C. The small army of Hannibal cut 85,000 Roman legionaries to pieces, catching the enemy from the flank with cavalry and surrounding him. Not crude potential superiority, but specific, actual preponderance is the goal of effective strategy. The famous Schlieffen plan, which despite emasculation nearly guided Germany to victory in 1914, was based on this conception. Schlieffen allotted two-thirds of the entire German army (fifty-three divisions out of seventy-two) to one single part of the front, the right wing, which was to march across Bel-

gium and northern France on Paris. He sought to augment
the fighting strength of the right by the latest instruments
of war, heavy howitzers and machine guns, which the army
undertook to accumulate in secret in order to obtain the
effect of Hannibal's special cavalry. After crushing the
principal enemy, France, the idea was to turn against Russia in the east. But the absence of two corps which were
shifted by von Moltke from the right wing as it was marching triumphantly through Belgium and northern France
was sufficient to block the realization of victory. The two
corps were dispatched to the eastern front to ease the pressure on East Prussia, home of the influential Junkers.

Today the new devices of warfare, airplanes and gas,
inflame the imaginations of ambitious specialists in violence. Can superior quantities of planes and gas, secretly
accumulated in advance, be sent against the strongest
enemy, reducing him to submission in a few days or hours,
enabling the victor to turn against weaker enemies, or possibly to crush rebellion at home? As a rule the lure of
technological supremacy has paved the way to disappointment. It has led to absorption in mechanical detail, and to
the neglect of the more delicate psychological and social
aspects of the total situation.

Successful violence depends upon coordinating such
other salient aspects of the total act as organization, propaganda, information. Since the demand to secede usually
appears in parts of the state inhabited by elements which
are differentiated from the state as a whole, it is often
feasible to defer large-scale violence until a government
within a government has been successfully organized.

Such a government within a government was, and is, the
Interior Macedonian Revolutionary Organization, the
IMRO, which was founded in 1893 by a group of young
Macedonian schoolteachers. It aimed by means of popu-

lar agitation to force Turkey to recognize Macedonian autonomy in line with the guarantees of Article XXIII of the Treaty of Berlin. It was open to all Macedonians, whether Serbian, Greek, Rumanian, Turkish, Jewish, or Bulgarian. In 1903 the IMRO fostered an uprising which, though crushed by the Turks, precipitated European intervention. It was not until 1906 that a constitution was ratified by a general assembly of the IMRO. "Macedonia for Macedonians" and "Evolution not Revolution" were the principal slogans. Local committees were elected by universal suffrage; each committee sent delegates to a rayon committee; above this was the okrug committee, corresponding to the vilayet. The okrug committee sent 47 delegates to the regular general congress, which elected the central committee of three. Another body appointed by the central committee represented the organization in the purchase of arms and ammunition from outsiders. No single person was ever given authority. Owing to the breakdown of Turkish administration, the IMRO took over the courts, suppressed brigandage, and maintained schools. Military groups executed the decrees of courts, and a secret village militia stood ready for emergencies.

The case of the IMRO is exceptional. The organization of economics and diplomacy is usually far less complete, especially in revolutionary movements. It is seldom possible in advance of violence to regiment those who are friendly to the objective sought. As a rule, therefore, successful violence is relatively more dependent upon proper coordination with propaganda. Successful violence in revolution depends upon the conjunction of a *coup d'état* with a crisis of mass discontent. The *coup d'état* can be executed by a small number of storm troops which are well informed, armed, and trained; but the chances of securing a loyal conspirative personnel, and of carrying through the action with mass support, depend upon long propaganda preparation in advance of crisis.

This propaganda preparation must be especially designed to win over or to demoralize a large fraction of the soldiery and the police. By the nature of the case, revolutionary forces are certain to be inadequately armed. Thus the 2,000 storm troops which engaged in one of the Canton uprisings had only 200 bombs and 27 revolvers. At Shanghai 6,000 men had weapons for only 150. The proletarian hundreds of Germany in 1923 numbered a quarter of a million, though only a few hundred were armed. Since it is imperative to capture arms early in the uprising, penetration of the armed forces of the established order is crucially important. Proper propaganda preparation ensured a pro-Bolshevik garrison in Petrograd in 1917.

Since the rank and file in any revolutionary rising is composed of comparatively inexperienced fighters who are laboring under enhanced emotional stress, the uprising must be planned to yield conspicuous successes at once. In the Hamburg rising of 1923 careful planning enabled the storm troopers to overpower the men at several police stations and to secure arms. And a little later the workers were clever enough to cut off some of the dreaded tanks by building ditches and barricades behind them.

The cooperation of the masses requires careful timing of the uprising to fit the psychological moment. At Reval the leaders failed to instigate mass protests, even when Tromp, head of the trades unions, was shot, which occurred three days before the rising. Hence the masses were uncertain what was afoot and hesitated instead of striking. The success of the Bolshevik coup in Petrograd was partly assured by the building up of an atmosphere of general expectancy. Posters and papers constantly asked how the masses were to seize power. The final uprising itself was timed to coincide with the meeting of the Second All-Russian Congress in Petrograd which could then act quickly as a provisional government. It was not even necessary to launch a general strike.

An act of violence becomes "propaganda of the deed" when it is expected that the effect on attitudes will be highly disproportionate to the immediate objective consequences of the act. An assassination is such an instance. The horror with which constituted authority contemplates its own assassination has reduced the amount of calm analysis of this method of obtaining results. Seldom is assassination treated with the detachment exhibited in a famous letter received by Lord Kimberley, Viceroy of Dublin, which began:

"My Lord, tomorrow we intend to kill you at the corner of Kildare Street; but we would like you to know that there is nothing personal in it."

An eligible target for "propaganda of the deed" is some personality whose loss will terrorize the enemy and weaken the unity of will of those who uphold an established order. Or a despotic official may be given a temporary lease on life in order to enable him to serve the cause of secession or revolution by continuing to provoke resentment against the established regime. Sometimes an act of assassination is intended to show that resistance is possible, to destroy legends of invincibility, and to incite mass upheavals.

But it now appears reasonable to conclude that selective assassination fails of its purpose as revolutionary propaganda. The People's Will which was formed in Russia in 1879 relied upon terrorism in the hope of inciting the masses. The actual terrorists were usually from families of the depressed gentry who were inclined to individ-ual romanticism as a means of social protest. The peas-ants did not rise; hence terroristic tactics passed into disrepute.

An important qualification must be made however, upon the judgment adverse to assassination as a means of propaganda. Nationalistic aspirations have been furthered by demonstrated willingness to assassinate and to sacrifice. Foreign antagonism to the ruling elite may be brought to a focus by such dramatic acts. Foreign elites may seize the occasion for intervention. This, at least, was accomplished when the IMRO rose against Turkey in 1903, often assas-sinating government officials.

Plainly it is often advisable for attackers and defenders of an established order to use assassination as a means of ridding themselves of dangerous persons; but other than propaganda considerations are involved in such cases.

In terror, as in assassination, propaganda goals are up-permost, and the overt acts are timed to produce the great-est possible psychological effect. Terror must be ruthless and swift. The destruction of some enemies without delay may paralyze the opposition and save many lives later on. Secrecy is essential; hence the arrests at night, and the dis-closure of no information to relatives and friends for weeks or months. The terror was effectively used by the Soviet authorities after the attempt on the life of Lenin in 1918, and after the assassination of Kirov in 1934.

The importance of coordinating violence with informa-tion, no less than with organization, is universally accepted. During the World War there were many brilliant exam-ples of how good intelligence about the armed forces of the enemy won battles or avoided losses. A spy in the Russian railway service kept the German staff in East Prussia ac-quainted with the Russian field cipher during the first two months of the war, enabling von Hindenburg and Ludendorff to take full advantage of the poor coordination between Generals Rennenkampf and Samsonoff, and to win the Masurian Lakes campaign.

Failure of adequate intelligence led to the withdrawal of the Anglo-French Mediterranean fleet under the British admiral, De Robeck, from the bombardment of the Dardanelles. The Turks, sure that Constantinople was doomed, had a train loaded with government archives ready to leave when the astounding news came that the Allied fleet had suddenly sailed away.

In 1917 when the morale of the French troops had been gravely undermined by the apparently insensate demands that had been made upon them for incessant offensive action, mutiny broke out in a certain sector. For the greater part of a day a pivotal point on the front line was held by a handful of artillerymen and sappers; but the Germans did not discover the situation in time to take advantage of the gateway.

Often good intelligence has been ignored by the high command. Witness the incredulity with which the reports were received that the Allies were preparing an offensive with tanks. After the sensational debut at Cambrai, the German experts saw how close they had come to a devastating reverse, had the attack been launched on a larger scale.

Counterespionage seeks to uncover enemy spies, and often scored sensational successes in the late war. British agents found that German espionage in Great Britain was organized so that all messages were sent along one channel. By shadowing the lesser agents, the entire German staff was discovered, and they were promptly incarcerated at the outbreak of hostilities in 1914. So complete was this interference with enemy intelligence that as late as August 23 General von Kluck advanced on Mons in ignorance that the entire British Expeditionary Force of 100,000 men was in front of him.

Final action in a revolutionary uprising must be based on a plan which rests on proper information about the vital positions to take. This requires careful survey of the distribution of armed forces in a given city, discovery of the arsenals and ammunition dumps; location of staff, guards, and lookouts; study of telegraphic, telephonic, radio, and other communication agencies of the high command, and the best ways to control or wreck them; knowledge of the tension between officers and men, and of their attitudes toward the revolutionary program.

The same detailed information should be available about the police forces, and about essential city services, like communication, transportation, water, light, electricity, gas, bridges and streams, principal thoroughfares and squares, addresses of editors and publishers of hostile papers; addresses of government heads, private industrial heads, bankers, and influential persons; location of prisons and the possibilities of freeing prisoners.

Superior local knowledge is one of the assets of the rank and file in revolutionary uprisings. When a genuinely revolutionary situation is chosen, mass uprisings have the advantage of desperate resolve and high morale. Knowing the local terrain, the rank and file can make effective use of it for hiding, sniping, sudden forays, quick escapes. The local police have the same intimate knowledge, but they can be put out of action by sudden attack. The infantry has less familiarity with the terrain in street fighting and is usually accustomed to move in larger units and in more orderly fashion than is most effective. Indeed, small squads may be isolated from their officers and won over to the revolution.

Since the execution of dangerous projects in war or revolution relies so heavily upon the motives and skill of personnel, the choice and handling of men are of the utmost importance. Loyalty to the ideology or mythology of the elite is the prime consideration. Hence the Soviet army trains those who come from the families of workers or the lesser peasantry; only auxiliary services are open to the sons of former officials, teachers, physicians, merchants, or manufacturers. The German army depends mainly on the sturdy and loyal peasantry, especially for military duty in connection with industrial and urban disturbances. In order to prevent fraternizing between soldiers and the local population, the Russian imperial army depended upon Cossack cavalry in critical situations, and the Dual Monarchy took care to mix nationalities and to depend on a peasant rather than a proletarian rank and file.

Revolutionists have learned to rely on a small band of seasoned professional revolutionaries in preference to a fickle swarm of dilettantes. This was one of the principal contributions of Lenin to the practice of revolution.

Since the use of violence keeps the individual confronted by the possibility of death, it is somewhat incongruous to pay him in cash. Hence the effort to exalt psychological rather than material rewards. Hence the stress on "honor," and the investing of citations and orders with as much mystical potency as possible. This diminishes the cost of maintaining a given volume of effort, and prevents too much reflection about the proportion between risk and return. Seeking to cultivate the spirit of honor, the Soviet army regulations provide for thirteen levels of distinction. Modern armies have come to rely upon honor, and upon systematic indoctrination as a supplement to drills and penalties.

Plainly the astute use of violence depends upon the constant translation of social change into terms of fighting effectiveness. The appearance of gas as a weapon has recently modified the balance of power between the beneficiaries and the challengers of an established order. Authorities have hesitated to use artillery to destroy men, women, and children in entire districts, since attempts of this kind may provoke indignant support of revolutionary action. Hence artillery units have been confined, for the most part, to destroying barricades thrown up in street fighting. Cavalry, of course, is practically unusable in narrow street fighting, since it affords a conspicuous target to snipers. Cavalry can be used in charges against unarmed masses in open squares, but otherwise it is serviceable only for communication. Tanks and armed cars are sufficiently mobile for use in street fighting, and they are not vulnerable to rifle and machine-gun fire. Sometimes, however, they can be stopped by bombs and cut off by barricades. Airplanes can be used to reconnoiter. Their bomb and machine-gun fire can clean out nests of rebels, and their noise is unnerving to the undisciplined populace.

But it is the development of gas that has put in the hands of authority a means of demolishing segregated opposition without holocaust. Rebels can be put out of action without killing the inhabitants of a whole district. It is safe to say that unless an adequate supply of gas can be accumulated in advance or captured at once, street fighting against constituted authority has become futile. But this may be but temporary, for cheap means of gas defense may be discovered, and the balance of fighting effectiveness may be back where it was before.

Whether used for war, secession, or revolution, it is plain that violence must be subordinated to the total operation of which it is a part. Sheer joy in sadistic excess must be chastened by expediency. In a world of limited possibilities, violence is rarely "absolute." Violence is a means to ends to be attained in the developing situation. The attitudes of those upon whom the success of the enterprise depends must be carefully conserved. In the search for predominance of destructive power at vital points, violence must be coordinated with organization, propaganda, information. Special attention must be given to the personal agents of the elite, and to the meaning of any social change for the shifting balance of fighting effectiveness.

CHAPTER IV

GOODS

The use of goods in elite attack and defense takes the form of destroying, withholding, apportioning. There may be sabotage or shutdown; strike, boycott, blacklist, noncooperation; rationing, pricing, bribing. Destruction of property is so closely connected with the use of violence on persons that it will receive no special treatment in this chapter, which is limited to withholding and apportioning.

Plainly an elite is subject to domestic attack when it fails to coincide with prosperity. Mounting insecurities may be discharged nonrationally against the symbols and practices of the established order. The result may be no more extensive than the substitution of Tom for Bill in a Democratic parish in Louisiana, or of the Republicans for the Democrats in a border state like Kentucky. But it may involve a revolutionary change in government, as in Germany (1918), or a revolutionary change in social organization, as in Russia (1917). In modern society the oscillations of economic life have become so flagrant that the security of elites is peculiarly bound up with shifts in goods and prices. Hence we are compelled to concentrate upon the strategy and tactics of "economic" relationships.

There are two principal means of directing the flow of goods and services, and elite security is often sought by combining them. We may distinguish systems of *rationing* from systems of *pricing*. Rationing is an act of assigning specific goods or services for consumption or for use in production. Pricing is an act of assigning nonspecific claims to goods and services.

Modern armed forces rely extensively on rationing. Specialists in violence may be rationed the use of specific fortresses, garrisons, age classes of the population, training fields, factories, railroads, motor transports, airplanes. Soldiers are rationed uniforms, guns, food; their schedule of activity is prescribed.

Besides rationed resources, the high command may have many nonspecific claims (dollars, pounds, marks, francs) put at their disposal. A given unit of purchasing power is a nonspecific claim, since it may be spent to buy man power or material equipment.

Rationing systems have often proved highly efficient in the use of resources. Especially during emergencies is it customary for the ruling elite to rely upon this method of controlling the acts and attitudes of the population. The civilian population may receive food cards which call for specified amounts of specific articles. Often, of course, the rationing may be directed primarily toward the control of collective attitudes, and have little to do with its ostensible purpose. During the World War, for example, volunteer sugar rationing was encouraged in the United States. To some extent the purpose was to save the shipping which would have been used to import raw sugar from Cuba and the Philippines, and to increase the amount of sugar and shipping available to the Allies. But perhaps the dominant objective was to bring a sense of the immediate importance of the war effort into the daily lives of American housewives, and hence to the nation as a whole.

The conspicuous disadvantage of rationing systems is that discontent may be massed against the members of the hierarchy who are visibly responsible for the system. Slow, clumsy, or ill-advised action may go so far as to undermine respect for constituted authority. It has been remarked that the recipes issued by the German food administration during the war so often gave ludicrous results that the faith of many simple souls in the infallibility of the agents of the state was undermined.

It is true that pricing methods may suffer from many of the shortcomings of rationing systems. When the price of labor and of commodities is set by conspicuous members of the hierarchy, responsibility is focused upon them. And price fixing may deprive the individual of alternatives just as effectively as a rationing arrangement. If wages and salaries are set sufficiently low by the price fixers, or if the prices on goods are put sufficiently high, money is first spent for such essential items as food, and there may be little left over. It is also possible by the use of direct or indirect taxes to limit the alternatives open to the individual. Contributions or bond subscriptions may be made to appear so necessary that the individual is severely circumscribed.

However, the pricing system may work to veil the responsibility for the apportionment of goods from the eyes of the community. This reduces the probability that some official of a public or private hierarchy will be taken as the target of common discontent. When prices are set in the course of bargains among many equal participants in a market, the price appears to be beyond the control of any determinate person. The apportionment of goods seems to be the outcome of a depersonalized procedure for which no one is responsible.

When the routines of the freely competitive market are running smoothly, an "invisible hand" would appear to guide the result, and the hand is the hand of one unknown to flesh and blood, incapable of being found and thanked or found and hacked to bits. All pervasive "laws of supply and demand," promulgated by no executive and passed by no legislature, seem to have laid down the slots along which human efforts run their predestined course.

The competitive market among bargaining equals has notoriously failed to stay put. Hence the apportionment of goods through this "impersonal" agency has failed to function to the general satisfaction of many communities. Sometimes those who control the supply (like the local telephone company) seem to get the upper hand; sometimes those who control demand (like the milling companies) seem to dictate the terms of the transaction. The growth of great private hierarchies of big business and big finance have come to the center of attention in capitalistic countries. Discontent, therefore, tends to discharge against them. For a time private hierarchies seek to "pass the buck" to the government, and save themselves by attacking the public hierarchy.

But blackguarding the government is a dangerous game for private business, the most influential elite in modern capitalistic nations. Blackguarding the government undermines respect for duly constituted authority, breaking up the habit of acquiescence in the established system.

The most drastic solution of the conflict between public and private hierarchies occurred in Russia with the abolition of the private hierarchies. Effective decision-making rests in the hands of the political committee of the Communist party. Contradictory viewpoints, however, persist; trades-union members want better conditions for factory workers in relation to agriculturists; some demand more capital goods production, while others insist upon more consumption goods production. Plainly the governmentalizing of social life does not abolish the contradictions which are generated by differentials in relation to production.

But the technique of administration in the Soviet Union

has shown how pricing systems can supplement and even supplant rationing systems in a governmentalized society. Goods are distributed by a complex combination of rationing and pricing. Through rationing it is possible to withhold limited supplies from "undesirable" elements, and to starve them out of existence or into submission. Through pricing it is possible to disguise the rationing elements in the system. Thus prices may be set for eggs; but no eggs may be on hand if it is suddenly decided to procure foreign valuta by dumping eggs on the foreign market. Owing to the many complex combinations of pricing and rationing, it has been possible to find several different prices side by side for the same commodity. Only careful inquiry into the rationing aspects of each separate situation enables one to account for the astonishing difference in price level. The price at the factory supply store may be less than in the "open" market; but there may be restricted (rationed) access to the factory store. Contrasting price levels can be preserved in outlets which are accessible to foreign engineers, native engineers, higher officials and party members, lesser officials and party members, skilled workers, semiskilled and unskilled workers, peasants, workers in plants or on farms which made their quota, workers in plants or on farms which failed to make their quota, and so on through a long list of distinctions.

During times of crisis scarcity, the possibility of effective concerted protest can be guarded against by such mixed systems of distribution. The presence or absence of goods becomes an all-absorbing topic of conversation and of fantasy. The clothing card may entitle the "bearer" to a pair of shoes; but will there be shoes at the commissary? The food card may entitle one to "butter"; but there has been no "butter" for two weeks, and perhaps the "oleo" gave out two days ago. Better hoard rubles or marks or lire and take chances with the profiteers in the illegal market?

Like worried, fretful animals, an entire population can be reduced to droves of anxious beasts, concerned with crusts, overresponsive to pats and kicks alike. During periods of "depression" in capitalistic countries the relief population can be reduced in self-reliance and in capacity for collective self-assertion by the demoralizing effect of uncertainty and the multiplication of time-consuming red tape, petty favors, and petty penalties.

It is plain that pricing and rationing are methods available to any elite, whether in Soviet Russia or in the United States. And it is plain that pricing is the safest device of "smooth-water" sailing, but that it requires a supplement of rationing when the breakers of discontent are at hand.

It has been amply emphasized that one of the besetting plights of capitalistic systems is the tendency of competition to pass into monopoly, and to break down the defense of "impersonality" which has stood the system in such good stead. Monopolies also give way to competitive units, but the net historical movement has been toward hierarchies, whether public or private. This has meant that more and more prices are "administratively controlled" [Gardiner Means], whether the administrative hierarchy is public or private. They are not arrived at by bargaining among "equals" in a market.

One way to think of the problem of preserving capitalistic societies is to diagnose the consequences of this development. During depressions the administratively controlled prices can often be sustained at a high level, while competitively determined prices sag. In the United States the prices of manufactured goods are subject to more administrative control at the beginning of a depression than are agricultural prices. Thus the prices of electrical goods like telephones remain stable, while farm products often sell at low levels. As the money income of the farmer declines, he increases his production in order to realize whatever he can so that he may pay taxes, interest, and other obligations dischargeable in money. This tendency toward flooding the market brings down the prices of farm commodities yet further, and limits the ability of the farmer to buy manufactured goods.

Is it possible to work out a concert of vested and sentimental interests which will support the peaceful readjustment of overrigid and overflexible prices?

The great instability of economic life under capitalism has recently been traced to the free creation of circulating media by private commercial banks. Commercial banks have learned how to operate by keeping on hand but a small proportion of cash reserve against liabilities. A loan of $100,000 by a bank is typically made by creating a deposit to the credit of the borrower. This deposit increases the liabilities of the bank; but the loan also increases the assets (accounts receivable) by $100,000 plus interest. On the assumption that the deposit will not be called for at once, the bank is able to lend most of these 100,000 units again, thus creating another deposit and another asset.

The effect of this mode of multiplying circulating media is to build up a vast system of dispersed and pyramided claims which are based upon the tacit assumption that withdrawals will not be made simultaneously. That is, it is assumed that only a small proportion of the participants in the economic process will want cash at any one time. The whole superstructure of interrelationships will collapse when everyone takes the basic assumption of liquidity with sufficient seriousness to demonstrate that when everyone acts upon it, the assumption no longer applies.

These developments of industrial and financial capitalism have produced consequences for which the early expositors of the system were evidently unprepared. Thus it was taken for granted that "saving" and "consumption" were two separate processes which did not go on side by side, but one after the other. This looks plausible to the individual who receives $2,000 a year, and knows that if he saves $500, he cuts down his consumption by $500. Harold G. Moulton, however, contends that it is unsound to project this mode of thought upon collective processes. Using the term "capital" to cover "implements, tools, machines, industrial buildings, railroad tracks, power houses, and other concrete material instruments which aid man in the processes of production," he shows that periods of rapid capital formation, and periods of rapid increase in consumption, march side by side, not single file. This means that the flow of funds to the investment market does not automatically increase the creation of capital equipment. Moulton's analysis shows that savings which entered the investment markets during the prosperous years of the twenties inflated the price of securities rather than promoted a proportionate growth of plant and equipment. And it was the free creation of credit by the commercial banks that made most of this possible.

Hence it is proposed to remodel the routines of capitalistic economy by abolishing commercial banks and separating the deposit from the investment function. This might be done by requiring 100 per cent reserve against demand or short-term deposits. Investing would then represent "real saving." It is anticipated that the most important source of instability would be eliminated. It is not yet plain what combination of vested and sentimental interests, aligned behind this suggestion, would refrain from nullifying policies, such as the direct inflation of the cir-

culating medium by the government. But this suggestion
has begun to become practical politics in the United States
in the recent depression.

A closely related aspect of modern economic instability
and mobility is the weakening of individual ties to particular situations. When we say that a feudal family owns
real property, this relationship is most inadequately described by the word "owned." The specific acres, villagers,
servants, houses, barns, and driveways are all rich in traditional meaning. Such extreme attachment to specific properties has been attenuated by modern industrial and financial developments. A man who runs a huge wheat farm
today may sell out tomorrow and enter the warehouse,
milling, or commission business. He is likely to have no
interest in passing on specific acres to his heirs.

The search for profits has led to the discovery of ways of
making quick transfers from one claim to another. Hence
there has been constant increase in the liquidity of claims.

A quantitative estimate can be made of the total volume
of liquid assets by ascertaining the debts or claims which
are assumed to be convertible within a relatively short
time. Stocks and bonds which are listed on exchanges may
be included in the computation, since ordinary trading
operations are supposed to constitute a mechanism for con-
verting these claims into cash on short notice. Bank deposits should be included, since they are debts of the bank
to the depositor, which are presumed to be withdrawable
on demand or within a short time. The cash surrender
value of life insurance policies has usually been regarded
as available to policyholders through a process of lending
on a few days' notice.

Plainly these various arrangements for maintaining
liquidity function smoothly when the volume of realizations is kept within limits. Wherever attempts are made to

collect all bank deposits at one time, to sell all bonds and stocks at one time, to borrow on all life insurance policies at one time, or to force collection of all debts or claims at one time, the whole structure ceases to function. Such stoppages of function are precisely what happens in "panics"; and the severity of these malfunctionings is in proportion to the complexity of the superstructure.

Berle and Pederson have analyzed the ratio of liquid claims to national wealth in the United States. The figure was 16 per cent in 1880, 15 per cent in 1890, 18 per cent in 1900, 20 per cent in 1912. The war decade brought up the ratio to 25 per cent, and by 1930 the figure was 40 per cent. By 1933, third year of the depression, the ratio was 33 per cent.

This vast change in the relationship of person to goods was undermining the attachment of the individual to specific claims to property, and diminishing the connection between claims (ownership) and management. In the early days of private enterprise there was a strong link between ownership and management; this has rapidly weakened. The ownership claims are more often purely formal, depersonalized claims for continued units of nonspecific income. The guarantee of income is the crucial consideration; an opportunity for management is less important. Hence the speed with which demands for guaranteed income spread during adverse years. Hence the profound psychological insecurities generated by the depersonalization of business.

The oscillating behavior of capitalistic economic life is self-destructive precisely in the sense in which any adversity breeds disillusionment with the established order. It would, however, be a mistake to exaggerate the self-destructive tendencies of capitalism. Even oscillation is self-mitigating as well as self-destructive. During prosperity the destiny of the individual or of his subgroup seems to stay in his own hands. Basic uncertainty gives business something of the fascination of a game and a crime: a game, because success depends on combinations of luck and ability; a crime, because success depends in part on deception. From one point of view capitalistic society is a great confidence game, for it feeds on fantastic hopes. Millions throb with the prospect of fabulous riches in an economic system which is inherently destined to disappoint most of them.

The "insecurity prices" on the New York Stock Exchange during the boom put paper riches in the hands of millions; yet the whole thing seemed a little unreal. Despite the famous "New Era Boys," there was an atmosphere of the incredible which cushioned the shock of disenchantment. There was no outburst of moral revulsion because all the time there had been a profound suspicion that success was not a matter of morals, but of luck, smartness, and impostorship. It was a "grand racket while it lasted," a "joy ride," a "swell jag." The bargaining Yankee is still admired because he knows how to use his head to outsmart the other fellow, and this easy-going toleration of mutual fraud is a major trait of capitalistic society.

During prosperity, moreover, persons brought up to live abstemiously, to save, and to work are accustomed to luxurious and self-indulgent ways of life. But many of them never escape the early conscience. When the tide turns, adversity yields its satisfactions: one endures depressions to expiate the claims of conscience.

During prosperity, too, the population "succeeds" by ways of doing and thinking which are inconsistent with effective revolutionary action during depressions. In prosperity the individual is confirmed in private planning, in the expectation that rewards will follow self-assertion, and in individualistic pride in personal responsibility. But mass movements depend on the identification of the individual with collective symbols, collective demands, collective hopes. Individualists persevere in individualistic ways of life well into the depression; and thus far capitalism has been able to recover in the major countries. Capitalistic oscillation would seem to generate the psychological safeguards during its expansion which preserve it during collapse.

There is nothing predetermined about self-recovery, however; and the proposals now current for the protection of the system are compelled to rely upon the motivations and skills which can be recruited within the system itself, subject to all the entanglements of the system.

Striking differences in the distribution of wealth and income, prevalent in capitalistic countries, create constant provocations to attack the system which permits them to continue. Hence the undertone of discontent in prosperity and the overtone of protest in adversity. It is possible to separate, for analytic purposes, the problem of stabilizing capitalism from the problem of equalizing incomes. But it is clear that those who get the largest incomes usually assume that their vested interests are to sustain practices whose objective result is to promote instability. This is the inner contradiction in the policies of the plutocracy bred by capitalism. Policies of concession are clearly dictated by long-run considerations; but what are the intervening steps by which a sufficient concentration of vested and sentimental interest may be elicited? To this question we shall return from time to time in the course of this book.

Since the ruling elite usually has the goods at its disposal, the counter-elites which lead the masses must depend more on propaganda than on goods or violence. The potential economic strength or fighting strength of the masses may be concentrated by patient and prolonged propaganda.

To some extent control over goods is indispensable to any revolution. But until the actual seizure of power the control over goods is more important in its symbolic, that is to say, its propaganda, aspect than in its specifically economic aspect.

Withdrawal from cooperation in consumption, production, and other collective activities has been a principal weapon of the disadvantaged. Sometimes the boycott has drawn attention to conditions which aroused action favorable to the disadvantaged. In 1920 the International Trade Union Federation at Amsterdam called for the boycotting of Hungarian goods in protest against the repressive measures of the Hungarian government against labor. The result was to bring into the news of the world the previously suppressed reports of how the "white terror" avenged itself upon those who had been connected with the "red terror." In 1909 some support was won in America for the Chinese by means of a boycott by Chinese of American goods. The protest was directed against the alleged mistreatment of Chinese in America.

On some occasions nationalistic sentiment has been cemented by means of boycotts and strikes. In 1919 the Chinese nationalists organized a boycott against the award of Tsingtao to Japan. As early as 1905 Indians boycotted British goods and began to encourage domestic production. Such widespread movements of noncooperation as those led by Gandhi in recent years could only occur where the practice of noncooperation is deeply embedded in the culture. To this day in India it is a recognized procedure for a man who has suffered wrong from his neighbor to sit down before the latter's door and starve himself to death.

The bare threat is usually sufficient because if the victim were to perish, his ghost would presumably haunt the wrongdoer.

At certain times great expectations have been entertained of the effectiveness of the general strike as a means of social revolution. But it seems to be a weapon of limited utility. A general strike has occasionally been successful when launched by labor organizations on behalf of a demand which was popular with some other class in the community. In 1893 the Belgian general strike, which was enthusiastically hailed as a triumph of labor, was for the extension of the suffrage, a demand with which the middle classes were in sympathy. Other general strikes, like that of Sweden in 1909, failed through lack of support from other classes. In fact, the more specifically "proletarian" the demands have been, the more social formations have been marshaled for defensive action against the strike. Hence a general strike must either be a brief demonstration strike, or intensify a major revolutionary crisis, a resort to violence, a seizure of power. Such was the unmistakable meaning of the general strike of 1926 in Great Britain. The striking unions were confronted by the government's cry of "civil war"; and technical students and other volunteers did sufficiently well operating motor trucks and other essential services to prevent extreme disorganization of vital supplies for the community. In 1917 the general strike was a serviceable weapon at the height of the crisis in Moscow, although it was superfluous in Petrograd. In 1920 the Kapp *Putsch* in Berlin, met by a general strike, collapsed. But the Kapp adventurers were without active support in the community at large.

Until an elite has been disintegrated and discredited by colossal ground swells of insecurity, born of defeat and depression, rationalized by spokesmen of new and rising social formations, it is unassailable by withdrawals from cooperation, like strike and boycott.

Plainly the external position of an elite with reference to rival foreign elites is gravely affected by its control over commodities and services. Goods are both a measure of potential fighting strength and a means of fighting effectiveness. One means for the successful prosecution of war is the management of goods to induce dissatisfaction among enemy peoples, to win over allies, to preserve neutrals, and to strengthen internal morale. In a crisis the resources of the entire community are at stake and profit from a unified emergency administration.

The Central Powers were slowly strangled by the Allied blockade during the World War. Blockade cut down the supply of rubber, tin, cotton, copper, lubricating oils, and fats. The deficit was only partly made up by substitutes. Oils from the distillation of coal were substituted for lubricating oils of petroleum origin, and food and clothes were constantly modified. But progressive scarcity, like creeping paralysis, undermined the physical stamina and the morale of the population.

The extent to which wealthy powers were able to aid their allies is shown in these figures:

Loans by Great Britain	$ 8,770,000,000
Loans by France	2,817,000,000
Loans by United States	9,523,000,000
Loans by Germany	2,047,000,000
Total (others added)	23,660,000,000

The control over goods is nearly as important in the inter-elite rivalries of peace as of war. During the seventeenth and eighteenth centuries the theories and policies connected with mercantilism led to the imposition of discriminatory duties and prohibitions on the products of hostile countries. Peace treaties often included or were accompanied by tariff agreements which provided for the abolishing of prohibitions, for the renunciation of duties, and sometimes for most-favored-nation treatment. Friendly powers were bound to one another by preferential tariffs, notably in the case of the Methuen Treaty of 1703 between England and Portugal.

Jacob Viner has come to the conclusion that during the nineteenth century there was less relation between tariff policy and diplomacy, although tariffs continued to be used as means of pressure. One protracted series of controversies between Italy and France ran from 1888 to 1899. Since the World War the trend toward self-sufficiency has led to the general adoption of export and import licensing and quota or contingent requirements. Discrimination may be practiced in administrative fact even in contravention of legal duty by means of arbitrary valuations for customs purposes, by boycotting goods of foreign origin in government purchases and contracts, by embargoes on imports of animal or vegetable products in the guise of sanitary regulations, by preferred transportation rates for domestic commodities, and by similar devices.

To some extent considerations of fighting effectiveness have regulated the flow of investment into foreign countries. Before the World War, however, British investments abroad were comparatively little affected by such considerations. For 1914 these investments have been valued at 20 billion dollars, or about one-fourth of the national wealth of Great Britain, and constituted the largest bloc of the world's export capital. Where the sense of international insecurity was acute, as in France, calculations of fighting effectiveness influenced the distribution of loans abroad. In 1914 French foreign investments totaled $8,-

700,000,000, or 15 per cent of the national wealth. They were more concentrated in government and municipal bonds than British investments, which were more commonly in private undertakings. Melchior Palyi observes that about half of the foreign investment of France was in countries which were allies of France in the World War, or which were expected to be allies. About a third of the total foreign investment of France was lost as a result of repudiation and of other circumstances connected with the World War. English ownership of capital abroad was reduced by about a quarter, chiefly through the repatriation of American securities.

Many of the transactions which attend the movement of capital across national lines confer special influence upon the lending country. Concessions, or special privileges, range from tax exemption, agreements to spend the proceeds of the loan in the lending country, to the turning over of military, diplomatic, and fiscal control to the nationals or the government of the lending country. These devices of penetration have been most common when the borrowing country does not possess the technology of Western European civilization, when its government is unstable, and when foreign obligations are directly assumed by the borrowing government. Economic penetration depends upon a relative surplus of capital for investment. Since prewar Russia, alone among the great powers, was little industrialized, her landed aristocracy favored direct annexation rather than economic penetration, even as the landholders of many Southern states sought to expand the United States toward the southwest before 1861.

The World War, it will be remembered, broke up the world-wide division of labor, and substituted two self-sufficient, or "autarchic," systems: one composed of the Central Powers, one of the Entente. The expansion of the world market had generated conflicts which put profit seeking into the background, and brought considerations of fighting effectiveness to the fore. Hence the quest for invulnerability, each state seeking to attain economic self-sufficiency by controlling its own centers of iron and steel and food production. A divided and weakened Europe reduced to some extent the pressure on less commercialized and industrialized peoples. This favored the expansion of strong states far removed from Europe (like Japan). Instead of an expanding world economy there are now congeries of contracting local economies. Reduced standards of living intensify insecurity; greater insecurity threatens the traditional system, and the elites which profit by it. Prolonged crisis imperils the dualistic system of private and public hierarchies under capitalism. Big business and financial elites find themselves menaced by agitators skilled in the management of the masses, and by militarists stern in respect for glory, not profit.

Threatened from within and from without, the elites of a given community resort to oscillating policies of centralized, then decentralized control of essential goods and services, rationing, then pricing, sometimes to induce, sometimes to coerce, sometimes to divert. Challenging elites, handicapped by the concentration of goods and services in the hands of the established elites, practice withdrawals of cooperation as a means of heightening the will to power of the disaffected.

CHAPTER V

PRACTICES

The ascendancy of any elite partially depends upon the success of the practices it adopts. These procedures comprise all the ways by which elites are recruited and trained, all the forms observed in policymaking and administration. The constitution, written or unwritten, embodies the practices which are deemed most fundamental to the governmental and the social order. Constitutionalism is a special attitude toward the efficacy of written words, "a name," writes Walton H. Hamilton, "given to the trust which men repose in the power of words engrossed on parchment to keep a government in order."

Since practices are changeable details within a changing whole, an established elite can use them to defend itself by catharsis, or by readjustment. Catharsis, the harmless discharge of tension, may be fostered by such humble devices as the act of showing solicitude for the bereaved. The ruler is wise to attend to the disasters of the community, and to signify his prompt and earnest sympathy to the survivors. Whether quake, flood, hurricane, drought, or pestilence, the resulting insecurities are potentially dangerous to the social order. Hence the canker of resentment must not be permitted to thrive in lonely sadness. Gestures of condolence plus bread are far more potent than bread alone. It is safer to economize on bread than on condolence.

For purposes of defense by catharsis and minor readjustment an established order can rely upon the rearrangement of its own details. During the nineteenth and twentieth centuries, capitalistic nations have avoided revolutionary upset by minor modifications of the institutional order. To some extent the devices of democratization and education diverted attention from the underlying property system. Discontent drained into crusades for universal suffrage, proportional representation, and free public education. The bourgeois revolution did not abolish undemocratic forms of franchise at one blow, but in a protracted series of taps.

Disabilities in legal status were slowly liquidated at vast expense of crusading zeal and energy. The emancipation of negro slaves held by whites, inaugurated in the British colonies in 1833, was not completed until the act of Brazil in 1888. Forms of domestic slavery were tolerated in the African spheres of influence of the great powers, but the traffic in slaves was illegalized in the Brussels convention of 1890. Alone among the Western nations, prewar Russia divided her people into classes having different legal capacity (nobility, clergy, citizens, peasants, besides Asiatics and Jews). The last trace of peasants' disabilities did not disappear in Germany until 1867. By comity and treaty, most modern nations came to accord aliens practically the same civil capacity as citizens.

Disability upon the wife in the marital community began to be removed by legislative reform in America about 1840, and England followed America, beginning about 1870. The personal control of the father over the child has been curtailed, starting first with criminal punishment for cruelty. Freedom of opinion in religion, art, literature, and science was the drift of the times.

The underlying property system was also preserved by the discharge of discontent into controversies over sumptuary legislation. The social program of the bourgeois revolution was not only negative, in the sense that it abolished restrictions on the market, but positive, in the sense that it turned attention to the possibility of molding a bourgeois style of life by means of legislative prohibitions. The mass of the people, struggling for material prosperity, cultivated the "middle-class" virtues of industriousness and domestic regularity, and with the rise of democracy, legislative policy became more aggressive toward such disturbing influences as gambling, drink, and vice.

Since the illegalization of gambling, drinking, and prostitution did not destroy the demand, the chief effect of prohibitory legislation was to withdraw legal protection from certain business enterprises. These were compelled to provide their own means of protecting their investment and enforcing contracts; hence they paid for gangsters and political favors. In the United States, where administration is decentralized, and there has been little direct control by the nation of urban and local life, the resulting administrative laxity frequently generates "reform waves."

Another safety valve for the discharge of discontents against something other than the property system was religious revivalism. English revivalism began with the Wesleys in 1743. The experiences of mass emotion and the practice of assembling, and to some extent of acting, together were of some importance in shaping the labor movement. But attention was diverted from secular symbols of reform and revolution. Waves of revivalism swept over Germany from 1814 to 1836, appealing to the new urban proletariat and galvanizing them into a semblance of collective action. In such years of depression as 1837 and 1853 the United States was the scene of many intense evangelistic campaigns in the cities where the suffering was greatest.

When the criticism of capitalistic individualism became practical politics, concessions took the form of "social legislation." Money had already been spent to provide educational opportunity for the young, but "social legislation" broadened the scope of the state to assume part of the burden of caring for the superannuated, the disabled, and the defective. Many of the consequences of industrialism shocked the sensibilities of influential groups in society, and it was also feared that certain influences were undermining the military effectiveness as well as the industrial efficiency of the masses.

Fear of monopoly led to demands for government ownership and operation, or at least for regulation. Influential business groups soon discovered that they had little to lose from regulatory commissions. In many cases state regulatory commissions were preferred to local or to national bodies. State control commissions reduced the number of authorities to be controlled, and at the same time retained a sufficiently large number of agencies to handicap any effort to use the government for effective socialization. Such commissions were bulwarks of defense against popular petulance and local exactions. The state as the "umpire of competition" could be induced to suffer from myopia.

The lapping waves of discontent continued, however, to erode the breakwaters which were constructed in defense of the established property arrangements. During depressions, battle lines tended to form more and more around slogans and expedients of basic social protest. In many places the reserve concessions of democratic government ran toward exhaustion. A new disillusionment with democracy was expressed in sharper criticisms of parliament, of the "mere legalism" of the old Bill of Rights, and of the "reality" of democracy.

Viewing the transformations of the nineteenth century in retrospect, A. V. Dicey came to the conclusion that criticism of democratic institutions meant that the task of democracy had changed. At first the goal was destruction; all were united in abolishing old restrictions. Now, however, the destructive task of democracy had been accomplished. It had entered upon a constructive phase; but there was little unity in the discovery of positive goals.

Another way to diagnose the situation was to say that the defensive possibilities of democracy for capitalism were becoming depleted. The forms of democratic parliamentarism were being devalued for the masses, who were more insistent upon the use of democracy for socialized purposes. Democratic practices, therefore, could no longer protect a beleaguered capitalism during recurring crises of discontent. Hence capitalism, it was predicted, would soon abandon democracy and rely upon dictatorship.

Every new revolutionary pattern has a vast repertory of minor changes which can be made in order to cope with the insecurities of the population. This was true of the bourgeois revolution, and it is equally true of the revolution in Russia. In the cataclysm of 1917 the fundamental property relationships were altered, and two major social formations—the landed aristocracy and the private plutocracy—were totally liquidated. Organized life is now governmentalized, and the devices at hand for coping with potential discontent are countless. A unified hierarchy of this kind, as long as it retains competent central direction, can deflect hostilities away from itself by changing from rationing to pricing and back again, if need be. It can appear to the community in protean forms, organizing, consolidating, exterminating, rechristening at will. Differences in money income, once so great under private capitalism, can be rearranged in thousands of minor gradations to stimulate the maximum of individual and small group effort. Many forms of honorific distinction can be invented, and discarded when stigma becomes attached to them.

Plainly it is not profitable to consider any practice apart from the principal features of the context in which it operates. Elite preservation is furthered by judicious combinations of efficiency and acceptability. It is dangerous to sacrifice acceptability for efficiency; and it is dangerous to allow momentary considerations of acceptability to obscure the long-run dangers of some forms of inefficiency.

Judgments about all the traditional patterns of policy making and administration require constant revision in the light of the purposes to be served in changing circumstances. The perils of overemphasis are only matched by the perils of underemphasis, whether the pattern in question is dictatorship or democracy, centralization or decentralization, concentration or dispersion, functional universalization or limitation, obedience or originality, bias or objectivity.

Crisis demands dictatorship, centralization, concentration, obedience, and bias. Intercrisis permits concessions toward democracy, decentralization, dispersion, originality, and objectivity.

Once reasonably certain of rather general support, a recently established elite can afford to democratize the basis of authority, and to use liberalities and restrictions as chips in the baccarat of catharsis and readjustment. Members of any successful revolutionary party want their friends to join for the sake of security and influence within the party, and there are members of the community who seek the privileges that come from belonging to the new "aristocracy." Hence the party is diluted by members who are insufficiently indoctrinated. These members are disposed to exercise their influence on behalf of conciliatory and temporizing policies. This alarms the "diehard" fundamentalists of a vigorous revolutionary party, and sharpens the contradiction between "orthodox" and "moderates." The men on top of the party pyramid can take advantage of this contradiction to hold first one and then another party element responsible for any recent failures. Hence the celebrated "purges" which expunge "wavering" or "irreconcilable" personalities from the party rolls. Then the process of accretion begins again. Roberto Michels has called the expansion and contraction of revolutionary parties the "accordion rhythm." As a general sense of security increases, the trend is toward democratization.

Although it is necessary to centralize in crises, when prompt, decisive action is safer than malcoordination and delay, centralization has notorious disadvantages. In order to mitigate the bureaucratic consequences of great centralization, authorities in the Soviet Union have encouraged many devices of mass criticism. Wall newspapers are prepared in plants and clubs, and the peasants' correspondence ventilates many grievances and fosters initiative. Plainly, however, mass criticism can be encouraged only when the elite is sufficiently secure.

Modern devices of "attitude measurement" have been applied to the task of keeping the elite informed of the changing waves of discontent. Data are carefully tabulated in "morale charts" to show the spores of disaffection and noncooperation.

The invention of certain technical devices has made it possible to compare the results of administrative effort, and to stimulate honesty and emulation. Sidney and Beatrice Webb have remarked that in the early part of the nineteenth century the business of government in Great Britain, whether national or local government, was honeycombed with "favouritism, corruption, and barefaced peculation." Most of this was swept away by the adoption of the audit, a device which is scarcely a century old. The practice of checking the cash transactions of all public officials by a special class of independent experts has improved the general standard of honesty no less than accuracy, and proved how the "habits of human nature" can be altered on a large scale.

As crisis recedes, governments can decentralize. It is important, however, to manage the decentralization in such a way that central agencies can resume control in lawful ways when future emergencies arise. This is the great technical advantage of the practice of devolution, which invests a subordinate authority with a broad competence, subject to specific reservations and future resumptions. Some of the "home rule charters" in American urban communities exhibit true devolutions of authority. But the scope of this principle in the nation as a whole is circumscribed by the federal practice, which delegates specific and limited authority to a central agency. A necessary concession to acceptability when the federal constitution was drafted, it has often barred the path to efficiency. It is inimical to respect for constitutionality when formal barriers are too high for prompt centralization in crises.

Intimately connected with the expedient degree of centralization is the problem of organizing public authority in legislatures or in assemblies. In nations like the United States, where there has been some degree of exemption from the fear of foreign attack, legislatures have been channels of regional trading rather than national policy. It is abundantly plain, of course, that any national policy implies the consideration of component interests and sentiments. But legislatures create vested and sentimental interests which weight national policy in the direction of patchwork rather than mosaic. The local legislator often devotes himself to the advancement of neighborhood projects by striking bargains on national issues.

Such consequences need not invariably be associated with legislatures. In Great Britain, for example, a singularly delicate set of understandings has been developed which render it possible to change the effective executive (the Cabinet) only after a general election. Special procedures have been invented to route local matters through channels which integrate them in terms of national policy. For modern governments, however, it is probably expedient to minimize the effect of interlocality trading by sharing authority with assemblies and not with legislatures.

Thus the Soviet Union operates with an assembly rather than a legislature. The assembly is composed of a great many delegates, meets for a short time, listens to broad reports and discussions of policy, expresses itself, especially by the choice of a continuing committee, and retires. This assembly is an important instrument for procuring acceptance of the policies of the central executive. But it need not be assumed that the tone of the assembly is without influence upon the men at the center.

No doubt there will be many efforts to extend the influence of the assembly and to transform it into an agency exercising the same detailed supervision over policy and administration in the Soviet Union which legislatures have obtained in many foreign lands. But it is doubtful if the authority of the assembly will increase appreciably in the visible future of the Soviet Union, because the specter of external danger is not laid, and in centralization lies preparedness.

There are many ways short of formal centralization by which united action may be attained. The "grant-in-aid"

offers tangible inducement to local authorities to conform
to centrally defined standards. The device of the executive
budget compels the consideration of the total communal
enterprise. Both the talk and the practice of planning focus
attention upon definite goals, and compel the justification
of local demands in terms of inclusive advantages.

Crises not only make it wise to centralize but to concentrate authority. In the acute struggles from 1917 through
1921 in Russia, influence became more concentrated in the
Communist party at the expense of rival agencies. Rival
parties were at first allowed to persist, but they were presently liquidated as the Communist party established a monopoly of legality. Other influential organizations, like the
army, the trades unions, and the cooperatives were all subordinated to the party. That decisive, though piecemeal,
liquidation of organized nodules of actual or potential opposition is essential to dictatorship was thoroughly learned
by Mussolini and Hitler from the Russian experience. Hitler moved with the utmost dispatch. On May 2, 1933, the
old trades-union officials of Germany were ejected from
their posts, their buildings and property seized, their members incorporated in a special organization of the National
Socialist party. Within a few more days all the political
parties were destroyed. Meanwhile hostile elements were
"purified" from the government services, and the "totali-
tarian" state was close to completion.

As crisis recedes in the Soviet Union, the political committee of the Communist party is able, in actual practice,
to share more authority with roughly coordinate agencies.
Initiative can be permitted in more centers and funneled
less narrowly through the principal party conduit. But the
committee will doubtless continue to integrate the life of the
entire Union whenever a sense of threat, or a chance of
expansion, inspires the ruling elite.

Such concentration is difficult in the United States, owing to the system of "checks and balances" which was set up under the influence of certain interpretations of the British constitution and of the laws of mechanics. In moments of extreme emergency when the nation demands action the presidency can eclipse the two coordinate branches of government, the Congress and the court. But when threats recede, the President must rely mainly on the patronage power to preserve discipline on behalf of a national policy, as W. Y. Elliott has recently reminded us. The President cannot force the legislators to contest their seats on matters of grave national concern, which is the alternative always open to the British Cabinet. It is a question to what extent the conflicts between the several branches of the federal government cast discredit upon the capacity of democratic government to act boldly for the collective advantage. Thus respect for constitutionality may suffer once more from its apparent role in the strangulation of action.

Authority can be dispersed along functional lines during intercrisis periods, especially in modern civilized communities, where organized activities play such decisive roles. Functional interests in the United States are quite directly expressed through the hundreds of special agencies which maintain headquarters in Washington or New York and direct lobbying activities toward officials and propaganda activities toward the electorate. This "Third House of Congress" is at least nominally legalized in the institutional plan of the "soviet" or the "corporative" states. In the Soviet Union, Italy, and Germany, crisis has been so continuous that the functional apportionment of authority has proceeded but a little way. The experience of Republican Germany with the Economic Advisory Council plainly showed that on political questions a functional body duplicates the territorial body, or that it is superfluous, since on technical questions sufficient contributions can be made by small administrative advisory committees. If a functionally selected legislature were substituted for the territorial legislature, almost no changes of alignment on political questions would take place.

During crises elites value obedience rather than originality. Suffering all the pangs of inner uncertainty, rulers covet the reassuring tones of respectful coordination. But obedience is often a notorious drag on initiative and efficiency. When regimes are less afraid of losing their position, they are wise to endure some lack of piety in the interest of ingenuity.

It is self-evident that during crises an elite is wise to recruit administrators and other agents primarily for bias and secondarily for objectivity. Bias in favor of the elite breeds self-confidence among the elite. But bias, like docility, has limitations. Skill in exhibitions of loyalty may become better developed than skill in shooting, accounting, or disciplining. Objectivity is itself a value, since it curbs the impulse to distort reality. Objectivity, or at least the appearance of objectivity, is especially useful in courts and quasi-judicial tribunals.

Objectivity can be fostered by many procedural devices which are intended to diminish the quick passage of impulse into action. Thus evidence presented to a court may be subjected to elaborate rules of inclusion and exclusion. Certain tones of voice and modes of address may be required in courts and legislatures. The function of chairmen may be to safeguard the interests of all who desire expression, and to prevent the discussion group from dissolving into a crowd.

Certain special problems present themselves to revolu-

tionary counter-elites. In general their task is to guide the
rebellious impulses of the moment into the ways of action
which give permanence and power to protest.

Modern revolutionary strategy takes it for granted that
sound procedure calls for the training of a body of professional revolutionaries who are capable of seizing revolutionary opportunities. But it is difficulty to state how far it
is wise to rely upon mass organizations, or to depend principally upon smaller bodies which specialize in the use of
symbols of mass appeal.

In the middle years of the nineteenth century, organizations which enunciated revolutionary goals were agita-
tional-conspirative, and hence small. In the ensuing years,
organizations in the name of the proletarian revolution
often grew to embrace many millions. Germany and
Austria were the scene of Social Democratic movements
which rivaled in structural complexity the intricacy of
capitalism itself. Such organizations and suborganizations
developed elaborate bureaucracies which were usually ex-
empt from physical danger in the performance of their
duties. They peacefully edited, orated, organized.

Where socialism spelt danger, as in Russia, the agita-
tional-conspirative methods came to prime expression. This
did not mean that tiny conspirative cells bore the brunt of
revolutionary struggle and committed acts of individual
terror. Very considerable organizations were constructed,
but they were limited to those who were seasoned to the
dangers of protest. Elsewhere, immense membership structures lacked fighting vigor. The sheer labor involved in
the internal management of these complicated organizations bound energy inside the organization in petty drudgery and ceremony. Oligarchiral tendencies, described by
Roberto Michels, produced a spiritless monstrosity when
the hour of opportunity struck. Evidently there had been

too much mass organization in proportion to mass appeal.

Operating from the triumphant center of revolution, the Third International undertook to subordinate national initiative to the decisions of the central hierarchy, which remained under Russian influence. Since a major revolutionary movement does not develop as a local but as a general movement of protest, the elite which arises to power is assured of moral support from abroad. The Russian elite was saved by the sympathetic cooperation of masses and mass organizations whose threats of revolution handicapped the hostile efforts of established governments. Thus Great Britain was prevented from giving unrestricted aid to Poland against Russia, and to White generals operating against the Soviets, because British statesmen were constantly hampered by the British workers.

The Third International tried to crystallize all this sympathy in a central organization in which, in fact, the Russian group would preponderate. This subjected the leaders of all foreign proletarian organizations to a damaging cross fire. If they supported "foreign" symbols of class war, they were open to devastating attack by spokesmen of the middle class, plutocracy, and aristocracy as antipatriotic and antinationalistic. But if they failed to subordinate themselves to the Third International, they were open to attack from some of the most dynamic and impatient elements inside the laboring class.

Even formal affiliation with the Third International did not assuage the crisis. Very often the measures demanded by the highly centralized organization in Moscow seemed much better adapted to serve the diplomatic expediencies of the new regime than to advance the cause of socialist revolution. Local communists were open to the jibe that they were the "Foreign Legion of Russia" rather than the vanguard of the socialist revolution.

The inner crises of German communism expressed these contradictory tendencies in the sharpest possible manner. There was a split in 1919 over trades-union policy, parliamentarism and Russian dictatorship. The Levi crisis came in 1921 after the unsuccessful "March days." In 1923 the failures in Saxony and Thuringia led to the expulsion of the Brandler group and the building of a communist opposition. In 1925 the "ultraleft" era of Ruth Fischer and Maslow was liquidated in another split. The history discloses many sharp dissensions over individuals and tactics which did not produce a serious break. Efforts were made to smash the Social Democrats by the formation of rival parties, trades unions, military and youth organizations. Plainly it was not foreseen that before the Social Democracy could be demoralized the defensive measures of the established order would find expression in a movement which would decapitate communists and Social Democrats alike. The overcentralized Third International, dominated by and for what were supposed to be the interests of the revolution as embodied in the Russian government, split the masses for the benefit of Fascism.

The implication is that when truly revolutionary movements have seized power anywhere it is wise to relax control from the center, and to permit foreign revolutionary processes to mature along separate national lines.

For elites and counter-elites alike it is wise to avoid rigid loyalty to specific devices. The ebb and flow of collective insecurity threatens whatever *is* with disgrace; and whatever is next will be discredited in time.

CHAPTER VI

SKILL

Political analysis is not only interested in the methods by which the influential are protected or superseded. It is also concerned with the characteristics of those who obtain such values as deference, safety, income. One aspect of the matter is the partition of values among the exponents of various skills.

A skill is a teachable and learnable operation, and skills include the technique of manipulating things or the symbols of things (skills of manual workers or engineers), the technique of manipulating ceremonial symbols, and the techniques of violence, of organization, of bargaining, of propaganda, of analysis.

It is plain that craftsmen and all who exercise the semiskills connected with the simpler manual operations seldom rise to eminence. The German Reichstag election of 1919 coincided with acute social crisis and the tide was running "left." Yet the new Reichstag had among its members only 2.4 per cent who were "workers," 2.1 per cent who were "salaried workers," and 1.9 per cent who were "craftsmen." The grand total for the manual skills was thus 6.4 per cent, which was remarkably similar to the situation in the Reichstag of 1912. Then the "workers" accounted for 0.5 per cent of the total membership, "salaried workers" were 1.8 per cent, "craftsmen" were 2.5 per cent, and the grand total was 4.8 per cent.

Agriculturists are almost universally underrepresented in proportion to numbers. Exceptions appear principally where agriculture is run according to a system which transforms the nominal farmer or estate holder into an administrator of persons rather than a manipulator of things. Small farming communities are prone to allow themselves to be represented by lawyers or other specialists in the handling of people by means of symbols.

It is noteworthy that engineering skill, so prominent in our society, has seldom led to the posts of greatest eminence. The heroes of the people have seldom been engineers or physical scientists. This remains true despite all the opportunities which have arisen as a result of the application of mechanical, electrical, and chemical energy to production. Wholly new specializations have arisen, concerned with chemistry, electricity, aeronautics, gas, steam, and radio; and older engineering branches have been profoundly modified. The sensational glut of new devices sometimes obscures the long history of specialization on the handling of nature. One may recall the attainments of Egyptians, Babylonians, and Chinese in grading, crowning, and bridging military roads; in constructing fortifications with walls, towers, gateways, moats; in laying out cities and supplying them with water and sewerage systems. Harbors included lighthouses, dredged channels, breakwaters, wharves, warehouses, cranes, windlasses, and water supply. Great works of land reclamation called for dams, irrigation, and drainage. Temples, cathedrals, monuments, and other public edifices and private dwellings are found in the ruins of early civilizations which flourished in Middle America and elsewhere.

So absorbed have the engineers been in the gratifications of their calling that they have been singularly free of outspoken occupational imperialism. They have rarely been articulate in demanding the control of high policy and administration, and in eliciting the support of the masses in the name of some complimentary mythology. In the United States the most elaborate case for the engineer has been made, not by an engineer, but by the economist Thorstein Veblen. In *The Engineers and the Price System* (New York, 1921) Veblen indicted the predatory captain of industry and proposed a system of economic organization in which production and distribution would be determined by engineers. The term "engineer," however, was so broadly defined that it far transcended the customary meaning of the word. The nearest approach to a popular movement spoke in the name of "technocracy," and reached a brief heyday of fame during the great depression after 1929. "Technocracy" was in many ways a very fortunate coinage; it avoided the doctrinaire implications of an "ism," and capitalized the prestige of the terms "technology" and "democracy."

The engineering indictment of the prevailing system runs in terms of waste, and the way to a utopia of plenty is by scientific management. The studies of waste which have been conducted by the Taylor Society in the United States are harbingers of a future when the engineers may rise to greater skill consciousness.

Those who specialize less in the management of things than in the management of the symbols of things are physical scientists. They suffer from the disabilities of the engineer in reaching for the highest posts of deference. It is true that Painlevé was a mathematician and a successful parliamentarian, that De Valera is a mathematician and an Irish nationalist, and that Weizmann is a chemist and a Zionist; but these are exceptional rather than typical.

The physician is an interesting combination of skills, for he learns much of physical technique, but he cannot wholly neglect interpersonal factors. Although the practice of healing brings the practitioner into intimate contact with people, few physicians have risen to posts of general prominence in modern public life. That Clemenceau was a physician in early life had little to do with his final career. In small communities where any learned profession may be believed to equip the individual to grapple on even terms with the "city slickers," physicians may enjoy deference in collective movements. Even so, it is unusual to find as many doctors as there are in the Irish Dail and the Irish Senate (14 in 213 members). Occasionally a physician to an influential king or dictator has won the confidence of his client and patron. When knowledge was less differentiated than today, persons who are reported to have studied medicine more often rose to diplomatic or administrative distinction. But it is not always possible to make out exactly what they studied under the name of medicine.

On the whole it seems reasonable to adhere to the view that heroes, and influential figures behind the scenes, are usually recruited from those who specialize in the management of men rather than the management of things. The control of conduct is the essential skill even when this is associated with elaborate technical skill in engineering or physical science.

The role of skill in violence among the heroes of mankind scarcely needs to be remarked. However, it is true that fighters have often been devalued for long periods of time. Western European civilization has assigned so much importance to the accumulation of property that the prestige of warriors has dwindled. In China the low regard in which fighting men are held has become proverbial.

But specialists in violence obtain a new lease on life when internal and external crises arise. It is notorious that every war and revolution leaves a legacy of military personages in its wake. In addition to General George Washington the list of candidates for the presidency of the United States who have had a military record includes Jackson, Harrison, Taylor, Scott, McClellan, Grant, Hayes, Garfield, Hancock, Harrison, McKinley, Theodore Roosevelt.

In some societies the road to eminence is not by fighting but by ceremony, as among the Zuni of the American Southwest. Within any society the most striking examples of those who sustain themselves by means of symbols are those who are devoted to ceremony. As the term is here understood, the true ceremonial act is one which involves a minimum of change in overt communal relationships, and is supposed to benefit the community as a whole. It is a true ceremony, in this sense, to perform a dance which is supposed to safeguard the fertility of the soil and the growth of crops. The dance works a minimum change in overt relationships, and is an act which we call "socially internalized." Such an internalized act may be contrasted with the act of judging between two claimants for property, or the act of joining in a raid on a neighboring community. Such acts modify overt relationships. They are "socially externalized."

In most communities there are persons who derive their influence and their livelihood by specializing in true ceremonies. Some ascetics spend their time in seclusion and prayer, obtaining expressions of deference and gifts of goods from the environment. Some priests spend their time in retreat or in the conduct of ritually prescribed operations which modify the emotional responsiveness of those who know about them, but work no other change in the situation.

In some societies the amount of specialization upon socially internalized acts is very insignificant. Every man may be his own priest and magician, communicating directly with a guiding spirit, and obtaining possession of objects and practices which are believed to have automatic power. Where a bit of stone is preserved because it is supposed to bring good luck, it is magic; when the stone is entreated and cajoled as if it were human, it is religion. As Ruth Benedict expresses the difference, magic is technological and mechanistic, while religion is animistic.

Field workers have estimated that a third of the time of some Pueblo Indians is given over to the rehearsal and performance of acts, principally dances, which are ceremonially important. But the number of those who specialize exclusively in ceremony is unimportant. It is notable, however, that many societies support a priesthood which mediates between the individual and the personalized universe.

Such priesthoods are found in varying degrees of helpfulness or rivalry with chiefs. Sometimes the ceremonial function becomes entangled with a host of additional functions. Chieftainship and priesthood are sometimes merged in a single office. Through consolidation chieftains have risen to wider control, and become emperors, fusing royal and priestly prerogatives. The Emperor of Japan, as Son of Heaven, is the highest priest of the land. The Emperor of Rome was Pontifex Maximus.

Sometimes the emperor has been immobilized through the exaggeration of his ceremonial duties. So it was in feudal China: the chief overlord preserved his peculiar potency by devoting himself entirely to the life of the court and to etiquette. Imprisoned by the court, webbed around by etiquette, the overlord reigned only on condition of remaining passive, of ordering nothing in detail, and of refraining from direct administration. He could act only through the simple efficacy of prestige, exercising less power of command than power of inspiration, more often associated with the chief of a sacred hierarchy than with the chief of a state.

The process by which a priestly elite may retain its sacerdotal symbols and add externalized functions as well can often be traced from historical data. The priestly elite which assisted in the performance of the priestly duties of the emperor developed into a priestly bureaucracy in China and a priestly caste in India. In Rome the various tribal priests were assimilated into a comprehensive *sodalitas;* but in Greece the tribal priests remained separated, never forming a unified priestly caste. In the new kingdom of Egypt the priestly caste was a serious challenge to the authority of the state. Although important from the earliest times in Babylon, the priests gained the upper hand in Israel only after the Exile. In Western Europe the priests predominated after the collapse of the Empire in the west, and they were curbed only as a result of movements which were usually led by secular authorities on the periphery of their sphere of influence. These authorities cooperated with the lesser clergy who were in revolt against the centralization of control at Rome. Such was the social composition of the most active elements in the Reformation.

Much of the history of Western Europe has pivoted on the rivalry of elites for the control of all the symbols capable of arousing submissive responses from the masses. Sometimes both "sacred" and "secular" symbols have been claimed by those who had previously been regarded as specialists in the one or the other. This was signalized in the struggles of Pope versus Emperor.

The effort to do away with "sacred" symbols of any kind, undertaken in the Soviet Union, is almost unique. The usual course of totalitarianism is to seize control of "sacred" symbols and to exploit them for control purposes. An influential element in the National Socialist party is

determined to develop a purely local system of sacred symbols which will detach Germans from loyalty to religious
vocabularies and customs beyond the frontiers of Germany.
As long as there are Germans who feel themselves "Catholic," "Protestant," "Jewish," or even "Christian," just so
long is a source of disunion at hand. It is feared that the
discontented will invoke support from abroad in the name
of these sacred symbols. Hence the plan is to abandon the
"Jewish-Christian" God and to return to the god symbols
which were current before the "Jewish-Christian God"
was "foisted" upon the "Aryans."

In the United States the secular elites have sought to
minimize the influence of priests and clergymen in politics
by proclaiming that they, themselves, championed Christianity and religion. The implication is that the participation of the clergy in government is unnecessary in order to
protect religion, especially since the clergy are associated
with the special interests of particular denominations. The
secular politician stands as the spokesman of the most inclusive symbols of piety, and is confronted by a disunited
front of ecclesiastical rivals.

This review of the ceremonial elite, as typified in the
priesthood, has shown how often the specialist on ceremony
has become a specialist on organization, enhancing his role
in the life of the community. He has sometimes moved over
to the control of marriage, family, inheritance, and many
other overt social relationships. Skill in organization, however, need not be associated with ceremonialism. Skills in
keeping accounts, collecting taxes, recording titles, handling correspondence, recruiting, training, supplying are
often independent avenues to wider influence. Skill in coordination becomes more essential as the division of labor
grows more complex, or as the scale of concerted action is
broadened in scope. Conquering chieftains have seen their

triumphs wither into dust in the absence of the organizing skill of a bureaucracy. The "bureaucratic culture pattern," traced with care by W. C. MacLeod, has exercised a standardizing influence over the course of political organization.

Skill in bargaining has been so important in the world of business and diplomacy that it may justifiably be singled out for independent consideration. With the gradual dissolution of customary restrictions on the terms of transactions, modern industrialism has, until recently, widened the scope of the competitive market. Skill in "buying cheap and selling dear" became a royal pathway to wealth and distinction.

Another major skill is advocacy, especially in the form of propaganda. There are forms of propaganda in which the personal convictions of the propagandist are important. This is true in the missionary activities of the proselyting religions, and it is true of the propaganda of revolutionary movements. Where personal danger is involved, conviction counts. But most modern propaganda is carried out under the direction of those who have no particular convictions about what their clients want. The modern public relations counsel or advertising agency or press agent has the same code as the lawyer, without the restraints which surround the lawyer. They accept fees to organize symbols to promote the attitudes desired by their clients. The late Ivy Lee rose to eminence as a counselor of the Pennsylvania Railroad, of the Rockefeller interests, and of other important clients. Shortly before his death he disclosed in a Congressional investigation that he had been retained by the German dye trust to advise on their problem of handling the attitudes of the American public toward the German government. Only after the World War did the propagandists begin to attain public recognition, and to overcome the earlier associations with the theatrical press agent or the loud-mouthed spieler at a side show.

Another important symbol skill is in the analysis of human relations. The extension to the relationships among men of the same objective attitude with which men approached physical nature is not qualitatively new. The classical writings of Kautilya, the East Indian, or Aristotle, the Greek, or Machiavelli, the Italian, testify with sufficient eloquence to the penetrating detachment with which some men have become equipped. But the growth of a sizable body of scholars devoted to history and the social and psychological sciences is quite recent. From the mother matrix of law, philosophy, theology, and history have come economists, political scientists, sociologists, social psychologists, individual psychologists, cultural anthropologists, human geographers, social biologists, and many other skill groups.

The connection between priestly skill and analytic skill has often been most intimate. Some priesthoods have specialized as seers, divining the future and stating the courses of action available in the present, thus rendering themselves of signal importance in policy and administration. Concern for the correct pronunciation of words in sacrificial incantations and cult songs made phoneticians and grammarians of the early Brahmans. With the growth of writing the priest often became historiographer and author of sacred codes, guardian of archives, editor of prayers and songs. As theologian he systematized teachings about the number of gods, and perfected the practice of dialectic.

In Western Europe the secularizing of intellectual skills has gone forward gradually through several centuries. Hanseatic merchants sought to emancipate themselves from the clerics by establishing municipal schools of their own. The growth of bookkeeping in Italian cities furnished an occupation for secular intellectuals. The prestige of Arabic and Greek knowledge during the Renaissance created a personality style for wealthy merchants who were supposed to support gentlemen of letters to flatter and instruct them. The rediscovery of printing from movable type, and the spread of cheap publishing, reduced the clerical monopoly of knowledge. The growth of bureaucratic posts multiplied the number of secular livelihoods available, and strengthened the secular gentry against upper secular and ecclesiastical groups. The breakup of the Roman Catholic Church fostered the fragmentation of Christendom and separated secular and sacerdotal authority more sharply than it had been before. With the spread of free public schools, the control of learning passed further out of the hands of the clergy and into the custody of the servants of the secular state.

The are several forms of intellectual expression which supplement, and which also rival, one another. The skill struggles among the practitioners of the intellectual arts often take the following shapes: *naturalistic* versus *normative, systematic* versus *impressionistic, expository* versus *depictive.*

The naturalistic style of discourse uses words which state conditions rather than preferences. The normative style abounds in terms like "ought," "good," "ugly." The modern social sciences emphasize the naturalistic modes of expression. Ethics, aesthetics, and some aspects of epistemology and metaphysics fall in the normative category. Political science is naturalistic; political philosophy is normative. In practice these distinctions are of relative emphasis rather than total exclusion.

Social conflicts afford ready opportunity for advancement by the use of "ought" words. Symbol specialists are demanded who can invent or elaborate the language of justification for the exercise, or the denial, of authority.

Contrasting demands are thus defended by appeals to legality, morality, or religion; and decisions among contending parties are couched in the same vocabulary. Lawyers, trained in the canon, Roman and common law, were conspicuous in the defense of the princes against the papacy, and of the monarchs against the nobility. During the eighteenth century when the tides of social criticism were running high against the monarchical system, the symbol makers were the *philosophies,* who as a rule were less professionalized than lawyers or theologians. In the same way it was nonacademic intellectuals who bore the responsibility of protesting against the advance of capitalistic society. There is some evidence that academic intellectuals were more conspicuous in nationalistic than in drastic revolutionary movements.

The prominence of polemical journalists, pamphleteers, lawyers, and theologians need not distract attention from the steady increase in the number of those who are supported in society because they can describe and compare many of the more complex routines of social life. They are constantly in demand for advice and support, whether they rise to popular recognition as members of a "Brain Trust" or no. Most of the current social sciences were once comprehended within the general term "moral philosophy." The first chair of "political economy" in the United States appears to have been occupied at Columbia University in 1818, and similar establishments spread gradually over the country. Political science took shape more slowly, although Dr. Thomas Cooper began to teach chemistry, politics, and political economy at South Carolina College in 1811. As a rule the connection was intimate with philosophy and law, and retained much of the normative tone of those disciplines.

Since the professional demand for lawyers was great,

efforts were made from time to time to broaden the curriculum of the law schools. When Francis Lieber was called to Columbia in 1857, it was hoped that he could overcome what was called the narrow specialization of law students by attracting them to courses in history and political science. This was a failure, and Lieber himself was finally transferred to the law school where he taught constitutional history and public law. The School of Political Science which was finally organized at Columbia University in 1880 at the initiative of John W. Burgess was the outcome of another unsuccessful effort to break down law school specialization.

The professors of moral philosophy were often so far out of touch with the new routines of business and government that they were at a loss for timely and relevant illustrations of classical aphorisms in terms of modern life. This discrepancy made it possible for new generations of specialists to gain attention by concentrating upon the task of describing the new routines of the expanding civilization in which they lived. This greatly increased the academic emphasis upon the naturalistic at the expense of the normative.

The processes just sketched in the United States were common to all the areas having contact with European civilization. Plainly a thirst for description and for comparison depends chiefly upon the appearance of novel phenomena. At first the impetus in this direction was "extensive" rather than "intensive." The age of discovery opened the minds of Western Europeans to the existence of cultures which contrasted notably with their own accustomed standards. The new world of the Americas and of the Orient, the rediscovered old world, revealed by the revival of classical learning and the excavations of the new archaeology, were refreshing experiences. Later stimulus was supplied by the "intensive" complication of the modern world through the growth of modern technology. The craving for naturalistic orientation went side by side with the growth of new demands and justifications. But so vast was the field of phenomena that normative preoccupations yielded ground to the naturalistic.

Another line of mutual support and of cleavage in the intellectual world is between systematists and impressionists. Systematizers are constantly moving toward an elaborate and logically consistent structure. Impressionists are content with less rigidity of form. In the former group is the treatise writer; in the latter, the essayist, the popular lecturer, the conversationalist, the editorial writer. In periods of stress, opportunities for distinction are open to those who know how to use a medium to arouse the emotions of the masses. Hence treatise making may be abandoned for pamphleteering or oratory by those who are able to master the impressionistic media.

But any new social order, or any slowly maturing movement of social protest, affords abundant opportunities for the systematizer. The Encyclopedists of the eighteenth century were interested in systematizing the new knowledge as a means of modifying the prevailing social system. Treatises like those of Marx and Engels could contribute to the literature of protest in a literate society where the currents of revolution gathered strength for many years. After a new regime marches to power in modern society, the work of codifying its symbolic defenses goes forward. The Italian Fascists used ephemeral media of communication during the seizure of power; but once in the saddle, began work on the Fascist encyclopedia.

Another distinction is between expository and depictive skills. Exposition tends toward the abstract; depiction moves toward the concrete. Depictive skill includes descriptive prose, poetry, drawing, painting, and related media. Some expositions are entirely devoted to the definition of terms and the formal statement of their interconnection. Such was Pareto's *Cours d'économie politique*. Sometimes the rich detail is summarized in elaborate quantitative form, as in Wesley Mitchell's *Business Cycles*. A more frequent form of exposition is to embellish the abstract definitions and propositions by illustrations. (The procedure in this book, for example.)

The skill struggle among exponents of different styles of discourse is often expressed with the utmost acrimony. The treatises of the systematists are often dismissed as idle pedantry, flights from reality, perversions of intelligence, and conspiracies at obfuscation. The essays of the impressionists, on the other hand, are often dismissed by the systematists as glib, irresponsible word-slinging. Academic environments foster the systematist; hence the acrid odor of the term "academic" in the nostrils of the impressionists.

No less pungent has been the exchange of discourtesies between expositors and depictors. Most of the "art" forms of our civilization are depictive. Spokesmen of the depictive may complain of the insufferable dullness of the expository style, and declare that the word moves with its "heart," not its "head." Expositors may dismiss the depictive as pandering to infantile ways of thought, prophesying that a more rational world will forsake the products of the "picture mind."

Those who excel in naturalistic analysis may proclaim the virtues of "objectivity" and refer with condescension to those who imagine the world is interested in the lengthy elaboration of their system of private preferences. The specialists on normative styles of speech may refer disparagingly to the absence of ethical fervor of the ostriches who bury their heads in the sand of science while the war of values is upon us.

Thus each of the skill specialists has at least the rudiments of a mythology in the name of which extra units of the available values may be elicited from his fellow men. The pattern for mythmaking by intellectuals was set for our society by Plato, who dreamed poetically of the "philosopher king" in whom omniscience was at one with omnipotence. For the symbol specialists as a group, both the intellectuals, in the narrow sense of those who specialize on the contentious, and the physical scientists, one of the most active mythmakers is H. G. Wells. Although he may single out the novelizing aesthete, the backward pedagogue, the otherworldly scholar, the smug university intellectual for opprobrious comment, Mr. Wells exalts the "mental worker."

We learn in the *Experiment in Autobiography* (page 2) of Mr. Wells that the mental worker leads not a subnormal, but a "supernormal" life. His is not an "escape"; it is a "way to power."

Mankind is realizing more and more surely that to escape from individual immediacies into the less personal activities now increasing in human society is not, like games, reverie, intoxication or suicide, a suspension or abandonment of the primary life; on the contrary it is the way to power over the primary life which, though subordinated, remains intact. Essentially it is an imposition upon the primary life of a participation in the greater life of the race as a whole. In studies and studios and laboratories, administrative bureaus and exploring expeditions, a new world is germinated and develops. It is not a repudiation of the old but a vast extension of it, in a racial synthesis into which individual aims will ultimately be absorbed. We originative intellectual workers are reconditioning human life.

Passing time includes the rise and fall of skill combinations of every description. It seems that during the feudal age in Europe skill in fighting was a major avenue to power. Later, skill in organization was essential to the consolidation of the national monarchies. Skill in bargaining brought the private plutocrat into his own during the nineteenth and early twentieth centuries. The insecurities of the world of the twentieth century, manifested in world war and revolution, have fostered the chances of the man of skill in propaganda (witness Lenin, Mussolini, Hitler). Once new ideologies have been consolidated in the sentiments of the community, the role of the propagandist will diminish: for the benefit of the man of violence? the bargainer? the ceremonializer?

CHAPTER VII

CLASS

Political analysis includes the class consequences of events. A class is a major social group of similar function, status, and outlook.

A revolution is a shift in the class composition of elites. The influence of the Southern landed aristocracy on American politics was curtailed as a result of the Civil War. On the world stage there was no significant novelty about substituting commercial and industrial capitalists for landed proprietors. This change had occurred under circumstances of catastrophic violence in France at the end of the eighteenth century. In world perspective, the American Civil War did not, but the French Revolution did, signify that a new social formation had risen to greatest influence. The French Revolution, therefore, may be called a world revolution. After the revolution in France the next world revolution took place in Russia in 1917.

World revolutions have been accompanied by sudden shifts in the ruling vocabulary of the elite. Said the absolutist James I of Great Britain, in the days before the gentry revolution:

"It is atheism and blasphemy to dispute what God can do . . . so it is presumption and high contempt in a subject to dispute what a king can do, or to say that a king cannot do this or that."

In the same strain are the words of Bishop Bossuet, commissioned by Louis XIV with the education of the Dauphin, before the bourgeois revolution:

"As in God are united all perfection and every virtue,

so all the power of all the individuals in a community is united in the person of the prince."

When the monarch and the aristocracy were swept away, a wholly new vocabulary was employed by those who sat in the seats of the powerful. Declares article 1 of the Declaration of the Rights of Man and the Citizen, adopted by the French National Assembly on August 26, 1789, "men are born and remain free and equal in their rights." Article 2 enumerates the "natural and imprescriptible rights of man."

When the monarchy, aristocracy, and plutocracy of Russia were supplanted, another potent vocabulary was invoked by those who seized authority. The proclamation issued by Lenin, as chairman of the Council of People's Commissars, November 18, 1917, read in part: "Comrades: Workers, Soldiers, Peasants, All who Toil! The workers' and peasants' revolution has finally been victorious in Petrograd, scattering and capturing the last remnants of the small bands of Cossacks duped by Kerensky. . . . The success of the revolution of workers and peasants is assured, for the majority of the people have already come out in its favor. . . . Behind us are the majority of the toilers and the oppressed of all the world. We are fighting in the cause of justice and our victory is sure."

From the "divine right of kings" to the "rights of man," from the "rights of man" to the "proletarian dictatorship"; these have been the principal vocabulary changes in the political history of the modern world. In each case a language of protest, long a utopian hope, became the language of an established order, an ideology. The ruling elite elicited loyalty, blood, and taxes from the populace with new combinations of vowels and consonants.

These sudden changes in class composition of elites introduced innovations in practice as well as in vocabulary.

The French Revolution introduced and presently established universal manhood suffrage, church disestablishment, relative freedom of agitation and discussion, the supremacy of parliament over the executive, and abolition of all manner of legal discriminations among classes. Policies favorable to the growth of commerce and industry were instituted by rearranging the system of tariff and taxation. Individual proprietorship was encouraged by transforming peasants into landholders. All this was legitimized in the name of the rights of man, and cemented in walls of intense nationalistic sentiment.

The pattern of the Russian Revolution of 1917 took shape at different phases of the revolutionary crisis. Conspicuous has been the governmentalization of all forms of organized social life. By the end of June, 1918, banks and insurance companies, large-scale industry, mines, water transportation, and the few railroads which were formerly operated by private companies were nationalized. Foreign debts incurred by the Czarist and the Provisional governments were repudiated, foreign investments in private industry were confiscated, and foreign trade monopolized. Presently was begun the abolition of the peasant as a distinct social formation by the development of great collective farms.

The control of affairs was gradually monopolized by a single political party which assumed a monopoly of legality. When the revolution got under way, there were several potent centers of influence in Russia, of which the Communist party was but one. The Soviets were centers of initiative which were by no means under the united discipline of the party; and there were rival political parties. The trades unions and the cooperative societies were only gradually brought under the iron rule of the party during the grinding years of bitter struggle against the

perils of intervention, famine, and revolt. Crisis forced
concentration or collapse, and the political committee of
the Communist party became the directive center of the
state.

Within the framework of the governmentalized society,
differences in money income were less striking than they
had been in the prerevolutionary society; this comparative
equality was particularly conspicuous during the period of
incessant conflict before 1921. The road to individual success now lay chiefly through the Communist party, which
gave access to the principal posts of influence.

This was a "dictatorship of the proletariat," or at least a
dictatorship in the name of the proletariat. It was not a
socialist state, because democratic forms were not yet permitted. It was not a socialist society, because the government was still constrained to use coercion; "the withering
away of the state" was an aspiration for the future, whenever a voluntary consensus among functional groups in the
new society should emerge.

World revolutions are valuable landmarks in the understanding of intervening events. Thus some events after the
French Revolution can be considered to facilitate, and
some to retard, the spread of the various details of the new
revolutionary pattern of symbol and practice. Some events
were moving directly toward the emergence of the pattern
which arose in Russia. Thus happenings can be construed
as transitions between one revolutionary emergent and the
next one.

After the French Revolution many details of the French
pattern of "democracy" were adopted and adapted. Great
Britain widened the parliamentary franchise in the direction of universal suffrage. Parliaments came to exercise
greater control over executives, even where revolution did
not eliminate monarchial authority (as in Prussia). There

were waves of land reform for the avowed benefit of peasants or small farmers; there were changes in public revenues designed to encourage commerce, industry, and finance; there was increasing use of the language of democratic internationalism.

Presently a significant political movement of protest arose in opposition to the property system which had benefited by democratic nationalism. Marxism outcompeted the "utopian" socialists and the anarchists, and furnished the dominant language in the name of which counter-elites sought to supersede the established order.

When construed with reference to the last and the next world-revolutionary patterns, the same event often possessed both revolutionary and counterrevolutionary implications. Demands for free public education and for universal suffrage often stimulated the wage earners, the peasants, and the lesser middle classes to assert themselves politically; this could be said to mark an advance toward the possible appearance of a new revolutionary impetus in the name of these classes. But some of the consequences of education and suffrage were inimical to the spread of world revolution. When concessions were made to these demands and political parties were able to obtain seats in municipal councils or national parliaments, revolutionary ardor was often lost. Party leaders became firmly incorporated in the national ideology and more intent on proving their patriotism than their proletarianism.

Correctly orientated persons living in the flow of historical happenings between the French and Russian revolutions would have seen the meaning of each situation for the spread or the restriction of these patterns of revolution.

Correct self-orientation in the world since the Russian Revolution consists in divining the meaning of current events for the passage from the last world revolution to the

next one. Since we are so close to the last epochal innovation, we shall no doubt be more successful in noting the
factors which influence its immediate fate than in discerning the outlines of the next significant upheaval. A search
for orientation is no once-and-for-all procedure; it is a
constant reappraisal of the march of time, construed self-
critically with reference to possible class consequences.

We are not wholly without guidance when we undertake
to construe the meaning of current affairs for the spread
and restriction of the revolutionary pattern of 1917.
World-revolutionary initiatives are not rare in the history
of mankind, but none has ever risen to total hegemony, and
unified the world in the name of one set of dominant symbols and according to one set of practices. The dialectic of
restriction has proved more potent than the dialectic of
diffusion, and world revolutions have always been stopped
short of universality.

It will be remembered that the men of France who seized
the power in the name of all humanity (*liberté, égalité,
fraternité*) were not accepted by all mankind. The claims
of those who seized the power in Russia to speak in the
name of the world proletariat have not been accepted by all
proletarians everywhere. Perhaps the same contradictions
which deprived the French elite of universality in fact, despite universality in rhetoric, will operate to circumscribe
the Russian elite. Evidently we have to do with a double
process of diffusion and restriction.

Possibly we may guide our attention to significant aspects of the total situation by adopting certain special
methods of collecting and exhibiting data. We deal with a
march of time, a stream of events. By intersecting the
stream at periodic intervals, and charting the geographical
distribution of selected symbols and practices, we may
contribute to sound understanding.

If we adopt rather wide intervals between cross sections, we may keep in contact with reality without getting lost in the sheer mass of detail. Perhaps five-year intervals will serve all the purposes in hand. Thus we may choose 1917, 1922, 1927, 1932. . . . Enough data are available to extend this five-year cross section backward between the Russian and French revolutions; were we to move further back, wider intervals would be a necessary concession to the scarcity of knowledge.

The features of the revolutionary pattern of 1917 may be briefly summarized here. Some of the positively sentimentalized words (plus symbols) were:

republic	proletariat
soviet	world revolution
socialist	communism

Some of the negatively sentimentalized words (minus symbols) were:

monarchy	imperialism
religion	parliamentarism
bourgeoisie	bourgeois liberalism and democracy
capitalism	

Some of the practices, not all of which were initiated at the beginning:

> governmentalization (of organized social life)
> equalization (of money income)
> monopolization (of legality by a single party)

At any given cross section through the stream of events the extent of diffusion and restriction would be shown. Such relationships may be classified as follows:

> Total diffusion
> Restriction by geographical differentiation
> Restriction by partial incorporation
> Restriction by functional differentiation.

Total diffusion would be indicated by universal membership in the Soviet Union, and in the adherence of the Soviet
Union to the symbols and practices proclaimed and inaugurated in 1917. Since the period of civil war and intervention, the Soviet Union has made little territorial progress, and hence total geographical diffusion has been
blocked. Whether the changes which have transpired within
the Soviet Union have fostered the cause of world revolution will be considered later on.

Restriction by geographical differentiation derives from
ideas and propaganda emphasizing the local, parochial,
provincial, circumscribed nature of the events at the center
of the new revolutionary movement. The appearance of a
revolutionary elite arouses the insecurities of all surrounding elites, who seek to protect themselves from external
and internal menaces to their ascendancy. They seek to
obtain the cooperation of their own masses against the external threat by stigmatizing it as foreign and alien, and by
emphasizing their own identification with the locality.
Hence a revolution in the name of humanity is treated as
the *French* revolution, and a revolution in the name of the
world proletariat is treated as the *Russian* revolution. The
struggle to restrict the external menace emphasizes parochialism: thus the Prussian dynastic and feudal groups
tolerated the language of German nationalism as a means
of rallying the rank and file of the community against the
French; thus the Poles and other newly independent peoples fought the Russians in 1919-1921.

Restriction by partial incorporation is the process by
which successful symbols and practices of the new revolutionary regime are borrowed as a concession to local sentiment. This "me, too, but" technique of identification and
distinction proceeds as follows: if "nation" is proclaimed,
then let there be a peculiar essence in the "German na-

tion"; if "socialism" be a virtue, then let it be "German National Socialism"; if "revolution" be a value, let it be our own national revolution.

The details of the revolutionary pattern which were most quickly paralleled abroad were the least novel ones. This may be shown by tabulating the changes which have occurred in the states of the world in forms of government. The overthrow of the Czar was in the best manner of the bourgeois revolutions, and similar movements went forward outside Russia, often draining off existing discontent and diminishing the chances of proletarian forms of policy. The following tables depict the situation in 1917 before the revolutionary movements of the year began. Otherwise the situation is shown as it was by the end of the year cited. Data are from such standard sources as the *Statesman's Yearbook* and the *Political Handbook of the World*. Arabi Saudi and Iraq are included for the first time in 1932. In general, colonial countries are excluded.

Year	Absolute Monarchies		Limited Monarchies		Parliamentary Monarchies		Presidential Republics		Parliamentary Republics	
	No.	%	No.	%	No.	%	No.	%	No.	%
1917	6	.10	7	.12	17	.30	21	.40	5	.08
1922	3	.05	5	.08	18	.29	21	.34	15	.24
1927	2	.04	4	.06	19	.30	22	.35	16	.25
1932	1	.02	7	11	19	.29	21	.32	17	.26

In 1917 there were 56 states of which 13, or 22 per cent, were absolute or limited monarchies. In 1922 the number of states was 62, of which 8, or 13 per cent, were absolute or limited monarchies. In 1927 there were 6 of 63 states, or less than 10 per cent, in these two categories. By 1932 there were 8 of 65 states, or 13 per cent, included. The greatest shift was toward parliamentary republics, in which are included both soviet and nonsoviet forms. Monarchies dropped from 52 to 42 per cent in favor of republics in the period.

Certain of these changes are accentuated when the forms of government are classified according to population. Figures are for the year nearest the year mentioned, when an official enumeration or estimate was unavailable. With the exception of China, the largest figure given in conflicting sources was used. Population is given in millions.

Year	Absolute Monarchies		Limited Monarchies		Parliamentary Monarchies		Presidential Republics		Parliamentary Republics	
	No.	%	No.	%	No.	%	No.	%	No.	%
1917	64	.04	675	.46	171	.12	189	.13	374	.25
1922	27	.02	401	.25	203	.13	200	.13	745	.47
1927	20	.01	396	.25	215	.13	210	.13	786	.48
1932	6	.01	455	.26	210	.12	231	.13	830	.48

It thus appears that 50 per cent of the population lived in absolute or limited monarchies in 1917. By 1922 the percentage was 27, and remained constant in the two succeeding samples. The expansion of parliamentary republics is emphasized in this table, since the proportion grew from one-quarter to about one-half of the total inhabitants of states.

The more novel details of the revolutionary pattern of 1917 have spread slowly. When the facts are assembled, it will no doubt appear that the governmentalization of organized life has proceeded apace outside the Soviet Union. This interpretation will apply if some allowance is made for the extension of governmental control during the period of the World War, comparing the situation as it was in

1912 with the transformations recorded in the postwar years. Civil emergencies connected with the great depression of 1929 have been met with notable extensions of governmental authority, even in the United States. The Reconstruction Finance Corporation was but one of the early and conspicuous examples of this trend.

In all probability there has been a general though very erratic movement toward the equalization of money income. The nonsoviet communities of Central and Eastern Europe sought to assuage popular discontent and to build up vested and sentimental support for their nonsoviet regimes by dividing up the large landed estates. Elsewhere high income and inheritance taxes have furthered tendencies toward equalization; but often such policies have been offset by higher exactions upon articles of general consumption. "Share the Wealth" has become a practical political slogan in the United States.

The monopolization of legality by a single dominant party is found in Germany, Italy, and in less evolved form in such countries as China, Turkey, and Yugoslavia.

Evidently, therefore, restrictions by geographical differentiation and by partial incorporation have made rapid headway in limiting the scope of the Soviet Union. To these processes may be added restriction by functional differentiation. The history of the past century shows that a turning point in political development was reached when it became common to refer to the French Revolution as the "bourgeois" revolution. The language which had been used by the original revolutionary elite of France was universalist in scope. By referring to the revolution as the "bourgeois" revolution, it was both implied and asserted that a special class had used the name of the many for the advantage of the few. Not all mankind, but the bourgeoisie were those who were supposed to have reaped most of the ben-

efits which accrued from the dramatic events of the years
following 1789.

A distinction of this kind strikes at the basic claim of the
revolutionary order, challenges the dominant myth, ex-
poses its fraudulent pretensions. Every elite which has become identified with any of the symbols and practices of
the last revolution is indicted. The symbolic foundation is
laid for a new revolutionary edifice; the new mythology of
protest, the new utopian promise, can be invoked against
the ideologies of the established elites. In the terminology
of the nineteenth century the alternative to the "bourgeoisie" was the "proletariat." With the perfection of Marxist
socialism a new formative myth was set loose, to gain allegiance during successive pulsations of discontent, and culminate when the bearers of the new symbols seized the
power in Russia.

Have lines of functional differentiation begun to cast
doubt upon the universality of the Russian Revolution?
Are these those who doubt whether the class consequences
of the revolution benefit the whole proletariat as much as
they benefit certain other class formations?

Perhaps, as some anarchosyndicalists have suggested,
the lower layers of the manual workers, especially the unemployed, have been grossly misled by the sloganeering of
the spokesmen of the Russian Revolution. Perhaps the rise
of modern political socialism is a phase in the struggle for
power, not of the manual workers, but of the "intellectuals"
who successfully allied themselves with the discontented
manual workers in wresting power from the aristocracy
and the plutocracy. Once established in power, they give
special privileges to special skill, capturing party and administration. Deference and higher money incomes go to
those who perform technical and organizational functions,
not to those who do manual work. Intellectuals have dem-

onstrated that Marx did not really intend to establish mechanical equality of money income. Hence the lowest layers of the population, possessed of less skill than the upper layers, are potential sources of disaffection, suspicion of "bureaucracy."

This line of analysis views the Russian Revolution as an incident in the rise to power of the lesser bourgeoisie, a Russian realization of the tendencies which are implicit in the march of events in Italy, Germany, and elsewhere.

It may be that the common factor in the seeming political confusion of our time is the rise to power of the middle-income skill group. Despite the contradictions and the aberrations of Russian Communism, Italian Fascism, and German National Socialism, a new world revolution may be on the march which will be realized independently of the inclusion of the world within the Soviet Union. In the name of the "nation's workers," and in the name of local patriotism, of antiforeignism, middle-income skill groups are rising to power at the expense of aristocracy and plutocracy.

Plainly the middle-income skill groups have not yet found a common name; nor have they discerned the inner principle of sacrifice on which their unity depends; nor have they risen to the full comprehension of their historic destiny. In Europe their disunion has bred the politics of catastrophe; but in America there may be more time for the attainment of a common name, a common policy, and a common sense of political destiny.

Lacking self-consciousness, the small farmers, the small businessmen, the low-salaried intellectuals, and the skilled workers have fought one another rather than acted together. The labor movements of the nineteenth and twentieth centuries have in many ways intensified rather than resolved the contradictions within the middle-income skill group. One element of the middle-income skill group has catered to the wage earners; it is composed of trades-union organizers, trades-union editors, trades-union secretaries, Socialist party organizers, Socialist party secretaries, and officials in cooperative societies. Such functionaries are often "renegades" from the older middle-income skill formations; their fathers may have been merchants, farmers, teachers, officials. Others rise from the ranks of the manual workers, learning to elude physical toil by cultivating oratorical skill, literary ability, and administrative technique.

The older middle-income groups have hated with deep intensity the skill group of proletarian origin or affiliation. One basis of this is the sense of outrage that those who exercise the same skill should get ahead by simple differences in vocabulary. The tool of preacher, teacher, lawyer, and journalist is the larynx and not the biceps. When fellow toilers of the tongue and typewriter ensconce themselves on pay rolls by saying "bourgeoisie" with a hiss and "proletariat" with a flaunt, resentment turns to bitterness and curdles into indignation.

All this seemed profoundly hypocritical to the older bourgeoisie, and insult is added to injury when the spokesmen of the proletariat indict this group as the tools of the exploiter. It is easy to understand why the National Socialists, when they seized power in Germany, swept official swivels free of "Communists," "Social Democrats," and "Democrats," and packed them off to concentration camps. In their place ruled men more closely identified with the older middle-income groups, but called "National Socialists."

Such intense inner strife is one mark of a social formation which has not yet come to itself, and attained full class consciousness. It lacks a consistent policy, a rallying name, and an invigorating myth of its historic mission. Quite typically, the energies of the middle-income skill group in America have been diverted toward the restriction of slavery and the restriction of thriftlessness by efforts to remove alcohol, gambling, and prostitution. Waves of indignation at the inequitable results of industrial concentration have been dissipated in struggles to regulate "unfair competition" and to obtain "easy credit." Farmers and small businessmen on the receding frontier followed the spell of "16 to 1," "antimonopoly," and the "new freedom"; but the principal effect of efforts to "restore competition" has been to complicate corporations. The lesser agrarian, business, professional, and skilled worker elements are left with no common body of effective political symbols.

The energy expended in Bryanism, Rooseveltianism, and Wilsonism might have organized sentiment around symbols capable of clarifying the special demands of the middle-income skill group. It is thinkable that during these many years the low-income farmers, storekeepers, schoolteachers, and clergymen might have learned to demand the rigorous use of the national taxing power to eliminate immoderate incomes. Had they become acquainted with the fact that America was run by a single party system, they might have ceased to divide their potential majority of ballots between the Republican and Democratic wings of the Republocratic party.

As it stands today the middle-income group is bereft of so much as an acknowledged name capable of distinguishing it from the proletariat and the plutocracy. There is something repugnant to the individualism of the middle class about the name "middle class." Apt for analysis, it is inept for propaganda. In order to distinguish themselves from the "alien" proletariat, the middle-income skill groups have warmed to such ambiguous expressions as "citizen," "American," "patriot," used by demagogues who were often sustained from behind the scenes by the bigger industrial, commercial, and financial interests.

Lacking an inspiring name and clear demands for national policy, the middle-income skill group has no myth of its virtues and its destiny. It can be contended that the bond which unites this class is both external and internal: external, since it loses monetary rewards to the plutocracy; internal, since sacrifice for the sake of obtaining socially useful skill is a common experience of moral worth. Self-discipline is involved in the acquisition of skill through specialized training, which is a basis of mutual esteem among mechanics, intellectuals, and enterprisers.

The middle-income skill group in various nations might conceive of its historic mission in these terms: to recapture the initiative in the struggle for social justice. In the eighteenth century the mission of the middle-income skill group was to collaborate with all comers in breaking the chains of feudal-monarchical society, and seeking to establish the principle of proportionality between sacrifice and reward.

During the nineteenth and twentieth centuries the expansion of modern industrialism has created a plutocracy, whose presence shows that the balance between sacrifice and reward has been drastically disturbed. Once more the political "destiny" of the middle-income skill group is plain: it is the remoralization of society by changing the practices of society in regard to reward and sacrifice.

As the middle-income skill group attains the dignity and insight of an effective social formation, it will see that it has been the victim of a psychological lag. The middle-income skill group has stayed loyal to the vocabulary of individualism after the practices sustained by this vocabulary generated great discrepancies between sacrifice and reward.

Despite every handicap, it might be argued that the middle-income skill group is on the way to ultimate victory.
The implacable processes of commercial, industrial, and
financial capitalism have stimulated it to political activity.
It may be that the middle-income skill group has suffered
no absolute decline in material income, but there is no mis-
taking the decline in psychological income, in deference.
The skill groups, especially the older ones, have been har-
ried on one side by the organized agencies which spoke in
the name of the proletariat, and on the other by the powerful combines of the plutocracy.

In Germany there were superimposed upon the psychological losses of a century, the adversities of war, defeat,
inflation, and depression. Goaded to desperation, the older
middle-income elements rose to partial self-realization in
the National Socialist movement, even supplying their
own leadership in the person of Hitler, son of a small customs official formerly in the service of the Hapsburgs. The
Italian Fascist movement had already been used by a man
who had previously made his living by employing the vocabulary of "proletarian" protest. Mussolini may be a
renegade in the sense that in adult life he altered his political convictions and persecuted his former friends, but in a
class sense Mussolini was a prodigal son returning to his
own.

Plainly the Italian and German movements are incidents
in the process by which the last world-revolutionary pattern
is both restricted and universalized. The domination of
Moscow is decisively rejected; but it would be a mistake to
suppose that revolution itself is dead. Restriction has proceeded by taking over some of the symbols and practices of
the new pattern, even as the French revolutionary pattern
spread after the emphatic rejection of the authority of the
French to administer the revolution.

This treatment of the Russian Revolution as the "Second Bourgeois Revolution" may foster the march to power of middle-income skill groups in other countries though not under the command of Moscow. It may also deflate the pretensions of the Russian revolutionary movement to invoke the name of the proletariat. The anarchosyndicalist appeal to the manual workers to rise against the bureaucratic state may embody the germ of the next great revolutionary upheaval "from underneath"; every indication is that this appeal will prove ineffectual in any visible future, while the "skill revolution" gradually will move toward universality.

This chapter has developed the implications of the view that political events may be seen as the passage from the dominance of one class form to the next. The French Revolution marked the rise of the bourgeoisie; the Russian Revolution may mark the rise of the lesser bourgeoisie, the skill groups. The next major revolutionary impulsion may come in the name of the manual workers against the bureaucratic state fostered by socialism. Meanwhile, the scope of the elite which seized authority in Russia is being circumscribed by the same processes which restricted the scope of the elite in revolutionary France. The main features of the new revolutionary pattern, however, continue to move toward universality, though in a disunited world.

CHAPTER VIII

PERSONALITY

What is the significance of social life for the survival of forms of political personality? In some respects this query about politics is closer to everyday attitudes in an individualistic society than is analysis by class or skill. Who has not dramatized politics as a struggle between Stalin and Trotsky, Roosevelt and Hoover? Whether the stakes are exile or dictatorship, presidency or private life, Washington or the old home town, the players are identifiable persons, and their fate is humanly exciting.

However, it is not the fate of the individual Tom, Dick, and Harry that holds our interest. Political analysis is more concerned with the general than with the unique. Our task is to examine the factors affecting success or failure of personality type. The Franklins, Benitos, Adolfs, and Josefs must be seen as instances of more general forms of personal development before we can compare them with predecessors, contemporaries, and successors.

Novelists, poets, and painters have long been preoccupied with the delicate nuances which bind men to one another, or condemn them to stare across seemingly impassable chasms of misunderstanding. Behind the façades of the class and skill struggle run the dialectics of personality. In the *Brothers Karamazov* are depicted the subtler shades of the subjective which divide one person, and one personality, from another. The modern student has sought to illuminate this obscure terrain in the language of exposition rather than depiction. Such expository works as those of Freud, Klages, Jung, and Kretschmer have become part of the common inheritance of cultivated men and women throughout Western European civilization.

Political life, in the narrowest sense of the word, is a life of conflict, and presupposes men who can bring themselves into active relationship to their surroundings. Impulses must be externalized upon the human environment. A fully developed political personality combines certain motives with certain skills, fusing an emotional capacity to externalize impulses with enough skill to secure success.

This requirement of externalized impulse at once eliminates from the arena of rough-and-tumble politics certain personalities who have failed to achieve an emotional life sufficiently free to enable them to express themselves in the world of reality. Witness the disintegrated wrecks who lie in the wards of institutions for the care of sufferers from severe mental disease. In some of these cases the evidence is convincing that systems of motivation within the personality clashed so decisively with other systems of motivation within the same personality that the whole energy of the individual was absorbed in the inner struggle, leaving nothing over for the task of remaining orientated toward surroundings. Such individuals may spend days and weeks quite motionless, seemingly oblivious to all beyond themselves.

Such pathological pictures of complete internalization offer the greatest possible contrast to the active political figure. The politician displaces his private motives upon public objects, and rationalizes the displacement in terms of public advantage. When this emotional and symbolic adjustment occurs in combination with facility in the acquisition of manipulative skill, the effective politician emerges.

Some of the problems connected with the synthesis of motive and skill involved in politics may be broached by considering the behavior of Abraham Lincoln during his mature years. Lincoln was firm in his public pronouncements and in his official acts, revealing a flexible capacity to adjust his tactics to the changing features of reality. He remained in strong though not in domineering control of the situation. He may be contrasted with Stanton, his secretary of war, whose tenacity and energy were so often tinged with sadism; with McClellan, the general who never felt quite prepared to fight, and whose unwillingness to proceed under pressure was not firmness but negativism, nourished by unconscious fear; or with Greeley, fiery journalist, who fathered many chimerical expedients.

Inseparable from the public picture of Lincoln was his gentleness. His clemency was famous everywhere and notorious among his colleagues. Those who came in closer contact with Lincoln saw that he was overgentle and lacking in firmness in intimate relationships. They saw how incapable he was of disciplining his own children, and how overindulgent he was of his exigent wife. The true measure of this gentleness was its continuation despite provocation. Very rarely did Lincoln allow flares of indignation to escape him. But once an officer who tried to "bulldoze" the President into granting his petition scornfully said, "I see you have made up your mind against doing me justice!" Lincoln's face convulsed with pain, and he is said to have grabbed the officer by the collar and unceremoniously bundled him out of the room.

His sadness impressed contemporaries, who saw the brooding brows, the sunken cheeks, the luminous eyes, the deliberate ways; and they saw his tears at Gettysburg. Those who knew Lincoln intimately found that sadness was one of the many evidences of depression; Lincoln was plagued by insomnia, feelings of inferiority, of bearing too much responsibility, of pessimism. At times the President was suicidal. During the battle of Chancellorsville when it appeared that General Hooker was in retreat, Stanton says that Lincoln threw up his hands and exclaimed, "My God! Stanton, our cause is lost! This is more than I can endure!" The President later said that he had fully made up his mind to end his life in the Potomac River.

Lincoln's sadness was sometimes relieved by wit, often in the homely form which offended the cultivated and delighted the rustic. His extreme devotion to duty cut him off more and more from intimate human contacts. His honesty, and his desire to deal with scrupulous justice with his fellows were obvious. Allied to patience and gentleness was toleration of personal criticism. And of course Lincoln's physical courage was not in question.

Without summing up in detail the manifold personality of the man, but pausing to consider the principal features, we cannot fail to be impressed by the discrepancy between his firmness in relation to technical objects (his public duties) and his dependent, passively enduring attitude toward his wife. It is clear, also, that Lincoln spent a great deal of his energy in antiself reactions, which ranged all the way from gloomy moods and depressing fantasies to the contemplation of suicide. The melancholy tinge of his waking life stands in stark contrast to the subjective tone of men who have few morbid moments and who live in serene self-assurance. Plainly much of Lincoln's great energy was not externally effective in dealing with his environment, but turned back against the personality; and much of the energy which was internalized took the form of morbid rather than grandiose reverie.

There is ample evidence of Lincoln's craving for the approval of a wide public. When the news of Chancellorsville burst upon him, his reaction was not only "Our cause is lost!" but the question, "What will the people say?"

Many another chief executive has lived through moments of apparent disaster without exhibiting so much dependence upon public sentiment, and without being moved to suicidal plans when public approval seemed lost.

Much of Lincoln's personality was a defense formation against extreme demands for wide appreciation. By tempering his conduct with incessant thoughts of the just rather than the popular, by neglecting as far as possible to take note of the avalanches of criticism which poured upon him, Lincoln was able to erect buffers against his own yearning for constant appreciation.

What of the conditions in which such personality type rise to eminence? Lincoln won the presidential nomination from Seward largely because his language was less peremptory than Seward's. When the Republican party met in convention, there was no doubt of the personal popularity of Seward. But the party wanted to win the election, and there were the doubtful states of New Jersey, Pennsylvania, Indiana, and Illinois to be taken into consideration. Against the outspoken Seward the Republicans would be at a disadvantage in dealing with the Democratic candidate, Douglas. Seward had appealed to the "higher law" above the Constitution. This was profoundly shocking at this stage of the developing crisis; it seemed to indicate an imperious determination to force the issue. The Northern states were divided among themselves. Quite apart from constitutional issues, antislavery sentiment was not unanimous. Lincoln had distinguished himself by firmness; yet he had spoken in terms which somewhat veiled the grimness of the crisis. Lincoln had talked of "moral codes" to supplement legal ones. As one of his biographers, L. Pierce Clark, wrote: "The principles of the two views are identical, but Lincoln knows how so to state the principle that it alarms few, although many must know that they are not essentially different." Lincoln was less ruthless and peremptory, more conciliatory and winning, than Seward; at this phase of crisis, his personality was more acceptable.

After winning the election, Lincoln gradually led the Northern states to a united front against secession and slavery. It was his capacity to chasten destructive drives, to temper them to reality, or to turn them against himself, that was well adapted to the situation. The Northern States, torn by local, regional, denominational, and other differences, edged rather than rushed toward the approaching war. The Southerners, unified in the name of "our sacred institutions," strode forward to meet the crisis. Lincoln's mixture of firmness and gentleness alternately commanded and wheedled the Northerners into unified action.

The chances are that Lincoln would not have found his way to the top if the North had been a united rather than a divided people. Certainly the Southern leadership contained few figures of the Lincoln stamp. United people are peremptory when attacked. As heterogeneous people become more united during crises, they become more ruthless, partly as a reaction against previous doubts and scruples. Conciliatory personalities tend to be swept aside as indecisive weaklings. Lincoln, it will be remembered, narrowly missed defeat in 1864.

It is correct to say that Lincoln was an agitator in the sense that he displaced strong cravings for emotional response from the intimate circle to the wider public, and that he acquired enough skill in oral and written discourse to succeed. He was not, however, restricted to a purely agitational role, for, unlike Greeley, for example, he was able to hold his destructive impulses in sufficient restraint to permit him to coordinate the efforts of others in organization.

Suppose we undertake to explain the type of development that was displayed by Lincoln. Three questions present themselves at once. Under what conditions is the demand for love displaced from the primary to the secondary public? Under what conditions is there extreme demand for love? When are aggressive impulses held in check and partially turned against the self?

The displacement of strong demands for response from the intimate to the wider public is favored by failure in the intimate sphere. We have seen that Lincoln's marriage was not an emotional success, and if we go further into his history, we discover that Lincoln exhibited some difficulties in relation to women. He left Mary Todd waiting at the altar on the "fatal first of January, 1841," plunging into a depression which was so serious that physicians still differ in diagnosing this reaction as neurotic or psychotic. Lincoln went into serious depression when Ann Rutledge died; and, further back than that, he suffered severely when his mother died when he was nine years old. Although shy and ineffectual with women of his own age, he got on with maternal women who were usually older than himself. His displacement onto the political public can be attributed to the focusing of his attention upon political activity in the environment where he was reared.

What was the origin of the great demand for love, which, since it could not be resolved in the primary sphere, was partly resolved by displacement? When we have to do with a living person who is willing to try to understand himself by the method of free association (psychoanalysis), by saying everything that comes into his mind, we are able to learn a great deal about early formative experiences. Many old and long-forgotten episodes are recalled, many old impulses are rediscovered. This method is unavailable for the study of Lincoln, of course; but psychoanalysts have often studied personalities who display the chief characteristics of Lincoln's life.

It is found that when the young child is overindulged by his mother in nursing, or in handling his body, the child may display great unwillingness to relinquish his demands to be nursed. Urges to incorporate objects through the mouth, to be dependent, to be cared for, to remain inactive, may become very powerful. Hence the individual stays relatively fixated upon early ways of reacting to the world, and encounters many difficulties in subsequent development. In ensuing crises the individual is prone to regress to this early fixation and to remain immature.

Lincoln's early environment was in some respects emotionally unstable. His father was often harsh and often overindulgent; this type of contradictory treatment arouses great uncertainties about being loved. There is no evidence that young Lincoln responded to the obstacles put in his way by his father by growing intractable. Nor is there any evidence that he gave up the struggle and retired completely within himself. But there is ample indication that Lincoln had strong tendencies to regress when difficulties presented themselves in his pathway. It is recorded that throughout his entire life the dream of a ship recurred when crises were intense. This dream is of a pattern which has often been met and described in our civilization for similar persons under similar circumstances.

In general, we can think of behavior as a system of acts which are running toward completion at varying rates along different channels. A completed act is a sequence of events running from impulse through subjectivity to expression, and to the reinstatement of a situation very like the situation before the impulse got under way. Thus hunger contractions may be followed and accompanied by the subjective sense of hunger, and by nursing, which completes the act by abolishing hunger contractions. The infantile organism is equipped to complete some acts, like sucking, swallowing, and defecating. When these acts are interfered with, substitutions may occur, or persistence and rage reactions may appear. If persistence and rage reactions are not successful in removing the obstacle, such reactions may be turned against the personality itself, establishing an internal resistance to the completion of the impulses in question. By this process a rigorous system of inhibition and compulsion may be developed.[1]

The mother or nurse not only indulges the infant and the young child, but denies; hence the mother is both "good" and "bad" to the child (whose attitude is thus ambivalent). The basis of depression is laid when the child is deprived of the loved one (as by death), and responds regressively, that is, by seeking to substitute fantasy for reality. The "good" mother is fondly remembered as the perfectly indulgent mother; but at the same time the rage at the "bad" mother is turned against the self. Hence the individual in extreme cases punishes a part of his personality on behalf of another part of his personality. When children undergo great deprivations during phases of great ambivalence, they often respond through this depressive mechanism. Subsequently they love persons after the ambivalent patterns of infancy, and if they are not constantly supplied with love, rage gets the upper hand, but this rage is internalized in the form of depression and perhaps even suicide.

[1] For technical purposes the original patterns of expression may be called libidinal channels; persistence and rage reactions may be called ego channels; other patterns may be named transformations. The transformations include total repression, partial repression, identification, projection, masochism, detachment, and several other reactions which will not be discussed here. For details, see the standard treatises by Sigmund Freud.

Just why does this internalizing occur? Because of acute fear of loss. The fear may be precipitated by fear of physical retaliation, by fear of losing future love, by fear of being treated with contempt. Failure in the tactics of persistence and rage may have occurred; but the urges toward defiance, though subdued, are not relinquished. A strong structure of inhibition is constantly in conflict with potent impulses. Such persons are overshy or even overconscientious. Lincoln, it will be recalled, was famous for his over-scrupulous honesty. Rarely did the underlying destructive tendencies break through to external manifestations. We know only of Lincoln's extremely sadistic attacks on Shields, and perhaps his damaging anonymous letters to the Grigsbys (their authenticity is in dispute).

Evidently, then, we must class Lincoln among the partially inhibited rage types. The relatively uninhibited rage types usually come into such incessant conflict with other people that they play little part in political activity. They are extremely willful, violent, domineering, and egocentric. The child who is accustomed to tantrums and to violence as a means of responding to denial may get little love at adolescence, and strengthen tendencies to remain resentfully fixed on primitive ways of dealing with the world. The uninhibited rage types are able to accomplish something by intimidation, but they are constantly encountering difficulty because of defensive behavior on the part of society. Many of these uninhibited rage types contribute to the ranks of the aggressive delinquent, unemployable and criminal.

Success in cowing the environment by wilfullness forms a personality predisposed toward imperious violence. The first Napoleon appears to have won through willfulness from the second year of his life. He grew into a quarrelsome and combative child; and when his parents, seeking to curb his truculence, sent him to a girls' school at the age of five, he was only spoiled by his teachers and school-mates, who tolerated the eccentricities of the only boy among them. Evidently Napoleon was deeply fixated on the mother imago, and resentful of the rivalry of his elder brother Joseph, whom he used to "thump and bite." His inordinate craving for deference was but partly gratified, even by success; for the picture of an inferior self, against which he struggled, was ever with him. Among his companions at the military school at Brienne he felt hopelessly inferior, for he was but five feet five in height. He was taunted as poor and Corsican. He secretly worried lest his sexual organs were atrophied, and lived an active sexual life as a constant means of reassuring himself of his doubtful masculinity. But throughout his life Napoleon was subject to moods of melancholy and to reveries of inferiority and isolation. To some extent these were mitigated by fantasies and claims to grandiosity: "I am no ordinary man, and laws of propriety and morals are not applicable to me." But he was haunted by exaggerated fears of a conspirative environment. In fundamental respects Napoleon was very close to the true political type. With his insatiable craving for gestures of deference to his ego from his fellow men, he had no durable interests in the objective processes of nature or the conditions of beauty. He sought the balm of success for his wounded ego, and he was forever licking his self-inflicted mutilations.

The inhibited rage types are often relieved of their inhibitions upon destructiveness during collective crises. They are prone to fortify their personalities by allying themselves with collectively acceptable symbols and practices. Hence they can play parts in political movements which are closed to the ill-tempered, uncontrolled, impatient rage types.

There is a rather completely inhibited rage type which is depicted in the popular phrase about a child "whose will is broken." Aggressive tendencies are disavowed by this personality, which treats the environment itself as overwhelmingly dangerous; hence the excessive timidity.

The partially inhibited rage group may be strongly masochistic. By enduring much mental anguish Lincoln was able to permit the expression of his aggressive impulses in the chastened form of firmness without accumulating a disastrous load of hampering guilt. The suffering expiated the guilt and released the impulse for expression. His apparent suffering won the sympathy of some who knew him intimately, and who felt impelled to minister to the protection of one who endured such inner anguish. True masochists are avid for affection, and, as Karen Horney has emphasized, they often use physical sexuality and experiences of intimate indulgence as means of being reassured against the anxieties generated by efforts to down the profoundly destructive components of their natures.

Such extremely masochistic types are often devoted to aggressive personalities who externalize their own aggressions. The entourage of every dominating leader is likely to contain such masochistic individuals who perform conscientious service to the "chief" and the "cause."

Another major mode of dealing with inner stress is detachment, which was also to some extent involved in the complex personality of Lincoln. Extreme detachment may be exhibited by conduct which seems to be "inhuman." The individual in question may be polite but never spontaneous. A thin barrier of barely perceptible ice freezes more expressive natures.

Excessive detachment marked the personality of a chemist who became entangled in practical politics rather by accident. He was known to his associates as exceptionally gifted in mathematics and experimental science. In personal relations he was quiet, soft spoken, gentle, polite, and acquiescent. Those who knew him best sensed that his inner life was tinged with no high light of enthusiasm, depression, rage, or love. He seemed to meet the world with poise and equanimity. He came to the attention of the police when he lay stunned by an explosion in the "bomb factory" which he ran for his revolutionary friends. Psychoanalytic interviews disclosed that he cared very little for the revolutionary philosophy of his associates. He ran the "bomb factory" as a side line, partly because he was interested in the technical problems involved, and partly because he wanted to be agreeable to his friends.

An important disclosure was made early in these interviews, however. He said that he had been seized by an irresistible impulse to hurl a bomb through the window of his laboratory and to destroy the whole building. Almost as if he were in a dream he had gone to the window overlooking the courtyard, thrown the bomb, which exploded prematurely and demolished the adjacent rooms.

Later on he recalled that on some previous occasions the same imperative impulse to destroy had seized control of him. Once when climbing an Alpine peak, he had noticed the reverie that if the rock by his hand were but slightly jarred, it would roll down the mountain and hit the next man beneath him. Some strange force seemed to take possession of his hand, which detached the rock, and his companion fell to death. The chemist felt no shock, but mild wonder. There was no feeling that the destructive impulse belonged to his own personality.

In extreme cases of "emotionlessness" the person often has a well-developed "spectator self" which seems to observe his own mental processes without feeling any sense of being personally involved. If such personalities figure in politics, it is usually as theorists or by accident.

The personality of Lincoln has often been contrasted with a persecutory agitator like Greeley. The basis of the Greeley type is probably the extensive use of projection and displacement as ways of coping with guilty and hostile tendencies. Such agitators share the common failure to obtain sufficient indulgence in relation to intimate objects, and transfer this craving to an enlarged world of objects. They succeed in externalizing their assertive impulses by projecting an inner sense of guilt upon the world outside; if the world is in the wrong, they are in the right by attacking it. The precarious nature of this adjustment is often shown by its collapse in adversity. When Greeley, for instance, suffered property losses and political defeat late in life, he developed a severe melancholia. His aggressions came tumbling back against the self, and he ceased to figure in the world of action.

Certain personalities are distinguished by haughty rather than persecutory behavior. The analysis of haughty people has often disclosed the functional basis of haughty behavior in the struggle against self contempt. By displacing contempt for the self upon the environment, and treating the world as contemptible, the personality is enabled to reduce the inner crisis. When a child is struggling for control of his excretions, verbal methods are often used to express disdain. To "smell bad" is to be treated with aversion, to be shamed. The tendency to accept the "you smell bad" as the correct self-valuation struggles with the tendency to project the valuation upon the environment. By haughtily treating the environment as foul smelling, self-esteem is often retained.[1]

---

[1] More vindictive, parsimonious, and secretive tendencies are connected with resentment at the interferences of the nurse with fecal and urethral indulgences. Infants and children may obstinately cling to pleasure in the retention of feces, and resent violations of privacy and urgings to adhere to routine.

Another way to resolve the stresses which arise from inhibited destructive impulses is to act obsessively and compulsively. Such reactions range all the way from Stanton, who amazed everybody by his fanatical devotion to work, which he carried on with concentrated intensity, bad temper, and cruelty, to the behavior of bureaucrats and ceremonializers who handcuff themselves in ritualistic repetitiousness. Hounded by destructive tendencies, they hold them in abeyance by means of order, red tape, routine, stereotype. The destructive impulses receive expression by annoying, exasperating, and rebuffing the world.

Some forms of extraverted personalities respond excitedly to the mood of the moment. The study of such personalities reveals a shallow subjective life. Often the individual passes suddenly between hyperactivity in relation to business, sex, or sociality, and great depression, lassitude, and sleep. Noisy and insistent promotional types often come from these extraverted personalities. They usually prove insensitive to the reactions of others, failing to detect boredom, handling persons as if they were things classified into a small number of simple categories. Deeper study often reveals acute developmental crises which were resolved by flight into extraversion.

It appears to be well established that philosophers and other elaborate thinkers about nature and the world are usually recruited from inhibited types. Alexander Herzberg collected intimate data about thirty world-famous philosophers in *The Psychology of Philosophers*. Most of them had been hesitant in embarking on a career, and were inefficient in their occupations. Most of them were unwilling or unable to earn money. The married life of the philosophers showed conspicuous peculiarities: fifteen of the thirty did not marry at all, six married very late, four were unhappily married, two separated from their mates. Most of them were diffident in social intercourse or unsuited to it. Herzberg found that they were equally inept in politics. Plato made abortive attempts to exercise practical influence, and Aristotle lost favor. Bacon was disgraced for accepting bribes, and Mill suffered many setbacks. Hume was the great exception. As secretary and later as deputy to the British ambassador in Paris, and finally as undersecretary of state, he was very successful. All these men seemed to possess a vigorous impulsive life which they had inhibited by consciences so stern that their efforts to cope with immediate reality were cramped; hence the resort to thought.

Since we have seen that many active politicians were driven by potent consciences, we may inquire after the factors which determine whether philosophy, neurosis, or politics will result. As far as can be judged from inadequate data, agitators are the politicians who have most in common with philosophers. The early environment was undependable. In the main the environment was very indulgent during formative years, but this indulgence was subject to interruption by sudden deprivations. An unstable relation between the parents in the home may have meant that the pleasant emotional weather was subject to upsetting storms; hence the child learned to respond sensitively to the changing barometer of human attitudes.

It is plain that severe crises may resolve the inner difficulties of the individual, freeing his inhibited impulses to express themselves on the world outside himself. Shy and timid boys who survive the harrowing experiences of shell-fire have suddenly blossomed out into calm, bold, and masterful persons. The anxieties were "abreacted" and overcome.

When crises intensify in the direction of violence, uninhibited rage types find more social sanction for the discharge of their sadistic drives; inhibited rage types, relieved somewhat of retaliatory fear, give greater scope to their aggressive tendencies; healthily assertive types resort to ruthlessness, though less tinctured with overactive cruelty and vindictiveness. During the initial phases of crisis, emotional solutions occur at different rates in different places. Conciliatory personalities are popular where indecision is bred of heterogeneity. They are passed over when imperious unity has been attained. In the aftermath of crisis, less dictatorial types rise in the scale of popularity.

The insecurities of the contemporary world, sharpened by the vicissitudes of a rapidly expanding and rapidly contracting economy, foster the conditions of perpetual crisis which favor the seizure of power by the agitator, and the retention of power by the man of ruthless violence.

CHAPTER IX

ATTITUDE

What is the meaning of social life for the political attitudes of successive elites? Plainly very different personality forms may share the same political outlook and belong to the same elite. At one time the predominating attitudes may be "local," "regional," "national," or "international." At another time the ruling attitudes may be loyalty to "class" or "skill." Under some conditions the ruling groups are "militant"; often they are "conciliatory." Politics is a changing pattern of loyalties, strategies, tactics; and political analysis may quite properly review the succession of predominant attitudes through the stream of time.

Acts of the most acute political interest are acts which change the social environment. Political acts are therefore externalized acts, since they implicate the environment as they run to completion. Internalized acts involve only the organism itself. If we observe any individual through a given period of time, we may perceive that he stimulates his personal environment, and that he in turn is directly stimulated by this environment. There is no doubt that his acts are *object orientations*. But if an individual is out of touch with the immediate situation for five minutes, we may be in some indecision about the nature of his subjective reactions. He may be solving a problem which will culminate in relevant action in some future situation. If so, his thought is *adjustive*. But it may be that he is plunged in gloomy meditation on his own deficiencies, merely intensifying the mood of depression and initiating no activity which would rectify his relationship to the world. His reveries would then be *autistic* (preoccupied with self). Yet another important reaction may be displayed by the subject of study. He may become incapacitated for love or work by stomach troubles, skin afflictions, or headaches which have no lesional basis. Such responses are *somatic* (bodily) *conversions*.

The four forms of reaction just sketched may be recapitulated thus:

> Object orientation
> Adjustive thought
> Autistic reverie
> Somatic conversion.

Politicians often show marked changes in their behavior which may be tersely described in these terms. When Mr. X, member of Congress, lost an election, he promptly established a new relationship to the world of practical politics by becoming a lawyer-lobbyist in Washington. When his wife died, he promptly married again. Other men have met similar reverses in professional and intimate life by withdrawing from immediate reality and devoting themselves to creative research or writing. A frustrated political career is responsible for the diversion of Machiavelli's energy into history and political science. Other men have reacted to rebuff by becoming incapacitated through reverie or bodily ailment. A certain councilman would grow depressed whenever he lost an election, refuse to eat, and retire to a sanitarium, where he elaborated morbid reveries of suicide. His friends would run him for office again, and when elected he would promptly forsake his difficulties and function as efficiently as usual. Still another councilman would develop gall-bladder and similar troubles when he was rejected at the polls.

Politics is itself often a substitute reaction which comes about because of deprivations in other spheres of life. Brigadier General Ezra Mannon in Eugene O'Neill's *Mourning Becomes Electra* discloses himself to his wife in these words:

"Maybe you've always known you didn't love me. I call to mind the Mexican War. I could see you wanted me to go. I had a feeling you'd grown to hate me . . . That was why I went. I was hoping I might get killed. Maybe you were hoping that too. . . . When I came back you had turned to your new baby, Orin. . . . I turned to Vinnie, but a daughter's not a wife. Then I made up my mind I'd do my work in the world and leave you alone in your life and not care. That's why the shipping wasn't enough—why I became a judge and a mayor and such vain truck, and why folks in town look on me as so able! Ha!"

In a biography of Joseph II, Saul K. Padover has shown the effect upon Joseph of the death of his wife, Isabel of Parma, an experience which was embittered by the discovery that his melancholy wife had never loved him. Thenceforth Joseph II was "hard, dry, and bitter," wholly immersed in administration, and harsh, cold, and contemptuous of women. In the incisive phrase of Casanova, even the face of Joseph expressed "conceit and suicide."

Even an indulgent environment does not always elicit uniform reactions. A promotion may release a whole new burst of activity; the new office manager may brim with new ideas and take a wife. The success of one book may stimulate a stream of books from the author. But sometimes the responses to success are singularly disproportionate. The individual may develop grave doubts of his own ability, grow gloomy and depressed. He may develop physical symptoms, or indulge in the excessive use of drugs. Or he may grow arrogant, peremptory, cruel, thus preparing the way for final failure. Freud was able to describe types who collapse when success comes. He found that they were often driven by unconscious guilt feelings when confronted by an opportunity to take the role of authority, to give orders, to demand attention.

It is possible to put individual incidents of the sort just named into the wider context of events in which they occur. Each deprivation and indulgence, each form of response is paralleled in any community by other incidents of the same kind, or deviates atypically from them. We can isolate sequences which are characteristic of particular groups.

Unemployment, for example, is a frequent deprivation which every community in the modern world inflicts upon its members. Individual responses run through the entire gamut of internalized and externalized solutions. There may be morbid self-accusations of failure, leading to suicide; or physical difficulties of functional origin may develop. There may be growing preoccupation with fantasy in the form of daydreams, adventure stories, or motion-picture romances. There may be private reading in order to learn new skills which will prove useful if new opportunities open up. There may also be serious reading and study devoted to economic conditions; this may lead up to express demands for overt changes in the real environment.

To some extent blocked assertive impulses may be displaced to people in the immediate environment; then the individual becomes quarrelsome. To some extent blocked interest in life may find expression in sexuality and sociableness. Or assertiveness may be worked off in socially stigmatized ways, like theft and robbery. In contact with representatives of authority, like public relief administrators, personal aggressiveness may increase. The person may justify these acts to himself and to others in the name of collective symbols, like "loyal citizen," "ex-service man who has suffered for his country." Individual acts of terrorism may be justified to "blast a rotten system."

Organized, as distinct from private, activity may be expressed in ceremonials which leave the overt environment unchanged. Persons may associate themselves with sects which spend hours confessing, singing, dancing, listening. Or an organization will sponsor simple and circumscribed demands. Thus committees of the unemployed may protest against "abuses" of power by administrators. Again, there may be elaborate demands for institutional reconstruction, like the socialization of production. And these larger demands may be associated with methods which are conventional, like electioneering and voting, or drastic and forbidden, like general strikes and armed uprisings.

The foregoing alternatives may be expressed in this general form:

> Privately internalized acts
> Privately externalized acts
> Socially internalized acts
> Socially externalized acts.

Political analysis is partly concerned with the discovery of which people act which way under which conditions. Conduct in a given situation can be partially predicted by noticing how those who are involved in it have responded to similar situations in the past, and with what success.

A study of the Chicago unemployed, by Gabriel Almond and the writer, was intended to contribute to our knowledge of *who* responded *how* to the deprivation of unemployment. Who would resort to "privately externalized acts" and who would resort to "socially externalized acts"?

Hyperaggressiveness in face-to-face relations was found to be an alternative to organized protest. Hyperaggressiveness was discovered by observing the conduct of clients when they came into personal contact with administrators of public relief. A sample of 100 hyperaggressives contrasted in certain respects with a sample of 100 members of protest organizations, like Workers' Committees or Unemployed Councils. The hyperaggressives, unlike the organized, had seldom belonged to parties, unions, or fraternal organizations before the depression; they had changed their jobs more often, and had been more often on private or public relief; they had more often committed impulsive offenses against the law, like assault; they had more often fled from personal responsibilities (deserted their wives, for example).

In general the hyperaggressives were psychopathic personalities who were so narcissistic that they had little love to give to organized activity, so overreactive against the submissive tendencies of their personalities that they resented discipline, so uncontrolled in relation to their impulses that they often clashed with their fellows. They were externalized rage types, capable of organized effort only during the most acute crises. When the organized effort first runs into difficulties, such personalities throw off the bonds of discipline and withdraw into isolation.

Hypersubmissiveness was likewise shown to be an alternative to organized protest. One hundred hypersubmissive clients, in contrast with 100 members of protest organizations, had few predepression affiliations with organizations (and especially few with protest groups). They had seldom committed offenses against the law or the mores; they had held modest jobs; they had come from rural districts in the United States and Europe; they had often been stigmatized by their environment (like the Negroes, objects of race prejudice).

Plainly those were most likely to assert themselves collectively who had been members of trades unions, fraternal societies, and similar associations. This mode of dealing with the world was carried over to the emergency situation as well.

More drastic assertiveness, in the form of membership in revolutionary parties, appealed to those who had been connected with radical parties before, and who had most flagrantly defied the mores. The leaders of the communist-led organizations were recruited from those who committed more impulsive violations of the law than had the leaders of the socialist-led organizations. The socialist leaders revealed a higher incidence of those who had committed crimes of calculation against property. The most radical leaders committed crimes of impulse, like assault rather than "crimes of calculation," like forgery. Such leaders had much in common with the hyperaggressive personalities previously described.

Leaders in unemployed groups came from leaders in the party, business, and social life of the predepression epoch; the rank and file came from the rank and file of predepression organizations. It was apparent that the training, skill, and social connections of the leaders of the radical and the less radical movements were more like one another than they were like the rank and file. The principal bond with the rank and file was the symbol in the name of which the leaders elicited support.

It is important to understand the obsolescence processes of political life. Organizations which fail to "get results" leave some of their members passive; others move over to competing symbols and practices. Comparative investigations seem to show that the ruling elite in any organized movement is less mobile than the rank and file; after all, the rulers are able to extract income, deference, and sometimes safety from their official positions. They build up vested and sentimental bonds to their jobs which are more tangible than those which bind the rank and file. A sam-

pling in 1931 of a branch of the Social Democratic party
in mid-Berlin showed that 60 per cent had been members
of the party less than five years. Another report on 75,000
members showed that 50 per cent were party members less
than five years. Youths, especially, moved from Social
Democrat to Communist to National Socialist organizations, and even back again, as recurring waves of success
or failure altered their estimate of the total situation. The
broad masses are seldom sufficiently active, or sufficiently
radicalized, to bind themselves firmly to special means of
expression. A self-critical Social Democratic writer showed
that, despite generations of proletarian agitation and organization, the proletarian organizations in pre-Nazi Germany exercised a feeble hold on the masses of those who
might be called proletarian. Of the forty million proletarians, only 2.5 per cent were to be counted as full members of proletarian parties (Social Democrat, Communist,
and fractional Communist parties). Sixty-five per cent of
the wage and salaried workers were not in trades unions,
and 28 per cent of those who were in trades unions were in
"bourgeois unions" (such as those controlled by religious
organizations).

The problem of readjustment is plainly connected with
the level of general insecurity, which is a function of the
way in which environmental changes are interpreted as inflicting indulgences or deprivations. Kautilya's *Arthasas-
tra,* the Indian classic, divides the discontented into the
"provoked," "alarmed," "ambitious," and "haughty," and
considers the methods which will arouse them against a
particular ruler or win them over. The principal contribution of modern analysis is no doubt the discovery of time,
and the emphasis upon the processes by which world movements are facilitated or impeded. Plainly the same volume
of unemployment may be more dangerous to an elite which

is close to the center of the current revolutionary wave than to an elite which is far away. Warsaw is far more menaced than New York.

The focus of discussion so far has been the relationship between person and person, or person and community. The same categories of analysis are relevant to the study of connections of community to community, especially of one state in relation to other states in the modern state system. The sudden defeat of a state may lead to a wave of suicides among its humiliated leaders, and to such internalized collective behavior as religious revivalism. Organized action may also undertake the economic and technical rehabilitation of the nation, for the recovery of status and the exaction of revenge (France after 1870; Germany after 1918).

The same major categories may be used to examine the consequences of contact between persons of contrasting cultures.

The expansion of European civilization has left in its wake a broad wave of cultural crises whose varied outcomes furnish examples of cultural adaptation as well as cultural collapse. An important factor in the outcome is the speed and magnitude of outside interference. But some cultures which have been subject to about the same degree of restriction through contact with Europeans have disintegrated quickly, while others have adapted themselves and survived.

By cultural survival is meant the preservation of the identifying name of the culture and many of its distinctive supporting symbols and practices, and the maintenance of a population to transmit the cultural heritage. Sometimes a smooth and gradual transition is made to effective participation as a member of the body politic of a state which is recognized in the Western European state system. The older tribal name is preserved as a respected social mark, but there are no demands to become a state. No doubt the Maori of New Zealand represent this form of adaptation.

In some instances the carriers of a primitive culture have internalized their behavior to such an extreme degree that the culture moved rapidly toward extinction, not only through the abandonment of its forms, but through the self-destruction of its bearers. W. H. R. Rivers proposed to explain the depopulation of Melanesia on this hypothesis, since he rejected the view that external interference had been more severe here than in areas where the results were less decisive. His interpretation was that the appearance of the white man who violated all sacred restrictions and suffered no harm created such frustration, depression, and lassitude that cultural patterns were neglected, and the people became too uninterested even to procreate.

The same process may occur less spectacularly when many individuals desert a primitive culture, find it impossible to establish a foothold in the larger environment outside, and ultimately destroy themselves by the excessive use of drugs or by the careless contraction of diseases. Those who remain loyal to the primitive culture may adhere strictly to old forms, sometimes failing to adopt enough of the new to make a smooth transition.

Sometimes the amount of socially internalized conduct increases in response to deprivation. New sects may multiply the amount of time and energy spent in dancing, praying, meditating. They may increase the frequency of autistic experiences among the members of the community, thus modifying the norms of the community. There is some evidence that where the peyote cult has made progress among Pueblo Indians, as at Taos, the importance of personal, subjective events has been increased. As Ruth Benedict has shown, the Pueblo Indians are predominantly matter-of-fact. They do not rely upon the dream as a means of personal contact with power, as do the Plains Indians. Those who chew the peyote (dried cactus) report elaborate visions, often in color, and this private autistic experience seems to represent a novel value in Pueblo life.

Socially externalized acts may use for targets not only the world outside the community but also the community itself. We have seen that when aggressive impulses are blocked, the aggression turns back against the targets which are close to the self. There is evidence that this process often appears in the growth of factions among defeated people, especially when they are accustomed to very assertive behavior. M. E. Opler has reported a striking example of this process among the Mescalero Apache. With the destruction of the buffalo herds and the suppression of marauding bands, the Mescalero were thrown into close proximity to one another on the reservation. The peyote cult spread rapidly among them, but in a peculiar form. Here the cult meetings were theaters of acute conflict among rival shamans, each trying to lead the other into the disclosure of his special secrets. Feuds and reprisals grew so bloody that another adjustment became imperative or the Mescalero seemed doomed to mutual extermination.

The symbols which spread among communities in response to deprivation are related to the previous patterns of external expression. The Indians on the plains were devoted to hunting and fighting, in contrast with the Pueblo Indians of the Southwest who were primarily agriculturists when the white man came; and it was among the Plains Indians that the Ghost Dance, which had many antiwhite features, spread most vigorously.

Some symbols organize collective impulses into acts which influence the overt environment. Conspirative uprisings, like the Boxer rebellion in China, may be full of determined hatred of the foreigner; but without the superior technique of the foreigner, failure is sure, unless other circumstances weaken the encroaching civilization. When the bearers of the superior fighting technique are divided among themselves, the pressure is released on peripheral people of simpler technique, who may then emerge from their remote mountains, deserts, and steppes, and sweep in to destroy alien communities or to settle down and become assimilated.

Socially externalized forms of adjustment occur when foreign techniques of agriculture, trade, craftsmanship, manufacturing, and fighting are adopted in the community.

Externalized forms of adjustment may also involve the borrowing of the symbols and the institutional practices of the limiting civilization. Thus nationalistic programs may be borrowed and spread, as the Chinese, for example, are taking over the Western conceptions of the competitive state system and nationalism, and turning them against the Western powers by abolishing extraterritoriality and other kinds of foreign privilege. Among feebler peoples, the precursors of nationalism may appear in the multiplication of native sects in competition with sects and denominations which are foreign controlled. It is reported that among the negro natives of Southwest Africa there are more than 500 native denominations which have been formed in recent years. This is no doubt a cultural activity which tides the negroes through a long period of watchful waiting for the external balance of power to shift to the advantage of the black and against the white.

The foregoing considerations have shown how contact may be met by internalized or externalized acts, some of which give impetus to passive or active programs. What are the factors which affect the geographical distribution of loyalties? Modern nationalistic movements have consolidated the loyalties of the inhabitants of many local areas around symbols of much larger communities. But the reverse has been equally true. The history-less nations of Central and Eastern Europe were stimulated to self-discovery or rediscovery in recent times. The result was to disrupt the continuity of administration in the Austro-Hungarian, Russian, and Turkish empires. Such demands for self-determination in the name of a national unity often follow old administrative lines. Great Britain and France were both organized around urban centers of old administrative districts. The speech of the capital became the standard language of justice, civil and military administration, debate, learning, society. Such unifying traits were often incompletely diffused into outlying provinces. Hence cultural differences could be inflamed into political separatism as national status came to be more highly prized.

Despite the persuasive or the militant pretensions of many self-styled world elites, the world is no unified community. It has no solidarity of sentiment and practice. Such unification has thus far been blocked by the spontaneous and partly deliberate play of the balance of power, or, more correctly, the balancing of power. The play of the balance restricts the scope of an ambitious monarch, an expanding bourgeois state, a militantly revolutionary society. It is the balance of power that has tipped the scales against every local aspirant to world hegemony, and left the nations of mankind loyal to symbols more inclusive than neighborhoods but less inclusive than the world. No external threat, no common hope of gain, no common code of right, has attained the ascendancy which would ensure the peaceful succession of an elite in a united world.

Loyalties may follow functional no less than geographical lines. The new division of labor inaugurated by machines created conspicuous differences between those who toiled in plants and those who owned or managed them.

When peasants moved to cities, multifarious insecurities arose. Older codes of morals and manners underwent terrific stress, and found expression in protest symbols directed against the ruling "class." When a revolutionary situation in Russia led to the seizure of power in the name of the "proletariat," processes of geographical restriction got under way at once, as foreign elites sought to protect themselves by emphasizing the parochial characteristics of the new elites. Whether insecurities will be expressed in symbols of geography or of function is largely a matter of their position in time and space with reference to the world-revolutionary process itself.

When are individual impulses displaced upon collective symbols? Periods of prosperity are periods of individualistic expression, when private plans are formed with reference to a benevolent universe. Periods of depression or of war are periods of submission to collective symbols.

When are conciliatory or militant attitudes most likely to be adopted? Cruelty is especially common among those who have felt guilty and inferior, and who seek to overcome submissive tendencies by overreaction. The externalized rage types and the partially inhibited rage types are those from whom destructive acts are to be expected under stress. Elites and communities which have felt guilty and inferior, and which struggle to overcome lack of self-confidence, are most disposed to orgiastic rage and to acts of collective destruction.

The attitudes which are of particular interest to the student of politics have been passed in terse review: externalized attitudes, community attitudes, militant attitudes, and their correlatives. When we consider these attitudes in the perspective of world development, we cannot fail to be impressed by the tenacity with which certain forms of attitude, included within the pattern of Western European civilization, have persisted in competition and conflict with rival attitudes. This civilization is favorable to externalization, militancy, and parochialism. Energies are directed outward toward the manipulation of man and nature. The expectation of violence leads to the incessant evaluation of social change in terms of fighting effectiveness. Local groups who participate in the technical processes of this civilization are split off from one another by the expectation of violence as a probable resolution of internal and external difficulties, and by the sentimentalizing of local differences. This sentimentalization of local differences has taken the modern form of nationality and nationalism. Nationalism is a mass demand to become or to remain a state among states.[1] Nationalism is a form of provincialism which was stimulated as modern commerce and industry emphasized the advantages of larger markets.

But tendencies to enlarge the local market were checked by conflict with others in the same civilization who were striving for the same extension of market. Tendencies to externalize human activities along profitable economic lines proved incompatible with tendencies to respect localism and to expect resorts to violence. No unified economic group rose to the direction of world-economic processes, since each economic group sought to strengthen its position by emphasizing patriotism and practicing violence, which in turn prevented complete unity with dominant economic groups elsewhere, who were stressing the same things.

Functional symbols rise from time to time to challenge the ascendancy of parochial symbols. The most recent at-

---

[1] For naturalistic as distinguished from certain normative (juristic) purposes, the state may be defined as a manifold of events. "That subjective event which is the unique mark of the state is the recognition that one belongs to a community with a system of paramount claims and expectations." (Quoted from the author's *Psychopathology and Politics*, chapter XIII, "The State as a Manifold of Events," p. 245.)

tack on parochialism has been in the name of a world-wide proletarian class. But the other characteristics of Western European civilization have nullified, or are nullifying, the success of these appeals for a functional path to a unified world. Those who seize power in the name of an all-inclusive symbol are promptly isolated by the play of the balance of power, which is particularly sensitive in a civilization that expects violence and sentimentalizes nationality and nationalism. In self-defense, the bearers of the new appeal to functional universality accept the basic conditions of survival in this environment, and emphasize their own local values in a world of potential violence. Hence we are not surprised to learn that the word *Rodina,* meaning birthplace or homeland, is permitted in the press of the Soviet Union in referring to the U.S.S.R. Phrases like "Socialist Fatherland" were formerly used to emphasize the idea of internationalism.

Everywhere the activism, militancy, and parochialism of Western civilization combine to overwhelm all whose attitudes stand opposed.

CHAPTER X

RÉSUMÉ

By the study of politics is here meant the study of influence and the influential. The influential cannot be satisfactorily described by the use of a single index. To some extent influence is indicated by claims over values, like deference, income, safety. But deference may not go to the rich, and safety may not go to the distinguished. Plainly different results may be obtained by different criteria of influence.

The results of political analysis depend also on the characteristics of the elite which it is proposed to explore. This book has spoken of skill, class, personality, and attitude groups, and discussed the meaning of social change for the relative ascendancy of such formations. The most important political analysis of modern times (the Marxist) has concentrated attention upon the class results of social change. This has diverted attention from many equally relevant ways of viewing the results of social life, such as the fate of skill, personality, and attitude groups.

Emphasis on class, like emphasis on skill or personality, is a methodological contrivance of systematic thinkers, a selected frame of reference to be held constant during the course of a *particular* act of analysis. The act of using new frames of reference for purposes of political analysis will, as usual, modify the preferences of those who use them. Those accustomed to think in terms of community attitudes (like nationality, nationalism) have often obtained new insights by the use of class analysis, and often modified their practical preferences. Sometimes they have turned from patriotism to proletarianism. Thinkers accustomed to class analysis may be led to new insights and new scales of preference by becoming accustomed to other ways of construing social results. They may want to identify themselves with the skill struggle rather than the class struggle, or to seek fulfillment in the name of nation or race or personality. Any act of analysis chastens preferences by the very act of exposing them to new naturalistic insights.

In communities which share Western European civilization the few, called here the elite, are more influential than the many, the mass. Lord Bryce said that government was always government by the few, whether in the name of the one, the few, or the many.

The ascendancy of an elite depends in part upon the successful manipulation of its environment. Methods of management involve symbols, violence, goods, practices. Counter-elites depend upon the same means.

Some methods are especially adapted to elite attack and others to elite defense. An established elite is usually so well situated in control of the goods, violence, and practices of a community that a challenging elite is constrained to rely chiefly upon symbols. After all, symbols are cheap and elusive; they can be spread by word of mouth beyond the eye of vigilant authority; they can organize concerted action among the disaffected and promote the crisis in which other methods are serviceable. Any established order possesses a dominant myth (ideology); but a symbol monopoly is less easy to protect than a monopoly of goods and violence.

A smoothly functioning political order has little need of thought about propaganda among members of its own community. An ideology, once accepted, perpetuates itself with remarkable vitality. The individuals born into the state direct some of their love toward the symbols which sustain the system: the common name, the common heroes, the common mission, the common demands. Some destructive tendencies are directed against rivals, traitors, heresies, and counterdemands. Individuals generate feelings of guilt in connection with the complex process of growing up; and some of this guilt is projected away from the individual and upon symbols of collective enemies, which are treated as shameful violators of the mores. Personal weakness, too, is projected upon the world outside; after all, is not the enemy destined to defeat in our victory?

The propaganda of revolution has at least one long-run advantage. Discontent, however created, tends to weaken the hold of the dominating system of symbol and practice. Any elite which fails to coincide with prosperity and victory may be rejected by the masses. Defeat, depression, and disaster, however, caused, raise doubt about the legitimacy of the Son of Heaven. When individuals are deprived, they tend to withdraw their love from symbols of the external world and to concentrate affection upon themselves; also to divert their assertive impulses from the world outside back against themselves. Extreme reactions result in a narcissistic psychosis, or suicide. Most people, however, avoid such extremes by substituting a new set of collective symbols for the old symbols. The problem of a revolutionary propagandist is to guide miscellaneous insecurities into channels suitable to his seizure of power. He seeks to control the projection of love, destructiveness, guilt, and weakness with reference to a utopia capable of becoming ideology.

Deprivations, alone, are insufficient to produce revolutionary upheavals. Social revolutions occur when new indulgences have been made possible by the growth of new social formations as an incident of technical development.

Only the new self-confidence of success gives strength for resentment against deprivation.

It is the recurring surge of insecurity that, however initiated, places a premium upon incessant innovation of detail, both in keeping and in taking power. Boredom with one symbol signifies the importance of another symbol; failure of the army emphasizes the importance of the air force; failure of free competition indicates the possibilities of monopoly; discontent with legislatures suggests the popularity of strong executives.

The harmless discharge of mass emotion (catharsis) can be induced by propaganda, by violence, or by the management of goods and practices. Adjustment, too, can be furthered by each method. But all methods are susceptible to defeat through ineptitude and unpropitious circumstances.

The results of social change are politically significant as they affect the distribution of values among elites of various kinds. Elites have been described here in terms of skill, class, personality, attitude.

Some types of skill have seldom led to eminence. Manual workers, peasants, physical scientists, engineers (manipulators of things) have been far less conspicuous than have managers of men. In Western European civilization, skill in violence, organization, bargaining, and symbol manipulation has been important at all times. But the relative role has varied. Skill in violence was a major way to power in feudal Europe. Skill in organization provided the cement which integrated the national monarchies. Skill in bargaining arose with the age of industrial expansion. In recent crises of world development, skill in propaganda played a decisive role, and skill in bargaining went into partial eclipse.

The growth of new classes, like the growth of new skills,

is intertwined with the appearance of new means of production. New technology was a major precondition of the decline of aristocracy and the rise of the bourgeoisie. This was in part signalized by the seizure of power in France (and elsewhere) during crises of great intensity. A world revolution is a seizure of power which benefits a new social formation. This seizure is local, and proceeds in the name of a new set of ruling symbols. The French Revolution, it will be remembered, was carried out in the name of the "rights of man," and some of the practices were universal suffrage, parliamentarism, church disestablishment, and the encouragement of businessmen at the expense of feudal aristocrats.

We have accepted the proposition that the revolution of 1917 in Russia was another world revolution. Those who seized power spoke in the name of the proletariat, and instituted relative equality of money incomes, governmentalization of organized social life, monopolization of legality in the hands of a single dominant party. Where do we stand with reference to this latest revolutionary upheaval and the next one?

Our analysis has drawn attention to the way that world-revolutionary initiatives are at once partially restricted and partially universalized. Those who seized power in France and Russia were restricted by the play of the external balance of power. Hence the world was not united by those who spoke in the name of the new political symbols. One of the means of defense was partial incorporation of symbols and practices connected with this pattern. Thus we interpret the present juncture of world affairs as a movement toward relative money equality, toward governmentalization of social life, and toward the monopoly of legality by single political parties.

From this point of view we are in the midst of a unified

world movement which is expressing itself in many contradictory forms during its early phases. In the United
States it is doubtful if these developments will pass through
a period of *"romantic" Fascism*, as in Italy and Germany.
Romantic Fascism is marked by a seizure of offices behind
a tenuous façade of legality by leaders of a mass movement. The backbone of the popular movement is the lower
middle class; the agitators at the top receive support from
big business and aristocratic groups as well. At first private
capitalism is conserved; but it seems probable that in the
face of the necessity for a united nation, private capitalism
will be liquidated in times of military stress. In a military
state, the movement toward equalization, governmentalization, and monopolization would no doubt proceed.

Another possible path to Fascism in the United States
would involve the steady encroachment of an impatient
community upon the use of the strike. This *"piecemeal"
Fascism* could come about as middle-class groups are
aroused against the "agitators," "reds," and "radicals"
by organized agencies of big business and big finance.

A more peaceful development of American life might
follow were the middle classes emancipated from their
present psychological dependence upon the agencies of
big business and big finance. At present spokesmen of na-
tionwide organizations of businessmen speak in the name
of American business as a unit, without emphasizing the
conflict of interest between independent business and monopolistic business. In the past the discontent of independent
business and professional groups at the monopoly tendencies of modern industrialism has been exhausted
through partisan channels. Effective action in the modern
world depends upon functional organizations which lie
behind parties and which confer strength upon partisan
action. Hence the growth of middle-class consciousness

depends upon organizing middle-class groups into effective national bodies which command their own executive staffs, their own means of communication, and which develop their own self-consciousness, outlook, and program.

As far as the United States is concerned, the organization of an Independent Chamber of American Business and Service would foster middle-class activism. Practical demands could be made to use the taxing power to curb big business and big finance, and to provide credit to independent groups. On this program, the smaller business and professional man can cooperate, within limits, with the organizations of labor, especially skilled labor. The smaller agricultural interests can be closely identified with antimonopoly demands. These several components of the middle class might be united for common purposes in an American Skill Congress, welcoming all Americans who have sacrificed to obtain socially useful skill, and who belong to the lesser-income group. In annual assembly, the American Skill Congress could coordinate the scattered programs of cooperating organizations and stimulate effective skill consciousness among them.

Such a capstone agency would stimulate effective self-consciousness among social formations which are now driven hither and yon by historical processes into which they have little insight. Perhaps the supreme paradox is that it is precisely the skill groups of the lower middle classes which are rising to control in modern world politics. In the Soviet Union present developments favor those who get skill in engineering, organization, propaganda, violence. Vast differences in money income were wiped out with the extinction of the landed aristocracy and hierarchies of private business. In the United States, where middle-class formations are still relatively flourishing, world developments to curb great differences of income may take somewhat distinctive form.

Recently independent druggists, hardware dealers, grocers, and other business men have undertaken to curb the chain stores. They have been supported by wholesalers who were alarmed by the possibility that their own markets would be dominated by the chains. Some small manufacturing concerns are run by men who are alert to the possible advantages to be derived from protecting their independence through organized action. The canning industry, widely dispersed over the nation in many small units, is typical of the most promising bases of middle class politics. Many business men were stimulated to greater awareness of their special interests when they saw their large competitors seek to monopolize the machinery of the National Industrial Recovery Act. Some have seen the advantages to be gained by them from cheap power furnished by such government enterprises as the Tennessee Valley Authority, the Boulder Dam, and the Grand Coulée project. A government "yardstick" can be used to control the rates of private utility companies.

It has recently been percieved that the devices of modern corporate control may be used as instruments of public, as well as private, policy. Large private utility companies, notably in the fields of power and communication, have spread their stock widely throughout the nation. It was hoped that the vested interests thus created would protect the utilities against demands for public ownership and operation. At the same time it was believed that the nominal owners were too widely dispersed to exercise any degree of effective influence over the small controlling groups which dominated the holding operating companies.

Public policy may require the use of "shares" not only

to propagate the illusion of control as a "public relations policy," but to provide the means of efficient control. Governments have already learned to use the publicly owned corporation, and there are many instances of joint subscription of share capital by public authority and private groups and individuals. An infinitely large variety of joint arrangements is conceivable. Important credit, power, transportation, and communication enterprises (regional, national, extra-national) could have voting shares assigned to significant functional groups, like Federal government departments and commissions, business associations (including dependents), farmers, organized workers, consumers, cooperatives, state and metropolitan governments.

At present it is common, as a public relations policy, to assign blocs of stock to a "preferred list" of individuals who are connected with banks, brokerage houses, investment trusts, insurance companies, engineering companies, and political parties. This practice can be "institutionalized" and brought under more responsible control by assigning shares to important functional groups in their corporate capacities.

If this, or any other, control device is set up, the results will depend upon the relative skill and strength of functional groups. If middle-income skill groups are to influence national policy in their own behalf, they must be nationally organized, capable of independent self-assertion. They must be represented by a set of spokesmen who will not be misled by the spokesmen of some big business groups who complain of "reds" when independent business, professional, and labor groups threaten to curb monopolistic practices.

Imaginative minds have already forecast the day when devices of corporate control would be adapted to the requirements of integrated national policy. They have foreseen the possibility of "every citizen a shareholder" in "U.S.A., Incorporated," enjoying a guaranteed basic income as a fixed charge on the national economic enterprise (contingent upon satisfactory participation in the national undertaking), and belonging to functional-territorial groups capable of exercising some formal, rather than clandestine or external, influence over policy.

Entirely apart from such ambitious projects are many less pretentious devices for coping with the "efficiency and acceptability" problems of large-scale undertakings in the American Republic. Many ingenious practices are proposed in the works of such seasoned students of modern society as Sidney and Beatrice Webb.

Some men of substantial property will see that the preservation of American business depends upon a healthy middle class of business and professional Americans. Big business needs smaller business, and can wisely adopt measures necessary to sustain it. Otherwise the cleavage between rich and poor, so disastrous for the preservation of republican institutions, will widen to alarming proportions. *The Federalist* faced these issues with the utmost candor during the critical days of debate on the adoption of the new Constitution. Plainly, "the most common and durable source of factions has been the various and unequal distribution of property." It was taken for granted that factions could not be eliminated, but that their effects could be controlled. And there were some among the early statesmen of the United States who saw that something might be done to preserve that considerable dispersion of economic control upon which the stability of republican government depends.

While the literature of class analysis is abundant, the meaning of social life for the relative success of personality types has been but little explored. Yet the ebb and flow of events favors now one, now another, style of personality. The principal trait of the politician, in general, is intense craving for deference; but this motive must be joined with appropriate skills and with propitious circumstances if success is to come. Within the general pattern of the politician several subtypes are discernible. Notable is the agitator, whose urge for deference is so intense that he is content with nothing less than the *excited* response of his contemporaries. As means to excitement he cultivates the skills of oratory and polemical journalism. The organizer is less bound to the need for excited response; he has more energy for coordinating human activity. Conciliatory personalities come from the partly inhibited rage types; ruthless and imperious personalities, from externalized rage types. Agitational and ruthless types are both favored by crisis, and they have been abundantly in evidence during the recent crises of world economic expansion-contraction. Organizers and conciliatory personalities are more favored by the periods between crises, and by the initial phases of stress.

Social developments may be seen with reference to their effect upon attitude groups. Though closely related to other frames of reference, attitude groups cut across all of them. The most diverse personality types may share the same nationalistic loyalty; the most similar personality types may be separated by class loyalties. Men whose skill is violence may be very group-conscious and politically assertive; men whose skill is engineering are notably less active in politics. The success of classes may be impeded by attitudes of national loyalty.

The civilization of Western Europe is distinguished by certain attitudes which survive the most varied local developments, and impose themselves upon successive generations. European civilization is activistic: it fosters the manipulation of man and nature; it favors the externalizing rather than the internalizing of human impulses. European civilization is parochial: it fosters local loyalties, like nationalism, and curbs the tendency to assert functional loyalties as a means of universal union. European civilization has the expectation of violence; it takes wars, revolutions, secessions, revolts, gang struggles, and homicide for granted; regardless of how violence may be deplored, the probability of violence is sorrowfully assumed by the overwhelming majority. There are other cultures ("primitive" cultures) which take none of these things for granted. But the Western European pattern now holds most of mankind in its clutches.

Perhaps the distinguishing and unifying political movement of our times is the emergence of the lesser-income skill groups to hegemony in a world where the partial diffusion, partial restriction of the world-revolutionary pattern of 1917 is taking place atop the world created by the revolution of 1789. Yet behind the grandeur of class façades a penetrating political analysis can disclose the additional, perhaps subtler, dialectics of personal skills, personality types, personal attitudes. Thus the study of politics can lead to no once-for-all accomplishment, no gratifying certainty; it can give some measure of orientation for the incessant reappraisal of the shifting lines of communal insecurity.

BIBLIOGRAPHICAL NOTES

CHAPTER I

The analysis of politics which is found in this book was briefly stated in the author's *World Politics and Personal Insecurity*, New York, 1935, Chap. 1, "The Configurative Method." Charles E. Merriam has been particularly influential in redefining the scope of political science in the United States. See *Political Power; Its Composition and Incidence*, New York, 1934. See also the works of Charles A. Beard. Among the younger writers reference may be made to G. E. G. Catlin, *The Science and Method of Politics*, New York, 1927, and Frederick L. Schuman, *International Politics; An Introduction to the Western State System*, New York, 1933, Chap. XIII. Similar formulations by European writers are not uncommon; see, in particular, Gaetano Mosca, *Elementi di scienza politica*, 2d ed., Turin, 1923; Max Weber, "Wirtschaft und Gesellschaft," in *Grundriss der Sozialökonomik*, III Abteilung, Tübingen, 1925; Part 1, Chap. 3; Part 2, Chap. 7; Part 3, Chaps. 1-11 incl. For data about the affiliations and successions of elites, see Pitirim Sorokin, *Social Mobility*, New York, 1927; Vilfredo Pareto, *The Mind and Society*, 4 vols., New York, 1935; Roberto Michels, *Umschichtungen in den herrschenden Klassen nach dem Kriege*, Stuttgart, 1934. Data on the United States are in *Recent Economic Changes*, 2 vols., New York, 1929; *Recent Social Trends*, 2 vols., New York, 1933; Arthur N. Holcombe, *The New Party Politics*, New York, 1933; and *The Political Parties of Today*, 2d ed., New York, 1925.

CHAPTER II

For detailed references consult *Propaganda and Promotional Activities: An Annotated Bibliography*, compiled by H. D. Lasswell, R. D. Casey, and B. L. Smith, Minneapolis, 1935. On the general categories of myth, ideology, utopia, see Georges Sorel, *Réflexions sur la violence*, Paris, 1908; Karl Mannheim, *Ideologie und Utopie*, Bonn, 1929. For the inculcation of patriotism and the spread of nationalism, see Charles E. Merriam, *The Making of Citizens: A Comparative Study of Methods of Civil training*, Chicago, 1931, summary volume of the "Civil Training Series," which contains monographs on the Soviet Union, Italy, Germany, Switzerland, France, the Dual Monarchy, Great Britain, United States, and primitive societies. For the new Germany, see Frederick L. Schuman, *The Nazi Dictatorship*, New York, 1935. For Italy, Herman Finer, *Mussolini's Italy*, New York, 1935. In this chapter I have drawn upon my article, "The Psychology of Hitlerism," *Political Quarterly*, 4:373-384 (July-September, 1933). The nature and effect of Entente propaganda against Germany are appraised in Hans Thimme, *Weltkrieg ohne Waffen*, Stuttgart, 1932. Propaganda to win and retain foreign aid is studied in Francis P. Renaut, *La politique de propagande des Américains durant la guerre d'indépendance*, 2 vols., Paris, 1922—. For revolutionary propaganda, Lenin, *What Is To Be Done?*, New York, 1928. For general propaganda in the United States, see E. P. Herring, Jr., *Group Representation before Congress*, Baltimore, 1929; *Public Administration and the Public Interest*, New York, 1936. A theory of propaganda is stated by Leonard W. Doob, *Propaganda: Its Psychology and Technique*, New York, 1935. In general consult Hardwood L. Childs, ed., "Pressure Groups and Propaganda," *Annals*, May, 1935.

CHAPTER III

On war, consult Quincy Wright, *The Causes of War and the Conditions of Peace*, London, New York, Toronto, 1935; Pitirim Sorokin, *Contemporary Sociological Theories*, Chap. VI, New York, 1928. S. Rudolf Steinmetz, *Soziologie des Krieges*, Leipzig, 1929. An early discussion of strategy and tactics is *The Book of War: The Military Classic of the Far East*, London, 1908. See Carl von Clausewitz, *Vom Kriege*, 3 vols., Berlin, 1832-1834. A recent brief treatise is by Sir Frederick B. Maurice, *Principles of Strategy*, New York, 1930. For separate aspects, refer to Adolf Caspary, *Wirtschaftsstrategie und Kriegsführung*, Berlin, 1932; Richard W. Rowan, *Spy and Counterspy; The Development of Modern Espionage*, New York, 1928; Maximilian Longe, *Kriegs- und Industrie-Espionage*, Vienna, 1930; H. D. Lasswell, *Propaganda Technique in the World War*, London and New York, 1927. Concerning police: Raymond B. Fosdick, *American Police Systems*, New York, 1920, and *European Police Systems*, New York, 1915; A. T. Vassilyev, *The Ochrana, the Russian Secret Police*, Philadelphia, 1930; Bruce Smith, *The State Police*, New York, 1925; J. P. Shalloo, *Private Police, with Special Reference to Pennsylvania*, Philadelphia, 1934; Edward Levinson, *I Break Strikes: The Technique of Pearl L. Bergoff*, New York, 1935. For the theory of armed revolutionary uprising, see A. Neuberg (pseud.), *Der bewaffnete Aufstand: Versuch einer theoretischen Darstellung*, Zurich, 1928 (secret literature of the Third International; imprint false). For the theory of assassination, see Netschajeff, *The Diary of a Revolutionist*.

CHAPTER IV

Case studies of rationing systems during the World War are to be found in Carnegie Endowment for International Peace, Division of Economics and History, *Economic and Social History of the World War*, ed. by James T. Shotwell. The conditions under which prices might be set by free competition are formulated in Frank H. Knight, *Risk, Uncertainty and Profit*, Boston, 1921. Studies of deviation from "perfect competition" are in such volumes as Erich Egner, *Der Sinn des Monopols*, Berlin, 1931; J. M. Clark, *The Social Control of Business*, Chicago, 1926; D. M. Keezer and Stacy

May, *The Public Control of Business*, New York, 1930; A. Salz, *Macht and Wirtschaftsgesetz*, Leipzig, 1930. On the Soviet Union, consult Calvin B. Hoover, *The Economic Life of Soviet Russia*, New York, 1931; William Henry Chamberlin, *Russia's Iron Age*, Boston, 1934; Sidney and Beatrice Webb, *Soviet Communism*, New York, 1936. For certain aspects of modern economic developments, see A. A. Berle, Jr., and Gardiner C. Means, *The Modern Corporation and Private Property*, New York, 1932; A. A. Berle and V. J. Pederson, *Liquid Claims and National Wealth*, New York, 1934; Harold G. Moulton, *The Formation of Capital*, Washington, 1935; Henry C. Simons, *A Positive Program for Laissez-Faire*, Chicago, 1934; J. M. Clark, *Studies in the Economics of Overhead Costs*, Chicago, 1923. On commercial policy, consult Josef Gruntzel, *System der Handelspolitik*, 3d ed., Vienna, 1928. Also Eugene Staley, *War and the Private Investor*, New York, 1935, and R. G. Hawtrey, *Economic Aspects of Sovereignty*, London, 1930. For special aspects of withholding, see Ernest Theodore Hiller, *The Strike: A Study in Collective Action*, Chicago, 1928; Wilfred Harris Crook, *The General Strike: A Study of Labor's Tragic Weapon in Theory and Practice*, Chapel Hill, 1931; Evans Clark, ed., *Boycotts and Peace*, New York, 1932; Charles F. Remer and William B. Palmer, *A Study of Chinese Boycotts with Special Reference to their Economic Effectiveness*, Baltimore, 1933; Clarence M Case, *Non-violent Coercion: A Study in Methods of Social Control*, New York, 1923.

CHAPTER V

The non-Marxist literature on government and administration has tended to minimize the elite consequences of institutional practices by considering relative "efficiency" or by using universalistic terms like "liberty" or "obedience." The study of governmental practices in relation to the total context was greatly stimulated in English-speaking countries by Graham Wallas, *Human Nature in Politics*, London, 1908, *The Great Society*, London, 1914, *Our Social Heritage*, London, 1921, and *The Art of Thought*, London, 1926. See also Thurman W. Arnold, *The Symbols of Government*, New Haven, 1935; Jerome Frank, *Law and the Modern Mind*, New York, 1930; E. S. Robinson, *Law and the Lawyers*, New Haven, 1935; Huntington Cairns, *Law and the Social Sciences*, New York, 1935; William A. Robson, *Civilization and the Growth of Law*, New York, 1935; Roscoe Pound, *An Introduction to the Philosophy of Law*, New Haven, 1922; A. Leist, *Privatrecht und Kapitalismus in neunzehnten Jahrundert*, Tübingen, 1911; A. V. Dicey; *Lectures on the Relation between Law and Public Opinion in England during the Nineteenth Century*, 2d ed., London, 1914; M. M. Bigelow, and others, *Centralization and the Law*, Boston, 1906. See also Harold J. Laski, *A Grammar of Politics, Part II*, New Haven, 1925; R. M. MacIver, *The Modern State*, Oxford, 1926; Franz Oppenheimer, *The State*, Indianapolis, 1914; J. W. Garner, *Political Science and Government*, New York, 1928; Alfred Weber, *Ideen zur Staats- und Kultur-Soziologie*, Karlsruhe, 1927; Georg Jellinek, *Allgemeine Staatslehre*, 3d ed., Berlin, 1914; Rudolf Kjellén, *Grundriss zu einem System der Politik*, Leipzig, 1920; J. R. Seeley, *Introduction to Political Science*, London, 1896; J. W. Burgess, *Political Science and Constitutional Law*, 2 vols., Boston, 1890; Henry Sidgwick, *The Ele-*

ments of Politics, London, 1891; Robert H. Lowie, *The Origin of the State,* New York, 1927; W. C. MacLeod, *The Origin and History of Politics,* New York, 1931; Frank J. Goodnow, *Politics and Administration,* New York, 1900; Ernst Freund, *Administrative Powers over Persons and Property,* Chicago, 1928, and *Standards of American Legislation,* Chicago, 1917; W. F. Willoughby, *Principles of Public Administration,* Baltimore, 1927: Leonard D. White, *Introduction to the Study of Public Administration,* New York, 1926. For new approaches, see the articles by Underhill Moore and collaborators in *Yale Law Review;* also H. D. Lasswell and Gabriel Almond, "Twisting Relief Rules," *Personnel Journal,* 13:338-343 (April, 1935).

CHAPTER VI

Data about the skills and affiliations of legislators are in Karl Braunias, *Das parlamentarische Wahlrecht: Ein Handbuch über die Bildung der gesetzgebenden Körperschaften in Europa,* 2 vols., Berlin and Leipzig, 1932. Eminent figures in Germany are analyzed by Fritz Giese, "Die öftenliche Persönlichkeit," Beiheft 44, *Zeitschrift für angewandte Psychologie,* Leipzig, 1928. In general, consult A. M. Carr-Saunders and P. A. Wilson, *The Professions,* Oxford, 1933. For engineers, see A. P. M. Fleming and H. J. Brocklehurst, *A History of Engineering,* London, 1925; for physical scientists, W. C. D. Dampier, *A History of Science and Its Relations with Philosophy and Religion,* Cambridge, England, 1929. For physicians, consult Arthur Newsholme, *International Studies on the Relation between the Private and the Official Practice of Medicine with Special Reference to the Prevention of Disease,* 3 vols., London, 1931. Priests: Alfred Bertholet, "Priesthood," *Encyclopaedia of the Social Sciences.* For chiefs, bureaucrats, civil servants: W. C. MacLeod, *The Origin and History of Politics,* New York, 1931; Max Weber, "Politik als Beruf," in *Gesammelte Politische Schriften,* Munich, 1921; A. A. Lefas, *L'état et les fonctionnaires,* Paris, 1913; O. H. von der Gablentz, "Industriebureaukratie," *Schmollers Jahrbuch,* 50 (1926): 539-572. Diplomats: Severus Clemens, *Der Beruf des Diplomaten,* Berlin, 1926; Dale A. Hartman, "British and American Ambassadors," *Economica,* 11 (1931): 328-341. Bargainers: Werner Sombart, *Des Bourgeois,* Munich, 1920; F. W. Taussig and C. S. Joslyn, *American Business Leaders,* New York, 1932. Teachers, philosophers, social scientists: Edward H. Reisner, *Historical Foundations of Modern Education,* New York, 1927; H. Rashdall, *The Universities of Europe in the Middle Ages,* 2 vols., Oxford, 1895; Gladys Bryson, "The Emergence of the Social Sciences from Moral Philosophy," *International Journal of Ethics,* XLII (1932): 304-323. Lawyers: Max Rumpf, *Anwalt und Anwaltstand: Eine rechtswissenschaftliche und rechtssoziologische Untersuchung,* Leipzig, 1926; H. D. Hazeltine, Max Radin, A. A. Berle, Jr., "Legal Profession and Legal Education," *Encyclopaedia of the Social Sciences.* Journalists: International Labour Office, "Conditions of Work and Life of Journalists," *Studies and Reports,* ser. L, No. 2, Geneva, 1928; G. Bourdon and others, *Le journalisme d'aujourd'hui,* Paris, 1931; H. D. Lasswell, "Research on the Distribution of Symbol Specialists," *Journalism Quarterly,* 12:146-157 (June, 1935).

CHAPTER VII

For fuller details of the class analysis of politics, consult H. D. Lasswell, *World Politics and Personal Insecurity*, New York, 1935; Max Nomad, *Rebels and Renegades*, New York, 1932; V. Pareto, *Les systèmes socialistes*, Paris, 1902-1903; Hendryk de Man, *The Psychology of Socialism*, London, 1928; Werner Sombart, *Der proletarische Sozialismus*, 2 vols., Jena, 1924; L. L. Lorwin, *Labor and Internationalism*, New York, 1929; Roberto Michels, *Zur Sozialogie des Parteiwesens in der modernen Demokratie*, 2d ed., Leipzig, 1925; Julien Benda, *The Treason of the Intellectuals*, New York, 1928. An important historical analysis is Eugen Rosenstock, *Die europäischen Revolutionen*, Jena, 1931. On dialectical materialism, see Sidney Hook, *Towards the Understanding of Karl Marx*, New York, 1933; Georg Lukács, *Geschichte und Klassenbewusstsein*, Berlin, 1923; N. Bukharin, *Historical Materialism*, New York, 1925; N. Lenin, *Materialism and Empirio-criticism*, New York, 1927; Karl Kautsky, *Die materialistische Geschichtsauffassung*, 2 vols., Berlin, 1927; Heinrich Cunow, *Die marxsche Geschichts-Gesellschafts- und Staatstheorie*, 2 vols., 4th ed., Berlin, 1923; V. Adoratsky, *Dialectical Materialism*, New York, 1934. See also Guy Stanton Ford, ed., *Dictatorship in the Modern World*, Minneapolis, 1935, notably essays by Max Lerner, Ralph H. Lutz, J. Fred Rippy, Hans Kohn; Harwood L. Childs, ed., *Dictatorship and Propaganda*, Princeton, 1936, especially essays by Oscar Jászi, Fritz M. Marx, H. D. Lasswell; Hermann Kantorowicz, "Dictatorships" (with a bibliography by Alexander Elkin), *Politica*, No. 4, August, 1935, pp. 470-508; M. T. Florinsky, *World Revolution and the U.S.S.R.*, New York, 1933; Harold J. Laski, *The State in Theory and Practice*, New York, 1935.

CHAPTER VIII

Modern methods of intensive personality study range from the prolonged interview of Sigmund Freud, in which the subject indulges in free association, through various abbreviated interviews to the systematic observation of the acts of subjects who are unaware that they are being investigated. Recent literature is focusing attention upon the position of the observer in his field of reference; his abstract language is thus construed in terms of his characteristic method. An appreciation of the range of intensive approaches may be obtained by referring to the summary volume by Pauline V. Young, *Interviewing in Social Work*, New York, 1935. John Dollard has undertaken to formulate *Criteria for the Life History*, New Haven, 1935. Ways of objectifying the prolonged psychoanalytic interview are discussed in H. D. Lasswell, *Psychopathology and Politics*, Chap. XI, Chicago, 1930, and in subsequent articles in *Psychoanalytic Review* and *Imago* (Vienna). A succinct introduction to modern psychological conceptions is found in Bernard Hart, *Psychology of Insanity*, Cambridge, England, 1912. For general psychiatry, see William A. White, *Outline of Psychiatry*, 13th ed., Washington, 1932. Among influential authors, reference may be made to Sigmund Freud, Alfred Adler, and Carl Jung. Emphasis upon symbolic expressions in relation to biological traits is found in Ernst Kretschmer, *Textbook of Medical Psychology*, translated by E. B. Strauss, London, 1934. Current development in the various fields of psychology may be followed through the handbooks edited by Carl Murchison at the Clark University Press, Worcester, Mass. For typological or for individual studies of special interest to political scientists, reference may be made to Richard Behrendt, *Politischer Aktivismus, Ein Versuch zur Sociologie und Psychologie der Politik*, Leipzig, 1932; Fritz Künkel, *Grundzüge der politischen Charakterkunde*, Leipzig, 1933; Alexander Herzberg, *The Psychology of Philosophers*, New York, 1929; L. Pierce Clark, *Lincoln, A Psycho-Biography*, New York, 1933 (extensively used in this chapter); H. F. Gosnell, *Negro Politicians*, Chicago, 1935; John Gunther, *Inside Europe*, New York, 1936; Fedor Vergin, *Subconscious Europe*, London, 1932.

CHAPTER IX

The analysis of specific attitudes is complicated by the fact that attitudes are influenced by other attitudes, as well as by material conditions. The psychological significance of the state is studied in Jacob Wackernagel, *Der Wert des Staates*, Basel, 1934. An elaborate research on the relation between the family and every form of authority is *Studien über Autorität und Familie*, Forschungsberichte aus dem Institut für Sozialforschung, Paris, 1936. Nationalism, nationality, and patriotism are probed from several standpoints in the writings of Charles E. Merriam, Hans Kohn, Carlton J. H. Hayes, Roberto Michels. See especially Heinz O. Ziegler, *Die moderne Nation; Ein Beitrag zur politischen Soziologie*, Tübingen, 1931. Concerning militant attitudes, consult Edward Glover, *War, Sadism and Pacifism*, London, 1933, and Robert Waelder, *Lettre sur l'étiologie et l'évolution des psychoses collectives*, Institut international de coopération intellectuel, 1933. For experiments on morale in modern industrial plants, consult Elton Mayo, *The Human Problems of an Industrial Civilization*, New York, 1933. An observational and interrogatory procedure for the study of positive and negative personal relations is found in J. L. Moreno, *Who Shall Survive? A New Approach to the Problem of Human Interrelations*, Washington, 1934. The psychological characterization of personality and culture is discussed in Ruth Benedict, *Patterns of Culture*, Boston, 1934. For an analysis of changing interrelationships, see H. D. Lasswell, "Collective Autism as a Consequence of Culture Contact," *Zeitschrift für Sozialforschung*, IV (1935): 232-247. An analysis of assertiveness in response to deprivation is Gabriel Almond and H. D. Lasswell, "Aggressive Behavior by Clients Toward Public Relief Administrators: A Configurative Analysis," *American Political Science Review*, XXVIII (1934): 643-655. On certain aspects of proletarian socialism, consult *Die Organization im Klassenkampf. Die Probleme der Arbeiterklasse*, Berlin, 1932, notably the essay by Fritz Bieligk. For the relation between changing collective attitudes and law, consult Svend Ranulf, *The Jealousy of the Gods and Criminal Law at Athens: A Contribution to the Sociology of Moral Indignation*, 2 vols., London and Copenhagen, 1933-1934; Jerome Hall, *Theft, Law and Society*, Boston, 1935.

CHAPTER X

On developments in the United States: Lewis Corey, *The Crisis of the Middle Class*, New York, 1935; Alfred Bingham, *Insurgent America: Revolt of the Middle Classes*, New York, 1935; Lawrence Dennis, *Coming American Fascism*, New York, 1936; "The Unofficial Observer" (pseud.), *American Messiahs*, New York, 1935; Raymond Gram Swing, *Forerunners of American Fascism*, New York, 1935; William Yandell Elliott, *The Need for Constitutional Reform*, New York, 1935; and especially T. V. Smith, *The Promise of American Politics*, Chicago, 1936. As for functional groups, there are a number of scattered publications on trade associations, federations of labor, farm organizations, etc. On devices of mixed government and private control, see Sidney and Beatrice Webb, *A Constitution for the Socialist Commonwealth of Great Britain*, London and New York, 1920; Harold A. Van Dorn, *Government Owned Corporations*, New York, 1926; Marshall E. Dimock, *British Public Utilities and National Development*, London, 1933, and *Government-Operated Enterprises in the Panama Canal Zone*, Chicago, 1934; Marquis Childs, *Sweden: The Middle Way*, New Haven, 1936; Kurt Wiedenfeld, "Wesen und Bedeutung der gemischt-wirtschaftlichen Unternehmung," in *Schmollers Jahrbuch* 55: 439-456 (1931); Julius Landmann, ed., *Moderne Organisationsformen der öffentlichen Unternehmungen*, Schriften des Vereins für Sozialpolitik, pt. 2, vol. 176, Munich, 1931; "Government Owned Corporations," *Encyclopaedia of the Social Sciences* (by Paul Webbink). On corporation forms, see James C. Bonbright and Gardiner C. Means, *The Holding Company; Its Public Significance and Its Regulation*, New York, 1932; Eliot Jones, *The Trust Problem in the United States*, New York, 1921; Robert Liefmann, *Die Unternehmungsformen*, 4th ed., Stuttgart, 1930.

Democratic Character

BY HAROLD D. LASSWELL

☆ ☆ ☆

THE FREE PRESS · GLENCOE · ILLINOIS

DEMOCRATIC CHARACTER

The Classical Tradition

The connection between individual character and the body politic is a recurring theme in the classical political tradition. "The type of character appropriate to the constitution," wrote Aristotle, "is the power which continues to sustain it, as it is also the force which originally creates it."[1] When he spoke of the constitution Aristotle was thinking of something broader than an "arrangement of offices." He had in mind "a scheme of life, directed to attain a particular quality of life," which is conception close to the inclusiveness of the modern idea of "a culture."[2] Writing of what we would today call a well-functioning democracy Aristotle emphasized the favorable effect of relying upon men of a middle condition in all "gifts of fortune." "Those who belong to either extreme—the over-handsome, the over-strong, the over-noble, the over-wealthy; at the opposite end the over-poor, the over-weak, the utterly ignoble—find it hard to follow the lead of reason." The privileged ones incline more toward "violence and serious crime," while the underprivileged tend to "roguery and petty offenses." Those enjoying too many advantages are "both unwilling to obey and ignorant how to obey." At the other end of the scale are the "mean and poor-spirited."

We thus have, on the one hand, people who are ignorant how to rule and only know how to obey, as if they were so many slaves, and, on the other hand, people who are ignorant how to

[1] Unless otherwise indicated quotations from the *Politics* are from Ernest Barker, *The Politics of Aristotle*, Oxford, 1946. The present phrase is at p. 332.

[2] Footnote one, *op. cit.*, p. 180.

obey any sort of authority and only know how to rule as if they were masters of slaves. The result is a state, not of freemen, but only of slaves and masters: a state of envy on the one side and on the other contempt. Nothing could be further removed from the spirit of friendship or the temper of a political community. A state aims at being, as far as it can be, a society composed of equals and peers.[3]

The greatest means of ensuring the stability of any constitution, continues the *Politics*, is "the education of the citizens in the spirit of their constitution," which attunes them to the "right constitutional temper."[4] It is also important to institute a magistracy "to supervise those who live in a way out of harmony with the established constitution."[5] When the selection of officials is the problem, several considerations must be kept in mind, especially loyalty, skill and character. The public good demands the capacity to command the "passions."[6]

Aristotle concedes that popular government is an acceptable principle when it is based upon genuine discussion. The judgment of the people individually is not as good as that of an expert, but taken collectively it is better "if they are not debased in character."[7] Moreover, if we have a body of persons who are both good men and good citizens, it is more likely that the entire body will be free from corruption than that one man is free from it."[8] The citizens of a state "must know one another's characters" if they are to "give decisions in matters of disputed rights, and to distribute the offices of government according to the merit of candidates."[9]

[3] *Op. cit.*, p. 181.
[4] *Op. cit.*, p. 233.
[5] *Op. cit.*, p. 227.
[6] *Op. cit.*, p. 231.
[7] *Op. cit.*, p. 126.
[8] *Op. cit.*, p. 142.
[9] *Op. cit.*, p. 292.

The most plastic and penetrating portrayal of the interplay of character and constitution is to be found in the
Republic, not the *Politics*. When one form of state changes
into another, Plato finds the cause, not in external circumstances, but in the spirit of men whose "soul-structure" is
changing as a result of faulty education. The changes in
soul-structure as set forth by Plato are correctly characterized by Warner Jaeger as a comprehensive "pathology
of human character."[10] Using Sparta as the model for the
first deviation from his ideal type of constitution, Plato
speaks of Spartan rule as the rule of honor, or timocracy.
The second deviation is oligarchy, for which the philosopher took the Athens of his time as the model. Then
comes what Plato calls democracy, understanding by the
democratic man "what we should call the typical indi-
vidualist."[11] Finally we arrive at tyranny. In all cases the
disturbance arises in the relationship between fathers and
sons, which is taken as the prototype of all education even
when the specialized teacher has taken over most of the
tutorial responsibilities of the parent. The disturbance begins when the father pushes impulses which, within limits
would have been justified, too far toward his own exaggerated ideal. Moved by the natural opposition of youth
to age, the youth refuses to copy his father and from one
generation to the next the social inheritance becomes faul-
tier. The young timocrat, for example, is described as
despising his quiet and retiring father. The son prefers ambition, but his son in turn thinks this is too unselfish, and
prefers money. Then *his* son despises the money-grubber
for rejecting so many pleasures in pursuit of wealth and
becomes a "democrat." His son again goes beyond his

[10] Werner Jaeger, *Paideia: The Ideals of Greek Culture,* New York, Oxford University Press, 1943. Volume II, p. 323.
[11] Jaeger, *op. cit.,* volume II, p. 336.

father in the gratification of superfluous desires, and culminates in a tyrannical character.

Changes in the constitution are therefore depicted as being the outcome of varying degrees of unbalance in the individual soul-state, which is described as composed of the desirous, the spirited, and the reasoning parts. Delineating the "state within us" Plato treats the ambitious man as the outcome of the victory of the spirited component over the reasoning part. The oligarch reflects the triumph of the desires over the spirited and the reasoning parts. The democratic man is produced by battles within the desirous parts of the soul, and the tyrannical type is the extreme expression of self-indulgence. More specifically, the democratic man comes from the luxuriant growth of *superfluous* desires, and the tyrannical man from *unlawful* desires.

In order to understand the tyrannical man it is necessary to probe beneath the conscious level. In passages which foreshadow Freud it is said that the clue to these subterreanean depths of desire is to be found in the interpretation of dreams. In dreams the soul casts off the restaining bonds which have been put upon it by reason, and the bestial part of man awakens, revealing a part of his nature which the individual does not himself know. Plato described the Oedipus-complex, the desire to have intercourse with one's own mother, and a host of other wish-complexes, likewise suppressed, which range from sexual intercourse with the gods to sexual deviations of every kind, and murder.

The Modern Approach

It would be an exaggeraton to say that for well over two thousand years Western man made no advances in the study of politics beyond Plato and Aristotle. But it is not exaggerating to say that no one went beyond Plato's insight into the dynamics of the human soul until Freud penetrated once again into the lurid depths of the unconscious, and brought to the surface once more "the state within us," and revealed again the niagara of love and destruction within every living person. Since Plato and Aristotle our advances have not been in the "universal" propositions concerning man, but rather in the invention and adaptation of procedures by which specific individuals and groups, operating in specific historic and cultural settings, can be understood, and hence opened to modification, under some circumstances, through self-understanding or through the self-understood action of others. In a word, the modern approach is toward the building of a body of scientific knowledge by perfecting the instrumentalities of inquiry.

It is customary to oppose Aristotle to Plato in this regard, and to emphasize the impatience of Plato with the apparatus of descriptive investigation. It is true that the spirit of Plato gave to everything "a certain plastic roundness, than which nothing more strenuously resists the analytical urge of Aristotle's thought, which is to Plato's as the anatomical diagram is to the plastic human form."[12] A lively historical sense is essential if one is to realize vividly how "strange and repellant" the procedure of Aristotle was to the average Greek of the fourth century, and what a revolutionary innovation he was making. "The technique of the orderly observation of particulars, methodically pursued, was learnt from the exact modern medicine of the end of the fifth century, and in the fourth century from the astronomy of the orientals with their century-long catalogues and records."[13]

mathematical, poetical and allusive, without thereby admit-

[12] Werner Jaeger, *Aristotle: Fundamentals of the History of His Development,* Second Edition, Oxford, 1948, p. 372.
[13] Jaeger, *op. cit.,* p. 336.

It is possible to concede that Plato was imaginative, ting that he was indifferent to the descriptive facts of human relations. If in his highest flights Plato thought of himself as celebrating, or even adumbrating, the "permanence" beyond "appearance," we do not need to believe that Plato was uninstructed by, or unintrigued by, human appearances. From the scrutiny of his life as a whole we recognize in Plato a thinker who was inspired by the urge to be immediately as well as ultimately relevant to human problems. He did not, nor could he, refrain from perceiving and interpreting human relationships, even though he might draw back from subjecting his own imagination to the discipline of prolonged, systematic and patient empirical inquiry. Nor could he fail to inspire successive generations of Aristotles who sought to enlarge the applicability of his insights, and to contribute to their continual correction, by erecting a process of perpetual annotation in the light of the data gathered by observing the evolution of man and his societies.

The emphasis which has been put upon Aristotle's pursuit of the conditioning factors capable of explaining human behavior has often neglected to give sufficient weight to the significance of the fact that the patterns of scientific thought and observation were part of a more comprehensive frame of reference. The modern approach, too, often fails to grasp the wholeness of the intellectual enterprise of dealing with human affairs, and thereby neglects to perceive the wisdom of keeping the scientific part of the endeavor properly related to the total context. But the modern approach is not indifferent to the pivotal importance of "goal thinking," which consists in the clarification of values. Those of us who strive for the dignity rather than the indignity of man in human relations sense the need of defining our goal values in terms that enable us to find a point of contact between lofty and enduring aspirations and the details of any concrete situation. Hence we seek to specify the meaning of such terms as "the dignity of man" in reference to the shaping and sharing of values in society.[14] This calls for the making of "operational" definitions in reference to the institutional patterns found, or capable of being realized, in the body politic.[15] Part of the present essay will devote itself to describing the nature of a democratic community, as we now conceive it.

Even as Plato and Aristotle were acutely conscious of living in a time of change, the modern approach proceeds with full stress upon time. And in this regard we have somewhat sharper tools of inquiry than were utilized by the Greeks. I refer particularly to the patterns of thinking about the future. Both Plato and Aristotle sought in forecasting the future to subject it to scientific or, equivalently, to "inner logical" restriction. Aristotle in particular explored the passage of one form of constitution into another, inspired partly by the analogy of the successive stages through which the human being passes from conception to death. There is, however, a way of thinking about the outcome of the past and present which makes use of, though is not subordinated to, such conceptions of "stages." We can set up "developmental constructs" which are not scientific hypotheses, but which refer only to the possible ordering of events in the "unique" past and present. For example,

[14] I am speaking of the clarification of the goals appropriate to the policy sciences of democracy. There can also be a policy science of tyranny. A science of total policy would select either set of postulates and analyze both. A useful historical inquiry into our preference for human dignity is *The Dignity of Man* by Herschel Baker, Cambridge, Harvard University Press, 1947.

[15] Although modern "operationalism" derives from many sources, an influential statement by a distinguished physical scientist is Percy W. Bridgman, *The Logic of Modern Physics*, New York, Macmillan, 1927.

when we say that the present day world may be moving from the predominance of "business states" to "garrison states," we are putting forward no "law of politics."[16] We are characterizing a possible ordering through time of the appearance of predominant state forms on the globe. The function of the "construct" is to further our critical thinking about the probabilities of future events. To this end we review what is scientifically known about conditioning factors, and we examine the trends in different parts of the world. Part of the scientific knowledge that bears on such interpretations has to do with the connections between "character and constitution" to which the Greeks made early and original contributions.

We likewise share with the Greek thinkers an active concern for policy. Jaeger remarks that what Plato had to say in examining character and constitution was designed as a "warning against what he knew to be the logically inevitable sequel of the present."[17] And we are aware of the story of Plato as the advisor of the tyrants of Syracuse, and of Aristotle also acting as an advisor. Plato, in particular, was absorbed with the connection between knowledge and choice. Indeed, as Jaeger remarks in interpreting his thought, Plato believed that the "only science which is valuable is the science of choice, which enables us to make the right decisions."[18] And today the recovery of perspective which is expressed in the term "the policy sciences" is symbolic of the same concern for the making of decisions

16 The "developmental construct" is characterized in Chapter I of my *World Politics and World Insecurity* (1935) reprinted in *A Study of Power* by H. D. Lasswell, C. E. Merriam and T. V. Smith, Glencoe, The Free Press, 1950. On the garrison state, see my paper reprinted in Lasswell, *The Analysis of Political Behaviour; An Empirical Approach*, New York, Oxford University Press, 1947, Part II. Section A, Chapter II.

17 Werner Jaeger, *Paideia, The Ideals of Greek Culture*, New York, Oxford University Press, 1943, volume II, p. 340.

18 Jaeger, *Op. cit.*, volume II, p. 370.

which, in our case, are intended to implement human dignity.[19]

The modern approach then, is configurational in the sense that comprehensive perspectives are sought over human affairs. We utilize several interrelated and mutually facilitating patterns of thought, which we may abbreviate as the clarification of goal *values*, the assessment of *trends*, the review of scientific knowledge of conditioning *factors*, the *projection* of developmental constructs of the future, and the invention and estimating of policy *alternatives* designed to increase the probability of the realization of the goal values. Hence the concern with the interconnection of character and democracy enters into our thinking at many points: at the level of goal, trend, science, projection, invention and evaluation of policy.

The Democratic Community

Since we are concerned with the significance of democratic character for the democratic community, our principal frame of reference is the community. Our conception of character, and our judgment of the impact of character upon democracy, will depend upon the empirical study of how the democratic community is solidified, undermined, or on the contrary, brought into being, on the basis of character.

Let us therefore begin by clarifying the characteristics of the democratic community, which is the form of society which it is our purpose to achieve on the widest possible scale in both space and time. A democratic community is one in which human dignity is realized in theory and fact.

[19] See Myres S. McDougal and H. D. Lasswell, "Legal Education and Public Policy" in Lasswell, *The Analysis of Political Behaviour; An Empirical Approach*, New York, Oxford University Press, 1947, Part I, Chapter III. Also H. D. Lasswell and Daniel Lerner, editors, *The Policy Sciences; Recent Trends in Scope and Method*, Stanford, Stanford University Press, 1951.

It is characterized by wide rather than narrow participation in the shaping and sharing of values. By the term "value" we refer to a category of "preferred events." The social process we conceive to be comprehensible as *"man striving for values through institutions upon resources."* For the statement of goal values, and also for descriptive purposes, it is convenient to operate with a short list of value categories. At present the following eight terms appear to provide a workable list: *power, respect, affection, rectitude, well-being, wealth, skill, enlightenment.* Sometimes it is useful to sub-divide this set of values according to the degree to which attitudes are important, or are supplemented by relatively impersonal standards. When the attitudes are prominent, we speak of *deference* values, and put in this category power, respect, affection, and rectitude. When attitudes are supplemented by comparatively impersonal standards, we speak of *welfare* values, and include well-being, wealth, skill and enlightenment.

Consider briefly the deference values. A power relationship is distinguishable by the prevailing expectation (or application) of violence, or of some other extreme deprivation of value used in support of a choice. No overt use of physical instrumentalities is essential, and it is this aspect of the relationship that justifies the inclusion of power among the deference values. It is obvious that respect is peculiarly bound up with the quality of the attitudes prevailing in an interpersonal relationship. Respect can be indicated by symbolic expressions concerning the total position of the "self" in relation to the "other." Affection, of course, is understood in terms of feelings and of the accompanying estimates of "self" and "other." By rectitude we understand the sense of responsibility for sustaining a given order of human relationships. Thus rectitude sustains democracy when there is a sense of responsibility which is interpreted in reference to patterns consistent with, and sustaining, the democratic commonwealth.

We consider well-being to be one of the welfare values, since somatic considerations occupy an important part in the evaluation of a given set of relations in terms of health or disease. Wealth often involves claims to the services of such tangible resources as land, buildings and other facilities. Skill so frequently involves some level of proficiency in the handling of resources that we think of the acquisition and exercise of skill as among the welfare values. The content of the communications which are made in connection with enlightenment are often amenable to relatively impersonal tests for truth or falsity, comprehensiveness or restrictedness.

Equipped with some such list of categories, we are in a position to consider any community according to the old formula: *Who gets what (values) when and how?*[20] If we think of democracy as general shaping and sharing, despotisms are at the other end of the scale, characterized by the concentration of values in relatively few hands.

Although these distinctions provide preliminary orientation, they do not carry us far toward "operational" definitions. We must specify the nature of the prevailing "myth" which we regard as in harmony with shared values. Moreover, we need to specify the patterns of "technique" which meet the minimum requirements of sharing. The myth, of course, is divisible into "doctrine, formula, and miranda," the doctrine referring to basic justifications, the formula

[20] In my *Politics* (1936) which is herewith reprinted I spoke of safety, income and deference as "representative" values. Safety can be treated as equivalent to well-being, income to wealth, and deference, if desired, to the sub-divided list comprising power, respect, affection, rectitude. This list is still to be taken as "representative" rather than "definitive."

to prescriptions for conduct, and miranda to popular lore pertaining to a given value.[21] Although it is beyond the scope of the discussion to deal with these matters in detail, it may be worth while to give some of the definitions that aid in the clarification of the concept of sharing.[22]

Power

1. Power is shared when the political myth favors the pattern of general participation in the making of decisions.

2. Power is shared when in fact there is general participation in decision-making.

3. Shared power means that it is assumed that office-holders can be criticized without fear of serious retaliation.

4. Shared power means that the shaping of decisions depends upon values to which access can be had on the basis of merit.

5. Shared power includes the freedom to challenge the lawfulness of applying general rules to concrete cases.

6. Power is shared when there is an effective presumption against the politicizing of human relations.

7. Power is shared when there is a presumption against the use of power in great concentration, particularly in the form of regimentation, centralization, and militarization.

Respect

1. According to the prevailing myth, individuals deserve respect because they are human, and also because of individual merit.

2. In practice, no deprivations are imposed which are incompatible with the merit of the individual as a human being. For example, basic human dignity implies that no "cruel and unusual" punishments are inflicted.

[21] These and other categories are elaborated in Lasswell and Abraham Kaplan, *Power and Society: A Framework for Political Inquiry*, New Haven, Yale University Press, 1950.

[22] The following paragraphs are from a working paper for the study, jointly with my colleague, Professor Myres McDougal of the Yale Law School, of "Law, Science and Policy: The Jurisprudence of a Free Society." See McDougal and Leighton, "The Rights of Man in the World Community: Constitutional Illusion versus Rational Action," *Yale Law Journal*, 59 (1949), pp. 60ff.

3. Access to the values on which prestige is based depends upon individual merit. That is, no discriminations are practiced. Opportunities are open for the maturing of individual talent into the means of acquiring power, wealth, and all values which influence the giving and receiving of prestige.

4. Positive aid is made available in order to overcome handicaps that would otherwise prevent the achieving of a full human experience. If an individual is handicapped by blindness, for instance, respect is not only a passive matter of offering the identical opportunities open to a person of normal vision. Special aid is needed to overcome impediments to learning imposed by blindness. We know that it is possible for handicapped persons to live a life of full or adequately compensated participation.

5. There is a strong presumption in favor of affording the widest scope to voluntary choice and to privacy. When we speak of a presumption, it is a matter of relative emphasis and not of an irrefutable prescription. In this instance, we are speaking of the presumption in favor of the individual's own judgment until the consequences of such judgments are dangerously destructive of community values.

Rectitude

1. The prevailing myth makes articulate a demand for a sense of personal and collective responsibility for perfecting a free society.

2. The myth includes standards upon which there is a high degree of consensus regarding the conduct consistent with, and facilitative of, human dignity.

3. The sense of responsibility and the standards of right conduct are applied on public matters.

4. The sense of responsibility and the standards of right conduct are applied in private judgments and in the private life of members of the community.

5. There is access on the basis of merit to the values which influence the conceptions and applications of rectitude standards.

Affection

1. The myth emphasizes the desirability of congenial human relationships, and emphasizes the capacity of human beings for entering into such relations.

2. Hostile attitudes are overcome by deliberate efforts to restore friendly attitudes, and these efforts are largely successful in practice. The implication is that positive relations are maintained by clarifying common goals and capacities, and not by substituting one set of hates for another.

3. Hostilities are prevented by reducing provocativeness, as well as by the exercise of self-control directed against impulsive expressions of destructiveness against others. An everyday example of non-provocative conduct is the cutting down of adverse and unnecessary criticism of individuals and groups. On a deeper level is the cultivation in all members of society of the ideal of giving calm consideration to one's impulses, rather than giving way to spontaneous anger and rage.

4. There needs to be equality of opportunity for the exercise of affection as a means of achieving affection; and this implies access to the base values which influence the channels and targets of affection. ("Base" values are those essential for "scope" values, in this case, affection.)

5. Denials of affection should be directed against conduct inimical to the free man's commonwealth. In the ideal commonwealth, affections would be so developed from infancy that incentives would be lacking for conduct inimical to freedom. The withholding of affection is a legitimate means of bringing about and sustaining congenial interpersonal relationships.

6. The scope of affection for human beings needs to be as wide as humanity. Less inclusive loyalties need not be abolished, but made compatible with the harmony of the whole.

Well-being

1. The myth emphasizes the importance of somatic and psychic well-being and interprets the ideal in a scientifically correct manner.

2. There is adequate treatment of the diseased, injured, and handicapped.

3. There are deliberate and successful efforts to prevent disease, injury, and handicap.

4. Progress is being made toward optimum somatic and psychic activity throughout life.

5. The motives and circumstances leading to suicide, murder, war and civil violence are reduced or eliminated.

6. Progress is made toward the lengthening of life (under the conditions indicated in 4 above).

Wealth

1. The myth emphasizes the importance of expanding production in order to have the possibility of expanding the standard of living; and the myth stresses the importance of a balanced (graduated) distribution rather than a division of the community into "rich" and "poor."

2. A progressively larger aggregate income is available for distribution.

3. The pattern of income distribution is in fact balanced (graduated) rather than dichotomous (bi-modal).

4. Security of basic income is guaranteed in theory and fact.

5. Opportunities are open to every capable person to earn more than the basic income.

6. Opportunities are provided to develop potential capacities as producers and consumers.

Skill

1. The myth attaches importance to the maturing of latent talent into socially acceptable skills and encourages excellence in performance.

2. Opportunities are provided for the full exercise of skills (full employment).

3. Opportunities are made available for the discovery of latent capacity, and for its development.

4. The base values upon which the acquisition and exercise of skill depend are accessible to merit.

Enlightenment

1. The myth emphasizes the importance of knowledge as a basis for sound judgment on questions of public policy.

2. Everyone has access to media of communication in which news of current developments is reported.

3. The media provide interpretations of the news which place them in relationship to a comprehensive context in which goals, alternatives, trends, factors and projections are included.

4. Members of the community have access to media for the dissemination of facts and interpretations.

5. The source of statements on which policy judgment depends are disclosed. (It is not essential for personal identity to be revealed; the facts about interest, bias, and competence need to be indicated. The separation of editorial and news statements is an example of a means by which attention can be called to the source and nature of the statement being made.)

6. There is a presumption against lying.

7. There is a presumption against non-rational statements (the irrelevant, for example). (Precautions are taken to nullify the non-rational by exclusion, equalization of affect, and the sharing of insight into the nature of the statement.)

8. There is a presumption in favor of statements from competent sources.

9. There is a presumption against advocacy or neutrality, and in favor of inquiry.

Character and Personality

When we speak of character we are referring to a part, not the whole, of personality. The comprehensive term for the enduring traits of an individual which are manifested in interpersonal relationships is "personality." Hence we are speaking of personality when we mention the aptitudes, skills (and knowledges) of an individual. We also refer to personality when alluding to the strength and direction of basic drives, such as the sexual. The personality also includes the automatic and unconscious restrictions and compulsions which modify the expression of basic drives. Such patterns can be made more explicit by considering the "mechanisms" upon which chief reliance is put in mediating among the drives, and between drives and the conscious processes of perception, imagination, recall and the like. The unconscious restrictions and compulsions can be viewed negatively, in terms of the "defenses" which have been evolved by the individual in the course of his experience with other people. Viewed positively, we consider the "ego ideals" which have been elaborated in the course of the same experience. The traditional psychoanalytic categories have divided the personality into the tripartite sectors of the "ego, the superego and the id." These are roughly equivalent to what we have just been calling the "basic impulses"; the "unconscious and automatic restrictions, compulsions and mechanisms" (viewed negatively and positively as defenses and ego ideals); and the "conscious processes."

In the study of interpersonal relations it is useful to examine the ego for the purpose of discovering "the self system."[23a] The self system, in turn comprises three main sets of patterns: identifications, demands, expectations.[23b] When we refer to ourselves in the privacy of meditation, we are aware of such subjective events as feeling a strong sense of "I" or "me" or "we." The primary symbols are the "I," "me," and "Harold Lasswell"; and they are linked with such secondary symbols as "family, friends, neighbors, nation" and the like. The "others" who are included in the "I-me-we system" are part of the identifications belonging to the self system as a whole. The "others" who are not so included are not part of the self.

We experience ourselves directly as loving and hating, liking and disliking, inciting and moderating many of the features of the self and of the "not-self." Such patterns of preference and determination may be called the "demand" system of the self. The demands can be conveniently classified according to the categories of value which were introduced above, including both the deference and welfare values. Moreover, the demand system includes demands

---

[23a] As Harry Stack Sullivan called it in his later articles.

[23b] The classification of the "identifications, demands and expectations" follows my usage in earlier publications. The fundamental distinctions were developed within the general frame of thinking made current by several scholars, notably George Herbert Mead, whose contributions are today receiving such active recognition in the textbooks of social psychology.

"by the self upon the self" and "upon others." And the demands may be linked with the various identification components of the self system. Thus the part of the identification system related to the "political party" may include demands for power as evidenced by success in winning elections and modifying policies. The identification system pertaining to the family or the fraternity may be concerned with different values, or with different interpretations of these values.

In some ways it is simplest to introduce the "expectation system" as the residual category comprising all of the subjective events not included among the identifications and demands. In general, it is a question of the assumptions entertained about past, present and future, irrespective of likes and dislikes, or of the drawing of the boundaries of the self. Therefore the expectations embrace all of the "fact assumptions" and "projections" (future-pictures) of the individual. The "expectation system," in turn, can be relatively specialized in sub-patterns which are closely linked with identification and demand sub-systems. Thus all that pertains to power may be closely integrated with the demand for power on behalf of the party or the nation or some other entity.

We are now in a position to introduce the term "character" for the purpose of conferring upon it a meaning which absorbs many of the conceptions which are current in much professional and lay usage. *By character we mean the self-system of the person, together with the degree of support, opposition or non-support received from the unconscious parts of the personality.* When we say that a man is of steadfast character it is implied that he has sufficient command of the resources of the whole personality to maintain the self system despite environing conditions which may be adverse. If we say that some one is "characterless," we are implying that he cannot be counted upon to perform a consistent role in human relations, whether where difficulties are to be overcome, or merely from one comparable situation to another. The implication is that inner energies are in such severe conflict that vacillation or weakness continually occurs; or that a level of functioning was never achieved in which consistent responses were integrated. However, the idea of "character" is not that of rigidity and repetitiveness. On the contrary, the preservation of the system as a whole depends upon suppleness in adapting to circumstances that might shatter a less versatile pattern. Pliability must be kept within the limits of the larger contours, so that the pattern "snaps back" when testing conditions are removed.

Conflicting Hypotheses

Why concern ourselves with the study of character? We have already encountered the flat assertion in the classical tradition that character is a factor of such importance in political life that it is capable of determining the constitution of a state. This viewpoint is alive in much of the social science of our time, although in less drastic form. The classical tradition, of course, also expressly stated that constitutions influence character, and that stability depends upon success in moulding an appropriate "temper." Some of the studies of the interplay of culture and personality appear to assign a significant place to the determinative role of "basic personality."[24] The studies of "national character" have undertaken to demonstrate, in many instances, that the functioning of the nation in politics is affected by the configuration of traits which are implanted upon the rising

[24] See Abram Kardiner and others, *The Individual and His Society: The Psychodynamics of Primitive Social Organization*, New York, Columbia University Press, 1939.

generation by the prevailing patterns of child-rearing.[25] The rise and fall of such political movements as German National Socialism have been in part explained on the basis of the personality structure of leaders and lead.[26] Many investigators have sought to connect position within the class structure of a culture with a distinctive personality profile.[27]

There are, however, dissenting voices to the proposition that character is to be taken as a significant dynamic in the living processes of society. The most emphatic dissent comes from the theorists of social development who assign a primary role to "material" as against "ideological" factors. The many varieties of Marxism are substantially at one in affirming the overwhelming impact upon the "superstructure" (ethics, law and other social norms and assumptions) of the "division of labor" which follows the "means of production." What we are calling the self-system, and the alignment of the self-system with the unconscious patterns of personality, obviously belongs to the realm of the "ideological," or secondary, factors in the Marxist version of the social process. Even in this domain there are, however, qualifications whose true weight is vaguely indicated. What, for example, can we make of Trotsky's rhetorical remark to the effect that "We do not at all pretend to deny the significance of the personal in the mechanics of the social process, nor the significance of the personal in the accidental"?[28]

[25] Notably Geoffrey Gorer and John Rickman, *The People of Great Russia*, The Cresset Press, London, 1949.

[26] Henry V. Dicks, "Personality Traits and National Socialist Ideology," *Human Relations*, 3, (1950), 111ff.

[27] The work of Lloyd Warner, John Dollard, Alison Davis, Robert Havighurst and associates may be noted in this connection.

[28] *History of the Russian Revolution*, New York, Simon & Schuster, 1936, volume I, p. 35. See the careful book of Vernon Venable, *Human Nature: The Marxian View*, New York, Knopf, 1945.

It is safe to say that among professional students of personality the "tendency to encompass the opposite" has displayed itself in a series of counter-marches which has somewhat modified the stress which was formerly laid upon the early conditioning of personality. Fifteen years ago, for example, the forefront of psychoanalytic theory was the discovery of the patterning influence of culture upon basic urges, and the elucidation of the process by which the situations encountered at successive phases of the career line might affect the individual. Karen Horney is an excellent representative of the pioneers in this direction.[29] The development of the psychology of the ego, long neglected in orthodox psychoanalysis, gradually focussed the attention of psychologists upon the structure of the environment available to perception.[30] The psychologists of the Gestalt school had already invented a kit of conceptual and experimental tools for the refined study of perception.[31] During this period a constant incentive was provided by the hope of obtaining the benefits of the depth therapies, like psychoanalysis, without using the prolonged, and therefore costly, procedures involved. It gradually became respectable to explore the potentialities of "short therapies"[32] and "group therapies,"[33] and this led to a wave of experimentation with combinations of "insight" experience with facilitative rearrangements of the environment.[34] The lat-

[29] Notably *The Neurotic Personality of Our Time,* New York, Norton, 1937.

[30] See Anna Freud, *The Ego and the Mechanisms of Defense,* The Hogarth Press and Institute of Psycho-Analysis, London, 1937.

[31] Kurt Koffka, *Principles of Gestalt Psychology,* New York, Harcourt, Brace, 1935.

[32] Franz Alexander, T. M. French and Associates, *Psychoanalytic Therapy: Principles and Application,* New York, Ronald, 1946.

[33] J. L. Moreno has been a pioneer in this field. See, for example, *Psychodrama,* New York, Beacon House, 1946.

[34] The most extreme position is stated by Marshall C. Greco, *Group Life: The Nature and Treatment of Its Specific Conflicts,* New York, Philosophical Library, 1950.

ter has long been the preferred mode of approach employed by social workers, and by gifted laymen, who look for opportunities suitable for the handicapped, whether the handicap is a criminal record, drug addiction, slow-mindedness, or "personality difficulty." The apparent success of such movements aiming at the creation of a supportive environment as Alcoholics Anonymous, and of boy's club programs to counteract juvenile delinquency, have stimulated new confidence in what can be done by "changing the situation" and thereby "remodeling the personality."

These several currents have challenged the conception of personality, and hence of character, as a relatively "finished" structure organized in early life which persists as a strong selective influence in turning all subsequent life situations to account. Gustav Ichheiser has suggested that the psychologists in our culture may be suffering from the same basic sources of "false social perception" as laymen, with the result that entirely too much unity has been "read into" the personality structure at any given time, and through life. He suggests, for example, that "our interpretations and expectations operate under the silent assumption that other people do not change fundamentally, even if actually they do undergo far-reaching transformations of their personality structure. Other people, so we assume, might have changed their views, convictions, attitudes, loyalties, and sentiments, but essentially they are still the same person. Specifically, John Smith at sixty is 'the same' John Smith when he was, let us say, twelve years of age." We therefore "overestimate the role of personal" and "underestimate the role of situational factors" in accounting for human behavior.[35]

[35] *Misunderstandings in Human Relations: A Study in False Social Perception* (Supplement to the September, 1949, issue of the *American Journal of Sociology*).

It may be that the "attrition of personality explanations" is a manifestation of deep-lying and pervasive trends in the structure of American life. David Riesman writes of the diminishing role of "traditional" and "inner directed" varieties of personality in modern American civilization, and of the rise of "outer directed" types who are sensitively oriented to the shifting pressures and opportunities of the specific circumstances in which they find themselves at any moment. To the extent that this interpretation is correct it is evident that the link between the past of the individual and any subsequent behavior is attenuated, if not altogether obliterated.[36]

When conflicting hypotheses concerning complex processes survive from decade to decade, the explanation may lie in the treachery of words, rather than in the structure of the phenomena. Undoubtedly there are many sources of ambiguity in the traditional and current formulations of the connections between character and culture. Against some of these ambiguities we must put ourselves on guard.

The Character-Culture Manifold

There is then, much confusion in opposing "character" to "culture" and seeking to assess the effect of one upon the other. The obvious fact is that terms like character and culture are attempts to refer to recurring features of the same process, namely, the interpersonal relationships of man. And it is exceedingly troublesome to define the intended referent of any term about the social process, since the outstanding characteristic of interpersonal relations is an unceasing zig-zag of interaction. We say "good morning" to the boss on Monday and Tuesday, but we may be in a very different frame of mind on Tuesday than on Monday, and the boss himself may differ in ways that modify his own part in the interaction. We may have received our draft

[36] *The Lonely Crowd*, New Haven, Yale University Press, 1950.

call, or the boss may have a sick child at home. Hence there may be a somewhat "abstracted" or "withdrawn" quality about the exchange of salutations. Our tone of voice may be less high pitched, and our tempo of speech less quick. The boss may hesitate a split second before noticing us, and "overreact" with a note of "false cordiality." How shall we fit these two observations which we, acting in the capacity of a scientific observer of human relations, have made on the interaction of the boss and his employee? From one point of view, we witness the bearers of the same culture playing roles which can frequently be observed under comparable circumstances. The routine of salutation fits the expected roles to be played by employer and employee in many work situations. From another perspective we can think of two characters as interacting, perhaps observing that the employer seems to deviate somewhat more from the usual pattern of salutation than the employee. This raises the question in our mind whether the character of the boss is as well-integrated as that of the employee, in the sense that the self-system of the employer was unable to mobilize sufficient command over internal energies to conform to the role playing appropriate to the morning contact. However, we might think that further information is needed for the purpose of assessing the relative magnitude of the changes in the total life situation of the two men over the twenty-four hour period. How can we compare the comparative severity of the deprivation represented by the draft call and by the illness of the child? This carries us to the study of the predispositions of the employer and employee in reference to all the major features of family life and of civic responsibility. As we consider these predispositions, we are continually reminded of the perpetual interplay of "patterns seen cross-sectionally" from one individual to another, and "patterns seen developmentally" in the perspective of the whole self- and energy-system of each person. We have defined a character trait as a relatively enduring response, and this implies durability in the recurring circumstances of life. A culture trait is defined as a relatively enduring pattern of action, also; and this implies that the response and the situation reappear together. But all this remains vague unless it is possible to specify the time span which is taken into account by the observing scientist. Do we satisfy our definition of a trait of culture or of personality and character by observations extending over a year or over several years? Must we establish "consistency" of personality trait from early childhood? Must the "consistency" of a culture trait be maintained over an entire generation? A decade? A year?[37]

The Incessant Interplay of Predisposition and Environment

When we remind ourselves of the complexities involved, we do not thereby assert that it is nonsense to explore the interrelations between that part of culture which we call politics, for example, and that form of culture which we call personality or character. We establish only the conditions that must be met before such talk makes sense.

In principle, the interactions among human beings are open to observation. If we think of the immediate personal contacts occurring in the course of a twenty-four hour period, the task of noting them is by no means insuperable. When a busy administrator asked his secretary to keep a record of his direct contacts, the following was not an unpresentative day (beginning with a brief conference with the private secretary): staff conference with six subor-

[37] Concerning the "event-manifold" see my paper on "Person, Personality, Group, Culture" in *Psychiatry* (1939), reprinted in *The Analysis of Political Behaviour: An Empirical Approach*, New York, Oxford University Press, 1947, and *A Study of Interpersonal Relations*, edited by Patrick Mullahy, New York, Hermitage Press, 1950.

dinates; staff conference with a superior and four colleagues; twenty-four office appointments; forty telephone
conversations; ten telegrams sent or received; fifteen letters
read; twenty-five letters dictated; lunch with twenty visit-
ors; brief appearance at cocktail party where fifty or sixty
persons were present; dinner with family of four; six guests
after dinner. Even an incomplete inventory of this kind is
a reminder of the ways in which direct interpersonal contacts are patterned in an "office culture," and at the work
bench, or in the household, or on the farm, or in school.
The preceding inventory could be extended to include the
"secondary" contacts through television or radio, or with
"name" persons in newspapers and magazines. Further-
more, the "content" of mass communication contacts can
be analyzed for the purpose of bringing out the geographical distribution and social role of the individuals or groups
referred to. Extending the interactions backward through
time, we eventually come to the early years of childhood
and infancy. During the first months of life it is not exceptional for the mother in her nursing role to have two thousand major occasions of contact with the infant.

The inventory of direct or indirect opportunities for
contact among human beings is a record of the unrehearsed
ballet of ordinary life. When we read a calendar of appointments we catch a glimpse of the "hoops of culture"
through which the individual carries his soma. Within this
changing configuration inner experiences of great intensity
or of utter superficiality are taking place. Such reflections
as these remind us of another source of ambiguity in talk
about character, personality, politics and culture.

The False Opposition of Inner and Outer

Often the connotation of words like character or attitude
is that, in contradistinction to culture, they refer to inner

experience rather than manifest activities. Hence inquiry into the interdetermination of personality and culture seeks to estimate the effect of the "inner" in shaping the "outer," or of the "outer" as stamping itself indelibly upon innermost thoughts and feelings. In the most generalized form this is often stated as opposition of "ideas" to "material" factors in society.

Now the plausibility of this way of talking is very great, since each of us is aware of his own subjectivity, and of his sense of separation from what is taken to be "out there." Indeed, the chasm may be so great that a sense of alienation is the dominant tone of inner life. Some of the most searching observations made about man in modern society have laid hold upon the disjunction between the inner and outer. One of the most successful formulations was made by Durkheim, whose conception of "anomie" has been firmly planted in the social science of the West.[38] Durkheim was seeking to explain the rising curve of suicide, and he found it in the desperation of the individual who, under modern conditions, is handicapped in arriving at a satisfactory identification with others. Erich Fromm is among those who have called attention to the inner infirmities occurring in the lives of human beings who live in a world in which they must make up their own minds, rather than depend upon traditional solutions.[39] Moreover, our civilization is competitive, and rewards successful mobility in the marketplace, or in the arena of politics, or in any distinctive locale. When the demands upon the "self by the self" are for infinite success in reaching a position of top influence, the likelihood of disappointment and self-depreciation are correspondingly enhanced.[40] The inner stress

[38] *Le Suicide,* Alcan, 1897.

[39] *Escape from Freedom,* New York, Farrar and Rinehart, 1941.

[40] See especially Part II of Sebastian de Grazia, *The Political Community: A Study in Anomie,* Chicago, University of Chicago Press, 1948.

generated as an incident of the clash between the biological inheritance of man and the requirements of getting along together has been graphically depicted by Sigmund Freud in *Civilization and Its Discontents*. It appears, therefore, that modern man has many sources of secret misery: the miseries of non-identification, of thinking for one's self, of self-appraisal in terms of competitive success, of carrying an "animal" nature into an effort at socialization.

Although the interpretations of our time which have just been reviewed are phrased in terms of inner experience, and appear to trace the miseries of the subjective life to the imprint of "outer" factors, such is not in fact the case. What is the "civilization" which is portrayed as pressing upon the individual? On analysis this "outside" pattern is seen to comprise both inner and outer traits. For if A withholds affection and respect from B, thereby provoking discouragement in B, A is engaged in subjective as well as expressive activities. Part of the pattern is for A to deny himself the free expression of whatever tendencies he has to give affection or respect regardless of B's economic or political success. Indeed, A may in turn suffer from the failure of C to admire and love him, even as he causes B to suffer.

It is evident, therefore, that we are not comparing an inner *versus* an outer relationship, but rather, we are comparing two patterns both of which are composed of inner and outer elements. If we speak of culture as including "the success pattern," we mean that the giving of indulgence or deprivation depends upon certain subjective appraisals and evaluations. If we think of "discontent" as a pattern of modern civilization, it includes not only subjective events, but the relating of these events to the acts of other persons, which are integrated with the subjective life of those individuals. Indeed, every interpersonal relationship, when complete, comprises a series of events in which each participant is furnishing the other with a stimulating environment, and is in turn initiating and interpreting what goes on. For some purposes it is convenient to think of the acts of A as constituting an "environment" for the "predispositions" with which B enters the relationship. We account for the response of B as a function of the two sets of determining factors, the environmental and the predispositional. It is equally valid and useful to think of both A and B as entering a situation with various predispositions, and to limit the meaning of the term environment to the initial cues which they provide for one another (together with whatever other features of the situation are also cues). The term response can then be applied to the ensuing pattern of interaction. The latter usage is especially convenient when the cues which we are seeking to describe are circumscribed, as when a drillmaster barks a command to disciplined troops, and the resulting behavior, such as discharging a variety of weapons, is patterned in easily characterizeable ways. The intensive study of each individual in a situation is indicated when the cues are not easy to distinguish, and when the ensuing patterns of conduct are exceedingly varied and changeable from one broadly comparable situation to the next.

It is not appropriate, therefore, to interpret the interplay of character and politics as an example of inner *versus* outer factors, but rather to consider the problem as one of discovering the determinative effect of various "practices." A "practice" is a relatively stable pattern composed of "perspectives" (the subjective events) and of "operations" (externally perceivable events).

Strictly speaking, of course, all inferences about the inner life of other persons are based upon inferences from "outer," that is to say, perceivable events. The significance of this distinction is reduced, however, when we recognize the phenomenon of communication. Very complicated inferences about the subjectivity of other persons can be made on the basis of "signs," such as the spoken words of a common tongue, or the written characters of a common language. The signs are directly perceivable events, but they are highly specialized to the function of providing a means of inference concerning the subjective state of the communicator. We interpret the sign made by another individual as part of our own subjective stream of events. But we interpret the common signs by inferring that certain interpretative intentions are part of the perspectives of the other. Any specific interpretation, of course, is subject to correction on the basis of further experience with, or examination of, the deeds and statements of the other person.[41]

Attempts have sometimes been made to strip the interpretations which are made of the other person to "perceivables," and to disallow any inference about the perspectives of the other. The supposed scientific justification of this self-denying ordinance was the "inconsistency" or "invalidity" of the results. But it has repeatedly been shown that "inconsistencies" can be held within known limits if observers have been trained to interpret cues in the same way. Moreover, it has often been shown that forecasts of future conduct (or predictions of what the facts were about past conduct) can be relied upon. Hence the problem of "reliability" and "validity" is to be settled, as in all empirical work, on the basis of empirical inquiry,

[41] The modern study of communication has benefitted from the work of many scholars, notably Charles W. Morris whose most comprehensive treatise is *Signs, Language and Behavior*, New York, Prentice-Hall, 1946. Morris uses "sign vehicle" for the physical event here called a "sign." We use "symbol" for the interpretation, which is the "sign" in the sense of Morris.

since methodologically there is no fundamental difference between observing the behavior of people or of other living beings (or the manifestations of inorganic events). If the scope of reliable and valid inference is less comprehensive in terms of time or space than in some empirical work on other organisms, this is to be discovered by investigation, and not "settled" by advance definition or arbitrary postulate.[42]

The Self-System in Democratic Character: The Open Ego

We may now proceed to formulate our conception of democratic character, an enterprise that falls in two grand divisions, the first of which has to do with the self-system, the second with the energy-system. The initial step in characterizing the self-system is to select the system of identifications which appears to be consonant with democratic character. It is, of course, to be understood that the present sketch is designed to serve as an aid to empirical inquiry, and that the "theoretical model" of the democratic character will undoubtedly undergo extensive modification as scientific work in this area gains in scope and depth.

Let us take as the outstanding characteristic of democratic character, in reference to identifications, *the maintenance of an open as against a closed ego.* By this expression our intention is to convey the idea that the democratic attitude toward other human beings is warm rather than frigid, inclusive and expanding rather than exclusive and constricting. We are speaking of an underlying personality structure which is capable of "friendship," as Aristotle put it, and which is unalienated from humanity. Such a person transcends most of the cultural categories that di-

[42] Some of the more technical aspects of this problem are considered in Lasswell, Leites and Associates, *Language of Politics: Studies in Quantitative Semantics*, New York, George W. Stewart, 1949.

vide human beings from one another, and senses the common humanity across class and even caste lines within the culture, and in the world beyond the local culture. In the extreme case we have "saints" who have undergone the deprivations of a concentration camp without losing the serenity of outlook that reaches out hopefully and tolerantly toward other human beings.

The conception of the open ego is something other than the capacity to enter into an intense and all-embracing sentimental bond with another person. Often such passionate attachments represent a socialization of fears and hostilities directed against other human beings. It operates as a preventive of the degree of detachment which enables the individual to sense the feelings and viewpoints of others in the life of an entire group, such as appears to be characteristic of those persons who are well-equipped to function in a' democratic manner.[43]

It is apparent that the prototypes of many later experiences are undergone in the early years of life, and especially in early infancy. So far as we can tell the "primary ego" evolved during the early weeks of life is a fusion of experiences which are not capable of being sorted into a sharply delimited "out there" and "me." Experiences connected with nursing (the intake of food and body contact) are divisible into those which are gratifying (the indulgences) and non-gratifying (the deprivations). Harry Stack Sullivan has suggested that the first or gratifying experiences become structured around the image of the

[43] Helen Hall Jennings; *A Study of Personality in Inter-Personal Relations,* Second Edition, New York, Longmans, Green and Co., 1950. "The universal characteristic of the leaders in this study may be a 'logical' carrying out of their larger insight into the needs of persons generally and at least partially a reflection of greater emotional maturity on their part than appears to characterize the average member," p. 201. This is a report of an investigation conducted by sociometric techniques of the 400 individuals in the New York State Training School for Girls.

"good mother," and that the second or non-gratifying experiences are attributed to the "bad mother," even though the boundaries of the ego are lacking in focus. Soon the limits of the "me" and the "not me" gain in precision, and this in turn redefines the possibilities for symbolizing and localizing the recurring patterns of indulgence and deprivation. When there is a "me," there is also a stream of characterizations emanating from the environment in terms of "good" and "naughty," which are usually integrated with a variety of comforts and discomforts on the physical level. The recurring sources of gratification become stably symbolized as "my mother," "my body" and the like, and the identification-system begins to include and exclude according to the prevailing stratifications of the social system into which the infant is becoming integrated.[44]

There is reason to believe that in some cultures the possibility of developing an outgoing democratic character is excluded at an early period. The prevailing patterns of child care appear to induce early despair that profound gratifications can emanate from other human beings; yet they prevent this despair from putting a stop to all externalized activity. Indulgences are wrested from the hostile, reluctant universe by a variety of sly maneuvers.[45]

The Self-System in Democratic Character: Values Multiple and Shared

Our characterization of the democratic community has provided a frame in which the demand-system of the democratic character can be rather clearly set forth. Let us speak of the democratic character as *multi-valued, rather*

[44] See especially, "The Meaning of Anxiety in Psychiatry and Life," 11 *Psychiatry* (1948) pp. 1ff.

[45] Ruth Benedict and Margaret Mead have been the most energetic explorers of the impact of child-rearing practices upon the other features of culture. I refer here to the interpretation of the Hobbesan life of Dobu.

*than single-valued, and as disposed to share rather than
to hoard or to monopolize.* In particular, little significance
is attached to the exercise of power as a scope value.

The characteristics of democratic character have often
been cast into relief by the study of individuals who are
infatuated with the pursuit of one value to such a point
that the integrity of the common life is imperiled thereby.
This is perhaps most obvious in studies that have been
made of the *homo politicus,* the man who, when compared
with others similarly situated in culture and class, relies
with relish upon the "pursuit of power by the use of
power." Since we understand that power relationships have,
or are assumed by the participants to possess, the element
of severe deprivation, it is apparent that the human being
who is fascinated by power is out of harmony with our
basic concept of human dignity.[46] The psychiatrist feels
at home in the study of ardent seekers after power in the
arena of politics because the physician recognizes the
extreme egocentricity and sly ruthlessness of some of the
paranoid patients with whom he has come in contact in the
clinic. To the power-centered person all human beings and
all contacts with others are opportunities for imposinig
his will, or for enlisting the other person in some manner
that contributes to the imposition of his own will in some
future situation. Hence he imposes a wall of insulation
and isolation between himself and others, with the result
that a growing sense of alienation from mankind becomes
one of the recurring complaints of those who attain power,
or only aspire with all the intensity of their being to
acquire it.

[46] In the Salmon Lectures at the N. Y. Academy of Medicine the present
writer developed some hypotheses concerning the power-centered man
which were first outlined in the *Psychopathology and Politics,* which is herewith reprinted. See *Power and Personality,* New York, Norton, 1948.

When the demand for respect is the consuming passion, other values are sacrificed for the sake of receiving symbolic acknowledgements of eminence. The vain man has a special position of dependence upon the human beings by whom he is surrounded, seeking to elicit a continuing flow of those reassuring postures, gestures and symbolic expressions which sustain the inflated image of the ego.[47] We are speaking of the individual who is so sensitized to the admiration of others that he may react with wounded pride to fancied slights, and burn with fierce jealousies and resentments against those who receive the plaudits to which he fancies himself entitled, or against those from whom he believes that the plaudits ought to come. The respect-centered character is often disposed to poison human relations "by taking everything personally" and by needing a perpetual stream of reassurance about "how am I doing." The clinician is accustomed to see in the over-sensitive neurotic, or in the grandiose delusions of the paranoid, the extreme manifestation of what is known to common sense as abnormal pride. The secret image is not necessarily connected with power, since coercive intentions are not always the cherished means of obtaining boundless admiration.

The excessive demand for affection carries with it a distortion of capacity for full participation in the life of a democratic community. The most extreme examples in our culture turn every human contact into a sexual invitation or assault, and are absorbed in the active indulgence or the fantasying of success in sexuality. Many of those who are preoccupied with sexual conquest have no con-

[47] See the examples of how the denial of respect can be used as a base value designed to influence power in Charles E. Merriam, *Political Power* (1934), reprinted in Lasswell, Merriam and Smith, *A Study of Power*, Glencoe, Free Press, 1950, chapter VII.

scious interest in affection, but gloat over sexual achievements as a demonstration of virility (well-being) or as a
means to fame (respect).[48] At the moment we are referring only to those whose lives are filled with sex as a mode
of giving and receiving affection, or who are absorbed in
giving and receiving love. The affection-centered person
may not be promiscuous in the choice of love objects, but
may, on the contrary, develop an intense and all-absorbing
bond with one individual. As we have already intimated
in connection with the identification-system, these exclusive
couplings may represent a withdrawal from fuller functioning in the community. In Western civilization, at least,
the woman is expected to specialize upon affection much
more than the man, and to stay within the primary circle
of the home. The distorting effect of this cultural pressure
upon the personality of the woman, and of many with
whom she comes in touch, have been described by many
observers.[49] An additional source of difficulty rises from
the fact that our civilization is in a transitional stage regarding its conception of women, who are gradually being
relieved of the disabilities from which they have suffered
in theory and in fact. But the "lag" effects are among the
sources of distress in modern life.

Hyper-specialization on rectitude produces another set
of character deformations. We are speaking of those who

[48] The "old-fashioned" literature on sexology was usually limited to an
account of the conscious perspectives of the subjects who were described.
Hence the re-classification of the material according to conscious interest in
affection (or some other value) is not difficult. Much of the work of Magnus
Hirschfeld and Havelock Ellis belongs in this category. See also George
W. Henry, *Sex Variants; A Study of Homosexual Patterns*, New York,
Hoeber, 1948 (One-volume edition).

[49] Notably Karen Horney, Clara Thompson, Helene Deutsch among psychoanalysts. See also Margaret Mead, *Male and Female*, New York, Morrow,
1949.

are continually beset with questions of right and wrong so that the entire career is transformed into perpetual judgments of the self and others in reference to such standards. These persons may wrap themselves in an impenetrable cloak of self-righteousness, and speak censoriously of the imperfections of their fellow men. They may, however, view themselves in a wholly different light, and engage in private and public confessions of sin and guilt. Human relations are transformed into occasions for the repetitive application of a limited set of rigid categories, a process that squeezes from sight the richness and variety of values which are essential to the democratic community. Physicians are accustomed to meet symptoms of the kind here described in their patients, whom they recognize as suffering from obsessional or compulsive difficulties.[50]

Some characters are taken up with goods (with wealth). When the fixation upon wealth is so intense that other values are almost deprived of meaning, we have miserly, greedy types who are eager to accumulate and to retain goods and services. Such acquisitive and retentive personalities are referred to in the folklore of many cultures with utter disdain, since public service, affection, or other values are all rejected in order to get hold of impersonal and tangible resources.

Over-preoccupation with well-being may take the form of anxious concern for health, which can reach the dimensions of hypochondria, or of disturbing interference in the lives of others in the name of their physical welfare.[51] Or

[50] Described in any textbook that includes the psychoneuroses, such as D. K. Henderson and R. D. Gillespie. *A Text-book of Psychiatry for Students and Practitioners*, Sixth Edition, New York, Oxford University Press, 1944.

[51] See David M. Levy, "Maternal Over-protection," *Psychiatry*, Vol. 1 (1938), pp. 561-91; Vol. 2 (1939), pp. 99-128, 563-97; Vol. 4 (1941), pp. 393-438, 567-626.

the cult of the body, and of virility as an end in itself, can exclude other values.

Devotion to the exercise of skill may become so complete that an absolute exemption may be demanded from all considerations of rectitude, affection, or any other value. "Art for art's sake" is a slogan which in our civilization is often matched by similar demands in the name of other skills. Scientists, for example, may resent any restraint on the direction or timing of their activities, even when the destiny of mankind is at stake.

Enlightenment, too, can become a "vice" when "being in on the know" becomes an end in itself.

The Self-System of the Democratic Character: Confidence in Human Potentialities

When we turn from the demand-structure of the democratic character to the consideration of the pattern of expectation we note at once that it is essential to have *deep confidence in the benevolent potentialities of man.* This affirmative trust is very different from the apathetic endurance of life in the manner of the apathetic orphan.[52]

Unless there is some early basis for trust in the benevolence of the surrounding world, we can hardly expect that the individual will develop predispositions capable of carrying him through adverse experiences. This is the deep significance of the "good mother" image in contributing to the formation of a perspective that fosters inclusive identifications with other people. It has become amply apparent in the course of research on the infant that the expectation

[52] Even though this response may enable the individual to survive under such drastically adverse conditions as a concentration camp in later life. See Ralph R. Greenson, "The Psychology of Apathy," *Psychoanalytic Quarterly XVIII* (1949), pp. 290-302.

of benevolence is a factor enabling the infant to put forth the energy to live.[53, 54]

Such rigid specializations as those which have been reviewed in relation to each of the eight values fly in the face of the needs of a democratic community, and prevent the consolidation of a democratic character.

The Energy System of the Democratic Character: Freedom from Anxiety

The ideal conception of democratic character *includes the specification that the self-system shall have at its disposal the energies of the unconscious part of the personality*. The deviations from this standard are in several directions. The energies may be so divided and opposed to one another that little is available to the ego, which may be relatively immobilized into the performing of an impoverished social role. The super-ego system of restriction and compulsion may remain at war with the recurring initiatives of the id-system, resulting in immobilization through physical incapacitation. The genesis of the "conversion" response is being traced in detail by modern specialists in psychosomatic medicine. A recent statement of the field by Franz Alexander, for example, reviews the research which confirms the psychogenetic factor in gastrointestinal disturbances, bronchial asthma, cardiovascular disturbances, skin diseases, metabolic and endocrine disturbances,

[53] Consult Margarethe Ribble, "The Significance of Infantile Sucking for the Psychic Development of the Individual," and "Disorganizing Factors of Infant Personality," reprinted in *Contemporary Psychopathology: A Source Book*, edited by S. S. Tomkins, Cambridge, Harvard University Press, 1947, pp. 1-15.

[54] The importance of recognizing the *potential* benevolence of human beings is emphasized, for example, in analyses of democracy by C. E. Merriam, T. V. Smith, A. D. Lindsay, R. M. MacIver, James Bryce, Hugo Krabbe, Hans Kelsen, and many others.

disturbances of the joints and skeletal muscles (including rheumatoid arthritis and the accident-prone individual), and of the sexual apparatus.[55]

The basis for ineffectual participation in society may lie in the sphere of fantasy (or autistic revery) rather than organic malfunctioning. We observe "autistic withdrawal" in forms of psychic suffering experienced by some persons who limit their human relationships more and more. Sometimes these disturbances are sufficiently light to be called "neuroses." But there are many kinds of grave, psychotic processes that carry the individual out of touch with other human beings. However, all internal conflicts do not result in such conspicuous restrictions of overt social activity. In varying degree the person who is suffering from a somatic disturbance with a psychological basis may be able to carry on a regular professional and sociable life. It may even be that the function of the somatic symptom is to dispose of energies that might otherwise interfere with the self-system of the democratic character.[56]

However, the self-system of the democrat may be betrayed chronically or occasionally by eruptions of conduct in flat contradiction to democratic perspectives. In many instances the person is fully conscious of occasional seizures that contradict his conscious demands upon himself. Some men "can't control their temper" on all occasions. Others go in for jags of alcoholism or sexual debauchery,

---

[55] *Psychosomatic Medicine: Its Principles and Applications*, with a Chapter on "The Functions of the Sexual Apparatus and Their Disturbances" by Therese Benedek, New York, Norton, 1950.

[56] It should not be supposed that the psychosomatic emphasis is altogether new to physicians. Ralph Waldo Emerson remarked in his essay on the poet that he knew "a witty physician who found the creed in the biliary duct, and used to affirm that if there was disease in the liver, the man became a Calvinist, and if that organ was sound, he became a Unitarian."

or for athleticism of a type that does serious damage to the body and endangers others. The deviation may be so pronounced that one can only speak of a psychopathic distortion of character.[57]

Often the self-system of the democrat is betrayed by *conduct* whose incompatibility with the perspectives of the system are invisible to the man himself, although clear to nearly anyone who observes him. I am not speaking of "hypocrisy," but of the "self-deluded." One familiar example is the humorless, sincere individual who unconsciously persecutes everyone with whom he comes in touch. He may be an extreme advocate of order, and puts everything on a timetable. His unfortunate wife, children and employees suffer the despotism of a man whose purity of motive is beyond self-dispute.

The energies of the unconscious system may also express themselves in deformations of *perspective* which the individual does not recognize. Although he considers himself to possess a democratic character, the person may cling to beliefs that stand in flagrant contradiction of his professed regard for human dignity. It is not a question in these cases of subtle distinctions, but of gross distortions, as when convictions about the equality of all members of the human race are contradicted by statements of belief about specific ethnic groups. Such contradictions within the self-system are screened from self-inspection by the automatic operation of unconscious channels and forces. These individuals differ from the persons cited above in

[57] On the history of this difficult conception see Karl A. Menninger, "Recognizing and Renaming 'Psychopathic Personalities,'" *Bull. Menninger Clinic*, 5 (1941), pp. 150-156. See Hervey Cleckley, *The Mask of Sanity; An Attempt to Clarify Some Issues About the So-called Psychopathic Personality*, Second Edition, St. Louis, Mosby, 1950.

that the distortion is within the belief-system and not between beliefs and conduct.[58]

There appears to be a common element in the organization of energies that distort or betray the self-system of an otherwise democratic character. The element is human destructiveness. We have noted that destructive drives may be *externalized* against other human beings, or *internalized* against the body of the person. In the former cases, the drives may be directed against groups who have never been included within the self-system. However, the targets may be selected from within the identification pattern of the self, ranging all the way from peripheral individuals and groups to nuclear groups and individuals. When destructiveness is directed against the primary ego, as in psychosomatic illness, the inner core of the ego system becomes the target. As indicated in the previous analysis, any given course of conduct can express a two-edged aggression, as when the value positions of the individual and of other persons are simultaneously reduced. Partial incapacitation may reduce not only the well-being of the sufferer, and cut down income and capital, political power and other advantages; the reduction in influence may hamper the family, in this way gratifying grudges of which the individual is quite unaware.

May not destructive tendencies contribute positively to the formation of a self-system and to the effective energies

[58] Numerous examples of the combinations referred to in the foregoing can be found in the volumes of the "Studies in Prejudice" published in 1950 by Harpers, New York, and conducted under the auspices of the American Jewish Committee. See especially *The Authoritarian Personality*, by T. W. Adorno, Else Frenkel-Brunswik, Daniel J. Levinson, and R. Nevitt Sanford, *Dynamics of Prejudice: A Psychological and Sociological Study of Veterans*, by Bruno Bettelheim and Morris Janowitz, and *Anti-Semitism and Emotional Disorder; A Psychoanalytic Interpretation*, by Nathan W. Ackermann and Marie Jahoda.

available to the democratic character? To take the latter part of the question first, it is apparent that the destructive energies of a person may be directed against enemies of the democratic community. Indeed, any other behavior would betray the opportunities and responsibilities of democratic citizenship. The reply to the first part of the question is less categorical. Modern studies of human development repeatedly show that democratic responses often arise from motives which are incompatible with it, and signify that the individual has achieved part of his democratic outlook by "reaction-formation" against tendencies of an opposite kind. Many democrats appear to develop in opposition to anti-democratic parents, for example. And yet, from the point of view of modern personality research, the characters which are achieved by a complex process of balanced defense are viewed as constituting less enduring formations than those which evolve more directly.

A significant insight into the dynamics of non-democratic character is contained in the studies of prejudice alluded to above. Prejudice was defined in several ways, ranging from denials of respect (as defined in our list of values), to denials of access to all values irrespective of common humanity or individual merit. The intensity of the prejudice might range from mildly derogatory reveries and remarks to militant activism designed to exclude target groups from the community (or from effective participation therein according to democratic norms). The research succeeded in demonstrating that prejudiced attitudes were not only connected with immediate, situational factors, but that they represented a carry-over from early experiences in which a certain pattern of character had been formed during early years of life. Within our culture, at least, the emerging picture of interconnection was summed up as follows:

The most crucial result of the present study, as it seems to the authors, is the demonstration of close correspondence in the type of approach and outlook a subject is likely to have in a great variety of areas, ranging from the most intimate features of family and sex adjustment through relationships to other people in general, to religion and to social and political philosophy. Thus a basically hierarchical, authoritarian, exploitive parent-child relationship is apt to carry over into a power-oriented, exploitively dependent attitude toward one's sex partner and one's God and may culminate in a political philosophy and social outlook which has no room for anything but a desperate clinging to what appears to be strong and a disdainful rejection of whatever is relegated to the bottom. The inherent dramatization likewise extends from the parent-child dichotomy to the dichotomous conception of sex roles and of moral values, as well as to a dichotomous handling of social ingroup-outgroup cleavages. Conventionality, rigidity, repressive denial, and the ensuing break-through of one's weakness, fear and dependency are but other aspects of the same fundamental personality pattern, and they can be observed in personal life as well as in attitudes toward religion and social issues.

On the other hand, there is a pattern characterized chiefly by affectionate, basically equalitarian, and permissive interpersonal relationships. This pattern encompasses attitudes within the family and toward the opposite sex, as well as an internalization of religious and social values. Greater flexibility and the potentiality for more genuine satisfactions appear as results of this basic attitude.[59]

We know that repetitiveness is one of the most frequent "defense mechanisms" by the use of which the ego prevents itself from being swamped in a flood of anxieties and hostilities. The rigidification goes so far that the perceiving processes of the ego system are affected, and relevant features of a novel situation are pressed into established

[59] *The Authoritarian Personality*, p. 971. The essential conclusion is confirmed in many respects by the Bettelheim-Janowitz and the Ackermann-Jahoda investigations.

moulds, thus preserving the older categories from the changes that rise from new knowledge. Hence the self-system, even when it conforms to democratic requirements, has at its command only some of the energy of the personality as a whole, much of which is tied down to the task of nullifying the hyperaggressive, destructive drives. The inner stability of the rigid person is imperiled in any situation which is comprehended with difficulty. Hence there is low tolerance for ambiguity, which may be one of the most diagnostic traits of such individuals, as Else Frenkel-Brunswik has pointed out.

What is the genesis of the anxiety reactions which play such an important role in personality development? The theory of anxiety is the most fundamental feature of psychiatric theory, since the disorders with which the psychiatrist is concerned are seen as unsuccessful modes of defending the ego against anxiety. By the term is meant something different from fear, which appears in response to such relatively impersonal stimuli in the early environment of the infant as gross temperature change, or falling. Harry Stack Sullivan described sudden severe anxiety in these terms: "(It) . . . is undergone in later life as what I call *uncanny emotion*, chilly crawling sensations, and the like, often meant by the words 'awe,' 'dread,' 'loathing,' and 'horror.' " According to Sullivan's theory the starting point of anxiety reactions can be discovered in infancy when the person who mothers the infant "*is anxious, angry, or otherwise disquieted.*" "This *interpersonal induction* of anxiety, and the exclusively interpersonal origin of every instance of its manifestations, is the unique characteristic of anxiety and of the congeries of more complex tensions in later life to which it contributes."[60]

[60] "The Meaning of Anxiety in Psychiatry and in Life." *Psychiatry*, 11 (1948), p. 5.

"While we may be unaware, at least temporarily, of milder degrees of any one of the other tensions connected with living, we are never unaware of anxiety at the very time it occurs. The awareness can be, and very often is, fleeting, especially when an appropriate security operation is called out." ". . . any event which tends to bring about a basic change in an *established pattern* of dealing with others, sets up the tension of anxiety and calls out activities for its relief. This tension and the activities required for its reduction or relief—which we call *security operations* because they can be said to be addressed to maintaining a feeling of safety in the esteem reflected to one from the other person concerned—always interfere with whatever other tensions and energy transformations with which they happen to coincide." "Anxiety appears not only as awareness of itself but also in the experience of some *complex* 'emotions' into which it has been elaborated by specific early training. I cannot say what all these are but I can use names for a few of them which should 'open the mind' to their nature: embarrassment, shame, humiliation, guilt, and chagrin." ". . . security operations . . . are the movements of thought and the actions of which we, as it were, impute to or seek to provoke in the other fellow feelings like embarrassment, shame, humiliation, guilt, or chagrin." ". . . fleeting moments of anxiety . . . mark the point in the course of events at which something disjunctive, something that tends to pull away from the other fellow, has first appeared or has suddenly increased. They signal a change from relatively uncomplicated movement towards a presumptively common goal to a protecting of one's self-esteem, with a definite *complicating* of the interpersonal action."[61]

When we observe an infant we are struck by two sets of patterns which can conveniently be distinguished from one another. There are some "terminal" relations in which the infant appears to be receiving gratifications, such as quiet nursing or some skin stimulation or sleep. And there are unmistakeable activities in which the infant does not appear to be receiving gratification, as when he cries and rages, or appears stricken with numb terror. Suppose we label the

[61] "Towards a Psychiatry of Peoples," *Psychiatry*, 11 (1948), 105-116.

first group of patterns "libidinal" activities, and the second group "defensive-assertive." Since the infant has not learned a conventional set of signs (language), we can apply the same direct observational methods that we use in studying other non-lingual organisms. Thus we can make an inventory of the "libidinal" patterns, specifying both the "terminal" events, and the antecedent operations which we choose to see as part of the patterns in question. The "defensive-assertive" patterns will often appear when it is obvious that some interference has occurred in the reaching and sustaining of the terminal state of gratification. The infant may cry when the bottle is empty, and such a manifestation is an example of what we call a defensive-assertive pattern. All human activity falls into these two patterns throughout life, but the task of describing the degree of libidinal and of defensive-assertive activity becomes more complicated when language has been acquired, and the self-system has been elaborated. The anxiety response is "defensive-assertive," and evidently derives its persistent and labile qualities from the vagueness of the discomforts induced by the mother, and the ambiguity of the means of expression open to the infant (and the post-infant) in getting rid of it.

We can usefully classify the activities displayed by any human being according to the categories of *ego, superego,* and *id* at any time after the brain becomes active. The ego includes the perceptual phase of all activities, and all other subjective events integrated therewith. The self-system, as defined above, includes the enduring patterns of ego activity. The primitive "libidinal" and "defensive-assertive" patterns of the infant include some "perceptual" features which we take as the most rudimentary part of the ego. The patterns of the superego are developed as various channels of expressive activity are denied or made compulsive on the basis of experience. The term id refers to the initial and unconscious energy-channels of the individual. These are also continually modified since the superego and ego systems are ever changing. The energy sources of the personality vary with such factors as glandular balance, and the position that such inner activities occupy when they are "triggered" by ego processes.

Subjective events occurring as part of the terminal state of a libidinal activity are positive gratifications (indulgences). Subjective events may deviate in the direction of non-gratification and anti-gratification (deprivations). The extremes of indulgence are euphoric events; extreme deprivations are dysphoric. We speak of "tensions" when referring to events within the personality which lead to the occurrence of dysphoria. Dysphoria may come about because gratification is deferred, as in the case of ungratified hunger; or the dysphoria may flood the ego before it can be reduced, as in the case of aches and pains. Our basic postulate in examining human activity is that the "maximization principle" applies in accordance with which the tendency is to maximize the indulgences of the system as a whole. It is evident why the reduction and avoidance of anxiety (an acutely dysphoric set of events) occupies such a pivotal position in the evolution of the personality.

The events which the individual accepts as occasions of positive gratification (or of deprivation) are by no means always immediate rather than remote. A self-system may be evolved in which the demands on the primary ego for success include long range plans in politics, business, scholarship, or in some other field of action. Over long periods the self-system (and its supporting energy system) may provide all the self-indulgences which are needed to keep the individual hard at work on his career aims. Although the self-system is to an overwhelming extent made up of acquired rather than innate patterns of activity, the acquired patterns may become relatively independent of receiving indulgences from the environment. We know, of course, that innate physiological patterns are so "built in" the organism that they provide internal sources of gratification which render them comparatively independent of indulgences and deprivations in the environment. For instance, we do not lose the basic reflexes even when we are subjected to grave deprivations as a result of their occurrence. (One of the favorite modes of torture is to penalize the individual for repeating a reflexive and therefore relatively "unconditioned" act, such as jerking the knee in response to a tap, and blinking the eyelids.) When we speak of democratic character, of course, we have in mind the development of self and energy systems which withstand adversity on behalf of democratic patterns of value and practice.

The task is nothing less than the drastic and continuing reconstruction of our own civilization, and most of the cultures of which we have any knowledge. Since the basic postulate of behavior is the maximization of indulgences over deprivations, our task is to consolidate democratic conduct by directing the indulgences toward those who act democratically, and the deprivations toward those who do not. This calls for a reconsideration of adult-to-adult and adult-to-pre-adult relationships for the purpose of achieving a pattern of adult conduct that, in accordance with the maximization principle, gives differential rewards to democratic practice, and thereby provides continuing support for democratic performance, and aids in the development of character systems which are capable of acting democratically in the face of adverse conditions. The aim is to bring into being a democratic equilibrium in societal relations in which deviations are promptly rectified. If we were designing a machine, it would be possible to "build in" a set of servo-mechanisms which perform this re-stabilizing operation.[62] Since human relations are not mechanized, our task of creating and sustaining a democratic equilibrium is more complex. And the complexity is augmented by the prevailing anarchy in the world community, which keeps alive the expectation and the application of violence in the arena of world affairs, and also in the civic arena of police states. Hence the tremendous task of reconstruction must proceed in the face of adverse contemporary conditions and of anti-democratic inheritances from the past.[63]

Towards a Continuing Survey of Character Trends

An essential step in the task of achieving and sustaining democratic character is the development of continuing surveys of the trends in the structure of character, and in the pattern of determining factors which are currently moulding character. If democratic goals are to be clarified in terms sufficiently explicit for policy, an intelligence network must be built up. Such a continuing survey must cover the entire community; in principle, therefore, it encompasses the globe, or as much of it as is accessible to democratic policy makers.

Such a continuing trend survey is essential for many reasons, one of which is connected with the "index instability" of the terms in which we must talk about the interrelations of character and society. It is gradually dawning

[62] Some of the specific hypotheses and procedures recommended in Norbert Wiener's *Cybernetics, or Control and Communication in Animal and the Machine* are original and promising. However, the pattern of equilibrium analysis, as a mode of conceiving of interpersonal relations, is not new, nor does it purport to be.

[63] Some indication of the scope of the problem is in William C. Menninger, *Psychiatry in a Troubled World; Yesterday's War and Today's Challenge*, New York, Macmillan, 1948. See further, Otto Klineberg, *Tensions Affecting International Understanding; A Survey of Research*, New York, Social Science Research Council, 1950; Hadley Cantril, editor, *Tensions That Cause War*, Urbana, University of Illinois, 1950.

upon psychologists and social scientists that it is necessary to find means of overcoming the variability of meaning which is inherent in the social process itself. An interpersonal relation is a "meaning manifold," and is a continuing process of more or less perpetual change. In a "meaning manifold" the significance of each detail is modified as the context alters. Hence the words used to provide an "operational index" with which to describe character and society in one situation are likely to be somewhat inapplicable to other situations. Our operational indices of power, respect, wealth, or other values, and of the institutions by which values are shaped and shared, must undergo modification from one culture to another, and frequently from one social class to the next.

Some of the trend information about character and society can be obtained on a scale that includes the whole community. We speak of such total coverage as a *census*. But the manpower and other facilities may not be available for conducting a census of many items. *Sampling*, therefore, must be used, and samples may be in the form of *case studies* or of *quantitative studies*. The sample investigations may be primarily *contemplative* or *manipulative*, the latter being pre-tests. Most of the research reports in the "Studies in Prejudice" are contemplative inquiries, since they were designed to explore interrelations, without attempting to pre-test a potential policy change in the prejudiced person or group.

Actually the entire battery of procedures which has been outlined is closely interconnected. If we have adequate scientific understanding of a given set of responses, obtained by "contemplative" methods, we should be able to predict the outcome of those deliberate interventions in the situation which we call "pre-testing." For instance, if our scientific analysis is complete, we can correctly foretell how a given group of subjects will be affected by exposure to a film with a given content. In practice, of course, our contemplative studies always leave something to be desired, and gain by the perspective and the outcome of pretests, since the pre-testing operation is itself a means by which the predispositions are disclosed of the participants in a given situation.

Pre-testing is to be distinguished from *policy innovation*, employing the latter term to refer to changes in the whole community which so alter the total picture that "control" situations cannot be found. Strictly speaking, a pre-test is to be viewed as a rehearsal on a small scale of a change that might be introduced on a comprehensive scale. Although we often speak of "experimenting" with Federal legislation, for example, this is not a useful application of the term "experiment." We have a vocabulary for talking about policy innovation, and the term "experiment" has the connotation, which is convenient to retain, of the control of all relevant factors. In most cases in the social and biological sciences this means comparing the results of exposing an "experimental" group to a change to which a "control" group is left unexposed.

By organizing the trend survey so that provision is made for many methods, we obtain the closest potential coordination with policy, and with the needs of scientific study. Moreover, we can make full use of a host of observation-making and processing procedures of varying intensiveness. Let us designate as *Procedure A: the member of the community* the least intensive perspective. Suppose, for example, that we observe X touching Y with a sword. Is this to be understood as a threat to the physical well-being of Y? By consulting members of the community we may learn that from the point of view of the local culture Y is being "invested" with an office. We are thus witnessing an indulgence of Y by X in terms of power. This tells us nothing, obviously, about the character of X or Y. But suppose we make further inquiries into the context from members of the community. We may discover that the advancement of Y is an act of discrimination against Z, who was more entitled to promotion than Y. Assume also that X is a public official elected by a political party opposed to the rapid improvement in the condition of the Negroes (and Z is a Negro). Can we say at this point that the character of X is undemocratic because he did an undemocratic deed? Before reaching this conclusion it is plainly necessary to review the conduct of X as a whole during the time-internal that we have chosen for studying X (or the community). How does he act as an employer? As trustee of an educational institution? As a member of an athletic club? As a participant in the social life of the neighborhood? If we draw all the data together we can prepare a character profile of X based upon information pertinent to democratic values (such as X's "discrimination score").

It is possible to intensify the study of X's character (and of characters in the community) by shifting from the standpoint of a community member to that of a person who is also an intimate friend. Perhaps the friend reports that X is strongly opposed to discrimination, and that he hopes to work into a sufficiently potent position to modify the traditional program of his party. It is now possible to revise our picture of the character of X from the observational standpoint of *Procedure B: the intimate friend.* (We are not adopting the interpretations made by the friend; we are sifting his testimony about the words and deeds of X.)

Our view of the character of X may be further intensified by taking his private picture of himself into account (as disclosed, perhaps, in a diary not meant for the eyes

of living friends). Our conception may be complicated by
the discovery that X is aware of an acute conflict on matters of discrimination, not only as Negroes are affected,
but whenever Catholics, Jews and "foreign" groups are
involved. X may confess that he has a strong distaste for
persons connected with these groups, but that, since he
holds such prejudices to be immoral, he tries to overcome
them. We may now re-edit our picture of X's character
from the standpoint of *Procedure C: intimate introspection.*

The most intensive perspective in which X can be studied undertakes to disclose the unconscious structure of his
personality. This is accomplished by means of special techniques which reveal the superego and the id. Psychoanalysts use the technique of free association for the purpose;
and several projective and other tests have been invented
to aid the process. The "depth" perspective may bring to
light new complications in our view of X. For example,
we may learn that hostility against ethnic groups represents a generalized reaction which has spread from early
(repressed) conflicts between impulses to touch the genitals of ethnic playmates and fear, guilt and shame for
having such interests. A battery of "defense mechanisms"
may have gone into action, including the projection of
feelings of apprehension, guilt and shame upon "bad"
symbols which were "colored," "remote," and "big." In
this way hostile expectations were perpetuated in relation
to "racial" and "alien" groups. At the same time, part of
the primary ego may have become identified with the al-
luring though forbidden, thus furnishing a basis of attrac-
tion toward individuals and problems connected with ethnic
images. Such connections can be disclosed if X is seen
from the vantage point of *Procedure D, or special disclos-
ures of the unconscious.*

Obviously there is a continuous "manifold" of observational procedures, varying in length of contact between observer and subject, and in elaborateness of the details disclosed, and of records made and processed. The "Studies in Prejudice" may again be cited as an example of a large-scale research enterprise in which observational procedures of varying intensiveness-extensiveness were employd.[64]

A further important possibility remains to be pointed out. Many of the theories of personality development undertake to characterize the entire career-line of the individual from infancy to maturity, and after. If it is necessary to verify such theories only on the basis of data gathered through entire career-lines, many years may elapse before the impact of early patterning on later phases can be ascertained. And by that time the factors that condition the first or second year of existence in the culture may have changed (as when there is a rapid shift from breast to bottle-feeding, or *vice versa*, or a rapid change from rigid to flexible feeding schedules). Some years ago I proposed that researches be organized to permit "interlapping" observations, in the hope of bringing into view the whole panorama of relationships with an important bearing upon the profile of personality development.[65] For instance, groups matched in as many particulars as possible (and deemed relevant) might be set up on a two-year cycle. Thus one set of observers would be watching infants as they passed through the first and second year at the same time that other observers were recording children who were living through the second and third year. Thus the character

[64] See for other examples H. A. Murray and others, *Explorations in Personality*, New York, Oxford University Press, 1938; *Assessment of Men*. Office of Strategic Services Assessment Staff, New York, Rinehart, 1948; and many of the studies cited in Gardner Murphy, *Personality; A Biosocial Approach to Origins and Structure*, New York, Harpers, 1947.

[65] Footnote 37, above.

exhibited by some of the three year olds could be traced back (by proper matching) to the significant constellations seen in the first year. In principle, the overlapping system could be applied throughout the entire career line.

Overlapping samples can be set up according to functional rather than chronological periods. For this purpose some of the more creative suggestions about the stages of human development can be used. Harry Stack Sullivan, for example, distinguished seven periods before maturity, which he schematized in one of his last papers as follows:[66]

1. *Infancy* to the maturation of the capacity for language development.
2. *Childhood* to the maturation of the capacity for living with compeers.
3. *Juvenile Era* to the maturation of the capacity for isophilic intimacy (like-sex intimacy).
4. *Preadolescence* to the maturation of the general lust dynamisms.
5. *Early Adolescence* to the patterning of lustful behavior.
6. *Late Adolescence* to maturity.

More closely connected with Freud's original scheme, Erik H. Erikson has recently sketched "eight stages of man" and suggested the polar processes which are the most significant adaptive opportunities and dangers for each. Thus:[67]

1. *Oral sensory*. Trust vs. Mistrust.
2. *Muscular-Anal*. Autonomy vs. Shame, Doubt.
3. *Locomotor-genital*. Initiative vs. Guilt.
4. *Latency*. Industry vs. Inferiority.
5. *Puberty and Adolescence*. Identity vs. Role Diffusion.
6. *Young Adulthood*. Intimacy vs. Isolation.
7. *Adulthood*. Generativity vs. Stagnation.
8. *Maturity*. Integrity vs. Disgust, Despair.

[66] Footnote 60, above.
[67] *Childhood and Society*, New York, Norton, 1950.

An obvious and great advantage to be derived from organizing a continuing survey of character in society is that working agreements concerning the meaning of words must be made among those who conduct the survey. Since we are interested in relating character formation to the attainment of a democratic commonwealth, it will be necessary to engage in a continuous process of clarifying the conception of such a community.

It will also be essential to agree upon the terms and indices to be employed in the study of character formation. However it will not be necessary to agree upon the probable truth of hypotheses, since it will be possible to study a large number of hypotheses at the same time, and to repeat the investigation so long as results are in doubt. Caution must taken to specify the observational procedures (of type A, B, C, or D, for instance) which are involved in verifying any hypothesis.

As a brief reminder of what is at stake, let us consider one of the most comprehensive hypotheses about the formation of democratic character. Stated negatively, the proposition is that *failure to develop democratic character is a function of interpersonal relations in which low estimates of the self are permitted to develop.*[68] Suppose we interpret this hypothesis in reference to situations which can be explored by such procedures as A. We may often find confirmatory evidence, as when we study the composition of anti-democratic movements, and learn that they are heavily recruited from salaried employees and members of the older artisans who regard themselves as losing out, relative to other social groups. On the other hand, it will be possible to find facts that point in another direction. The anti-democrats may be recruited from the top aris-

---

[68] See my *Power and Personality*, p. 162 ff.

tocracy, and therefore appear to possess a tradition of superior worth.

The general proposition is more likely to be in harmony with data disclosed by intensive procedures of the C or D type. But it is necessary to specify in detail how the key terms are to be interpreted. For instance, "low estimates of the self" should include indirect as well as direct presentations of the primary ego in the material produced in psychoanalytic interviews. *Direct* statements, of course, may affirm that the primary ego is, was or will be weak (in terms of power), poor (in relation to wealth), contemptible (in reference to respect), guilty (in terms of rectitude), unloved (in relation to affection), uninformed (regarding enlightenment), clumsy (in reference to skill), and diseased (in terms of well-being). The primary ego can also be presented as deprived, rather than indulged, in *indirect* statements. The assertion, for instance, can be attributed to someone else; or an alleged reminiscence or fantasy can portray the patient as deficient without putting it in words. Reminiscences of early anxiety would thus be among the relevant indices of a low self-estimate. This is reasonable, since acute dysphoria is a subjective event which swamps the primary ego. "Low estimates of the self" ought also to be interpreted to facilitate the study of infants and young children by direct and intensive procedures of observation. Satisfactory indices would be the manifestations of anxiety on the part of the infant which Sullivan was attempting to describe. (It will be recalled that such "defensive-aggressive" expressions may have no focal points of origin such as are evident when fear-responses occur.) [69]

[69] Useful hints for studying the first years of life are in Part IV of John Dollard and Neal E. Miller, *Personality and Psychotherapy, An Analysis in Terms of Learning, Thinking and Culture*, New York, McGraw-Hill, 1950. A much-needed restatement of psychoanalytic theory is now being carried

When we study the equilibrium of factors sustaining or undermining the equilibrium of democratic activity in a specific community, or on the part of a person, during a selected period, it may sometimes appear that democratic conduct does not depend, to a significant degree, upon democratic character. It may seem, for example, that the giving of immediate indulgence to democratic responses, and the inflicting of immediate deprivation upon anti-democratic acts, will outweigh the factors making against democratic conduct. The continuing survey of character and culture is essential if we are to comprehend the interplay of factors affecting democratic behavior, including the importance of the practices called the "self" and "energy" system. By utilizing proper procedures it will be possible to give the classical terms such as "character" and "constitution" a contemporary meaning, and to estimate the impact of practices upon one another.

The following questions are among those whose relevance will not diminish: To what extent is it possible to achieve democratic conduct in adult life without forming democratic character in early life? To what extent can democratic character formed in early life persist against anti-democratic environments in later life? In what measure can democratic conduct in later life form democratic character among adults (and the pre-adults influenced by them)?

Freedom and the Sciences of Man

To some extent descriptive probing into the processes of political life has been held back by inapplicable analogies

forward by Drs. Kris, Hartmann and Löwenstein. The choice of operational indices and of "testable" hypotheses should be much facilitated thereby. The equating of anxiety with repressed fear is a point requiring further clarification in the Dollard-Miller treatment, and in much psychoanalytic literature.

from the natural sciences. It is insufficiently acknowledged that the role of scientific work in human relations is *freedom* rather than prediction. By freedom is meant the bringing into the focus of awareness of some feature of the personality which has hitherto operated as a determining factor upon the choices made by the individual, but which has been operating unconsciously. Once elevated to the full focus of waking consciousness, the factor which has been operating "automatically and compulsively" is no longer in this privileged position. The individual is now free to take the factor into consideration in the making of future choices.

This enlargement of the scope of freedom is the most direct contribution of the study of interpersonal relations to democracy. If more individuals can be made aware of the distorting effect of anxiety upon their judgments of personnel and of public and private issues, the continuing reconstruction of civilization toward the more perfect realization of democratic values will be expedited. Hence it is the growth of insight, not simply of the capacity of the observer to predict the future operation of an automatic compulsion, or of a non-personal factor, that represents the major contribution of the scientific study of interpersonal relations to policy. It is by exposing and perhaps destroying the interpersonal relationships which have held true in the past that scientific effort produces the most far-reaching results. Hence all propositions about character or society which are made by the scientific specialist must always read "subject to insight." In a sense the aim of the science of man is to make such a science superfluous. This is achieved in the degree that insight into value goals, past trends, and past conditioning factors increases the scope of policy choice touching upon the future realization of a commonwealth in which the dignity of man is respected in theory and fact.

We cannot, at this moment in history, pride ourselves upon what we know or what we put into practice about human relations. Nor can we rely upon any one path to the understanding of politics and society.[70] We can, however, congratulate ourselves upon possessing many of the procedural tools which are capable of penetrating further into the interrelations of man in society than has been possible hitherto. And we possess a new sense of direction and of urgency for the effective application of the instrumentalities of science and policy.

From the classical inheritance we have no static tradition, but a vast panorama of inspiration and suggestion for the reshaping of all civilizations and all cultures toward the goal of free men in a society at once universal and free.[71]

[70] There are other ways than direct participation by which we can explore power in society, although we do not exclude the active and self-observing life. "If a man don't occasionally sit in a senate how can he pierce the dark mind of a senator?" asks Ezra Pound in *The Pisan Cantos*, New Directions, 1949.

[71] Reflected in the work of such a modern minded scholar as the late Karl Mannheim. See his posthumous *Freedom, Power, and Democratic Planning*, New York, Oxford University Press, 1950.